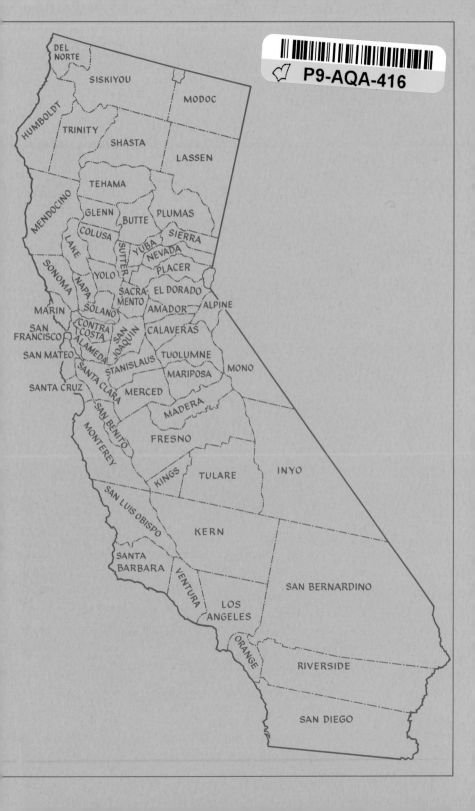

DEL
NORTE

SISKIYOU

MODOC

HUMBOLDT

TRINITY

SHASTA

LASSEN

TEHAMA

MENDOCINO

GLENN

BUTTE

PLUMAS

COLUSA

SIERRA

LAKE

SUTTER

YUBA

NEVADA

SONOMA

YOLO

PLACER

NAPA

SACRA-
MENTO

EL DORADO

MARIN

SOLANO

AMADOR

ALPINE

SAN
FRANCISCO

CONTRA
COSTA

SAN
JOAQUIN

CALAVERAS

ALAMEDA

SAN MATEO

STANISLAUS

TUOLUMNE

MONO

SANTA CLARA

MARIPOSA

SANTA CRUZ

MERCED

SAN BENITO

MADERA

MONTEREY

FRESNO

KINGS

TULARE

INYO

SAN LUIS OBISPO

KERN

SANTA
BARBARA

VENTURA

SAN BERNARDINO

LOS
ANGELES

ORANGE

RIVERSIDE

SAN DIEGO

The Democratic Party and California Politics 1880-1896

R. HAL WILLIAMS

The Democratic Party and California Politics 1880-1896

STANFORD, CALIFORNIA

STANFORD UNIVERSITY PRESS

1973

Stanford University Press
Stanford, California
© 1973 by the Board of Trustees of the
Leland Stanford Junior University
Printed in the United States of America
ISBN 0-8047-0847-9
LC 73-80626

For Linda and Lise

Preface

HISTORIANS have not, on the whole, been very kind to the late nineteenth century in the United States. Partly by design, mostly by default, they have viewed the 1880's and 1890's as an unfortunate interlude, representing either the bleak aftermath of Reconstruction or the unhappy prelude to Progressivism. Although recent scholarship has brought fresh interpretations, relatively few historians have scrutinized these decades, whose issues and preoccupations now seem remote. Consequently, the protective tariff system has been dismissed as evidence of a corrupt alliance between politicians and businessmen, and events and issues involving patronage, currency, and business regulation have suffered from similar distortions. Studies of Mugwumps and Populists—groups, to be sure, that are well worth examining—greatly outnumber studies of Democrats and Republicans, who after all retained the allegiance of 90 percent of the national electorate.

This study was undertaken half a dozen years ago to test previous assumptions and to investigate in detail some of the problems and accomplishments of the late nineteenth century. Drawing on the copious evidence in Pacific Coast archives, it traces the course of the California Democratic party from the early 1880's through the important election of 1896. It does so not only through close scrutiny of the principles and policies of Pacific Coast Democrats, but also in the context of economic and social development, and with frequent reference to the activities of the Republicans and Populists. Where pertinent, comparisons with events in other states and regions have been suggested. Finally, since party developments on the national level inevitably shape local prospects, the study examines the critical impact of national events, particularly the policies pursued by President Grover Cleveland, on the California Democrats' fortunes.

Rich in symbolism, sources, and issues, California has obvious attractions for the historian. The period under examination marked the beginnings of the state's swift rise to its present prominence. Rapid change challenged political leaders. Reflecting California's diversity in population and in resources, it fostered regional tensions, altered issues in sometimes bewildering ways, strained the political system, and made enduring statewide alignments difficult for politicians to construct. Economic depression, extending through much of the era, led to popular discontent and raised serious questions about the nature and direction of the state's development. Political flux, exhibited in shifting intraparty alliances and the spread of such movements as Nationalism, Populism, and the Farmers' Alliance, tested the abilities and probed the commitment of party leaders. Out of depression and flux, these party leaders advanced solutions and created patterns that would shape Pacific Coast politics for decades to come.

As the domain of the Southern Pacific Railroad, California offers still another valuable perspective. During these decades, it is commonly thought, the Southern Pacific ruled an "invisible government" that dominated both major political parties, corrupted the press, dictated policy to the legislature, and controlled the judiciary. But research has revealed little to sustain this view. Although the Southern Pacific's influence was felt throughout the state, it functioned in complex and limited fashion. Certainly, Collis P. Huntington and other railroad leaders came to know the limits of the Southern Pacific's power, as politicians and public opinion resisted their plans, circumscribed their authority, and sought tight controls over their railroad. California politics in the late nineteenth century was far more than a branch of the Southern Pacific Railroad.

It involved, instead, a hard-fought contest over meaningful issues between two evenly matched political organizations. One of these, the Democratic party, is the focus of this book. For Democrats and the Democratic philosophy, the 1880's and 1890's were a time of critical challenge. The party's final recovery from its Civil War defeats brought to power the first Democratic president in 24 years. Party doctrines of states' rights, limited government, and decentralization won widespread support among Americans who distrusted federal intervention. In applying these doctrines to the problems of an increasingly interdependent urban-industrial society, the Democrats pursued a legitimate vision that produced some beneficial results. But by century's end the vision had collapsed, unsustained and unsustainable, the victim of inadequate leadership, changing outlooks, and economic hardship. Today, when the states are again being called on to meet a welter of responsibilities—some of them regional or national in scope—policy-makers might profitably examine the successes and defeats of the Democratic party in the late nineteenth century.

California has been blessed with a number of excellent historians. John W. Caughey, Earl Pomeroy, Gerald D. Nash, Walton Bean, Andrew F. Rolle, and Robert Glass Cleland, to name a few, have treated some of the events covered in this book. But these events have here been placed, I think, in a fresh context, and since much of the material is new, I have dealt with fundamental questions as well as involved ones. Who were the California political leaders, both Democratic and Republican? What were their outlooks and objectives? What was the quality and effect of their relationships? How effective were their responses to challenge and change? In what ways did the state party organizations reflect national party developments? Finally, how does the California experience relate to the broader framework of American political history?

Answering these questions, among others, has been my own challenge. What follows, of course, is the record of my findings. It is not an analysis of voting behavior, though I have profited greatly from the studies of political scientists and historians who have examined the shifting patterns of voter allegiance in California and the nation during the late nineteenth century. Rather, it adopts the view that political history is the result of a complex interaction among political leaders, issues, and voters, in which skillful leaders respond to issues and work on voters in ways designed to meet perceived needs and keep themselves in power. The book focuses on that interaction, relating the story of a political party, its leaders, and its efforts to win a state and serve a nation. Hopefully, it will enhance our understanding and appreciation of a neglected era.

It is a pleasure to acknowledge the many debts I have incurred in preparing this study. I am particularly grateful to Ralph W. Hansen, Patricia J. Palmer, and the staff of the Manuscripts Division, Stanford University Libraries, for generous assistance during my months of research in Palo Alto. Miss Mary Isabel Fry and Miss Haydée Noya guided me through the valuable manuscripts at the Henry E. Huntington Library. Saundra Taylor provided gracious and efficient help in the Division of Special Collections, University of California at Los Angeles. I also owe a special debt to Douglas A. Bakken of the Nebraska Historical Society.

The dedicated staff at the National Archives shared their knowledge of California sources and helped me uncover new material in the records of government departments. I also am grateful to the staffs of the Manuscript Division of the Library of Congress, the H. H. Bancroft Library, the University of California General Library, and the Yale University Library for their assistance. At Yale, Archibald Hanna and Arthur C. Schwaner gave me indispensable help by making California newspapers available for my use. Above all, I wish to thank W. Stuart Debenham, whose warm friendship and zest for scholarship never faltered despite the demands of an insistent historian.

Brief portions of this book appeared originally in an interpretive essay on the national Democratic party in H. Wayne Morgan, ed., *The Gilded Age* (Syracuse, N.Y., 1970); they are used here in modified form with the permission of the publisher, Syracuse University Press.

David M. Kennedy, of Stanford University, and Michael F. Holt, of Yale University, read the manuscript in its early stages and contributed valuable suggestions. I owe a great deal to them, and to two former colleagues at Yale, Timothy H. Breen and R. Laurence Moore, who offered me their friendship and encouragement. I also am indebted to John M. Blum, of Yale University, whose advice and assistance over the past years have meant much to me. Two other friends deserve particular thanks. Lewis L. Gould, of the University of Texas at Austin, read the entire manuscript several times, offered detailed and searching criticism, and shared with me his broad understanding of American politics in the late nineteenth century. In commitment, insight, and craftsmanship, he sets an example for us all. Howard R. Lamar, of Yale University, has given me generous assistance since the study's inception. During an extremely busy period of his own career, he scrutinized every chapter with great care and gave me oft-needed guidance and perceptive criticism. For this, and much else, I am deeply thankful. Of course, any errors of fact or interpretation in the book remain my responsibility.

Above all, I am grateful to my parents for their encouragement, and to my wife, Linda, and my daughter, Lise, who both contributed to the book in countless ways. The dedication, perhaps, expresses some measure of my gratitude.

R.H.W.

New Haven, Conn.
June 1973

Contents

꿍ᴥ꿍

Eight pages of photographs follow p. 154.

Abbreviations

꧂

Alta Cal: *Alta California* (San Francisco).

AP: Appointment Papers, National Archives, Washington, D.C. Cited by Record Group (RG) number.

CP: Grover Cleveland Papers, Manuscript Division, Library of Congress.

HP: Benjamin Harrison Papers, Manuscript Division, Library of Congress.

JA: State of California, Legislature, *Journal of the Assembly* (Sacramento).

J App: State of California, Legislature, *Appendix to the Journals of the Senate and Assembly* (Sacramento).

JS: State of California, Legislature, *Journal of the Senate* (Sacramento).

LA *Times*: Los Angeles *Times*.

PHR: *Pacific Historical Review*.

SF *Bul*: San Francisco *Bulletin*.

SF *Chron*: San Francisco *Chronicle*.

SF *Exmr*: San Francisco *Examiner*.

WP: Stephen Mallory White Papers, Borel Collection, Stanford University Libraries.

The Democratic Party and
California Politics
1880-1896

CHAPTER ONE

California in the 1880's and 1890's: The Setting

THE GENERATION that spanned the 1880's and 1890's confronted unprecedented challenges. A burgeoning urban-industrial society, impressive in scope and diversity, posed complex questions. Corporate expansion, urban growth, recurrent economic depression, and large population movements strained inherited institutions and probed the public's ability to accommodate to change. These developments also tested political parties and their leaders, who for the most part responded in meaningful fashion. Democrats fought Republicans over significant issues, and presented different remedies for national ills. Long before the progressives, late-nineteenth-century party leaders experimented with varied solutions to the problems of modern society. Though tempered always with respect for the past, innovation and growth pervaded the era. By 1900 new patterns had appeared that would mold the life of succeeding generations.

No state enjoyed immunity from these nationwide trends. Through much of the period, in fact, the states were the focal point of important activity. While events in Washington captivated newspaper readers across the country, they raised mixed emotions among a populace fascinated with the byplay of power but fearful of centralized authority. Recent experience during the Civil War and Reconstruction accentuated the distaste for federal bureaucracy, and the conviction spread that state and local governments must resume the vital role in the governing process. Although this feeling gave the Democratic party, with its emphasis on states' rights and limited government, an initial advantage in the era's political battles, Republican leaders also paid close attention to state affairs. A watchful electorate and a concern for their own careers ensured that they would. Even to be elected United States senator, the highest office to which most politicians could realistically aspire, depended on the actions of state legislatures meeting in Albany, Harrisburg, Columbus, or Sacramento.

In large measure Californians shared these characteristics, though environment and distance from Eastern political centers introduced modifications. In 1880, at the outset of the period, California already ranked among the ten most urban states in the country. Its population, a mixture of foreign and American immigrants, had increased on the average by over a quarter of a million people each decade since 1850.[1] In most cases climate, natural resources, and an aura of wealth and rapid advancement—the last a lingering vestige of the Gold Rush years—had lured the newcomers. The state, concluded a perceptive English traveler, Lord Bryce, "is in many respects the most striking in the whole Union, and has more than any other the character of a great country, capable of standing alone in the world. It has immense wealth in its fertile soil as well as in its minerals and forests." Californians agreed. In an era known for promotional activities, they won notoriety for the distinctive vigor of their own boosterism.[2]

Expansive confidence in the future gave a special cast to California politics. Few Californians would have understood the outlook of a young visitor in 1887 who urged relatives not to move to the Pacific Coast: "I cannot tell why, but I despise this country—not the people exactly, for they are most of them Easterners who live here under protest and pretend to be glad of it.... California is not for me. It has no past, its future reveals nothing but an ignominious scramble for dollars, its politics are odious and its population mongrel."[3] Such sentiments bewildered Californians. They possessed an enormous faith in their state and often discussed its unique Manifest Destiny, "where the civilization of American freedom shall culminate in all

[1] Earl Pomeroy, *The Pacific Slope* (New York, 1965), pp. 120–28; Carey McWilliams, *California: The Great Exception* (New York, 1949), p. 82; *Compendium of the Tenth Census* (Washington, D.C., 1888), pp. 4, 408.

[2] James Bryce, *The American Commonwealth*, 2 vols. (New York, 1908), 2: 439; Henry George, "The Kearney Agitation in California," *Popular Science Monthly*, 17 (1880): 436; Kate Sanborn, *A Truthful Woman in Southern California* (New York, 1893), p. 18.

[3] Charles Dwight Willard to Harriet E. Willard, Feb. 20, 1887, Charles Dwight Willard Papers, Huntington Library.

that is greatest, best and glorious." As an early historian noted in introducing his 1863 account, "I write of a land of wonders."[4]

For more than two decades after 1850 conditions sustained this confidence. During these years Coast residents concentrated primarily on the exploitation of the region's virgin resources. Gold, of course, supplied the first impetus, but agriculture soon surpassed mining as the chief industry of the state. Wheat began to supplant gold in the popular imagination. "Such wheat-fields!" exclaimed an early visitor to the San Joaquin Valley. "You look at them, and try to look across them, but can't; your vision yields to the endless waves of wheat-spires." By 1880 California placed seventh in the nation in wheat production, first in barley, and second in wool. Important developments in viticulture and fruit growing foreshadowed future agricultural patterns. Consequently, when gold output declined after the early 1850's, California escaped almost entirely the "boom-bust" pattern experienced by mining states with less varied resources, like Colorado and Nevada. Instead, the state entered a period of prosperity marked by major advances in farming, transportation, and manufacturing.[5]

A serious flaw marred the facade. Expansion was uneven. Most newcomers shunned the southern part of the state, with its arid climate, relative absence of minerals, and regional economy dependent on the cattle industry. Travelers found the area delightful, "a land of perpetual spring" where people led a placid life unknown in the bustling North. But glowing reports could not mask economic stagnation and hardship, particularly after 1863, when severe drought killed thousands of cattle and brought eventual ruin to the region's dominant industry. With few exceptions the unbalanced pattern of settlement and development within the state would continue until the land boom and railroad competition of the late 1880's attracted large numbers of settlers to the "cow counties" and stimulated inten-

[4] LA Times, Jan. 1, 1887; John S. Hittell, The Resources of California (San Francisco, 1863), p. iii.

[5] H. C. R[oberts], Journal: April 5–May 20, 1882 (n.p., n.d.), p. 27; Gerald D. Nash, State Government and Economic Development: A History of Administrative Policies in California, 1849–1933 (Berkeley, 1964), pp. 29–30, 63–64; Tenth Census, pp. 660–67, 948–49; Ira B. Cross, A History of the Labor Movement in California, Univ. of California Publications in Economics, vol. 14 (Berkeley, 1935), p. 29; Vincent P. Carosso, The California Wine Industry: A Study of the Formative Years (Berkeley, 1951), pp. 74–101.

sive agricultural growth. In 1880, economically backward and beset by depression, Southern California had less than 10 percent of the state's population.[6]

For almost forty years after the Gold Rush, therefore, no important rival challenged the influence of the northern counties, and especially of a single city, San Francisco. By far the major urban area west of Chicago, with nearly 234,000 inhabitants in 1880, San Francisco indeed dominated a state whose second largest city, Oakland, had only 34,555 people and whose capital, Sacramento, had only 21,420. In that year San Francisco accounted for 27 percent of California's entire population, and its political and economic power was correspondingly great. Representing about one-fourth of the state's voters, the city's political delegations enjoyed a preponderant position in conventions, elections, and the legislature. With its harbor and investment capital, San Francisco had become the focus of economic development from Alaska to Arizona. It "dwarfs the other cities," noted Lord Bryce, "and is a commercial and intellectual centre, and source of influence for the surrounding regions, more powerful over them than is any Eastern city over its neighbourhood."[7]

Visitors to San Francisco, the "queen of the Pacific" and center of Far Western society, found a mixture of wealth and squalor, of civilization and the frontier, that both fascinated and repelled them. The wealthy and socially prominent frequented the city's opulent Palace Hotel and the Nob Hill mansions of the railroad and Comstock magnates. Others less fortunate crowded into Chinatown and the city's slums. Nearly half the residents were of foreign birth. "San Francisco is a mad city—inhabited for the most part by perfectly insane people," wrote Rudyard Kipling in the spring of 1889. There, within a period of thirty years, several vigilante committees formed to administer law to the populace and three newspaper editors succumbed to bullet

[6] Ludwig Louis Salvator, *Los Angeles in the Sunny Seventies: A Flower from the Golden Land* (Los Angeles, 1929), pp. 3, 124–25; Margaret S. Gordon, *Employment Expansion and Population Growth: The California Experience, 1900–1950* (Berkeley, 1954), p. 164; Robert Glass Cleland, *The Cattle on a Thousand Hills: Southern California, 1850–1870* (San Marino, Cal., 1941).

[7] *Tenth Census,* p. 380; Bryce, *American Commonwealth,* 2: 443; Henry George, "What the Railroad Will Bring Us," *Overland Monthly,* 1 (1868): 299–300; Hugh Quigley, *The Irish Race in California, and on the Pacific Coast* (San Francisco, 1878), p. 255.

wounds. There, too, reigned for two decades a bankrupt businessman, Joshua Norton, who proclaimed himself Norton the First, Emperor of the United States and Protector of Mexico, issued proclamations dissolving the United States, and collected taxes from local merchants. "In what other city," asked Robert Louis Stevenson, "would a harmless madman who supposed himself emperor...have been so fostered and encouraged?"[8]

Most Californians envied San Francisco; few admired it. "I don't like this railroad-ridden boss-ruled city at all," complained one traveler from Los Angeles. "There is no life about it, no enterprise. It is Ireland over again, owned by foreign landlords." Nativism and a general distrust of urban mores contributed to the hostility, as did the widespread conviction that San Francisco businessmen stifled local competition and overcharged rural customers. Above all, outsiders resented the city's political power, and this resentment shaped political patterns throughout California. Politics commonly aligned "city" against "country," San Francisco against the rest of the state. Discontent sharpened in the 1870's, when Californians became convinced that their region shared the national tendency toward political corruption. Dishonesty and mediocrity seemed to dominate every branch of the government, especially the legislature, which became a symbol of venality and inefficiency. "It has been usual in California to say of every Legislature that it was worse than its predecessor," remarked an observer in 1880.[9]

Blame for this situation fell on San Francisco. "Just so long as San Francisco sends a solid delegation of boodlers so long will the Legislature be a failure," suggested a Southern California legislator. "When one fourth of the body is bad to commence with how many others will fall into line.... In all likelihood this thing will continue until some of 'the boys' drop out of windows with ropes around their necks

[8] Rudyard Kipling, *American Notes* (New York, 1930), p. 17; John S. Hittell, *A History of the City of San Francisco* (San Francisco, 1878), p. 443; Irving McKee, "The Shooting of Charles de Young," PHR, 16 (1947): 281–83; Stevenson quoted in Allen Stanley Lane, *Emperor Norton: The Mad Monarch of America* (Caldwell, Idaho, 1939), p. 80.

[9] Cornelius Cole to Olive Cole, Oct. 14, 1887, Cornelius Cole Papers, Division of Special Collections, Univ. of California, Los Angeles; Theodore H. Hittell, "The Legislature of 1880," *The Berkeley Quarterly: A Journal of Social Science,* 1 (1880): 240.

& the indignant tax payer at the other end." Criticism extended beyond California, for in the 1870's and 1880's San Francisco politics attracted international attention. In a series of public letters Rudyard Kipling scathingly described "the august spectacle of a Government of the people, by the people, for the people, as it is understood in the city of San Francisco." Saloon-keepers and Irish immigrants, Kipling concluded, controlled the city's politics. Lord Bryce, using California to study American democracy on the state level, reached similar conclusions. And Jules Verne chose a San Francisco political gathering for an obstacle in the path of Phileas Fogg in *Around the World in Eighty Days*. After a mob had stripped him of most of his clothing, Fogg inquired at the railroad station about the cause of the riot:

> "It was a political meeting, sir," replied the porter.
> "But I thought there was a great deal of disturbance in the streets."
> "It was only a meeting assembled for an election."
> "The election of a general-in-chief, no doubt?" asked Mr. Fogg.
> "No, sir; of a justice of the peace."[10]

Dissatisfaction with their political system did not lead Californians to withdraw from it. Instead, they tried to reform it, by adopting such devices as the Australian secret ballot; they tried to modify it, by transferring authority over some matters to expert commissions; and finally they tried to use it to solve the welter of complex difficulties that confronted the state. In none of these ventures were they entirely successful. But their efforts made the late nineteenth century a period of introspection, experimentation, and intense political contention as Californians endeavored, generally through the party system, to find solutions to problems of economic depression, urban and industrial growth, foreign immigration, and corporate expansion. In this regard these decades "may seem less like an era of corruption and inaction, than a period of intensive experimentation, in which men tried to adapt the political institutions inherited from an agrarian age to new problems of industrialism."[11]

[10] Stephen M. White to J. E. McComas, May 12, 1889, WP; Kipling, *American Notes*, pp. 41–45; Bryce, *American Commonwealth*, 2: 439–64; Jules Verne, *Around the World in Eighty Days* (Boston, 1873), p. 212; Oscar Lewis, *This Was San Francisco* (New York, 1962), p. 228.
[11] Gerald D. Nash, "The California Railroad Commission, 1876–1911," *Southern*

II

Two problems in particular preoccupied Californians during these years: the Chinese and the railroad. By the close of the 1870's, the former had assumed an important role in the local economy. Beginning in the Gold Rush, immigration from China had steadily continued until in 1880 there were more than 75,000 Chinese in the state. This total represented about one-tenth of the state's population, and nearly three-fourths of the Chinese in the United States. Numerical strength combined with habits of industry and thrift to establish the Chinese in mines, laundries, restaurants, and farms across California. Fifteen thousand of them found employment in the construction of the Central Pacific Railroad, and Chinese labor also figured prominently in the clothing, furniture, and cigar industries.[12]

The success of the Chinese aroused widespread hostility. Perceptive observers stressed the racism that underlay this feeling and noted its similarity to the proslavery position of the 1850's. But Californians insisted that their opposition to the Chinese rested solely on economic and moral grounds. Their major grievance was that the Chinese lowered wage scales, replaced white laborers, and added to unemployment. "They do not constitute," argued a San Francisco newspaper, "as European immigrants do, an addition to the industrial element; on the contrary, they are substitutes and supplanters, every one of them who obtains employment taking the place of a white man, and depriving him of work."[13] Californians also attacked the exclusiveness of the Chinese community, complained that the Chinese spread leprosy and encouraged the use of opium, and described San Fran-

---

California Quarterly, 44 (1962): 303. See also Nash's "Bureaucracy and Economic Reform: The Experience of California, 1899–1911," *Western Political Quarterly*, 13 (1960): 678–91; Erik Falk Petersen, "The Struggle for the Australian Ballot in California," *California Historical Quarterly*, 51 (1972): 227–43.

[12] Gunther Barth, *Bitter Strength: A History of the Chinese in the United States, 1850–1870* (Cambridge, Mass., 1964), pp. 77–128; Mary Roberts Coolidge, *Chinese Immigration* (New York, 1909), p. 31; *Tenth Census*, p. 334; Alexander Saxton, *The Indispensable Enemy: Labor and the Anti-Chinese Movement in California* (Berkeley, 1971), pp. 3–66.

[13] Quoted in G. B. Densmore, *The Chinese in California* (San Francisco, 1880), p. 119; Elmer Clarence Sandmeyer, *The Anti-Chinese Movement in California*, Illinois Studies in the Social Sciences, vol. 24 (Urbana, Ill., 1939), p. 39; Irish to Parker, July 26, 1888, "Letters Written by John P. Irish to George F. Parker," *Iowa Journal of History and Politics*, 31 (1933): 426; Roberts, *Journal*, p. 17.

cisco's Chinatown as "the rankest outgrowth of human degradation that can be found upon this continent." In 1877 a special committee of the legislature pronounced Chinese immigration "a dangerous unarmed invasion of our soil."[14]

Anti-Chinese agitation resulted in three decades of local and state attempts to curb further immigration and discourage those Chinese already in California. Governing bodies on all levels adopted vigorous anti-Chinese measures, among them an 1882 San Francisco "Laundry Ordinance" that sought to limit the areas of the city in which laundries could be established.[15] But such laws generally foundered in the federal courts. In the Supreme Court a Californian, Justice Stephen J. Field, repeatedly invoked the Fourteenth Amendment, the Burlingame Treaty of 1868 with China, and the 1870 Civil Rights Act to block state and local action.

Field's decisions sparked bitter resentment. As one critic commented, after the Justice voided the Laundry Ordinance because it discriminated against inoffensive Chinese laundries: "If you have never had the pleasure of passing by a Celestial washhouse you cannot arrive at any sort of a correct conclusion as to the structure of Field's Judicial nose and if you ever visit San Francisco... and approach such an institution you will wonder *what does offend* Field's senses."[16] But besides generating personal animosity, Field's rulings alerted Californians to the desirability of a federal solution to the Chinese problem. With state regulation blocked by the courts, Coast residents turned in the 1880's and 1890's to the federal government for legislative and diplomatic controls over the Chinese.[17]

Californians attacked the railroad just as vehemently as they attacked the Chinese. Believing it would encourage immigration, pro-

[14] Willard B. Farwell, *The Chinese at Home and Abroad* (San Francisco, 1885), pp. 44, 84–111; George A. Nourse to William E. Chandler, April 21, 1882, William E. Chandler Papers, Manuscript Division, Library of Congress; Samuel Gompers, *Seventy Years of Life and Labor: An Autobiography*, 2 vols. (New York, 1925), 1: 305.

[15] Barth, *Bitter Strength*, pp. 129–56, 210–13; Coolidge, *Chinese Immigration*, pp. 69–82.

[16] Stephen M. White to Daniel Manning, April 23, 1885, WP; Elmer C. Sandmeyer, "California Anti-Chinese Legislation and the Federal Courts: A Study in Federal Relations," *PHR*, 5 (1936): 191–93; Carl Brent Swisher, *Stephen J. Field: Craftsman of the Law* (Hamden, Conn., 1963), pp. 206–26.

[17] Field himself advised Californians that "the remedy for the apprehended evil is

mote trade, and spur economic expansion, they had anticipated great benefits from rail connection with the rest of the country. And in the long run, of course, the Central Pacific more than fulfilled their original hopes. It linked the Pacific Coast to the rest of the country, introduced California into the national economy, and ultimately, with its related lines, opened vast areas of the state to future development. Land values soared along the railroad's route, especially through the San Joaquin Valley and Southern California, and settlers flocked to newly opened regions. The advent of rail transportation stimulated agricultural growth, primarily in grains and fruits, and fostered industrial expansion. Ultimately the railroad led to a more diversified, less exploitative state economy.

To many Californians, however, the immediate effects of the Central Pacific's completion in 1869 seemed more harmful than beneficial. Thousands of unskilled laborers were suddenly released from railroad work into an economy unable to absorb them. The railroad did bring the promised spurt in immigration, the largest since the early 1850's, but the newcomers swelled the unemployment rolls and depressed wage scales. Unable to farm or obtain jobs in the mines, the unemployed gathered in San Francisco, where businessmen and merchants also found themselves adversely affected; instead of entering outside markets, as they had confidently expected, the merchants discovered that their own preserves were being invaded by aggressive Eastern salesmen. For nearly twenty years Californians had pleaded, lobbied, and worked for a railroad, only to find the results bitterly disappointing. Their initial disillusionment with the Central Pacific would affect California politics for decades to come.[18]

Along with these difficulties, the railroad brought a pervasive economic and political power that aroused widespread discontent. With

to be sought from the General Government, where, except in certain special cases, all power over the subject lies." Chauncy F. Black and Samuel B. Smith, eds., *Some Account of the Work of Stephen J. Field as a Legislator, State Judge, and Judge of the Supreme Court of the United States* (n.p., 1882), p. 404.

[18] Stuart Daggett, *Chapters on the History of the Southern Pacific* (New York, 1922), pp. 173–74; Nash, *State Government*, p. 62; Cross, *Labor Movement*, pp. 61–63; Lucile Eaves, *A History of California Labor Legislation*, Univ. of California Publications in Economics, vol. 2 (Berkeley, 1910), p. 135; *California and the Pacific Coast: Address of Mr. Lloyd Tevis, President of Wells, Fargo & Company, San Francisco, Before the American Bankers' Association, at Niagara Falls, August 10, 1881* (n.p., n.d.), pp. 10–11.

6,799 employees in 1880, the Central Pacific easily ranked as the state's largest employer. Federal land grants amounting to more than eleven million acres made it also the largest landowner. Most important, the railroad enabled its owners, the "Big Four"—Collis P. Huntington, Leland Stanford, Charles Crocker, and Mark Hopkins—to achieve in the 1870's a virtual monopoly of California transportation. By 1877, besides the original Central Pacific, the Big Four had organized or absorbed the Western Pacific, the California Pacific, the Northern Railway, and the Southern Pacific. They controlled over 85 percent of the railroad mileage in California. Their purchase of the California Steam Navigation Company in 1869 and later agreements with the Pacific Mail Steamship Company effectively limited competition from water transportation. Until the late 1880's, moreover, when the Santa Fe entered Los Angeles, the Big Four managed to exclude rival railroads from the state. A visit to the Coast convinced Lord Bryce that "no State has been so much at the mercy of one powerful corporation."[19]

The manner in which the Big Four exercised this power evoked much hostility. Critics noted that various construction companies, essentially like the Union Pacific's notorious Crédit Mobilier, had allowed the associates to amass large personal fortunes, often at the expense of other stockholders. Merchants and farmers complained that California freight rates discriminated among areas and among shippers, and were generally higher than those in the East. Californians also charged that land grants had motivated the Southern Pacific's decision to build down the Central Valley, rather than along the more populous Coast, and that the railroad demanded special subsidies from communities through which it might pass. "They start out their railway track and survey their line near a thriving village," asserted one contemporary. "They go to the most prominent citizens of that village and say, 'If you will give us so many thousand dollars we will run through here; if you do not we will run by,' and in every instance where the subsidy was not granted, that course was taken, and the effect was just as they said, to kill off the little town."

---

[19] Bryce, *American Commonwealth*, 2: 441; *Report on the Agencies of Transportation in the United States* (Washington, D.C., 1883), pp. 276–79; E. Pomeroy, *Pacific Slope*, pp. 95–119; Daggett, *Southern Pacific*, pp. 104–41, 222–36.

The company exerted pressure of this kind on Visalia, Stockton, and even San Francisco; it persuaded Los Angeles to donate over $600,000 in subsidies.[20]

Opponents also accused the Big Four of corrupt involvement in politics. They claimed that the railroad controlled both political parties, influenced the legislature and judiciary, and subsidized much of the California press. Almost without exception they traced the corruption to the dominant railroad figure Collis P. Huntington, who looked after company affairs in New York and Washington. "I have a great many enemies," Huntington himself once told a Senate committee, "and I am proud of them, for I always hewed to the line and where there were fingers in the way they were pretty sure to be cut." Thrifty, energetic, and fiercely devoted to the company, he pursued its interests with a persistent ruthlessness that won success for his railroad, unpopularity for himself. "During the whole of my life," commented a prominent Californian, "I never met a man who was so full of selfishness and so devoid of the commonest principles of fairness and integrity as C. P. Huntington.... [He] has never knowingly favored a good man or an honest measure. He is the very essence of selfishness, the organization of cruelty and a complete compiled edition of business falsehood."[21]

Substantiation for this feeling came in 1883 with the publication of Huntington's letters to a California associate, David D. Colton, in which the railroad magnate described his Washington activities. The correspondence, according to the San Francisco *Chronicle*, exposed the fact that "for years past the Central Pacific Company has been systematically engaged in debauching Senators and Representatives,

[20] Quoted in Daggett, *Southern Pacific*, p. 28; Felix Riesenberg, Jr., *Golden Gate: The Story of San Francisco Harbor* (New York, 1940), pp. 198–200; William C. Fankhauser, *A Financial History of California: Public Revenues, Debts, and Expenditures*, Univ. of California Publications in Economics, vol. 3 (Berkeley, 1913), p. 208; James J. Ayers, *Gold and Sunshine: Reminiscences of Early California* (Boston, 1922), pp. 263–64; Maurice H. Newmark and Marco R. Newmark, eds., *Sixty Years in Southern California, 1853–1913: Containing the Reminiscences of Harris Newmark* (New York, 1926), pp. 502–7.

[21] LA *Times*, Feb. 22, 1896; Morris M. Estee to James S. Clarkson, Jan. 11, 1896, James S. Clarkson Papers, Manuscript Division, Library of Congress. Detailed accounts of Huntington's activities can be found in David Lavender, *The Great Persuader* (New York, 1970); Cerinda W. Evans, *Collis Potter Huntington*, 2 vols. (Newport News, Va., 1954); and Oscar Lewis, *The Big Four: The Story of Huntington, Stanford, Hopkins, and Crocker, and of the Building of the Central Pacific* (New York, 1938).

buying up Legislatures, presenting fraudulent reports, declaring dividends with borrowed money, buying up newspapers ..., and other kinds of wickedness too numerous to mention." Throughout the letters ran suggestive sentences: "I stayed in Washington two days to fix up [the] Railroad Committee in the Senate"; "If we are not hurt this session it will be because we pay much money to prevent it"; "We should be very careful to get a United States Senator from California that will be disposed to use us fairly and then have the power to help us." To Californians already troubled by railroad power, the letters supplied evidence of company interference in politics and confirmed the popular conviction that Huntington's ethical code read: "Whatever is not nailed down is mine. Whatever I can pry loose is not nailed down."[22]

In their bitterness against the railroad, Californians understandably exaggerated its influence and oversimplified its complex relationship with the political system. Dependent on state and federal government for loans and subsidies, and fearful of regulatory and repressive measures, the railroad entered politics to protect and enlarge its numerous interests. The process was gradual and often reluctant; but once involved, the company found it necessary to maintain and even to extend its political activities. Although he practiced the art with consummate skill, Huntington repeatedly made clear his distaste for continual conflict with political conventions, legislative bodies, and the courts. "This Washington business," he once wrote, "will kill me yet, if I have to continue the fight from year to year, and then every year the fight grows more and more expensive, and rather than let it continue as it is from year to year, as it is, I would rather they take the road and be done with it." Huntington and his associates made occasional efforts to withdraw the company from politics, but the process had become a circular one in which initial railroad involvement and the public's demands for regulation interacted to draw the company further into politics. The Big Four felt, as a sympathetic congressman explained in 1873, that "railroad companies cannot be kept out of the lobby or out of politics, if the people are continually incited

[22] SF *Chron*, Dec. 23, 1883; Cornelius Cole to Olive Cole, Dec. 25, 1883, Cole to Olive Cole, Feb. 5, 1884, Cole Papers; David Starr Jordan, *The Days of a Man: Being Memories of a Naturalist, Teacher and Minor Prophet of Democracy*, 2 vols. (New York, 1922), 1: 479.

to elect only their 'reliable enemies,' and projects are discussed and promoted by Legislatures to regulate their business and diminish their revenues, where malice or even well-meaning ignorance may plunge them into bankruptcy. 'Self-defense is the first law of nature.' "[23]

Even when involved in politics, moreover, the railroad did not always act as a cohesive unit; nor did it enjoy unbroken political success. A notable division occurred in 1885, when Huntington opposed Leland Stanford's senatorial ambitions, and the railroad leaders suffered several major reversals in the 1880's and 1890's. Most Californians, however, believed otherwise, and it was around this belief in railroad oppression, rather than around actual instances of it, that state politics during these years often revolved. Henry Adams would later note that "the generation between 1865 and 1895 was already mortgaged to the railways, and no one knew it better than the generation itself." In some respects the generation in California knew it too well. There the railways came to be regarded as a monolithic and malevolent force whose policies retarded economic development and whose power corrupted all levels of government. This conception stressed simplicity at the expense of accuracy and sometimes hindered a realistic approach to the state's railroad problem. But it swelled anti-railroad sentiment, gave reform-minded citizens a heightened sense of mission, and made the railroad the constant focus of political discussion.[24]

Grievances against the railroad sparked numerous attempts to supervise and regulate its operation. An advisory commission, formed in 1876, possessed insufficient powers; it lasted only two years. Another effort accompanied the revision of the state constitution in 1879. The new document erected safeguards against railroad influence and included vigorous regulatory provisions. It established a railroad commission, with authority to set maximum rates and prevent unjust discrimination, and divided the state into three districts, each to elect

[23] Huntington to David D. Colton, Nov. 15, 1877, in SF *Chron*, Dec. 23, 1883; Evans, *Huntington*, 1: 303; George T. Clark, *Leland Stanford: War Governor of California, Railroad Builder and Founder of Stanford University* (Stanford, Cal., 1931), p. 291.
[24] Henry Adams, *The Education of Henry Adams* (New York, 1931), p. 240; Thomas R. Bacon, "The Railroad Strike in California," *Yale Review*, 3 (1895): 248. See also SF *Exmr*, Sept. 14, 1889; John T. Doyle to Abram S. Hewitt, March 4, 1885, CP.

one commissioner. But this commission, like the first, failed to satisfy Californians, who overlooked its experimental nature and grew impatient with its slow progress. They believed it overly sympathetic to the railroad, "a new Southern Pacific literary bureau maintained at public expense." This feeling increased when an 1883 investigation by a committee of the legislature concluded that one commission member had accepted favors from Leland Stanford, while another's conduct "admits of no other explanation than that he was bribed." Both commissioners, the committee charged, had "acted in the interests of the railroad corporations rather than of the people."[25]

State and local efforts to regulate the railroad by law met the same difficulties that Californians experienced in connection with the Chinese question. The federal courts intervened in a manner that served to protect the company and limit the effectiveness of local control over the railroad. Resentment again centered on Justice Stephen J. Field, whose decisions broadened corporate rights at the expense of state authority. As a San Francisco newspaper complained after one case, "While the hireling sheets of monopoly are exulting over the decision, another class is mourning the fact that the circuit in which California is unfortunately included is presided over by Justice Field. . . . Whenever he has a case before him in which the community and the corporations are arrayed against each other, his lights always lead him to discover points against the people."[26] In the decades after 1880 Field's judicial pronouncements and the problems initially encountered by the state's regulatory experiments spurred Coast residents to search for more effective means to supervise the railroad. By demonstrating the limitations of state authority, these difficulties also brought a gradual and important change in outlook among reform-minded Californians, who continued to rely on state action but added a belief that the federal government was a necessary instrument for corporate control. By the mid-1890's, measuring the distance they had come, large numbers of Californians would demand government ownership of the Central Pacific Railroad.

<hr>

[25] S. E. Moffett, "The Railroad Commission of California: A Study in Irresponsible Government," *Annals of the American Academy of Political and Social Science*, 6 (1895): 476; Daggett, *Southern Pacific*, pp. 190–93; Nash, "California Railroad Commission," pp. 287–305.
[26] Quoted in Swisher, *Field*, p. 256.

III

Anti-railroad and anti-Chinese sentiment peaked under the unsettled conditions of the 1870's. Geographically isolated and not yet fully integrated into the national economy, California remained for several years relatively unaffected by the 1873 panic and depression in the East. But the state faced serious economic troubles within its own borders. The southern "cow counties" still suffered from the results of the drought of the previous decade, and insufficient rainfall, particularly during the winter of 1876–77, cut mineral and agricultural production in all sections. Speculative involvement with Nevada's Comstock Lode also had an adverse effect on California's economy. In 1877, after the Consolidated Virginia Mine passed its usual monthly dividend, bank failures spread across the state. Real estate values dropped, businesses closed, and unemployment mounted. The unemployed flocked to San Francisco, where in a three-month interval during 1877, more than four thousand persons applied for relief. In San Francisco alone that year, an estimated thirty thousand were without work.[27]

Economic hardship soon fostered a pervasive discontent. In agricultural areas, especially in the arc of grain-growing counties surrounding San Francisco Bay, depressed conditions aggravated long-standing grievances over oceanic and railroad freight rates, confused and monopolistic landholdings, uncertain water rights, and inequitable tax policies. Agrarian unrest was reflected in the swift expansion of the Grange movement, which claimed almost fifteen thousand members at its peak in the mid-1870's.[28] Another, more militant, organization arose among workingmen in the cities. On July 23, 1877, aroused by the railroad strikes in the East, eight thousand laborers and unem-

[27] Cross, *Labor Movement*, pp. 61–72; Carosso, *California Wine Industry*, p. 94; Ayers, *Gold and Sunshine*, pp. 275–77; Theodore H. Hittell, *History of California*, 4 vols. (San Francisco, 1885–97), 4: 542–49; Rodman W. Paul, *California Gold: The Beginning of Mining in the Far West* (Cambridge, Mass., 1947), pp. 181–82; Gerald T. White, *Formative Years in the Far West: A History of Standard Oil Company of California and Predecessors Through 1919* (New York, 1962), pp. 36, 64.

[28] For details on agricultural grievances, see Clarke A. Chambers, *California Farm Organizations: A Historical Study of the Grange, the Farm Bureau and the Associated Farmers, 1929–1941* (Berkeley, 1952), pp. 9–12, 205; Rodman W. Paul, "The Great California Grain War: The Grangers Challenge the Wheat King," *PHR*, 27 (1958): 331–49; Ezra S. Carr, *The Patrons of Husbandry on the Pacific Coast* (San Francisco, 1875), pp. 81–83, 131–35.

ployed massed on the sandlots before San Francisco's City Hall to express support for the strikers and to air their own grievances. The meeting, resulting in sporadic violence, prompted San Franciscans to form the city's third vigilance committee. More significant, it also led ultimately to the formation on October 5, 1877, of the Workingmen's party of California.

Headed by Denis Kearney, an Irish drayman and a skilled orator, the Workingmen's party spread quickly to Oakland, Sacramento, Los Angeles, Santa Barbara, and other communities. Kearney blamed corporate privilege and the Chinese for California's economic troubles. Large crowds gathered on the sandlots and before the Nob Hill mansions of the Big Four to hear him declaim on the menace of the Chinese and the railroad. "The reign of bloated knaves is over," he told them. "The people are about to take their own affairs into their own hands, and they will not be stayed by vigilantes, state militia, nor United States troops."[29]

As established politicians watched in dismay, the new party grew so rapidly that for a time it appeared likely to become a permanent fixture in California political life. At the beginning of 1878 it won legislative elections in Alameda and Santa Clara counties; in March it elected the mayors of Oakland and Sacramento. By then the party claimed fifteen thousand members in San Francisco. During the following months it published its own newspaper, established branches in 40 of the state's 52 counties, and achieved victories in several municipal elections. Its most important triumph came in June 1878, only nine months after its formation, when it elected one-third of the delegates to a convention that had been called to revise the California constitution.[30]

The convention produced a document that reflected the demands of the dissatisfied laborers and farmers. In response to Workingmen's grievances, the new constitution called for an eight-hour day on

[29] Carl Brent Swisher, *Motivation and Political Technique in the California Constitutional Convention, 1878–79* (Claremont, Cal., 1930), p. 12; Ralph Kauer, "The Workingmen's Party of California," *PHR*, 13 (1944): 278–81; Winfield J. Davis, *History of Political Conventions in California, 1849–1892* (Sacramento, 1893), pp. 377–86, 396–400.

[30] Kauer, "Workingmen's Party," pp. 282–86; Davis, *Political Conventions*, p. 375; Cross, *Labor Movement*, pp. 116–17; T. Hittell, *History of California*, 4: 610–14.

public works and prohibited the employment of Chinese by public agencies and California-chartered companies. The courts soon struck down the anti-Chinese provisions, but in any event the lasting significance of the 1879 constitution lay elsewhere. In its controls over corporations and revision of the state's basic tax structure, the document represented an early phase of a nationwide ferment that would continue into the twentieth century. Several times as long as the 1849 version, it also exhibited the Middle Period tendency to remove broad areas of policy from the discretion of elected lawmakers. It detailed fundamental procedures that molded state actions until the progressives, profiting from the experience of the late nineteenth century, introduced constitutional revisions in 1910 and after. Until then, in tax provisions and other respects, California and its new constitution served as a "weather gauge" for experts and legislators across the country.[31]

More than anything else, observers watched the California attempt to establish state controls over the modern industrial system. In regard to corporations, the most visible element in the system, the constitution naturally focused on the railroad. Declaring transportation companies "subject to legislative control," it created a railroad commission, which it endowed with unprecedented authority to oversee railroad rates and practices. Of equal significance, the constitution endeavored to bring industrialism's "new," intangible wealth under government sway. In terms subsequently copied by other states, it expressly included as taxable property "moneys, credits, bonds, stocks, dues, franchises, and all other matters and things, real, personal, and mixed, capable of private ownership."[32] The inclusion of franchises, a novel approach, captured wide attention among lawmakers who faced similar corporate and financial problems in their own localities. Such innovations also intrigued tax experts concerned with the dis-

---

[31] C. K. Yearley, *The Money Machines: The Breakdown and Reform of Governmental and Party Finance in the North, 1860–1920* (Albany, N.Y., 1970), p. 196; *California Blue Book, or State Roster, 1893* (Sacramento, 1893), pp. 17–38; Isidor Loeb, "Constitutional Limitations Affecting Taxation," *Proceedings of the National Tax Association* (New York, 1908), pp. 75–78; Newton W. Thompson, "Separation of State and Local Revenues," *ibid.* (Ithaca, N.Y., 1915), pp. 42–49.

[32] *California Blue Book, 1893*, pp. 31–33; Yearley, *Money Machines*, pp. 16, 37–74; Edwin R. A. Seligman, "Finance Statistics of the American Commonwealths," *Publications of the American Statistical Association*, 1 (1889): 411.

integrating tax structure of the era, and they were the forerunners of policies pursued two decades later by Theodore Roosevelt, as governor of New York, and other progressive leaders.[33]

The events in California, including the Workingmen's agitation and the adoption of the new constitution, promptly aroused controversy. Conservative organs in New York and other Eastern cities assailed Pacific Coast radicalism, while in London Karl Marx asked an American friend for details on local conditions. "California is very important to me," he observed, "because nowhere else has the upheaval most shamelessly caused by capitalist centralization taken place with such speed."[34] Both viewpoints misjudged the extent of the upheaval, but the ferment of the 1870's had a profound impact on California politics. In immediate terms it encouraged the rise of numerous splinter parties, disrupted established political patterns, and led all parties to adopt pronounced positions on the railroad and Chinese issues. By the end of the decade no party platform could fail to include a vigorous denunciation of railroad oppression and a demand for increased government regulation of corporate affairs.

More important, among the satisfied and the dissatisfied alike, the discontent of the 1870's focused attention on the course of California's development and posed questions that would dominate state politics through the remainder of the century. In their broadest form these questions involved the role of government in society, the position of large corporations in the economy, and the relevance and responsiveness of the political process. All of them, in one way or another, touched specifically on the power of the Central Pacific and Southern Pacific railroads. Though these issues affected every political organization, they received their fullest expression within the California Democratic party.

[33] Edwin R. A. Seligman, "The Taxation of Corporations," *Political Science Quarterly*, 5 (1890): 438; G. Wallace Chessman, *Governor Theodore Roosevelt: The Albany Apprenticeship, 1898–1900* (Cambridge, Mass., 1965), pp. 133–57; William Henry Harbaugh, *Power and Responsibility: The Life and Times of Theodore Roosevelt* (New York, 1961), pp. 115–18.

[34] "The Taxation of Personal Property," *The Nation*, 32 (Feb. 10, 1881): 86–87; C. T. Hopkins, "Taxation in California," *The Californian*, 3 (1881): 139–48; Marx to Friedrich A. Sorge, Nov. 5, 1880, in Alexander Trachtenberg, ed., *Karl Marx and Frederick Engels: Letters to Americans, 1848–1895* (New York, 1953), p. 126.

By the close of the 1870's, the Democratic party was a declining force in state politics. As it had twenty years before, when controversies over slavery, secession, and the Civil War had torn the Democrats asunder, trouble had again befallen this once-proud party that had dominated California politics during the first decade of the state's existence. Exploiting hostility toward the Chinese and the growing weariness with the Republicans' war issues, Democratic leaders had worked through the 1860's to reconstruct the party, only to see the product of their labor virtually dissolve in the political flux surrounding the rise of the Workingmen's party. In the space of a few years during the late 1870's the Democrats lost thousands of voters to the Workingmen. The gubernatorial election of 1879 measured the extent of their losses. In the corresponding election four years earlier the Democrats had polled 50 percent of the vote; in 1879 they polled only 30 percent, while the Workingmen polled 28 percent and the Republicans 42 percent. The 1879 results also gave the Workingmen's party eleven senators, seventeen assemblymen, and a larger number of seats in the legislature than the Democrats.

The Democrats' losses were particularly heavy in San Francisco, formerly a center of Democratic strength. There in 1879 the Workingmen elected the mayor, sheriff, treasurer, auditor, tax collector, district attorney, and most other municipal officers. The Democratic vote dropped precipitously, from some 22,000 in 1876 to less than 4,000 in 1879, as discontented laborers and other groups deserted to the Workingmen's camp. "Scarce a grease spot was left to mark its place," one Democrat recalled of the San Francisco party. In addition to votes, the Democratic party lost a number of prominent leaders, among them William F. White, who accepted the Workingmen's nomination for governor in 1879 even though he had been a member of the Democratic state central committee for the past two decades.[35]

In the late 1870's, therefore, Democrats found themselves in a

---

[35] James H. Wilkins, ed., "The Reminiscences of Christopher A. Buckley," SF *Bul*, Dec. 25, 1918; Kauer, "Workingmen's Party," pp. 285–87; Saxton, *Indispensable Enemy*, pp. 67–137; Cross, *Labor Movement*, pp. 120–22; Edith Dobie, *The Political Career of Stephen Mallory White: A Study of Party Activities Under the Convention System* (Stanford, Cal., 1927), pp. 23–28.

struggle for survival, as they fought to regain their scattered membership and reverse the abrupt decline of their party's strength in San Francisco and the state. They soon accomplished these objectives, but in the process their party underwent fundamental alterations. Unexpected assistance came in 1880, when dwindling support and internal dissension over Kearney's leadership caused the demise of the Workingmen's party. Most of its adherents returned to the Democratic fold, bringing with them the economic grievances, anti-monopoly sentiments, and anti-Chinese demands that had originally sparked their defection. "It is true," one Democrat later remarked, "that this new party finally collapsed and mostly returned to the Democratic party, but its former members still retain many of its old views and still ride many of its old hobbies. Others, not original members, have largely adopted its sentiments." That development, together with the Democrats' efforts to appeal to the disaffected elements, meant a more emphatic party stand on the railroad and Chinese questions. Both issues had been stressed in Democratic platforms throughout the 1870's, and now, in the years after 1880, they became the heart of the party's program.[36]

Not all Democrats welcomed the party's new outlook. The party contained a number of well-known men who scorned anti-monopoly sentiment and resented the Democratic position on the railroad issue. At the head of this group, giving it immediate prestige and authority, was California's most prominent Democrat, Stephen J. Field. A famous member of a celebrated family, Field had earned personal renown by virtue of hard work, legal skill, and luck. In 1849, at the age of 33, he had left the New York law office of his brother, David Dudley Field, to join the Gold Rush to California. Spurning the mines, he continued his law practice and within a year of arrival won election to the legislature. In 1857, following an unsuccessful attempt to capture a seat in the United States Senate, he secured a place on the California Supreme Court. Six years later, on the recommendation of Leland Stanford and others, Field received from Abraham

---

[36] Samuel M. Wilson to Thomas A. Hendricks, April 29, 1885, CP; Kauer, "Workingmen's Party," pp. 288–89. An example of Democratic efforts to appeal to the Workingmen is William S. Rosecrans to P. B. Tully, Oct. 3, 1880, William S. Rosecrans Papers, Division of Special Collections, Univ. of California, Los Angeles.

Lincoln an appointment to the United States Supreme Court, a position he held for over 34 years.[37]

Buttressed by an imposing judicial demeanor, Field's career on the Court since 1863 had won wide attention and some support. It had also manifested his inclination to provide maximum protection for personal and corporate property, and after 1880, when his state party began increasingly to reflect anti-monopoly sentiment, the Justice did not conceal his displeasure. Field made it clear that he regarded such sentiment as "agrarian and communistic" and as nothing more than a desire "to break down all associated Capital by loading it with unequal and oppressive burdens." In this view he was joined by other leading Democrats, among them Samuel M. Wilson, a San Francisco attorney; J. DeBarth Shorb, a Southern California viticulturist; and John P. Irish, a journalist.[38]

Like Field, Samuel M. Wilson had been deeply disturbed by the events of the late 1870's. A prominent delegate to the constitutional convention, he had led the resistance to change, whether it involved the creation of a strong railroad commission or the decision to tax stocks, bonds, and franchises. But he had lost, and Californians had adopted a new constitution whose "absurd, unwise and injurious" provisions threatened revered principles. Worse, Wilson's own party now contained many who favored further extensions of state authority, particularly in relation to business regulation. To Wilson their views not only represented a betrayal of the party's Jeffersonian legacy but signaled a failure to recognize that "great corporations, with large aggregate capital, are necessary to the vast enterprises of the age and to modern civilization and progress." Against anti-monopoly feeling Wilson set a fervent determination to uphold Democratic traditions and resist "paternalism" in any form. In the years after 1880 he worked to discredit those Democrats who believed, in his words, that "the hand of government should be felt in all the affairs of life; the acquisition of wealth should have a limit; the laws should make it an unhappy thing for those already having too much; and

[37] Swisher, *Field*, pp. 2–116; Gustavus Myers, *History of the Supreme Court of the United States* (Chicago, 1912), pp. 501–2; John Norton Pomeroy, "Introductory Sketch," in Black and Smith, eds., *Some Account of the Work of Field*, pp. 7–61.

[38] Field to George Ticknor Curtis, Dec. 14, 1884, CP.

by the mysterious workings of a new system no one should any longer suffer poverty or distress."[39]

The conservative attorney found an able ally in John P. Irish. A latecomer to the state, Irish had first won prominence in his native Iowa, where he had edited a party newspaper and pursued a political career that included the chairmanship of the Democratic central committee, three terms in the legislature, and unsuccessful campaigns for Congress and the governorship. His brief association with the Iowa Anti-Monopoly party in the early 1870's must have stemmed from a moment of political expediency or youthful exuberance, for Irish spent the remainder of his life fighting "radical" doctrines. On moving to California in 1882, he gained immediate influence as editor of the Oakland *Times* and later the prestigious *Alta California*. A famed orator, his light hair, engaging blue eyes, bushy mustache, and somewhat portly figure became familiar to audiences across the state. On the stump and in print, Irish was a respected and formidable advocate of the conservative Democratic philosophy. Soon after his arrival he joined Wilson and Field in the struggle against "the dissemination of socialistic and communistic doctrines" by anti-monopolist Democrats.[40]

The anti-monopoly wing of the Democratic party had formed gradually in the period following the collapse of the Workingmen's party. At first an informal union of like-minded men throughout the state, it was composed of some who, like William F. White, had returned to Democratic ranks from prominent positions in the Workingmen's party and some who, like Christopher A. Buckley, had remained in the Democratic party to profit from its internal dislocations. Although diverse in membership, the anti-monopoly coalition was bound together by a mixture of political ambition and honest desire to establish some measure of control over the power of the

[39] Wilson to Thomas A. Hendricks, April 29, 1885, CP; Carl C. Plehn, "The Taxation of Mortgages in California, 1849 to 1899," *Yale Review*, 8 (1899): 48.

[40] Details on Irish's life can be found in two articles by Mildred Throne: "The Anti-Monopoly Party in Iowa, 1873–1874," *Iowa Journal of History*, 52 (1954): 289–326; "The Liberal Republican Party in Iowa, 1872," *ibid.*, 53 (1955): 121–52. See also Benjamin F. Gue, *History of Iowa*, 4 vols. (New York, 1903), 4: 142–43; Edward H. Stiles, *Recollections and Sketches of Notable Lawyers and Public Men of Early Iowa* (Des Moines, Iowa, 1916), pp. 785–89; "Letters Written by Irish to Parker," pp. 421–22.

railroad. By the early 1880's it included William D. English and Michael F. Tarpey from Alameda County, Stephen M. White and Reginaldo F. Del Valle from Los Angeles, and Barclay Henley from Sonoma County. In San Francisco it was represented by Buckley, Delphin M. Delmas, and George Hearst.

Stephen M. White, Buckley, and Hearst exemplified the diversity of the anti-monopoly movement. One of a new group of California-born political leaders, White had graduated from Santa Clara College and in 1874, at the age of 21, had settled in Los Angeles to practice law. Influenced by his father, William F. White, he early became involved in politics. He served in local Democratic councils and won his first elective office in 1882. Thereafter White rose rapidly to prominence. His subsequent career, during which he gained nationwide attention as a silver spokesman in the United States Senate and as chairman of the 1896 Democratic national convention, revealed him to be a remarkably deft politician, a talented speaker, a firm believer in effective party organization, and in the words of a friend, a "master of invective." A generation of Southern Californians knew him simply as "Our Steve" and followed his achievements with pride. At his death in 1901 a Republican newspaper called him "the most distinguished son the State has produced in the half-century of her existence." Handsome and full-bearded, the "Little Giant of California," White was genuinely concerned about the implications of railroad power for the state, and in the early 1880's he became the acknowledged head of the anti-monopoly forces in Southern California.[41]

Sincerely committed to railroad reform, White never completely trusted the anti-monopoly convictions of his two powerful allies, Christopher A. Buckley and George Hearst. The former, born in Ireland in 1845, came to California in 1862 from New York City, where he had spent his youth. After working as a horsecar conductor and bartender, Buckley opened a saloon on Bush Street in San Francisco and entered city politics, first as a Republican and then as a Democrat. His opportunity came in the chaotic conditions of the late

[41] John Steven McGroarty, *Los Angeles: From the Mountains to the Sea*, 3 vols. (Chicago, 1921), 1: 358; LA *Times*, Feb. 22, 1901; SF *Chron*, Feb. 22, 1901; Los Angeles *Weekly Mirror*, Nov. 1, 1884; Peter Thomas Conmy, *Stephen Mallory White: California Statesman* (San Francisco, 1956), pp. 1–6; Dobie, *White*, pp. 24–27.

1870's, when the Workingmen's party virtually demolished the Democratic organization in San Francisco and then suddenly collapsed itself. "It was then," he later recalled, "the effort of the public-minded to cast a lifeline to these derelicts and haul them back safely to the stanch Democratic ship. I became interested in this noble rescue work and that is how I first took an active hand in politics."[42]

By 1882 Buckley had erected his own political machine on the ruins of the city party. Known as the "Blind Boss" and the "Blind White Devil" because he had lost his sight (from habitual drunkenness, his enemies alleged), Buckley won respect—even from opponents—for his generosity, intelligence, and keen memory. A deft sense of organization, a determination to maintain low municipal tax rates, and an ability to persuade respected San Franciscans to head his tickets enabled him to remain in power. To disarm opposition, Buckley used charm. "He looks one full in the face with his large sightless orbs below his smooth and serene forehead, and seems to be all innocence and candor," an enemy acknowledged.[43]

Exploiting these talents Buckley dominated San Francisco political life for almost a decade. "The game of politics is not a branch of the Sunday school business," he once remarked, and at his death in 1922 the onetime bartender and saloon-keeper left an estate valued at nearly one million dollars. In the early 1880's, having just witnessed the appeal of an anti-railroad platform to local voters, the Blind Boss added his considerable influence to the anti-monopoly wing of the Democratic party. Although the other anti-monopolists were always wary of Buckley, they needed his control over the San Francisco organization.[44]

While Buckley supplied the anti-monopolists with votes in conventions and elections, George Hearst contributed money and journalistic support. A "multi-millionaire, untidy of dress, almost illiterate, an assassin of grammar, a lover of poker and good bourbon, and an

[42] Wilkins, ed., "Reminiscences of Buckley," SF *Bul*, Dec. 25 and 28, 1918, Jan. 24, 1919; Alexander Callow, Jr., "San Francisco's Blind Boss," *PHR*, 25 (1956): 261–71; James H. Wilkins, ed., "Martin Kelly's Story," SF *Bul*, Sept. 5, 1917.

[43] Jeremiah Lynch, *Buckleyism: The Government of a State* (San Francisco, 1889), p. 12.

[44] Wilkins, ed., "Reminiscences of Buckley," SF *Bul*, Dec. 25 and 28, 1918, Jan. 24, 1919; Callow, "Blind Boss," pp. 261–71.

inveterate tobacco chewer whose long beard and shirtfront were generally stained with juice," Hearst had been nearly penniless when he arrived in California in 1850 at the age of 30. He then embarked on a series of lucrative mining ventures, acquiring the ownership of the country's largest gold mine, the Homestake in South Dakota, and the richest vein of copper in the world, the Anaconda in Montana. In 1880, his fortune made, Hearst bought the San Francisco *Examiner*, the leading Democratic newspaper on the Pacific Coast, and actively pursued a public career. Two years later, his ambitions apparently directed toward the governorship and ultimately a seat in the Senate, he formed an alliance in San Francisco with Buckley and, his opponents charged, with the railroad as well. At the Democratic convention, however, his gubernatorial candidacy failed when "country" delegates united behind another aspirant and when, again according to his opponents, the railroad deserted him. Whatever actually occurred between Hearst and the railroad, it was at about this time that the influential *Examiner* joined the anti-monopoly movement and began its long campaign to reduce the power of the Central Pacific in the state.[45]

Brought together in uneasy alliance, Hearst, Buckley, White, and their fellow anti-monopolists soon occupied a dominant position within the California Democratic party. Anti-monopolists took control of local Democratic organizations across the state. The extent of their influence became evident in the campaign and election of 1882. Although Hearst lost in his bid for the gubernatorial nomination, the party selected as its candidate another anti-monopolist, Gen. George Stoneman, a Southern California winegrower who was a member of the railroad commission established under the 1879 constitution. Stoneman's claim to office rested solely on his having advocated lower rates while on the commission, and he ran on a platform

---

[45] W. A. Swanberg, *Citizen Hearst* (New York, 1961), p. 3. Overshadowed by his son, William Randolph Hearst, George Hearst has not yet received adequate study. Mr. and Mrs. Fremont Older, *George Hearst, California Pioneer* (Los Angeles, 1966), remains the only full-length treatment. Brief accounts can be found in Swanberg, *Citizen Hearst*, pp. 3–23; Oliver Carlson and Ernest Sutherland Bates, *Hearst: Lord of San Simeon* (New York, 1936), pp. 5–30; John K. Winkler, *W. R. Hearst: An American Phenomenon* (New York, 1928), pp. 33–35; and John Tebbel, *The Life and Good Times of William Randolph Hearst* (New York, 1952), pp. 101–2.

that included five vigorous resolutions on the railroad question. The platform condemned the "faithlessness" of Stoneman's two commission colleagues, demanded an immediate 15 percent reduction in freight and passenger rates, urged "speedy and effective measures" to compel railroads to pay their taxes, and promised Californians relief from "the exactions and injustice now practiced with impunity by the railroad corporations."[46]

The election results far exceeded the Democrats' expectations. Alert to the obvious trend in popular sentiment, their Republican opponents had also adopted a strong anti-railroad platform and had nominated Morris M. Estee, an attractive candidate with a reputation for independence and anti-monopoly opinions. But the Republicans' strategy failed to overcome the party's vulnerability on the railroad issue. Stoneman received 55 percent of the vote, carried 44 of the state's 52 counties, and defeated Estee by more than 23,500 votes. Democrats captured nearly all state offices, the entire railroad commission, all six congressional seats, and an overwhelming majority of seats in the legislature. In San Francisco, the scene of the party's recent setbacks, Stoneman emerged with 62 percent of the vote and a plurality of 10,500 ballots. The anti-monopolists celebrated what one of them called "our glorious victory." The 1882 outcome, seemingly a complete vindication of their stand, convinced them as well as many previously uncommitted Democrats that the party had chosen the correct course. Democratic triumphs early the following year in Oakland, Stockton, Sacramento, and Los Angeles reinforced this conviction. "I think this anti-monopoly fight is bound to win in the end," exulted an Oakland Democrat, "if our friends do not become discouraged at minor defeats."[47]

Events would soon test the anti-monopolists' fortitude in the face of defeat. Promises made in 1882 would have to be kept if the victors

[46] Davis, *Political Conventions*, pp. 431–36; Nash, "California Railroad Commission," pp. 289–93; John T. Doyle to Abram S. Hewitt, March 4, 1885, CP; H. Brett Melendy and Benjamin F. Gilbert, *The Governors of California: Peter H. Burnett to Edmund G. Brown* (Georgetown, Cal., 1965), pp. 205–7.

[47] William W. Foote to Stephen M. White, Nov. 16, 1882, Foote to White, Sept. 2, 1883, WP; LA *Times*, Sept. 2, 1882; SF *Exmr*, Nov. 5, 1884; Dobie, *White*, p. 251; Davis, *Political Conventions*, pp. 439–44, 453; Samuel M. Wilson to Thomas A. Hendricks, April 29, 1885, W. S. Rosecrans to Grover Cleveland, March 3, 1886, CP.

wished to consolidate their newly won gains in the party and the state. Above all, the anti-monopolists would have to solve the complicated matter of railroad taxes and bring about prompt rate reductions. They would also have to dislodge the remnants of opposition within their own organization, for they quickly found that conservative Democrats refused to be impressed by party triumphs based on unacceptable doctrines. Denunciation and dialogue between the two factions continued in the years after 1882. At its most visible level, this factionalism involved struggles for patronage, party control, and personal advancement, as various individuals and groups maneuvered to secure their objectives. More important, it also reflected the progress of a significant internal debate over party philosophy, the proper use and extent of government authority, and the consequences of corporate growth. To some Democrats, like Stephen M. White, the solution to California's problems with the railroad lay in supervisory and regulatory action by the state. To others, like Stephen J. Field, such action constituted arbitrary and unwarranted interference in the natural operation of the economy. The struggle between these men, their allies, and their differing approaches to the issues confronting the state would mold California politics for much of the next decade.

CHAPTER TWO

Efforts at Reform
1883-1884

❦

THE ANTI-MONOPOLISTS' confidence soared in the wake of their 1882 election victory. Nothing, it appeared, could thwart the adoption of the reform program and the consolidation of Democratic hegemony in California. Democrats controlled the state government, and public opinion seemed ready to back vigorous regulatory measures. The intensity of anti-railroad sentiment carried the reform issue across party lines. With unusual unanimity, Republican and Democratic journals joined in denunciations of the "monster Monopoly" and demanded stern curbs on the "blighting policy, the iniquitous practices of the great railroad corporation which, octopus-like, is coiling its tentacles about every industrial interest in the State." The publication of the Huntington-Colton correspondence late in 1883, combined with revelations about the conduct of the first railroad commission, accentuated this sentiment and broadened support for reform. "This is a bad year for the Huntington crowd...," rejoiced Cornelius Cole, a Southern California Republican and former United States senator. "Those Colton letters have done him & his associates a 'power' of harm. If their sleep is disturbed by them, it will be no more than they have inflicted on us in times gone by."[1]

Like all reform groups, however, the anti-monopolists found it difficult to translate ideals into action. Taking office in January 1883, amid promises to check the "insolent and tyrannical" railroad, they first attempted to respond to the mounting clamor over railroad rates. But the new Democratic railroad commission refused to institute substantial reforms, even though its three members, William P.

---

[1] LA *Times*, Sept. 2, 1882; Cole to Olive Cole, Feb. 5, 1884, Cole Papers.

Humphreys, Gideon J. Carpenter, and William W. Foote, had each pledged to lower rates and end discrimination. Instead, the commission became mired in a damaging internal debate over government prerogatives and the extent of its own functions. A mixture of serious differences and petty squabbling, the debate stemmed in part from the experimental nature of the commission framework. In the sense that it reflected widespread public attitudes—respect for private property, fear that state interference might retard economic progress, and distaste for government intrusion in the affairs of the individual—it illustrated problems common to all commissions in the late nineteenth century.[2]

The railroad commission's difficulties began immediately. Early in 1883, in accordance with his campaign pledge, Foote proposed a maximum passenger fare of three cents per mile on the Central Pacific and the Southern Pacific. He met determined resistance from the railroad, which denied the commission's jurisdiction over a federally franchised corporation and took advantage of inadequate commission procedures to hinder effective regulation. Foote had anticipated railroad opposition, but he also encountered unexpected opposition from his two colleagues. Arguing that rate adjustments should await a detailed investigation of company revenues, Carpenter and Humphreys rejected the proposed fare reduction. Five months later, with the investigation concluded, Foote reintroduced the resolution, adding a provision for a 20 percent decrease in freight rates. Once again the two other commissioners voted it down.[3]

In the following months Carpenter and Humphreys justified the confidence of those Californians who had predicted that a commission would protect rather than damage railroad interests. Inexperience and an understandable hesitancy to adopt uninformed policies that might seriously harm the company helped explain their initial quiescence. Their continued inaction, however, owed more to their espousal of the business values and limited government doctrines of the con-

[2] Theodore H. Hittell, *History of California*, 4 vols. (San Francisco, 1885–97), 4: 673.
[3] "Fourth Annual Report of the Board of Railroad Commissioners," *J App*, 26 sess. (1885), 5: 13–16, 27–28, 63–66; Gerald D. Nash, "The California Railroad Commission, 1876–1911," *Southern California Quarterly*, 44 (1962): 290–93.

servative Democrats. In tones reminiscent of Stephen J. Field and Samuel M. Wilson, the two commissioners pursued a course of "intelligent conservatism," in which they relied for guidance on "truisms of transportation and of industrial self-government." They confined the commission to advisory functions, avoided "meddling supervision," and shunned interference with private property. As for the railroad, Carpenter and Humphreys asserted, "those engaged in the various useful callings of life and severally minding their own business, can and do manage it better than the State."[4]

To the dismay of the anti-monopolists, the conservative commissioners also devoted increasing portions of their annual reports to lavish praise of the railroad's contributions to California. "Nowhere and by no agency," noted one report, "is better, cheaper, or more accommodating service rendered to the traveling public than by companies owning and operating railroads in this State." The commission itself, they declared, was an "alien" and "communistic" innovation. It "has but one prototype, and that is the bureaucratic system of jealous and oppressive espionage, by which European despots size down their subjects, and supervise their private affairs.... With its minute ramifications, red tape, and routine, it has been and is the scourge and curse of countries where, unfortunately for them, it is more at home than in this broad land of free industrial opportunities and possibilities."[5]

The commission's inaction embittered a public that had been promised prompt reform of railroad rate schedules. Rotten eggs were thrown at its San Francisco office, and hostile crowds greeted Carpenter and Humphreys as they toured the state. "The RR Co. are thus far having their own way as you see," wrote the enraged Cornelius Cole. "There is no way but to kill one of those traitorous com-

---

[4] "Fourth Annual Report of the Board of Railroad Commissioners," *J App*, 26 sess., 5: 16; "Sixth Annual Report of the Board of Railroad Commissioners," *ibid.*, 27 sess. (1887), 5: 19–21; "Seventh Annual Report of the Board of Railroad Commissioners," *ibid.*, pp. 29–32. For a prediction of the commission's conservative course, see *California and the Pacific Coast: Address of Mr. Lloyd Tevis, President of Wells, Fargo & Company, San Francisco, Before the American Bankers' Association, at Niagara Falls, August 10, 1881* (n.p., n.d.), p. 18.

[5] "Fifth Annual Report of the Board of Railroad Commissioners," *J App*, 26 sess., 6: 15; "Seventh Annual Report of the Board of Railroad Commissioners," *ibid.*, 27 sess., 5: 31.

missioners, & it ought to be done."[6] No one followed Cole's advice, but many Californians shared his impatience. They had expected [...] system, only to find that for [...] referred argument to action. [...] would learn from this early [...] oners gradually gave way to [...] ates waned, and procedural [...] fectiveness. But subsequent [...] lifornians in the early 1880's. [...] ater and Humphreys shaped [...] ommission through the re-

[...] ilt problems for the anti-mo- [...] sion's failure to fulfill party [...] . "There is a good deal of [...] on the fact that nothing has [...] White reported to Foote in [...] popular outcry to pressure [...] s only drove them further [...] nined anti-monopolists had [...] arl in which we have been [...] nphreys is enough to make [...] k by careful work we may

[...] xes proved an even greater [...] numerous issues that linked [...] xation and the problem of [...] d lawmakers in virtually every state. Democrats in California, Republicans in the Midwest, Populists on the Great Plains, Gov. Theodore Roosevelt in New

[6] Cole to Olive Cole, June 4, 1883, Cole Papers; "Sixth Annual Report of the Board of Railroad Commissioners," *J App*, 27 sess., 5: 20.

[7] White to Foote, Aug. 14, 1883, White to H. I. Willey, Aug. 24, 1883, WP. See also White to Foote, Aug. 31, 1883, White to Foote, Oct. 3, 1883, Foote to White, Oct. 8, 1883, WP.

York, and post-1900 leaders in "backward" Alabama, "conservative" Massachusetts, and "progressive" Wisconsin all responded to the urgent need for fiscal modernization. To the California anti-monopolists of the early 1880's, the tax question possessed additional significance, for it cut to the heart of their struggle to establish the supremacy of the state over the corporation. More than the railroad commission, it involved, in the words of one Coast observer, "the right of the Commonwealth to regulate and control the artificial beings it has created."[8]

Unfortunately, the question's importance blinded most anti-monopoly Democrats to its inherent problems. It would take years to resolve; it embraced complex issues easy for opponents to cloud and difficult for voters to follow; and it entailed renewed conflict with Stephen J. Field, whose position on the federal bench gave him a commanding voice in the debate. By the time the controversy was over, it had stymied a special session of the legislature, evoked a series of major decisions in the federal courts, and seriously damaged the anti-monopolist cause. In the end, despite a few accomplishments, the anti-monopolists had failed even to demonstrate conclusively the state's preeminence over the railroad. As a Los Angeles newspaper noted of the tax problem in 1886, "There could be no more forcible illustration of the fact that a power has grown up in the State greater than the State itself."[9]

The controversy stemmed from the manner in which the 1879 constitution had distinguished between railroad property and other property for the purposes of taxation. In response to grievances against mortgagors who paid no taxes on their holdings, the constitution had provided that except for "railroad and other quasi-public corpora-

[8] White to Daniel Manning, April 23, 1885, WP; Edwin R. A. Seligman, "Recent Reforms in Taxation," *Yale Review*, 3 (1895): 353; David P. Thelen, *The New Citizenship: Origins of Progressivism in Wisconsin, 1885–1900* (Columbia, Mo., 1972), pp. 203–11; C. K. Yearley, *The Money Machines: The Breakdown and Reform of Governmental and Party Finance in the North, 1860–1920* (Albany, N.Y., 1970), pp. 225–50; G. Wallace Chessman, *Governor Theodore Roosevelt: The Albany Apprenticeship, 1898–1900* (Cambridge, Mass., 1965), pp. 133–57; Sheldon Hackney, *Populism to Progressivism in Alabama* (Princeton, N.J., 1969), pp. 139–40, 256–61; Richard M. Abrams, *Conservatism in a Progressive Era: Massachusetts Politics, 1900–1912* (Cambridge, Mass., 1964), pp. 131, 235; Herbert F. Margulies, *The Decline of the Progressive Movement in Wisconsin, 1890–1920* (Madison, Wis., 1968), pp. 44–71.
[9] LA *Times*, June 8, 1886.

tions," property owners should pay taxes on the value of the property less the amount of the mortgage, with the latter assessed to the mortgage holder. For railroads, however, it prescribed assessment at "actual value" and lodged the taxing power in a State Board of Equalization, with authority to assess the franchise, roadway, roadbed, rails, and rolling stock of railroads operated in more than one county.[10]

Similar boards, designed to remove certain taxing powers from local hands, already existed in a few other areas, but the California mortgage distinction represented a marked innovation. Endorsed by leading tax scholars who differentiated between personal and corporate debt, regarding the latter as simply another way to add to working capital, the distinction reflected the conviction that railroad debts far exceeded the value of railroad property and that the taxation of company bonds, held mostly by nonresidents and the federal government, would present insurmountable difficulties. Promptly imitated by Massachusetts, Pennsylvania, and several other states, it became—as one tax expert recalled in 1899—a famous "experiment in taxation."[11]

Experimentation of that kind held little attraction for the railroad. Protesting against the inequity of the mortgage scheme, the company withheld its taxes for 1880–81 and moved to challenge the constitutionality of the new tax system. It suffered momentary defeat in January 1882, when the California Supreme Court, in two unanimous decisions, upheld the authority of the State Board of Equalization, rejected the Central Pacific's contention that its special relationship with the federal government exempted its franchise from state taxation, and denied the railroad's assertion that the mortgage distinction violated the Fourteenth Amendment to the Constitution. The company quickly maneuvered into the federal courts and meanwhile continued to withhold its taxes. The latter tactic threw state and county governments into disarray. Deprived of anticipated revenue amounting to more than $500,000 a year, they had to borrow money and cut back on essential services. As the state controller reported in

[10] *California Blue Book, or State Roster, 1893* (Sacramento, 1893), pp. 33–34.
[11] Carl C. Plehn, "The Taxation of Mortgages in California, 1849 to 1899," *Yale Review*, 8 (1899): 66; Edwin R. A. Seligman, *Essays in Taxation* (New York, 1895), pp. 102–3, 142, 214; Yearley, *Money Machines*, pp. 37–95; John T. Doyle to Abram S. Hewitt, March 4, 1885, CP.

1883, the railroad tax delinquency caused "widespread consternation. The whole revenue system of the several counties was disarranged thereby; the ordinary obligations of the counties could not be fully met, and in many of the counties the public schools were closed for want of funds."[12]

In desperate need of revenue, various counties brought a total of 63 suits against the railroad for recovery of the delinquent taxes. They attempted to keep the matter in the hands of sympathetic state courts, but in July 1882, Justice Stephen J. Field accepted jurisdiction in the case of *County of San Mateo* v. *Southern Pacific Railroad Company*, an action to recover $414,150 in unpaid taxes together with the prescribed 5 percent penalty for nonpayment, 2 percent per month interest, and attorneys' fees.[13] Field's decision, delivered in circuit court on September 25, was a sturdy defense of corporate rights. It acknowledged "the opinion prevailing throughout the community that the railroad corporations of the state, by means of their great wealth and the numbers in their employ, have become so powerful as to be disturbing influences in the administration of the laws; an opinion which will be materially strengthened by a decision temporarily relieving any one of them from its just proportion of the public burdens." This widespread sentiment had given him some concern, Field admitted, but he declared that it could not be allowed to affect the court's judgment. "Whatever acts may be imputed justly or unjustly to the corporations, they are entitled when they enter the tribunals of the nation to have the same justice meted out to them which is meted out to the humblest citizen. There cannot be one law for them and another law for others."

The remainder of the decision had great significance for later constitutional law. Unlike the California Supreme Court, which had ruled that the Fourteenth Amendment provided no protection for

---

[12] *San Francisco and North Pacific Railroad Company* v. *The State Board of Equalization*, 60 Cal. 12 (Jan. 19, 1882); *The Central Pacific Railroad Company* v. *The State Board of Equalization*, 60 Cal. 35 (Jan. 19, 1882); "Biennial Report of the Controller," *J App*, 25 sess. (1883), 1: 23–24; William C. Fankhauser, *A Financial History of California: Public Revenues, Debts, and Expenditures*, Univ. of California Publications in Economics, vol. 3 (Berkeley, 1913), pp. 300–306.
[13] *County of San Mateo* v. *Southern Pacific Railroad Company*, 13 Fed. 145 (July 31, 1882). Details on the background of the suits can be found in *JS*, 30 sess. (1893), p. 461; and in the record in *County of San Mateo* v. *D. J. Oullahan et al.*, 69 Cal. 647 (May 28, 1886).

corporations, Field rejected the "narrow view," advanced by attorneys for the county, that the amendment was intended to safeguard freedmen "and should not be extended beyond that purpose." It had, Field declared, "a much broader operation" as a restraint on state legislation. To the critical question "Is the defendant, being a corporation, a person within the meaning of the fourteenth amendment, so as to be entitled, with respect to its property, to the equal protection of the laws?" he responded with a vigorous affirmative.

"Private corporations are, it is true, artificial persons," Field observed, "but ... they consist of aggregations of individuals united for some legitimate business. ... Indeed, there is nothing which is lawful to be done to feed and clothe our people, to beautify and adorn their dwellings, to relieve the sick, to help the needy, and to enrich and ennoble humanity, which is not to a great extent done through the instrumentalities of corporations. ... It would be a most singular result if a constitutional provision intended for the protection of every person against partial and discriminating legislation by the states, should cease to exert such protection the moment the person becomes a member of a corporation." Consequently, the California tax scheme, with its "palpable and gross" discrimination in the assessment of railroad property, was invalid.[14]

Virtually repeated a year later in another important case, *County of Santa Clara* v. *Southern Pacific Railroad Company*, Field's tax decision fostered bitter protest. It voided several years of assessments and convinced many of the impossibility of taxing the railroad. The Justice himself subsequently referred to the "misapprehensions" prevalent in the community since the San Mateo case and sought to defend his court against public attack.[15] The decision also spurred action on the county level, where worried officials despaired of collecting suffi-

[14] *County of San Mateo* v. *Southern Pacific Railroad Company* (The Railroad Tax Cases), 13 Fed. 722 (Sept. 25, 1882); Howard Jay Graham, *Everyman's Constitution: Historical Essays on the Fourteenth Amendment, the "Conspiracy Theory," and American Constitutionalism* (Madison, Wis., 1968), pp. 403–14. *The Central Pacific Railroad Company* v. *The State Board of Equalization*, 60 Cal. 35 (Jan. 19, 1882), gives the judgment of the California Supreme Court on the Fourteenth Amendment question.

[15] *County of Santa Clara* v. *Southern Pacific Railroad Company*, 18 Fed. 385 (Sept. 17, 1883); SF *Chron*, Sept. 27–28, 1882; LA *Times*, Sept. 28, 1882; SF *Exmr*, Sept. 18, 1883. The Santa Clara case involved fundamentally the same issues as the San Mateo case. It later assumed more importance when the United States Supreme Court used it as a test case on the California tax system.

cient revenue. Few followed the example of one tax collector, who placed railroad property on sale for tax delinquency and forced the company to pay. More frequently, they sought to compromise with the railroad in order to secure part of the money. San Mateo officials, for instance, accepted a "donation" from the company in lieu of taxes, while other county governments ordered legal representatives to reach similar private settlements with the railroad. At the behest of the state attorney general, the California Supreme Court forbade this practice when the agreement involved sums less than those authorized by the State Board of Equalization, but the movement toward compromise continued.[16]

It received unexpected impetus from the railroad leaders themselves. Alert to the compromise trend, and apparently concerned about growing public indignation, they decided to attempt a statewide resolution of the tax dispute.[17] On October 20, 1883, Creed Haymond, the attorney for the company, sent Gov. George Stoneman an offer to remit the unpaid taxes for the years 1880 through 1882. Haymond stipulated, however, that the railroad would discharge its obligations only on the basis of the 1882 assessment, which amounted to several million dollars less than the assessments for the surrounding years. He also offered to pay about 60 percent of the taxes for 1883 when they came due. Stoneman solicited the opinion of Edward C. Marshall, the state attorney general, who replied on November 8 by refusing the offer and warning against "the almost menacing attitude

[16] *San Francisco & N.R. Co.* v. *Dinwiddie and Others* (The Sonoma County Tax Case), 13 Fed. 789 (Sept. 23, 1882); *County of San Mateo* v. *Southern Pacific Railroad Company*, 116 U.S. 138 (Dec. 21, 1885); White to Edward C. Marshall, May 11, 1883, White to Marshall, June 26, 1883, White to Marshall, Dec. 1, 1883, WP; *County of Sacramento* v. *The Central Pacific Railroad Company*, 61 Cal. 250 (Aug. 22, 1882).

[17] In the absence of the papers of railroad leaders such as Stanford and Huntington, it is impossible to determine the precise reasons behind their decision to compromise. Some observers (see, e.g., SF *Chron*, Nov. 7, 1883) believed the decision stemmed from the realization that the United States Supreme Court would ultimately reject the railroad position. In view of the company's recent victories in federal circuit court, however, this explanation seems unlikely. Instead, it appears that two considerations prompted the company's decision: its court victories put it in a strong legal position from which to offer a settlement, while public indignation seriously weakened its political position and necessitated a compromise. The closing of schools and the impact of the railroad's tax delinquency on government agencies, including the state prison, whose directors had to borrow funds to support the convicts, aroused a popular outcry that apparently surprised the railroad leaders and persuaded them to compromise. See SF *Exmr*, June 12, 1884; John T. Doyle to William F. White, July 31, 1883, WP; Doyle to George Stoneman, Feb. 5, 1884, John T. Doyle Papers, Bancroft Library, Univ. of California, Berkeley.

assumed by the railroads." Declared Marshall: "If the amount of tax levied for State and county support is subject to reduction by State or county officers, or if the Courts themselves can give judgment for less than the lawful demand of the Government, our form of Government is a failure."[18]

A few days later Haymond tried again. In a letter to the San Francisco *Chronicle*, he agreed to the newspaper's suggestion that in view of the relatively small margin between the opposing claims, the railroad should voluntarily pay the face of the taxes as assessed for 1880, 1881, and 1882.[19] In return the company asked two concessions: the dismissal of the various suits against it, except those destined for appeal to the Supreme Court, and the withdrawal of the state's demand for penalty, interest, and fees. Some questioned the offer. "I do not go a great deal on compromises myself in such matters," one county official told Haymond. "It appears to me that the Supreme Ct. will either sustain our system or indicate a plan which will meet with their approval & all will concede that the State ought to know *how* to tax."[20]

But the apparent fairness of the company's proposal, combined with the discouraging tenor of recent court decisions, inclined others toward acceptance. On January 29, 1884, Attorney General Marshall gave his approval. Unlike the first, he advised Governor Stoneman, this offer sought no reduction in taxes and therefore did not dispute the supremacy of the state. "It concedes the right of the State to levy and collect a tax which the companies aver is excessive, thus yielding the supremacy, and submitting to the sovereignty of the State. The sums demanded in the suits against the companies as penalty, interest, and attorney's fee, do not appear to me to involve the vital doctrine of your Excellency's refusal of their first offer, nor any vital doctrine. It is a question of costs—of procedure—not of revenue or principle."[21]

[18] *JA*, 25 (extra) sess. (1884), p. 140; SF *Chron*, Nov. 10, 1883.
[19] According to the newspaper's figures, the state claimed $1,444,805.25 in railroad taxes for the three years. On the basis of the 1882 assessment, the railroad had offered to pay $1,297,965.77. Now that it had finally agreed to pay at least some taxes, suggested the paper, the railroad could easily afford the difference. SF *Chron*, Nov. 12, 1883.
[20] White to Haymond, Dec. 8, 1883, WP; SF *Chron*, Nov. 13, 1883.
[21] *JA*, 25 (extra) sess., pp. 140–41.

Stoneman vehemently disagreed. "This office protests, and will continue to protest, against the acceptance of the offer of defendants, and against the acceptance of any offer which acknowledges and includes less than the whole demand of the State against the defendants," he notified Marshall on February 12. As of that date the Central Pacific and Southern Pacific owed $2,730,303.39 in delinquent taxes and penalties, and Stoneman was determined to collect the full amount. To ensure Marshall's compliance, he secured an injunction in San Francisco Superior Court forbidding the attorney general to compromise any of the tax cases.[22]

Marshall simply ignored the governor. On February 28, 1884, he appeared with Creed Haymond in circuit court to hear final judgment in 41 of the original 63 suits, including the Santa Clara case. As opposing attorneys argued in the crowded courtroom, Haymond suddenly interjected: "I will tell these patriotic gentlemen, in order to stop all this talk, that the Central Pacific Railroad will pay its taxes before 4 o'clock today." He then formally renewed the railroad proposal to set aside the court's decision in its favor and permit judgments to be entered, for the face value of the taxes alone, in favor of the state and counties. Asked if he consented to such a settlement, Marshall replied that his participation was unnecessary, but the court refused to act without it. On the following day the attorney general told the court that he would disregard Stoneman's injunction and agree to the compromise plan. A Central Pacific check for $375,872 concluded the arrangement. A week later most of the remaining cases were settled in the same manner.[23]

Instead of ending the tax controversy, Marshall's action enflamed it. With the San Francisco *Examiner* leading the attack, denunciations of the settlement overwhelmed its supporters and dampened earlier sympathy for the difficult position in which the attorney general had been placed. Protest grew in succeeding weeks as Marshall managed to hurt his own cause. In an angry outburst, later retracted, he claimed not to have read the 24-page stipulation signed

---

[22] *Ibid.*, p. 141; "Biennial Report of the Controller," *J App*, 26 sess., 1: 24; SF *Exmr*, Feb. 28, 1884.

[23] SF *Exmr*, Feb. 29, 1884; SF *Chron*, Feb. 28–March 1, 1884; *JA*, 25 (extra) sess., pp. 141–42; *JS*, 30 sess., p. 461.

in circuit court. Called before a legislative committee investigating the affair, he contended that the stipulation had recognized the state's right to appeal to the Supreme Court for recovery of the penalties demanded in the various suits. Requested to produce a portion of the document, he could not. It had been mislaid, he said, during a recent move. Nearly a month passed before the stipulation appeared in circuit court records, and in June the attorney general still had not begun appeal proceedings in the tax cases.[24]

Finally, Marshall blamed the whole affair on the railroad leaders, whose obstinacy, he explained, had convinced him that the government had little chance of recovering its full claims. "The State was then out of money ...," he pleaded to a hostile crowd of Democrats in the summer of 1884. "Let the confession be humiliating or not, we could not make those people pay. The likelihood was that ... we never could make them pay."[25]

To the anti-monopoly Democrats, the confession was indeed humiliating. They had feared this result all along. Their chagrin over the lost revenue was overshadowed by their certainty that the attorney general had given way before railroad power, forfeiting the state's preeminence over the corporation. Private bargains with the railroad, they thought, accorded the company the status of a sovereign authority the state might negotiate with but could not govern, and granted it privileges denied the average citizen. "I ask you," charged one anti-monopolist, "can a poor man walk into the Federal Courts and settle the taxes he owes to the State for four or five years without paying the penalties? I think not." Governor Stoneman left no doubt of his feelings in the matter. With his approval the state treasurer and controller both refused to accept the tax payments Marshall had received from the railroad. And on March 5, 1884, less than a week after the circuit court settlement, the governor called the California legislature into special session.[26]

[24] SF *Exmr*, March 1, June 12, 1884; *JA*, 25 (extra) sess., pp. 138–43. Stephen J. Field subsequently praised Marshall's "wise and judicious" course. SF *Chron*, May 11, 1886.
[25] SF *Exmr*, June 12, 1884.
[26] *Ibid*.; White to Daniel Manning, April 23, 1885, WP; SF *Chron*, March 6, 1884. The two officials continued to refuse to accept the money, which remained in Marshall's care, until the California Supreme Court ordered them to do so in May 1886. *County of San Mateo* v. *D. J. Oullahan et al.*, 69 Cal. 647 (May 28, 1886).

California, Stoneman declared in summoning the lawmakers, had
been placed in a "humiliating attitude" that "must fill the heart of
every public-spirited citizen with regret and mortification." To remedy this situation he urged the legislature to act on all aspects of the
railroad problem. Citing the "comparative inaction" of the railroad
commission, he asked for the removal of the present commissioners
and proposed a new method for electing their successors. He also
advocated laws to end rate discrimination and a constitutional amendment to set maximum freight and passenger fares. Turning to the
tax question, Stoneman advanced a series of stringent recommendations. The legislators should first nullify "all compromises, consent
judgments, and agreements wherever and by whomsoever made, in
which the State has lost, or is about to lose, any portion of the tax,
penalty, or interest due by law." They should then enact stiff penalties to discourage future settlements. Recent court pronouncements,
the governor noted, probably made it necessary to provide for the
assessment of railroad property on the same basis as other property.
But this must not result in a victory for the corporation. The legislature, he suggested, should impose an income tax on the company's
gross receipts, proportioned in such a manner that, combined with
the reformed property assessment, it would "at least" equal the taxes
and penalties currently under dispute. Since these measures met the
railroad's previous objections, Stoneman added slyly, "I apprehend
you will experience no opposition from that source."[27]

As often happened in the late nineteenth century, a period when
elected officials confronted untested procedures and hostile courts in
dealing with new problems, the California governor cited court decisions and the experience of other states in support of his proposals.
He closed his instructions to the lawmakers with a cogent expression
of anti-monopoly views. Stoneman's remarks displayed the ambiva-
lent attitude of many anti-monopolists, whose concern over the political and social consequences of industrial progress tempered their
admiration for its economic benefits. In particular he decried the ten-

[27] SF *Exmr*, March 6, 1884; *JS*, 25 (extra) sess., pp. 8–10.

dency to protect corporate privileges more aggressively than human rights. "The natural person, he who is a *part* of the Government, ought at least to have rights equal to the artificial person, which is but a *creature* of the Government . . . ," Stoneman asserted. "But it is claimed that railroad corporations have materially assisted in the development of the State, and for that reason we should not interfere with them by legal enactments. Concede all that is claimed for them, it does not follow that they should be allowed to exercise unrestrained power and oppress our people. History proves that unrestrained power is only limited and controlled by the opportunities for its exercise. If the development of the State and the accumulation of private fortunes shall go hand in hand with disobedience of authority and resistance to law, it would be far better that private fortunes were smaller and the development of the State less rapid."[28]

When the special session opened on March 24, anti-monopoly Democrats foresaw little difficulty in enacting Stoneman's suggestions. Their party possessed an overwhelming numerical advantage, with margins of 32 Democrats to 8 Republicans in the senate and 61 to 19 in the assembly. The legislature's narrow agenda, limited exclusively to the railroad question, barred the dilatory tactics typical of regular sessions; by centering public attention on the lawmakers, press coverage promised to tighten Democratic ranks and prevent suspected recalcitrants from avoiding the issue. Christopher A. Buckley's powerful San Francisco organization, numerous Democratic county committees, and the state party hierarchy all adopted resolutions in support of the session's purposes. It also seemed possible that some Republican legislators would join the anti-monopoly effort, for California's leading Republican journal backed the attempt to "curb the insolence and rapacity of the Central Pacific monopoly."[29]

The anti-monopolists' confidence appeared justified during the opening weeks of the session, as both houses of the legislature moved quickly to consider the governor's recommendations. Even an an-

[28] *JS*, 25 (extra) sess., p. 10.
[29] SF *Chron*, March 24, 1884; Edith Dobie, *The Political Career of Stephen Mallory White: A Study of Party Activities Under the Convention System* (Stanford, Cal., 1927), p. 251; SF *Exmr*, March 1, 7–12, 26, 1884.

nouncement by Republican leaders that they would oppose stringent
legislation failed to dampen enthusiasm. Reginaldo F. Del Valle, a
close friend and ally of Stephen M. White, was elected president pro
tem of the senate, and Democrats in the assembly introduced 63 bills
to enhance the state's control over railroad affairs. They included proposals to oust commissioners Carpenter and Humphreys, provide
means for the recall of future commission members, strengthen the
commission's authority, set maximum passenger rates, and levy a
graduated income tax on persons and corporations with annual revenues of more than $10,000.[30]

Two measures in particular became the focus of the anti-monopoly
effort in the extra session. The first, offered on March 25 by Thomas
F. Barry of San Francisco, carried the title "An Act to Prevent Dis-
criminations and Abuses by Railroad Corporations." Like most anti-
monopolist remedies, a large portion of the bill sought simply to
assert the public's interest in railroad property. Railroads, it declared,
were "public highways" over which passengers and freight should be
transported "on equal and impartial terms." It forbade rebates and
special contracts unless they were granted to all shippers, and stated
that when a company's charter expired or was forfeited, its road and
right-of-way devolved to the state for public use, not to the stockholders. A provision requiring railroads to post rates conspicuously
in every station reflected the anti-monopolists' belief in publicity as
an effective weapon against rate abuses and their desire to force the
Central Pacific to simplify its 282-page rate schedule. Responding to
fears that reincorporation elsewhere might enable the company to
escape local control, the bill also barred from operation in California
any railway corporation chartered in another state. For violations it
prescribed unusually strong penalties. Railroad officials who dis-
obeyed its provisions could be punished by prison terms of thirty
days to six months, and any railroad that offered rebates, failed to
keep its tracks in good repair, or refused to comply with railroad commission directives would "forfeit its charter and be dissolved."[31]

[30] SF *Exmr*, March 24–27, April 23, 1884; *JS*, 25 (extra) sess., pp. 3, 123; *JA*, 25 (extra) sess., pp. 11, 209–10.
[31] The terms of the bill appear in *J App*, 25 (extra) sess., pp. 3–4. See also the supporting statements from Barry and John T. Doyle, in *ibid.*, pp. 160–63, 202–10.

The second measure, which the San Francisco *Chronicle* called "the corner-stone of the anti-monopoly fight," came in the form of three resolutions presented on March 27 by Assemblyman William T. Wallace of San Francisco. Because railroad construction had been dependent on public grants and subsidies, claimed the first resolution, the railroads "do not in law or fact constitute the private property of said railway corporations, but are affected with a public use, and the beneficial ownership of said railways belongs to the people, and said railways are possessed and managed by said corporations as mere public agencies." The other two resolutions placed railroads under legislative supervision and pronounced that Field's decision in the Santa Clara tax case, which required the assessment of corporate and private property on the same basis, had substantially assumed railroad property to be private property. This assumption, concluded the resolution, "involves a grave judicial and political heresy, alarming in its consequences, and tending to subvert the rightful legislative authority of this State."[32]

In their mixture of concrete reforms and broad assertions of state power, the two measures mirrored the anti-monopolists' strengths and weaknesses. A few provisions, particularly the exclusion from California of outside corporations and the various endeavors to establish public ownership of railroad property, would certainly have foundered in the courts. Other provisions blended the practical and the naïve. If unoriginal, the Barry bill's prohibition of rebates and special contracts offered some welcome reform, as did the effort to employ publicity to lower tariffs and simplify rate structures. The bill's penalty clause represented an innovative attempt to ensure company obedience and prevent railroad officials from escaping behind the corporate facade. In somewhat different fashion the Wallace resolutions sought to provide a general definition of the relationship between the state and the railroad. Wallace's clearly intentional choice of the phrase "affected with a public use" recalled the

Doyle, a prominent lawyer, a former state commissioner of transportation, and an expert on railroad affairs, reportedly wrote the measure. SF *Exmr*, March 26, 1884; Rev. Francis J. Weber, "John Thomas Doyle: Pious Fund Historiographer," *Southern California Quarterly*, 49 (1967): 297–303.

[32] SF *Chron*, March 28, 1884; *JA*, 25 (extra) sess., pp. 22–23.

1877 Munn decision, implied judicial approval of the anti-monopolist position, and undoubtedly stung Justice Field, who had dissented in the Munn case.[33]

Both measures quickly and easily passed the assembly—the Barry bill by a margin of 72 to 2—but they encountered stubborn opposition in the senate. There thirteen conservative Democrats, led by Charles W. Cross of Nevada County, ignored the pleas of the anti-monopolists and joined with the Republican minority to weaken or block the proposed legislation. The Wallace resolutions died in committee without ever reaching the senate floor. The Barry bill emerged relatively unscathed from committee hearings, only to succumb to a flood of crippling amendments. One amendment deleted the entire section relating to railroads chartered in another state; another affirmed that railroad property belonged to the stockholders, not to the public or the state. Most discouraging to the anti-monopolists, the vote on each amendment resulted in a tie, and in both cases the Democratic lieutenant-governor, John Daggett, cast the deciding ballot against the original bill.[34]

Resorting to their sole remaining weapon, the anti-monopoly forces tried to put external pressure on Daggett and the conservative senators, including a mass meeting in San Francisco at which erring Democrats were threatened with "lasting censure, moral disgrace and political ostracism." Such efforts had no effect. In early May test votes on the Barry bill showed neither senate nor assembly prepared to recede from its position. The final blow came on May 7, when the senate considered a proposal to remove the railroad commissioners from office. A tie vote again ensued, and again Lieutenant-Governor Daggett cast his ballot against the measure. In despair, Democratic leaders decided to adjourn the session before further damage was done. The extra session, which had cost the state about $80,000, ended on May 13, 1884. It had passed two appropriation bills and a few

---

[33] In the Munn decision, over Field's vigorous objections, the Supreme Court upheld a state's power to regulate businesses affected with "a public interest." *Munn* v. *Illinois*, 94 U.S. 113 (March 1, 1877).

[34] *JA*, 25 (extra) sess., pp. 37, 45; *JS*, 25 (extra) sess., p. 51; "Testimony Taken Before the Judiciary Committee of the Senate of California, in Considering Assembly Bill No. 10, Concerning the Regulation of Railroads," *J App*, 25 (extra) sess., pp. 4–211; SF *Exmr*, May 1–2, 1884.

minor laws. "Measured by its results," complained the San Francisco *Chronicle*, "it is the worst Legislative abortion the State has ever produced."[35]

Called to answer "the groans of an oppressed people," as Wallace had put it, the special session had accomplished essentially nothing. Despite wide popular support and their control of the party organization, the anti-monopoly Democrats had been defeated by a small group of determined legislators. There is no firm evidence that these lawmakers opposed the Wallace resolutions and the Barry bill because they "preferred railroad gold to railroad regulation."[36] Rather, their opposition clearly stemmed in great part from their conviction that the two proposals unduly enlarged the sphere of government and endangered "the rights of property upon which the welfare of society depends." Acting in this belief, conservative Democrats had rallied to defeat the "strange doctrines" and "extreme views" advanced in the extra session.[37]

In the end the reform program had succumbed to Democratic factionalism, aided by legislative procedures that inflated minority influence. As Charles W. Cross explained in defending his actions, there were two wings of the Democratic party in California: one advocated substantial government intervention in economic affairs, and another believed that "government is organized to *protect persons* and property." The anti-monopoly "pirates," Cross declared, had attempted to push radical laws through the extra session. "But a conservative sentiment and a good deal of manly firmness prevented this monstrous legislation from transpiring."[38]

The genuineness of their opponents' convictions, however, did nothing to soothe the feelings of the anti-monopolists, who had staked their hopes and much of their political prestige on the extra session. The work of several years, during which they had gathered

[35] SF *Exmr*, April 20, May 8, 1884; SF *Chron*, May 14, 1884; *JA*, 25 (extra) sess., pp. 181–84; *JS*, 25 (extra) sess., pp. 81, 111–12, 124–25.

[36] Railroad "gold" conclusion in Alexander Callow, Jr., "San Francisco's Blind Boss," *PHR*, 25 (1956): 274; Wallace quoted in SF *Exmr*, March 25, 1884. See also W. S. Leake, "When King Mazuma Ruled," SF *Bul*, April 2, 1917.

[37] *Alta Cal*, Oct. 27, 1885; Samuel M. Wilson to Thomas A. Hendricks, April 29, 1885, CP.

[38] Cross to Grover Cleveland, April 3, 1885, printed in *Alta Cal*, undated clipping in WP.

public and party support for railroad reform, had been thwarted by a handful of men. With the 1884 election scarcely five months away, voters were certain to resent the anti-monopolists' failure to fulfill their promises to invigorate the railroad commission, force the payment of railroad taxes, and institute tighter supervision over corporate power. Discouraged, a few Democrats suggested compromise with the conservatives and urged the anti-monopolists to "act *judiciously* & with a view to *harmonizing*, rather than *antagonizing* the party." The anti-monopoly leaders would have none of it. Anger and bitterness had supplanted the frustration of earlier months, and they resolved to continue the struggle, as one put it, "come what may." In the days after the legislature adjourned, they decided to defend the special session, reaffirm their anti-monopoly commitment, and rid the party once and for all of those who resisted their reform demands.[39]

The decision made, the anti-monopoly faction promptly displayed its continuing domination of the party. George Hearst's San Francisco *Examiner* rushed to the defense of the extra session, which it described as an "earnest and honest" effort to carry out the Democratic platform. Party organizations across the state responded to appeals that they endorse the governor's action in calling the extra session and also "the men who stood by the proclamation and endeavored to carry out the wishes of the people." Buckley's local committee declared, "Words fail to express our indignation and resentment toward those representatives, who, deserting duty, have made merchandise of honor and sale of sacred trusts." Most important, the county organizations selected anti-monopolists to attend the Democratic state convention scheduled to meet at Stockton in June. "The delegates so far *even* from San Fran. are all O.K.—and the Country will come in solid," exulted Reginaldo F. Del Valle in late May. "All conventions and central committees have spoken out boldly and without equivocation."[40]

[39] David R. Risley to White, May 29, 1884, White to Risley, May 18, 1884, WP.

[40] SF *Exmr*, May 14, 16, 1884; Del Valle to White, May 19, 1884, Del Valle to White, May 27, 1884, WP. Examples of county committee resolutions can be found in SF *Exmr*, June 1–6, 1884.

With their control of the party confirmed, another objective of the anti-monopolists was to block the presidential aspirations of Justice Field. Mentioned as a possible candidate as early as 1868, Field in recent years had received political encouragement from a number of nationally prominent Democrats. In the 1880 Democratic national convention he had ranked fifth among the candidates on the first ballot, and though his support had quickly vanished in the subsequent boom for Gen. Winfield S. Hancock, the experience had whetted Field's ambition. The approach of the 1884 campaign brought rumors that his admirers again planned to press for his nomination. Congressman Hilary A. Herbert of Alabama tested the reaction of northern Democrats to a Field candidacy. "His decision on the legal tender questions would commend him to business men and his sound views of the Constitution to all who think it worth while to preserve local self-government," Herbert argued. California newspapers noted in February the circulation of an anonymous inquiry in favor of the Justice's nomination, and there were reports from San Francisco that Buckley might back Field in return for *"dollars* and *patronage."* Alarmed by the rumors, the anti-monopoly Democrats worked to undermine the Field movement. By June, 22 county organizations had adopted resolutions that expressly rejected Field as the party's presidential nominee.[41]

When the Democratic convention opened in Stockton on June 10, 1884, it became apparent that the anti-monopolists had succeeded. As a conservative Democrat subsequently complained, "The extremists were nearly the entire body—they were absolute masters,—and the most unhappy use, for the harmony of the party, was made of the arbitrary power they possessed." The outcome was forecast when Stephen M. White, introduced to the convention as "a life-long anti-monopolist," was elected temporary chairman without opposition. White promptly appointed a sympathetic platform committee, with

[41] Herbert to Manton Marble, April 2, 1884, Manton Marble Papers, Manuscript Division, Library of Congress; SF *Exmr*, Feb. 12, 1884; David R. Risley to White, May 29, 1884, WP; Carl Brent Swisher, *Stephen J. Field: Craftsman of the Law* (Hamden, Conn., 1963), pp. 282–301. See also Field to Don M. Dickinson, Nov. 10, 1887, Field to Dickinson, Dec. 2, 1893, Don M. Dickinson Papers, Manuscript Division, Library of Congress.

Delphin M. Delmas, a San Francisco attorney who had been prominent in the prosecution of the railroad tax cases, as its chairman.
The committee was "in the main composed of our best men," White
remarked to Governor Stoneman after the convention. "I gave the
opposition some representatives simply to keep them quiet & I succeeded in the main."[42]

On the following day, June 11, Delmas strode to the stage to read
the proposed platform. A striking figure known for his legal cun-
ning and lavish attire, the 40-year-old Delmas was accustomed to
headlines and controversy. Much later, after the turn of the century,
he would gain national fame as defense attorney in the celebrated
trial of Harry K. Thaw for the murder of the architect Stanford
White. But there was no need for his courtroom eloquence on this
day in 1884, as the excited delegates repeatedly interrupted him with
cheers and applause. In all, Delmas's committee recommended 23
resolutions, nearly half of which were related to the railroad question. Leaving no doubt where the committee stood, the first resolution reaffirmed the party's "unwavering fealty and adherence to the
anti-monopoly principles which have ever been the doctrine of democrats." The platform also urged measures to resolve the tax problem and condemned the "interference of the Federal judiciary" in the
matter. Two planks stressed continuing support for the aims of the
extra session, and another declared that it was "the duty of a party,
if it is true to itself and to the people, to expel from its ranks and
denounce as unworthy of public trust and lost to all sense of honor,
traitors and pledge-breakers."

On this ground, Attorney General Marshall, commissioners Carpenter and Humphreys, Lieutenant-Governor Daggett, and the thirteen conservative senators were all formally expelled from the Democratic party. In conclusion, the platform named Samuel J. Tilden
California's presidential preference, with Sen. Allen G. Thurman of
Ohio as the second choice. Tilden's selection reflected no more than
a sentimental acknowledgment of his 1876 defeat; the anti-monopolists actually planned to work for Thurman, who had won their sup-

[42] James O'Meara to Samuel J. Tilden, April 2, 1885, CP; SF *Exmr*, June 11, 1884;
Dobie, *White*, pp. 46–47; White to Stoneman, June 23, 1884, WP.

port as the author of legislation to compel the Central Pacific Railroad to meet its obligations to the federal government. But for the moment the convention's leaders had a more pressing concern than a presidential endorsement. The final plank in the platform, which Delmas read to a storm of cheers, resolved "that the democracy of California unanimously repudiates the presidential aspirations of Stephen J. Field, and that we hereby pledge ourselves to vote for no man as delegate to the national convention of July 8, 1884, who will not before this convention pledge himself to use his earnest endeavors to defeat these aspirations."[43]

The last resolution brought an angry protest from Francis G. Newlands, a young San Francisco lawyer and later a United States senator from Nevada, who spoke in favor of a motion to delete the attack on Field. But Newlands's appeal was greeted by hisses from the floor and a successful motion to recess because "the doctrine the gentleman is announcing is too much for a Democrat with an empty stomach." The exultant Delmas, delighted to have another opportunity to rally the convention, asserted in reply that he hoped never to see California "in the attitude that some Democrats would have placed her in, licking the hand that smites her and accepting from the railroad corporations their chosen candidate, Stephen J. Field." When the applause died down, the pro-Field motion met overwhelming defeat, 453 votes to 19. Just before adjournment, each delegate to the approaching national convention pledged himself for "Tilden first, Thurman second and for Field never."[44]

More than any other event of the early 1880's, the Stockton con-

[43] Winfield J. Davis, *History of Political Conventions in California, 1849–1892* (Sacramento, 1893), pp. 456–60. Marshall addressed the convention in his own defense, asking fellow Democrats to withhold judgment until the tax cases reached the Supreme Court. But the delegates retained the original plank after narrowly defeating a substitute motion to censure Marshall for negligence rather than faithlessness. "The only kicking was as to whether Marshall should be called an ass or a knave," White later told Stoneman. White himself thought the attorney general was "more negligent than anything else but the Convention took the position that he was a scoundrel." White to Stoneman, June 23, 1884, WP.

[44] SF *Exmr*, June 12–13, 1884; William Lilley III, "The Early Career of Francis G. Newlands, 1848–1897" (Ph.D. diss., Yale Univ., 1965), pp. 159–61. Buckley later recalled that at Stockton he had doubted the wisdom of the attack on Field, but the temper of the delegates made resistance impossible. His San Francisco delegation voted 107 to 4 against the motion to delete the attack. James H. Wilkins, ed., "The Reminiscences of Christopher A. Buckley," SF *Bul*, Jan. 4, 1919.

vention split the California Democratic party. Conservative party
members resented the platform's "monstrous heresies" and regarded
the convention as "un-Democratic, proscriptive, disruptive and indecent." Asked his opinion of the gathering, John P. Irish replied
tersely: "The disreputable elements of the party captured it."[45] For
Irish and his allies the convention's anti-monopoly temper was disturbing enough. Far worse, they thought, was the personal attack
on Field and the censure of loyal Democrats who dissented from
radical policies. Samuel M. Wilson was outraged. The convention,
he wrote, had chosen to assault "one of the [country's] ablest jurists,
one of the most profound constitutional lawyers, and one who always
heroically delivers his judgments according to his conscientious convictions, however unpopular they may be.... This convention of pro-
fessed Democrats wantonly assailed the most renowned Democrat on
the coast." Field himself reflected the hardening of party attitudes in
the aftermath of Stockton. He abandoned judicial silence to challenge, as "dangerous to the rights of property," the "radical element
in California politics."[46]

For their part, the anti-monopoly Democrats were jubilant over
the outcome of the convention. During the three days it had met,
they had strengthened the Democratic commitment to anti-monopoly
reform and had demonstrated their recovery, at least within the party
organization, from the adverse effects of the extra session. They had
elected a new state central committee and had placed at its head
William D. English, an Alameda County politician with close ties
to both White and Buckley. Finally, they had expelled from the
party a number of their most prominent opponents and had publicly repudiated Field. These actions, they hoped, would reassure
voters, attest to the sincerity of Democratic platforms, and prepare
the party for a difficult national campaign. Writing shortly after the
convention adjourned, White expressed the anti-monopolists' general

---

[45] *Alta Cal*, Dec. 18, 1884, clipping in WP; Irish interview in SF *Exmr*, July 8,
1884.
[46] Wilson to Thomas A. Hendricks, April 29, 1885, CP; Field interview in *Alta
Cal*, June 18, 1884, quoted in Swisher, *Field*, pp. 308–9. See also Field to Charles W.
Cross, May 13, 1885, untitled and undated newspaper clipping in WP.

satisfaction. "The Dem. party is now *clearly* the anti-monopoly party of Cal.," he exulted. "Of this there is no question."[47]

IV

Stockton represented the high point of the anti-monopolists' fortunes during 1884. Five months later, following a hard-fought campaign in which only the anti-monopolist faction participated, the California Democrats suffered a resounding defeat when James G. Blaine drubbed the Democratic presidential candidate, Gov. Grover Cleveland of New York. Though Cleveland was of course the national winner, he carried only 17 of California's 52 counties, most of them in less populated interior sections. Virtually unknown in the state, he ran substantially behind the 1880 pace of Winfield S. Hancock. In compiling a victory margin of 13,128 votes, Blaine captured large pluralities in Alameda and Sacramento counties, as well as in much of Southern California. In San Francisco, where the Democrats had won by nearly 2,400 votes in 1880, the "Plumed Knight" emerged with a plurality of more than 4,300 votes. The Democrats' defeat extended to offices throughout the state. Republicans would represent five of California's six districts in the next Congress, whereas six Democrats had been elected in 1882. The party's representation in the state legislature underwent a similar reversal. From a minority position in both houses, the Republicans pulled even in the senate and regained control of the assembly. As one Democrat lamented after the election, "We did get the devil in Cala. this year."[48]

The devil had come to California in the person of James G. Blaine. The railroad commission fiasco, the failure of the extra session, and internal party factionalism all contributed to the extent of the setback, but it was primarily Blaine's candidacy that administered defeat to the California Democrats. The Plumed Knight enjoyed immense popularity on the Pacific Coast. Years of devoted party ser-

[47] White to Stoneman, June 23, 1884, WP. See also SF *Exmr*, June 21, 1884; English to White, July 1, 1884, White to E. M. Ross, July 24, 1884, Michael F. Tarpey to White, Jan. 11, 1885, WP.

[48] White to E. M. Ross, Nov. 28, 1884, WP; W. Dean Burnham, *Presidential Ballots, 1836–1892* (Baltimore, 1955), pp. 257, 292–305; Dobie, *White*, p. 251.

vice, during which he had become a spokesman for the increasingly important tariff issue, had endeared him to California Republicans. Coast voters admired his vitality, respected his ability, and remembered with approval the anti-Chinese record he had compiled as a United States senator. News of Blaine's nomination in early June had caused California Republicans to celebrate and California Democrats to worry. With unusual candor for a party newspaper, the *Examiner* had acknowledged the Republicans' advantage: "Blaine is perhaps, so far as California is concerned, the strongest man whom the Republicans could have placed upon their ticket, and they are therefore in this State overwhelmed with enthusiasm."[49]

As a result the Democrats had found themselves on the defensive from the outset of the campaign. Their delegation to the party's national convention, held in Chicago during early July, had supported Thurman as planned and in the process had emerged as a leader of the anti-Cleveland forces. After the nomination the Californians had fallen into line, but they recognized Cleveland's limitations as a candidate. His brief experience in government contrasted sharply with Blaine's extensive public career.[50] Blaine's long-standing popularity on the Coast also blunted the Democrats' efforts to raise doubts about his personal integrity, though concern over this issue did cause some Republicans to hesitate. One Republican editor complained to an associate: "Write me what you think of the Blaine Scandal. Will it interfere with our support of him? It seems as though the devil was after me at every turn. If I should support Jesus Christ, if he were a candidate for office, I believe they would spring something upon

[49] SF *Exmr*, June 7, 1884; SF *Chron*, May 1, 1884; Davis, *Political Conventions*, pp. 454–55; *Official Proceedings of the Republican National Convention* (Minneapolis, 1903), pp. 141–62; David Saville Muzzey, *James G. Blaine: A Political Idol of Other Days* (New York, 1934), pp. 152–55, 308–9. Perceptive appraisals of Blaine and the Republican party can be found in H. Wayne Morgan, *From Hayes to McKinley: National Party Politics, 1877–1896* (Syracuse, N.Y., 1969), and Lewis L. Gould, "The Republican Search for a National Majority," in H. Wayne Morgan, ed., *The Gilded Age: A Reappraisal*, rev. ed. (Syracuse, N.Y., 1970), pp. 171–87.

[50] *Official Proceedings of the National Democratic Convention* (New York, 1884), pp. 21–95, 224–45. Recalling Blaine's popularity and Cleveland's obscurity, Christopher A. Buckley later remarked: "So I had no question whatever before the campaign had gone very far that the State was lost to the Democracy on the national issues." Wilkins, ed., "Reminiscences of Buckley," SF *Bul*, Jan. 6, 1919. See also SF *Chron*, July 12, 1884; SF *Exmr*, Sept. 4, 1884; John T. Doyle to Abram S. Hewitt, March 4, 1885, CP.

him at the last minute." But this editor was soon thanking his friend for assisting "a decent *flop* on the Republican side," and along with most other California Republicans, he remained loyal to Blaine. In the end the Democrats were unable to attract enough of the "dude Republican vote," as the San Francisco *Chronicle* labeled it, to affect the outcome in the state.[51]

Unlike the pattern in other states, therefore, the California campaign matched a divided Democratic party, distracted by its own internal troubles, against a united and confident Republican party. Promising future reforms and pointing proudly to their repudiation of those who had broken party pledges, the anti-monopoly Democrats tried to restrict the campaign to the railroad issue. But the Republicans, except for sporadic attacks to keep the anti-monopolists off balance, felt strong enough to ignore the railroad. Instead they stressed Blaine's record on the Chinese question, profited from their candidate's appeal to the state's large Irish population, and raised fears about the effects of a Democratic low-tariff policy on California's wine, wool, fruit, and sugar industries. Vigorous protests from the Democrats, including reminders that the Stockton platform had favored "incidental protection to home labor and home industries," could not overcome the Republicans' strategy. "The Republicans have had three meetings here, and have been putting in heavy licks on the tariff question," an Anaheim Democrat reported a few weeks before the election. "There is considerable disaffection."[52]

Disaffection spread in the aftermath of the election, as angry recriminations tore the Democratic party again. Barred from participation in the campaign, opponents of the Stockton wing had watched with growing indignation as the anti-monopolists dispatched speakers

[51] E. C. MacFarlane to Ambrose Bierce, Sept. 20, 1884, MacFarlane to Bierce, Sept. 23, 1884, Ambrose Gwinett Bierce Papers, Stanford Univ.; SF *Chron*, July 12, 1884. On the strength of the Blaine campaign, see Lee Benson, "Research Problems in American Political Historiography," in Mirra Komarovsky, ed., *Common Frontiers of the Social Sciences* (Glencoe, Ill., 1957), pp. 113–83. Benson notes that in California Blaine ran a stronger race in 1884 than the Republican presidential candidates did in either 1880 or 1888.

[52] Davis, *Political Conventions*, p. 458; Thomas B. Brown to White, Oct. 14, 1884, WP; SF *Exmr*, Oct. 8, 1884; LA *Times*, Oct. 21, 1884; E. C. MacFarlane to Ambrose Bierce, Sept. 23, 1884, Bierce Papers; T. H. Merry to Thomas R. Bard, Oct. 21, 1884, Merry to Bard, Oct. 29, 1884, Thomas R. Bard Papers, Huntington Library; White to Samuel J. Randall, March 7, 1885, WP.

across the state to explain and defend the events at Stockton. The
conservatives, in Samuel M. Wilson's words, "were compelled to hear
in the campaign harangues in support of the Stockton Convention
platform, and the proposed radical measures of the Extra Session,
and arguments in favor of confiscating property and other communistic schemes." Resentful, they welcomed the party's defeat and regarded it as a complete justification for their opposition to the anti-
monopolists during the past year. The defeat stemmed, they boasted
in repeated letters and newspaper articles, from the "apathy and disgust and anger of thousands of democrats, of those who disapproved
of the anti-monopoly crusade of the extremists, of the unprecedented
proscription of Judge Field, of the extra-session, and of the Stockton
Convention throughout."[53]

For Stephen J. Field the Democratic setback was particularly satisfying. Despite the early rumors and the appearance of a small band
of "Field Fighters" at the party's national convention, the Justice had
not even been nominated. In view of the strength of the Cleveland
forces, Field should not have been surprised by the convention's outcome. But he blamed his defeat on "the very strange action in California," insisting that "had I received the cordial support, instead of
opposition of that State, my candidacy, according to the judgment of
my friends, would have stood great chances of success." Now, he
wistfully told an acquaintance, "my political life may be considered
as substantially at an end. It is not at all likely that my name will ever
again be used in connection with any political office. I had, of course,
some ambition to carry out certain measures which I believed would
be of great advantage to the country.... But all this must be placed
in the category of dreams that might have been but will not be realized." Field was consequently delighted with the Democratic debacle
in California. Calling it "the result of a revolt of men of property
against the communistic and agrarian course of a set of agitators and
sandlotters who had got the ascendancy there," he joined other con-

[53] Wilson to Thomas A. Hendricks, April 29, 1885, James O'Meara to Samuel J.
Tilden, April 2, 1885, CP. See also *Alta Cal*, Dec. 24, 1884, clipping in WP; John P.
Irish to Manton Marble, Sept. 16, 1884, Marble Papers.

servative Democrats in demanding that the party oust the anti-monopolist "conspirators" from power.[54]

The anti-monopolists did their best to refute these assertions. While acknowledging that the conservatives had worked against the party, they denied that the conservatives had been strong enough to affect the election. "They are so insignificant in numbers & influence that I do not charge them with any considerable portion of our losses," observed White. In reply to claims that radical doctrines had defeated the party, the anti-monopolists pointed out that their candidates had consistently run well ahead of the presidential ticket. Five of the six congressional nominees, including the anti-monopolists Barclay Henley and Reginaldo F. Del Valle, had outpolled Cleveland by substantial margins. Finally, they noted that the election had brought voters to the polls in record numbers, enabling Cleveland to garner nearly 9,000 more votes than his predecessor in 1880. But at the same time Blaine had captured some 22,000 more votes than any previous Republican candidate. Blaine's predominant role in the election's outcome, they argued, proved that the voters had not repudiated the Stockton platform. "Our discomfiture in the late election," concluded Michael F. Tarpey, California's representative on the Democratic national committee, "is in no wise an index of the public feeling upon that question—and it did not enter into the questions then being considered in the least." The contention that Stockton had injured the party, declared Tarpey, was "mere bosh and drivel."[55]

Despite the essential validity of their argument, the election had nevertheless been a severe blow to the anti-monopoly Democrats. Needing an emotional boost to offset recent rebuffs, they had recognized the importance of a satisfactory showing in the fall contest. "Work like h—l and carry that Co[unty]. We must win California for the honor of the Stockton Convention," William D. English had

[54] Field to John Norton Pomeroy, July 28, 1884, in Howard Jay Graham, ed., "Four Letters of Mr. Justice Field," *Yale Law Journal*, 47 (1937–38): 1107–8; Field to Edwards Pierrepont, Dec. 14, 1884, CP; *Alta Cal*, Dec. 18, 1884, clipping in WP; SF *Exmr*, July 8, 1884.

[55] White to Daniel Manning, April 23, 1885, Tarpey to White, Jan. 11, 1885, WP; Burnham, *Presidential Ballots*, pp. 257, 293–305; SF *Chron*, Nov. 3, 1886.

written White in October. "We have got to win," he had repeated.[56]
But the anti-monopolists had lost. In firm control of the party machinery and responsible for the conduct of the campaign, they had
failed to carry California for Cleveland, and this while Cleveland
was winning in the nation at large. The election, which had changed
the 1882 Democratic plurality of 23,500 votes into a Republican plurality of about 13,000, appeared to provide an easy opportunity for
dissidents within the party to discredit and challenge their leadership.
The success of this challenge, both factions believed, would depend
in large part on the distribution of federal patronage in California.

Almost immediately, therefore, there began a bitter contest for patronage as the two factions appealed for recognition to the incoming
Cleveland administration. The Stockton Democrats had suffered a
serious setback, but they were not yet ready to concede defeat. In the
weeks following the election, they again rejected all efforts at compromise in the party. They retained their hold on the Democratic
state organization, which customarily dictated the allocation of federal offices, and they remained convinced of ultimate success if the
railroad issue, unobscured by national considerations and loyalties,
could be brought before the people of California. As White told Barclay Henley, the only Democrat elected to Congress: "Henley, if we
stick to the Stockton Convention the honest anti-monopolists in the
Rep. party—& there are thousands of them, will come to us. At the
last election they saw nothing in the Democratic national nominee
to woo them from their party fold." Replied Henley: "The fact is,
friend White, if we take no backward step—and stick to the principles of the Stockton Convention we will *win*."[57]

[56] English to White, Oct. 19, 1884, WP.
[57] White to Henley, Feb. 8, 1885, Henley to White, Feb. 17, 1885, WP.

CHAPTER THREE

Patronage and Reform

꧁꧂

THE STRUGGLE between conservative and anti-monopoly Democrats
for control of federal patronage began within a few days of the 1884
election. It dominated Democratic politics in California for much of
the next two years. In the mid-1880's, with some 110,000 positions
uncovered by civil service requirements, federal patronage had critical significance for Democrats in any state; among California's divided Democrats it assumed even greater significance. Rather than
being simply a means to supply salaried places for party hacks, the
spoils system played a vital role in all aspects of late-nineteenth-century politics, permitting political leaders to mold and strengthen local
organizations, reward past party service, punish deviations from party
doctrines, arbitrate internal disputes, confirm an individual's political
influence, and give coherent direction to the party's efforts. During
these years it "functioned as a carefully graded and recognized system
of institutional standing."[1]

It was this symbolic side of the spoils, as much as the actual offices
themselves, that became the primary concern of the two California
Democratic factions in the aftermath of Grover Cleveland's victory.
Long before Cleveland's inauguration, the *Alta California*, the journalistic spokesman for the party's conservative wing, urged the president-elect to repudiate the "dangerous delusions and unwise radical-

---

[1] Eric L. McKitrick, *Andrew Johnson and Reconstruction* (Chicago, 1960), p. 381.
See also Geoffrey Blodgett, *The Gentle Reformers: Massachusetts Democrats in the
Cleveland Era* (Cambridge, Mass., 1966), pp. 40, 48–49. The tendency of historians
to dismiss the spoils system as corrupt and inefficient has resulted in a failure to ana-
lyze the critical role it played in American politics as a system of reward and pun-
ishment.

ism" of the Stocktonites. The paper expressed confidence that "none
but good conservative men will be appointed to office in this State."
In a similar vein Stephen J. Field and Samuel M. Wilson sought to
use patronage to discredit their opponents' "agrarian and communistic notions." Field in particular bombarded the incoming administration with advice to give "the Federal patronage to conservative
men there, men who believe in order, in law, in property, and the
great institutions of society."[2]

The anti-monopolists countered with claims of their own. Dominant in the party organization, they were certain of success in a fight
over the spoils. Field's patronage hopes "are simply ridiculous," insisted the San Francisco *Examiner*. "The people may rest assured
and feel every confidence that Grover Cleveland will do nothing to
strengthen the power of monopoly in California, and that no man
who has shown any disposition to betray the people will be viewed
with any favor by the Administration or have any part in its councils." William D. English, the chairman of the state central committee, agreed. "Can 75 men prevail against 75,000?" he demanded. "I
have confidence in Mr. Cleveland's judgement & believe he will consult the large majority of the party and not a factional & very small
minority."[3]

II

English's confidence masked an underlying worry. Patronage presented danger as well as opportunity. By making it the momentary
focus of their dispute with the Field faction, the Stocktonites had
entrusted their cause to an outsider whose past record suggested a
conservative outlook and whose nomination they had openly fought
at the party's 1884 national convention.[4] They knew their foes had
welcomed Cleveland's convention success; one had boasted to Governor Stoneman that it represented "in the highest degree a vindication of the conservative sense of the people of this State and a just

[2] *Alta Cal*, Jan. 3, May 14, 1885; Field to George Ticknor Curtis, Dec. 14, 1884, CP.
[3] SF *Exmr*, Nov. 17, 1884; English to White, Nov. 22, 1884, WP. See also White
to George Stoneman, Nov. 18, 1884, White to Stoneman, Nov. 23, 1884, WP.
[4] *Official Proceedings of the National Democratic Convention* (New York, 1884),
pp. 93–95, 159, 224–45; SF *Exmr*, July 7, 12, 1884.

rebuke to the radicals of our party." The anti-monopolists' disappointment had increased as the presidential campaign clarified Cleveland's views. "Looking the thing squarely in the face and talking between ourselves," White had lamented in the midst of the campaign, "there can be no genuine anti-monopoly victory won this year. I believe Cleveland will make a careful and good Executive but not an active reformer."[5]

In the course of his political career before 1885, Grover Cleveland had supplied ample evidence of his commitment to honesty and thrift in government. He had also imparted to discerning politicians clear indications that he shared the ideas and sentiments of the Democratic party's conservative leadership. Born in 1837 in Caldwell, New Jersey, the burly Cleveland had settled in Buffalo, New York, where he established a moderately lucrative law practice. His early political ventures, including an unsuccessful campaign for district attorney in 1865 and a narrow triumph in an 1870 race for sheriff, had not seemed especially auspicious, but during the early 1880's he rose rapidly to national prominence. Between 1881 and 1885, through a combination of fortunate circumstances, Cleveland became in swift succession mayor of Buffalo, governor of New York, and finally president of the United States.[6]

As mayor and governor Cleveland had acquired a reputation for conservatism, political independence, and integrity. California anti-monopolists might have found encouragement in an 1882 Cleveland pronouncement: "If a citizen is oppressed by a creature of the state, to wit, a corporation, he should have proper and firm relief. A citizen who is part of the state has rights which should not be infringed upon by a creature of the state." George Stoneman had used almost identical words in his message to the 1884 extra session. But Cleveland's record as governor of New York had indicated that in common with the conservatives of his party, he more often took a severely limited view of government interference in the economy. Demonstrating an

---

[5] J. DeBarth Shorb to Stoneman, July 29, 1884, James DeBarth Shorb Papers, Huntington Library; White to Charles A. Sumner, Aug. 12, 1884, WP.

[6] Allan Nevins, *Grover Cleveland: A Study in Courage* (New York, 1932), pp. 37–106; Horace Samuel Merrill, *Bourbon Leader: Grover Cleveland and the Democratic Party* (Boston, 1957), pp. 3–55.

essentially negative conception of government, he had sought primarily to carry out the principles of thrift and efficiency in public office. Among the many measures he vetoed as governor were ones that would have lowered the fare on New York City's elevated railroads and set maximum working hours for the drivers and conductors of horse-drawn streetcars.[7]

Such actions manifested Cleveland's sympathy with the ideals of only one among several factions within the national Democratic party, which in the years after the Civil War consisted of a complex coalition of groups with differing and often conflicting interests. Critics in California labeled the party "a sort of Democratic happy family, like we see in the prairie-dog villages, where owls, rattlesnakes, prairie-dogs, and lizards all live in the same hole." With the rural South and the Democratic machines of the urban Northeast forming its most reliable sources of strength, the party claimed among its membership natives as well as immigrants, and farmers, industrial laborers, and small businessmen as well as merchants, bankers, and railroad magnates. This diversity, and the disparity in outlook it entailed, fostered internal conflict and frequently undermined the Democratic coalition's stability.[8]

During the last three decades of the century, the party was generally dominated on the national level by its conservative or Bourbon wing. The Bourbons—Cleveland among them—believed that society functioned according to immutable natural laws with which government should not interfere. The primary task of government, they thought, was to remove any man-made obstacles that might hinder the natural operation of these laws. Thomas F. Bayard, a prominent Delaware

[7] Pearl Louise Robertson, "Grover Cleveland as a Political Leader" (Ph.D. diss., Univ. of Chicago, 1937), pp. 169–70; Merrill, *Bourbon Leader*, pp. 27–31; SF *Exmr*, March 12, 1883.

[8] Oliver Carlson and Ernest Sutherland Bates, *Hearst: Lord of San Simeon* (New York, 1936), p. 28. The Republican party, of course, also represented a union of differing interests, but the Republicans usually managed to maintain a degree of party cohesion that eluded their opponents. See, e.g., O. O. Stealey, *Twenty Years in the Press Gallery* (New York, 1906), p. 113. For a more detailed treatment of the national Democratic party, see R. Hal Williams, " 'Dry Bones and Dead Language': The Democratic Party," in H. Wayne Morgan, ed., *The Gilded Age: A Reappraisal*, rev. ed. (Syracuse, N.Y., 1970), pp. 129–48.

Democrat and Cleveland's first secretary of state, concisely expressed the Bourbon philosophy when he recalled a visit to a busy canal near the Great Lakes: "I can still shut my eyes," Bayard declared, "and see the stately procession of majestic vessels, freighted with the native products of the vast North-west moving noiselessly along the pathway of beneficent exchanges. What a lesson is here against governmental interference! How wisely the well-instructed spirit of self-interest works in self-directed channels, and is developed by natural competition without fear of contact with maleficent statutes!" If such views echoed the rhetoric of the antebellum Democrats, Bayard and his fellow Bourbons did not resent the comparison. Temperamentally bound to the past, they offered a negative and simplistic guideline for the nation's future: a return to individualism and an end to "governmental interference" through a low tariff, a sound currency, and administrative economy.[9]

Many Democrats, however, including a large number in California, did not completely share the Bourbons' confidence in the "well-instructed spirit of self-interest" and doubted the wisdom of rigid restrictions on government activity. In recent years these Democrats had become increasingly concerned about the inequities and hardships that had accompanied the country's economic development. While their specific aims differed from state to state, they generally sought some measure of supervision over the economy, especially over corporations, and they consequently grew restive under Bourbon political domination. In many respects conservative themselves and willing to function within the framework of American capitalism, these Democrats desired primarily to rectify imbalances in the system, to alter rather than to abolish it. They demanded government regulation as well as promotion of economic enterprise. They subscribed to the basic Democratic tenets of states' rights, decentralization, and limited government, but urged modifications in party philosophy to fit the nation's changing needs. In a number of states

[9] Bayard to Don M. Dickinson, July 11, 1891, Dickinson Papers. See also Horatio Seymour, "The Political Situation," *North American Review*, 136 (1883): 153–58; Horace Samuel Merrill, *William Freeman Vilas: Doctrinaire Democrat* (Madison, Wis., 1954), pp. 3–4, 30–43.

they, and not the Bourbons, had been responsible for the party's electoral victories before 1885.[10]

In California, Democrats of this persuasion had wrested control of the party from Stephen J. Field, Samuel M. Wilson, and other conservatives, had made the railroad the focus of their reform efforts, and had attempted to carry out a limited program of government regulation. Finding their proposals blocked in the courts and the state legislature, they turned to the Democratic national administration for assistance. They did not ask federal action in connection with the railroad problem; their own states' rights beliefs forbade that. Rather, they requested recognition in a form that would enable them to overcome conservative opponents and put their program into effect within the state. Aware of the new president's personal views, they relied for victory on the weight of their numbers, the justice of their proposals, and their dominance of the party organization. As Inauguration Day approached they waited anxiously along with the conservatives to see whether Cleveland would respond to their requests.

III

Although Cleveland's record appeared to give the Field wing an advantage in the patronage battle, neither faction reduced its pressure on the incoming administration. On January 15, 1885, anti-monopolist leaders convened a party conference in San Francisco to discuss the patronage question, bringing together delegates appointed by Democratic county committees throughout the state. Indicating the matter's importance, Stephen M. White journeyed from Los Angeles to attend. Buckley, English, Delphin M. Delmas, and Michael F. Tarpey headed the Bay Area delegation, and Clarence R. Greathouse, editor of the *Examiner*, spoke for George Hearst.

[10] William J. Cooper, *The Conservative Regime: South Carolina, 1877–1890* (Baltimore, 1968), pp. 45–83, 125–33; Horace Samuel Merrill, *Bourbon Democracy of the Middle West, 1865–1896* (Baton Rouge, La., 1953), pp. 33–138. The Wallace resolutions and the Barry bill of the 1884 extra session are both examples of attempts by some Democrats to assert the public's interest in railroad activities. These Democrats dissented from those in the nineteenth century who, as Wallace D. Farnham has noted, asked the government to "subsidize without governing." Farnham, " 'The Weakened Spring of Government': A Study in Nineteenth-Century American History," *American Historical Review*, 68 (1963): 680.

The conference resulted in a complete triumph for the anti-monopoly forces. By a vote of 65 to 9, they defeated an ambiguous resolution in favor of Justice Field and tabled a proposal that Democrats "lay aside past and present differences." By a comparable margin they endorsed the Stockton convention and asserted that the party "stands strong, united and harmonious, devoted to the principles enunciated in its platforms and confident of their ultimate success." With reference to patronage the conference named Congressman Barclay Henley the party's official representative in Washington, and anti-monopoly leaders agreed in private to "send on a select crowd of our own to do the requisite work."[11]

As the *Alta California* charged, the conference had "declared in favor of war rather than peace." The Stocktonites readily admitted the truth of the accusation. As yet they had no desire to compromise with their foes and end their battle against the railroad. To them, as Henley exulted when the news reached Washington, the San Francisco proceedings had been "just right. We must take no step backward in this matter. It is a strange spectacle to see a small junta, the most of whom are in the pay of the Railroad, undertaking to control our party—and through Field here declaring that no member of, or sympathizer with, the Stockton Convention should be recognized by this Administration!!" "That is what Field told me," Henley added, "and right then the fight commenced. Field is simply a d—d fool and can't begin to win this fight."[12]

If the San Francisco conference drew the lines in the patronage battle, events at the state capitol reinforced them. A new session of the legislature opened during the first week of January, and conservative Democrats seized the opportunity to issue their own declaration of war. None of the legislators who had been read out of the party at Stockton had won reelection, but staggered terms had kept Lieutenant-Governor Daggett and five conservative senators in office. As Democrats caucused on the afternoon of January 5, the six "read-outs" demanded public recognition of their party standing through the

[11] SF *Exmr*, Jan. 16, 1885; White to English, Jan. 7, 1885, WP; SF *Chron*, Jan. 16, 1885; *Alta Cal*, Jan. 16–17, 1885.
[12] *Alta Cal*, Jan. 19, 1885; Henley to White, Jan. 27, 1885, WP.

election of one of their number, Benjamin Knight, as president pro tem of the senate. When the "straight-outs"—those Democratic legislators loyal to the Stockton platform—refused, nominating instead Reginaldo F. Del Valle, Daggett and his cohorts withdrew from the caucus.[13]

Thereafter, for 184 ballots and almost two weeks, the "read-outs" exploited the even balance of party forces in the senate to block its organizational proceedings. "It is all very droll," a newspaper remarked of the six-man mastery of the legislature, but any humor in the situation escaped the anti-monopolists and a public incensed by the wasteful stalemate. Protests deluged Sacramento, blaming both Democratic factions for the "foolishness."[14] Finally, fearful that further delay might allow Governor Stoneman to fill a vacant United States Senate seat, Republicans agreed to trade votes with the "read-outs." On January 16, the day after the anti-monopolist triumph at San Francisco, the coalition of Republicans and conservative Democrats in the senate elected Benjamin Knight president pro tem.[15]

Daggett followed with the announcement of senate committee assignments. Conservative Democrats supplanted anti-monopolists as chairmen of the critically important committees on corporations, labor, and finance, and the conservative Charles W. Cross remained in command of the influential judiciary committee. Del Valle, in contrast, was placed in charge of the committee on the state library. The Stocktonites, as a reporter noted, were "boiling with rage."[16] In one move Daggett had rendered them virtually powerless for the remainder of the session and precluded committee clearance of major anti-monopoly legislation. The subsequent passage of a constitutional amendment to replace all existing railroad taxes with an annual tax of 2.5 percent on the railroad's gross receipts sharpened their anger. They argued that sweeping tax revision should await the Supreme Court's judgment on the present system, objected to the amendment's loosely drawn assessment procedures, and labeled the measure "a

---

[13] SF *Chron*, Jan. 6, 1885; SF *Exmr*, Jan. 6, 1885; White to Daniel Manning, April 23, 1885, WP.
[14] SF *Chron*, Jan 10, 1885; LA *Times*, Jan. 8, 1885.
[15] *JS*, 26 sess. (1885), pp. 5–76; SF *Exmr*, Jan. 17, 1885; LA *Times*, Jan. 6, 1885.
[16] SF *Chron*, Jan. 22, 1885.

most patent fraud. It is really an amendment to permit & empower the RR corporations to assess themselves."[17] With its course dictated by a small group of men, the session by now presented a familiar pattern to the anti-monopolists. Legislative achievement, they had learned once again, often eluded divided parties.

Equally disturbing to the Stocktonites, the session also endangered one of their primary objectives: the maintenance of their own unity within a fractured organization. In 1884, under the external pressures of the tax dispute, the extra session, and the presidential campaign, they had managed to sustain a large degree of cohesion. To that achievement, as well as to skilled leadership and widespread local support, they owed their continued control over the party. But with these pressures removed, and with Democrats involved in a divisive patronage fight, apprehension increased that the anti-monopoly coalition might weaken or dissolve. Showing his concern, White wrote on January 18, 1885, "The Senatorial struggle comes up soon & then no doubt the fur will fly."[18]

The danger lay in the uncompromising desire of both George Hearst and Barclay Henley to secure the party's nomination for United States senator. The press called the nomination a "barren honor," for no Democrat could be elected over the substantial Republican majority in the legislature. The two candidates recognized, however, that the endorsement of the party caucus would assume great importance in the event of a later senatorial vacancy or a Democratic sweep in the next election. Meeting on January 22, with thirty Democrats present and sixteen votes required for nomination, the caucus took eighteen ballots before reaching accord on a nominee. Hearst led from the start, receiving fifteen votes to Henley's eleven and another candidate's four, but he was unable to attract the necessary additional vote. Finally, two Democrats switched to Hearst, and the caucus made the endorsement unanimous.[19]

The contest exposed tensions between "country" and "city" anti-

---

[17] White to Stoneman, March 13, 1885, WP; Theodore H. Hittell, *History of California*, 4 vols. (San Francisco, 1885–97), 4: 690–91, 705. California voters rejected the amendment in the 1886 election.
[18] White to Henry T. Hazard, Jan. 18, 1885, WP.
[19] SF *Chron*, Jan. 24, 1885; SF *Exmr*, Jan. 23, 1885.

monopolists, caused the ambitious Hearst to question the value of his anti-monopoly alliance, and confronted the anti-monopolists with possible disaffection in their ranks. Believing himself more entitled to recognition than "Uncle George," as Hearst was called, Henley deeply resented the outcome of the caucus. To White he complained bitterly of the *Examiner*'s course in the matter and charged that "Hearst is and always has been friendly to Field." Relying on victory to pacify Hearst, the "country" anti-monopolists moved quickly to soothe the feelings of the defeated candidate. "I think a judicious application of the proper quantity of explanation to Henley will make him all right," White predicted.[20] In two letters to Henley, White held out the possibility of a gubernatorial nomination in 1886, while confiding his agreement that Hearst "is in no respect fit for Senator." He also wrote to English, who had ties in both camps, that Henley "is a little off since his non-success in the caucus but I think you can talk him round without trouble." In this way the anti-monopolists averted discord. Hearst took comfort in his caucus endorsement, Henley consented to avoid public attacks on the winner, and for the moment at least, unity was preserved.[21]

The Republicans had not been so fortunate. From their point of view the 1885 senatorial contest had produced a result that damaged their own party, encouraged the Stockton Democrats, and even divided the Big Four. Since the previous November the leading Republican candidate had been Aaron A. Sargent. A loyal defender of the railroad during earlier terms in Congress, Sargent apparently had been promised company support in the spring of 1884, and the subsequent Republican triumph had made him confident of election. "I have a good fight, and believe I am going to win," he explained to a legislator. "I do not invite you to a losing cause." Sargent now appealed to Leland Stanford to fulfill the railroad's promises: "It is very necessary that you come out soon.... I have a good majority of those elected, and can see success ahead. But your presence here, and your strong, influential words would make assurance doubly sure. I know

---

[20] Henley to White, Feb. 17, 1885, White to Michael F. Tarpey, Feb. 26, 1885, WP.
[21] White to Henley, Feb. 8, 1885, White to Henley, March 4, 1885, White to English, Feb. 26, 1885, WP.

your personal friendship for me will induce you to comply with my earnest request."[22]

By early January 1885 Sargent had lost much of his confidence. Stanford's support had not been forthcoming, and instead there were reports that the railroad magnate intended to secure the senatorial seat for himself. "What was last night a joke, this morning a curious speculation, is this evening a serious consideration," a Sacramento correspondent observed on January 5 in reference to Stanford's candidacy. On January 11 the harried Sargent, taking note of the rumors, warned Stanford, "There are men around you with personal ambitions, who hope to personally profit by confusion." And he reminded the railroad leader, "The path of honor and safety is in my speedy election."[23]

Two days later the outlook for Sargent's cause brightened with the publication of a letter in which Stanford denied reports of his candidacy. But on the same day Sargent notified Stanford that Creed Haymond and another railroad attorney were still attempting "to pull away my votes in the Legislature. As this is so inconsistent with your letter of yesterday, I call your attention to it directly, that you may stop it." These attempts, Sargent then bluntly declared, "trifle with your honor.... I have this fight by twenty majority if these gentlemen would speak a word of encouragement for me instead of opposing me; and I would have a fair majority if they would be neutral."[24]

News of Stanford's senatorial ambitions had meanwhile reached Collis P. Huntington in New York City. He immediately sent an angry telegram to Stanford in California: "It is reported here that you are in field against Sargent. I cannot believe it, please telegraph

---

[22] Sargent to H. H. Markham, Nov. 16, 1884, Henry Harrison Markham Papers, Huntington Library; Sargent to Stanford, Nov. 11, 1884, Timothy Hopkins Transportation Collection, Stanford Univ. See also Oscar Lewis, *The Big Four: The Story of Huntington, Stanford, Hopkins, and Crocker, and of the Building of the Central Pacific* (New York, 1938), p. 243; David Lavender, *The Great Persuader* (New York, 1970), pp. 344–45; Thomas R. Bard to Stephen Bowers, Nov. 13, 1884, Bard to George Steele, Nov. 26, 1884, Bard Papers.

[23] SF *Chron*, Jan. 5, 1885; Sargent to Stanford, Jan. 11, 1885, Hopkins Collection; LA *Times*, Jan. 6–8, 1885.

[24] Stanford to Claus Spreckels, Jan. 12, 1885, in SF *Exmr*, Jan. 13, 1885; Sargent to Stanford, Jan. 13, 1885, Hopkins Collection.

me at once." Much to his later regret, Stanford ignored his associate's warning and on January 20 received the Republican caucus nomination with 47 votes to only 16 for the unfortunate Sargent. The caucus endorsement ensured Stanford's election to the Senate on January 28, 1885.[25]

Considering that it came after a decade of anti-railroad agitation, Stanford's victory aroused noticeably little outcry. Cornelius Cole expressed the reaction common even among railroad opponents: "I am, upon the whole, rather pleased with the election of Stanford—better him than any puppet of his, or a mere pettifogger. S. is the best of the C.P.R.R. lot." Although Stanford was a bland figure whose dignified demeanor belied an undistinguished intellect, he had always been the most popular of the Big Four. A prominent role in the formation of the California Republican party and a term as Civil War governor gave him respected political credentials. Coast residents admired his service as railroad president and identified him with the railroad's positive contributions to the state, seldom including him in their indictments of the corporation he headed. In a senatorial battle limited to Sargent and Stanford, most Californians would clearly have favored the latter. As the San Francisco *Examiner* remarked, "The people, as a rule, prefer the master to the man—the creator to the creature."[26]

Behind the mild public reaction, however, ran a current of discontent that would affect California politics for years to come. Fervently devoted to the railroad, Huntington never forgave an action he deemed injurious to its interests, and he began a long, secret campaign to undermine Stanford's position in the company. The small band of anti-railroad leaders in the Republican party shared Huntington's profound distaste for the affair, though for different reasons. Seldom a coherent coalition, this group included the defeated gubernatorial candidate Morris M. Estee, the strong-willed Harrison Gray

[25] Huntington to Stanford, Jan. 12, 1885, Hopkins Collection. The telegram was actually sent in coded form: "Everett diagonal that soppy in field aft nomade driver believe it please omen apple." For Stanford's election, see SF *Exmr*, Jan. 21, 1885; *JA*, 26 sess., pp. 111–20.

[26] Cole to Olive Cole, Jan. 21, 1885, Cole Papers; SF *Exmr*, Jan. 22, 1885; SF *Chron*, Jan. 20, 1885; *Alta Cal*, Jan. 29, 1885. "If I've got to choose between the devil and his imp, I'll choose the devil," commented one legislator. LA *Times*, Jan 18, 1885.

Otis of the Los Angeles *Times*, and Michael H. De Young, the publisher of the influential San Francisco *Chronicle*. Its opposition to the railroad represented a blend of anti-monopoly conviction, political expediency, and eagerness to exploit the issue to destroy Stanford's power in the party. Although dismayed by Stanford's triumph, these Republicans took solace in the thought that the outcome perhaps better suited their ends. As Sargent had warned Stanford, they "think your election will drive the Republican party into anti-monopoly, because they say you can only get it by spending a great deal of coin, which will be notorious, & disgust the party with the railroad."[27]

Evidence of dissatisfaction in the Republican ranks surfaced in the weeks after the election. Rumors spread that Estee, who also blamed the railroad for his 1882 setback, might abandon the party. Hopeful Democrats followed his activities closely and reported that "he was still fighting the RR, & was bitterly denouncing the election of Stanford as Senator."[28] Estee ultimately decided to remain in the party, but in the meantime he had been joined by other disgruntled Republicans, including Thomas R. Bard, a young Southern Californian and later a United States senator himself. Outraged by the senatorial vote, Bard believed that it doomed Republican prospects and constituted "a betrayal of our Party and of the People of the State."[29] "Creed Haymond sits behind the throne that has immense power," Bard complained to a friend. "He has opportunity of wielding the machinery by which the Great Corporation makes and unmakes Governors of this State and sends whom it chooses as the Representative of the State in the U.S. Senate."[30]

[27] Sargent to Stanford, Jan. 11, 1885, Hopkins Collection; SF *Chron*, Jan. 20–21, 1885.
[28] English to White, Aug. 14, 1885, William W. Foote to White, Aug. 14, 1885, WP. Observed White: "I have not much confidence in ever getting Estee into our ranks though I do believe we will in time have a large accession from the Rep. rank & file." White to English, Aug. 17, 1885, WP.
[29] Bard to George Steele, Feb. 9, 1885, Bard Papers. "That the election of Mr. Stanford should be followed by so few expressions of dissatisfaction can be accounted for by the supposition that the People of the State were at first dumbfounded, and have since given up in despair," Bard wrote. "The fires have been smothered but will in my opinion be fanned to intense heat at our next election." Bard to C. F. Bassett, March 27, 1885, Bard Papers.
[30] Bard to Charles Fernald, Oct. 26, 1885, Charles Fernald Papers, Huntington Library; W. H. Hutchinson, *Oil, Land and Politics: The California Career of Thomas Robert Bard*, 2 vols. (Norman, Okla., 1965), 1: 320–22.

Anti-monopoly Democrats derived perverse encouragement from these developments. Stanford's victory both distressed and delighted them. It supplied conclusive proof of the Southern Pacific's interference in politics and gave added weight to their demands for close government supervision of railroad affairs. If properly handled, the issue seemed likely to alienate voters and drive unhappy Republicans into the Democratic camp. English, for one, was pleased: "I believe in our next fight we will have a great many of these people with us," he wrote. Most important to the Stocktonites, the election promised to rejuvenate their own flagging fortunes, damaged by repeated failures during 1884. "When Stanford was elected Senator how humiliated Cal. was," declared White. "He boldly denied the State's right to interfere with his charges. He refused to pay taxes. He defied the law." And now he represented California in the United States Senate. This outcome, White and other anti-monopolists predicted, could only result in "the solidifying and uniting of the anti-monopoly sentiment of this State and its rapid gravitation towards the Democratic party standing upon the principles announced by the Stockton Convention."[31]

IV

The events in the legislature also had an immediate impact on the fight over federal patronage. Successful maneuvers by Daggett and Stanford fueled animosities between conservative and anti-monopoly Democrats and enhanced the importance of patronage to each faction. As a result the anti-monopolists quickly arranged for a delegation, composed of English, William W. Foote, Michael F. Tarpey, and Thomas J. Clunie, to press their demands in Washington. "This is necessary," observed White, "because the enemy in the person of Field is on deck." Congressman Henley hurried to Albany for a talk with the president-elect who, he reported, "surprised me by his intimate knowledge of Pacific coast politics and politicians."[32] Through a friend Field made an urgent request for a similar interview. Noting that Cleveland had consented, White remarked: "I do not attach

[31] English to White, Aug. 14, 1885, White to Henley, Feb. 8, 1885, White to Daniel Manning, April 23, 1885, WP.
[32] White to Tarpey, Jan. 6, 1885, WP; interview with Henley in SF *Chron*, Jan. 6, 1885. See also White to English, Feb. 7, 1885, English to White, Feb. 13, 1885, WP.

much importance to this because I presume the Pres. desires to hear from both sides."[33]

During the following weeks Cleveland heard frequently from both sides. As he assumed office on March 4, 1885, delegations from California poured into Washington. Three representatives of the San Francisco party, Blind Boss Buckley among them, joined the anti-monopolist group already there. John P. Irish and Jesse D. Carr, a Kern County conservative, visited the capital on behalf of the Field wing. Lieutenant-Governor Daggett, armed with an introduction from Samuel M. Wilson, also came.[34] All called on the various government departments to present their version of the California situation. By the end of March, 42 "California Pilgrims" were in Washington on a patronage mission.[35]

Those who remained on the Pacific Coast also besieged the president with advice. Conservative Democrats warned that "it would be a calamity to Democracy in California if the conspicuous men of the Extra Session folly and blunder, and of the Stockton Convention woeful indiscretion, should be appointed to important Federal positions in this State." The anti-monopolist John T. Doyle, on the other hand, cautioned that "the future of the democracy in this state will be determined practically for success or failure, by the distribution of the federal offices." Stanford's election to the Senate, Doyle argued, "will send into our ranks many republicans, dissatisfied with their party's subservience to the Companies—unless of course we can be charged with being equally so." In the event that Cleveland's appointments "show that he recognizes the men whom the Stockton convention read out, as party leaders or party men, he will break us down here."[36]

Prevented by his law practice from making the trip to the capital, White followed English's suggestion that he present to the administration a written statement of the party's condition. "English thought

[33] William Dorsheimer to Cleveland, Jan. 16, 1885, CP; White to English, Feb. 7, 1885, WP.

[34] SF *Exmr*, March 8, 15, 1885; English to White, April 26, 1885, WP; Wilson to Cleveland, April 10, 1885, CP.

[35] R. E. Doyle to Thomas F. Bayard, April 27, 1885, Thomas F. Bayard Papers, Manuscript Division, Library of Congress; SF *Exmr*, March 15, 24, 1885; *Alta Cal*, April 8, 1885.

[36] James O'Meara to Samuel J. Tilden, April 12, 1885, Doyle to Abram S. Hewitt, March 4, 1885, CP. See also Hewitt to Cleveland, March 12, 1885, CP.

it might be well to keep the fire up so I have turned a fraction of my munition loose," he told Henley.[37] White's fraction consisted of a 29-page letter in which he outlined the anti-monopoly program and asked for assistance from the national party. Much of the letter focused on Field, "our political patronage Judge," and his position on the railroad issue. "The continuity of his decisions in favor of the Corporations has suggested a uniformity which is probably constitutional — at least with him...," White wrote. "If the Courts declared, as does Field, that we have not the power to control these beings we would 'abandon hope' as do the fellows below. There is *something* in having the *power* even where it is not exercised. The tyrant is restrained when he knows that too much oppression will work his ruin."

"The Field people will not control the party of this State, even if they—which the Gods forbid—control the Federal patronage," White added, indicating the depth of factional feeling. "They will be repudiated by the organization in the future as they have been in the past. Whenever one of them creeps into the ranks, he will be treated as a fungus and promptly removed to avoid infection." In conclusion White noted rumors that Cleveland might withhold patronage from both factions in order to promote harmony. "The party here do not desire any compromise," he insisted. "It is not wished that some nonentity should be appointed. Those who have 'no opinion' are Field men & their selection would mean a Field victory. There are no dissensions to heal."[38]

Field made no attempt to conceal his involvement in the patronage struggle. He first campaigned to secure a Cabinet position for Samuel M. Wilson, "a man of great abilities and of spotless character" whose appointment would assure "conservative men ... that agrarianism in no form would find favor in the counsels of the Government." The failure of this attempt caused Field to redouble his efforts in connec-

[37] White to Henley, April 30, 1885, WP.
[38] White to Daniel Manning, April 23, 1885, AP, Cal., Collector of Customs for the Port of San Francisco, Treasury Dept., Record Group (RG) 56. A copy of this important letter, which details the aims of the anti-monopolists and the background of the party dissension, can be found in the White Papers. See also Doyle to Samuel J. Tilden, May 7, 1885, Doyle Papers; English to White, May 3, 1885, WP.

tion with other offices. Eastern newspapers assailed his activities, charging that a Supreme Court justice "should not soil his robe by becoming an office broker."[39] But to Field the issues at stake demanded bold action rather than silence. In a public letter to Charles W. Cross he promised to fight appointments that might imply administration approval of "the communistic rulings of the Stockton Convention mob": "You and other friends may rest assured that no dainty rules of propriety laid down for my conduct by those who seek harm to our State will ever deter me from such effort as I may be able to make to thwart their mischievous purposes."[40]

To counter Field's plans the anti-monopolists obtained resolutions from county committees "reiterating once more [their] love and affection for the things done at Stockton."[41] They also held a mass meeting on August 10, 1885, to celebrate Henley's return from Washington. Six thousand people crowded into San Francisco's Grand Opera House to hear speeches by Henley, Tarpey, and Delmas. Several thousand others were turned away. In the evening's major address Delmas scornfully rejected compromise "with an insignificant knot of factious malcontents, deserters and readouts." "There can be no compromise with evil, no unholy pact with corruption, no truce with tyranny," he proclaimed to the cheering crowd. The California Democratic party "is marching onward in the accomplishment of a great purpose. It has taken its stand in the front rank of the battle now waging between the people on one side and aggregated capital on the other; between the equal rights of all on one side and the exclusive and oppressive privileges of the favored few on the other."[42]

The meeting was designed to impress Cleveland with the unity of

[39] Field to George Ticknor Curtis, Dec. 14, 1884, Field to Edwards Pierrepont, Dec. 14, 1884, CP; New York *Times*, May 17, 1885.

[40] Field to Cross, May 13, 1885, untitled and undated newspaper clipping in WP. In one recommendation Field noted that the applicant "is free from all agrarian and socialistic tendencies which unfortunately have affected so many men in California." Field to L. Q. C. Lamar, July 16, 1885, AP, Cal., Surveyor General File, Interior Dept., RG 48.

[41] English to White, May 3, 1885, WP. For committee resolutions see SF *Exmr*, May 23–June 14, 1885; English to White, April 26, 1885, English to White, May 7, 1885, English to White, May 30, 1885, White to Henley, June 3, 1885, WP.

[42] SF *Exmr*, Aug. 11, 1885; *Alta Cal*, Aug. 11, 1885; White to James Smith, Aug. 7, 1885, English to White, Aug. 14, 1885, White to English, Aug. 17, 1885, WP; Henley to Cleveland, Aug. 19, 1885, CP.

party and people behind the Stockton platform, but he did not seem moved. Deluged with contradictory information from Californians, Cleveland and his advisers understandably concluded that dissension, not harmony, characterized the party on the Coast. The initial result was a delay in the appointment process while members of the administration studied the situation. "Your California affairs," remarked the secretary of the treasury, Daniel Manning, to a newspaper correspondent, "are so mixed by conflicting statements made by your representative men, that I see no other way for us than to wait." After an interview with Cleveland a Californian reported that the president said "he had heard so much of the Democratic dissension that he was perplexed." Cleveland wrote across the bottom of one petition for office: "The applicant offered the resolutions at the famous Stockton Convention."[43] Although George Hearst's *Examiner* defended the administration's cautious approach to the patronage question, local Democrats became increasingly impatient with the delay.[44]

In fact, the disunity in California had made Cleveland decide to withhold patronage from prominent members of either wing of the party. Several California Democrats had suggested that he "steer clear of factions" as the best method to promote harmony, and Samuel J. Tilden of New York, who had numerous contacts in California, proposed the same solution. "The general conclusion is," Tilden wrote Daniel Manning, "that the anti-Field interest vastly preponderates in the Democratic party and among the people, but that it would be judicious to select for Collector [of Customs at San Francisco] and the other principal places, men who are not identified with the particular controversies which have afflicted the Democratic party in California."[45] In May 1885 Cleveland confirmed this policy to a Californian who after visiting Washington repeated the president's opinion

[43] SF *Exmr*, March 29, 1885; Cleveland's remark on petition from Margaret Hetzel to Cleveland, July 2, 1885, AP, Cal., Sacramento Land Office, Interior Dept., RG 48.
[44] SF *Exmr*, July 7, 1885; John Boggs to Henley, May 28, 1885, AP, Cal., U.S. Marshal File, Justice Dept., RG 60.
[45] John H. Wise to Cleveland, May 15, 1885, AP, Cal., Collector of Internal Revenue, First District, Treasury Dept., RG 56; Tilden to Manning, June 2, 1885, CP. See also P. D. Wigginton to Cleveland, May 11, 1885, AP, Cal., Collector of the Port, San Francisco, Treasury Dept., RG 56; J. F. Linthicum to Cleveland, Nov. 25, 1885, CP.

that " 'it would be good politics to build from the ground up'—thus ignoring all existing factions and factionists there, with a view to selecting the Servants of the Government from another and different class."[46]

To Cleveland, who had taken personal charge of the distribution of the offices, such a course would have seemed attractive for a number of reasons. It would relieve him of the role of judge between the factions and place him instead in that of impartial mediator. It would accord with his distaste for presidential interference in state politics. Finally, it might demonstrate the futility of intraparty dissension and foster a satisfactory compromise once the two factions realized they were both to be disappointed in the patronage matter.

Along with these advantages, however, the policy had two major weaknesses: it meant that Cleveland's patronage selections would ultimately satisfy no one, and it required the president to find, in a state party long engaged in a bitter dispute, able Democrats who were as yet uncommitted to either faction. In the end Cleveland's patronage policy foundered on both points. Designed to restore Democratic unity, it instead angered conservative Democrats as well as anti-monopolists, and alienated the state and local organizations that found themselves bypassed in the appointment process. As a result each faction secured a few offices, managed to unite with the other to secure offices for several particularly popular Democrats, and fought for the control or dismissal of the "neutral" Democrats appointed to the most desirable posts. Two cases in particular proved representative of the nature and outcome of the California struggle for the spoils.[47]

The first involved the selection of a collector of internal revenue for Southern California, a position English described as "the most important in a political sense in the state" because hundreds of subordinate offices were at its disposal. Ignoring the candidates recommended by the various factions, Cleveland chose Asa Ellis, a Los An-

[46] Frank McCoppin to Cleveland, May 21, 1885, CP; John T. Carey to Cleveland, Dec. 9, 1887, AP, Cal., U.S. Attorney, Northern District, Justice Dept., RG 60.
[47] Two popular Democrats who attracted support from both factions were Samuel H. Brooks (AP, Cal., Subtreasurer File, Treasury Dept., RG 56) and Thomas Beck (AP, Cal., Appraiser File, Treasury Dept., RG 56).

geles County resident who had not applied for the position and had no papers on file in Washington but who had apparently been casually mentioned to the president by the anti-monopolist William T. Wallace. To English the appointment came as "a great surprise," for neither Cleveland nor Wallace had consulted the party organization. On behalf of the conservative wing, Field wrote to the president vehemently protesting the decision. Ellis, he charged, had anti-railroad sentiments and had participated in a "vicious assault upon myself." Unless immediately reversed, Field continued, the selection of Ellis would be "taken as your judgment that there is nothing in his infamous imputations upon myself to unfit him to hold the second office in your gift" in California.[48]

Realizing that it would be futile to urge the president to change his mind, the Stockton Democrats quickly maneuvered to bring Ellis into line with their own desires: "We must use every effort," English directed, "to get the power of his office thrown in favor of the Party." White, who knew Ellis well and reported that "the old fellow paddles his own canoe as a usual thing & is not I think under the control of anyone," wrote the new collector a letter implying that he had been instrumental in Ellis's success.[49] The anti-monopolists were given an unexpected opportunity to ingratiate themselves with Ellis when charges of past dishonesty endangered his appointment. They rushed to his defense, sending telegrams to Washington and printing denials in local papers; and White extracted an endorsement of him from the Los Angeles County committee.[50] In this way the Stocktonites skillfully won the collector's gratitude and support. Ellis remained in office, and President Cleveland's effort to alleviate dissension and avoid factional appointments had failed. On June 3, 1885, only two

[48] English to White, May 25, 1885, WP; Field to Cleveland, June 7, 1885, Ellis to Wallace, May 20, 1885, CP; LA *Times*, May 23, 1885. Field was also outraged by Wallace's role in the appointment. In his letter to Cleveland of June 7, 1885, he called Wallace "a man utterly without principle" and of "extreme communistic views."

[49] English to White, May 25, 1885, White to Sherman P. Stow, May 30, 1885, White to Ellis, May 23, 1885, WP. "Those San Francisco sharps must be surprised at the outcome," White remarked to Ellis.

[50] White to Manning, May 25, 1885, William S. Waters to Manning, June 3, 1885, AP, Cal., Collector of Internal Revenue, First District, Treasury Dept., RG 56. White later recalled how Ellis had come to him in "hot haste" when the trouble arose and how he had "shoved through" the endorsement. White to William F. White, July 12, 1886, WP.

weeks after the president's decision was announced, White reported to Henley, "Asa Ellis will act & work with us."[51]

The second case, the appointment of a collector of customs for the port of San Francisco, dominated the patronage struggle from the beginning. Both factions viewed it as the crucial test of strength, the outcome of which would demonstrate conclusively the administration's position on the issues that divided the party. Besides the symbolic importance of his post, the collector controlled several hundred subordinate posts and disbursed about $200,000 in annual salaries. The appointment, White emphasized to the president on May 15, "is anxiously looked for. It is regarded as the turning point upon which hinges the question whether the party can have officers who have served it & who are wanted by those who compose the organization or whether the same Corporate power which has foreclosed on Republicanism has also a lien upon Democracy."[52]

The appointment's significance lay not only in the nature of the office but in the identity of the candidates. The conservative faction backed Jesse D. Carr, a wealthy landowner loyal to Field. To oppose Carr the anti-monopolists named English, the titular head of the California party. English marshaled impressive support in his bid for the position, including recommendations from Governor Stoneman, most party leaders, and two-thirds of the Democratic county chairmen. His rejection by the president would clearly imply a repudiation of the state party organization. With so much at stake the ensuing campaign became exceptionally bitter. Both candidates appeared in Washington in a personal effort to secure the office. As late as August 1885 English was confident that he would be chosen.[53]

Aware of the matter's importance, Cleveland delayed his decision until mid-September, when he passed over English and Carr, and announced the selection of John S. Hager as collector of the port. An

[51] White to Henley, June 3, 1885, WP.
[52] White to Cleveland, May 15, 1885, WP. See also Henley to Manning, July 29, 1885, AP, Cal., Collector of Customs, San Francisco, Treasury Dept., RG 56; Henley to Cleveland, Aug. 19, 1885, James O'Meara to Samuel J. Tilden, April 2, 1885, CP.
[53] Stoneman to Manning, May 21, 1885, Henley to Manning, March 1885, Robert Tobin to Manning, May 19, 1885, AP, Cal., Collector of Customs, San Francisco, Treasury Dept., RG 56. The endorsements from county chairmen are in the same file. English's confidence is expressed in English to White, Aug. 14, 1885, WP.

El Dorado County Democrat who had earlier served briefly in the
United States Senate, Hager, like Asa Ellis, had not applied for the
office and had no recommendations on file in Washington. The appointment, he told the president, "was unexpected and unsolicited."[54]

The logic behind Cleveland's move remains obscure. Although
somewhat more moderate than English, Hager had long been recognized as a leading proponent of anti-monopolist views. A participant
in the Stockton convention, he had also attended the January conference in San Francisco, where he had helped prepare the strong endorsement of the anti-monopoly program. As English acknowledged
on September 22, Hager's nomination "was quite a surprise to all of
us, but it is not an unmixed evil. I believe him to be square with the
state organization. The other squad are not using their lungs very
lustily for Hager." The new collector immediately expressed his anti-
monopoly sentiments to the administration and advised against "con-
ferring favors on our rail road men, or their stipendiaries." In October
English reported, "Hager tells me he is with us in the fight and speaks
very harshly of Judge Field."[55]

In effect, therefore, Cleveland had gained nothing from the appointment of Hager. The conservative Democrats were angered by his
recognition of an anti-monopolist, and the Stocktonites, while wel-
coming the selection of one of their own number, resented the president's refusal to appoint the organization candidate. Henley called
Cleveland's action "an unmitigated outrage.... The President will
find that he can't run a successful administration in that way, before
he is through." When the telegram announcing Hager's nomination
arrived, Foote had just finished a letter notifying the administration
that English's rejection "would fall like a wet blanket upon us." He
returned to his desk to add a postscript expressing the anti-monopolists' appreciation for the appointment. That done, he continued on
a less grateful note: "But after all this is said, he was not the choice

[54] Hager to Cleveland, Oct. 17, 1885, CP; SF *Exmr*, Sept. 16, 1885; *Alta Cal*, Sept.
16, 1885.
[55] English to White, Sept. 22, 1885, English to White, Oct. 3, 1885, WP; Hager to
Manning, Nov. 16, 1885, AP, Cal., Surveyor of the Port of San Francisco, Treasury
Dept., RG 56. Secretary of State Bayard, who knew Hager, possibly had a role in the
appointment. Hager to Bayard, April 23, 1885, Hager to Bayard, Nov. 14, 1885, Bayard
Papers.

of the Democrats of California for the position.... The news of his selection has caused a feeling of gloom among Democrats. You can rest assured that we will still carry the party banner in the forefront of battle but we expect little aid from the administration if this is a sample of the appointments yet to be made."[56]

The rejection of English and the nomination of Ellis as collector of internal revenue set the pattern for Cleveland's distribution of patronage in California during the remainder of his first administration. The number of his removals gave Democrats little cause to complain, for despite early pronouncements in favor of civil service reform, Cleveland wielded a heavy patronage hand. Superseding the postmaster general and other traditional dispensers of patronage, he devoted hours each day to the matter himself. His frequent directives, carrying detailed instructions in his small, precise handwriting, left only the most minor appointments to the discretion of subordinates. By 1888, through Cleveland's orders, Democrats had supplanted Republicans in nearly all the California offices. The president's most prominent attempt to retain a Republican—at the behest of the head of the American Express Company—foundered when charges of embezzlement were brought against the person in question.[57]

In replacing those he had dismissed, however, Cleveland displayed marked ineptitude. It would have been difficult for any president to quench the voracious demands of an organization that had been excluded from federal spoils for 25 years. Factional disputes in California and other states added to the task. But Cleveland, whose short career had not included training in the symbolic and practical importance of patronage to local party structures, viewed the spoils as the sordid side of politics. He did not conceal his contempt for office seekers, once remarking that "when a man begins to talk about office

---

[56] Henley to White, Oct. 1, 1885, WP; Foote to Manning, Sept. 15, 1885, AP, Cal., Collector of Customs, San Francisco, Treasury Dept., RG 56. The defeat discouraged English. "What can we do?" he wrote White. "Hard fighting is the only thing left for the leaders of the party. The appointments are not at all satisfactory to many of us, but we will have to take our medicine, in order that the party may not suffer; an assault upon the administration by any of us would greatly weaken our chances in the state fight next year." English to White, Sept. 26, 1885, WP.

[57] Cleveland to Manning, Jan. 11, 1886, Cleveland to Manning, Jan. 13, 1886, Cleveland to Wilson S. Bissell, Jan. 30, 1886, James Moore to Cleveland, Feb. 24, 1886, Moore to Cleveland, March 4, 1886, CP; SF *Exmr*, March 24, 1886.

I begin to get irritable and my head begins to ache." Sound advice on patronage came from experienced politicians like Samuel J. Tilden, who urged the administration to pay respectful attention to the suggestions of party leaders, but Cleveland generally ignored it. Within a year of his inauguration, Democratic organizations across the country were in open rebellion against his patronage decisions.[58]

To the California Democrats, at least, Cleveland's appointment policies appeared capricious and ineffective. In the end the president pleased neither faction and largely forfeited the support of the state party hierarchy by disregarding its recommendations. Although he devoted much of his time to the appointment process, his actions revealed a penchant for detail rather than an awareness of the larger concepts involved in the spoils. He scorned the advice of Democratic leaders; yet when it suited his own purpose, he named a well-known cohort of Buckley to the San Francisco postmastership, the most important postmastership in California.[59] He shelved lengthy analyses of candidates' qualifications and appointed individuals mentioned by Californians, sometimes inadvertently, in brief visits to the White House. This method may have satisfied the visitors, but it upset politicians and produced a class of office holders no more able than those suggested by the party organization. It also bewildered Democrats. "I do not really understand upon what theory the President acts," complained White. "He may be able to solve the conundrum himself, but if he can do so he has more intelligence than he has hitherto displayed."[60]

Despite the conservative temper of the administration, Field and his allies had been almost completely bypassed in the distribution of patronage. An offer of a distant position to Samuel M. Wilson, which

[58] Cleveland to Wilson S. Bissell, April 22, 1883, in Allan Nevins, ed., *Letters of Grover Cleveland, 1850–1908* (Boston, 1933), p. 21; Tilden to Manning, June 9, 1885, in John Bigelow, ed., *Letters and Literary Memorials of Samuel J. Tilden*, 2 vols. (New York, 1908), 2: 687; George F. Parker, *Recollections of Grover Cleveland* (New York, 1909), p. 81; James C. Olson, *J. Sterling Morton* (Lincoln, Neb., 1942), p. 329. See also Grover Cleveland, "The President and His Patronage," *Saturday Evening Post*, 174 (May 24, 1902): 1–2.

[59] Edward Curtis to Cleveland, May 21, 1886, Curtis to Cleveland, undated (1886), A. C. Bradford to Cleveland, June 12, 1886, William S. Rosecrans to Cleveland, July 6, 1886, CP.

[60] White to English, Dec. 22, 1886, WP.

he turned down, did nothing to assuage their anger. Inexplicably, Field had even found it difficult to obtain interviews with the president, a discourtesy he resented as much as Cleveland's failure to heed his counsel. "Judge Field called to see me last evening after I was in bed," Congressman Samuel J. Randall of Pennsylvania informed Cleveland's secretary on one such occasion. "He is 'wounded.' "[61]

The anti-monopolists shared Field's disgust with the president's course. Their recommendations, too, had been ignored, and English voiced their deep resentment in December 1886, more than a year after his own patronage setback: "How long are we to [be] cursed with Cleveland and his policy? Nothing he can do in the future can palliate his treatment of the California Democracy. He has treated us like a brute & as though we were a band of bridge burners. Foote & Tarpey say they will take the stump against him if he is nominated in '88. . . . Faithlessness is a passport to recognition by this mass of Presidential fat. Our people are howling against him over the whole country. With this feeling existing, can it be possible he is again to be our nominee? God grant otherwise. He will not get a vote from the Pacific Coast."[62] Ironically, Grover Cleveland had given the two California factions something on which they could agree.

[61] Randall to Daniel S. Lamont, June 13, 1885, CP. Wilson was offered the position of ambassador to China. Wilson to Bayard, March 30, 1885, Bayard Papers. For Field's efforts to obtain an interview with Cleveland, see Field to Lamont, March 25, 1885, Field to Lamont, May 25, 1885, Field to Cleveland, June 7, 1885, Field to Cleveland, June 8, 1885, CP. In 1890 Field remarked that his personal relations with President Harrison "are very pleasant, infinitely more so than they were with his predecessor." Field to Don M. Dickinson, Jan. 3, 1890, Dickinson Papers.

[62] English to White, Dec. 24, 1886, WP.

CHAPTER FOUR

Compromise

❧

THE DEPTH of the party split in California, reflected in the virulence of the patronage contest, threatened an indefinite continuation of the struggle between conservatives and anti-monopolists. Throughout 1885 the Stockton Democrats laid plans for the coming year's campaign. Nominations and elections, like patronage, had symbolic as well as practical uses. The anti-monopolists, declared English, must "fight like h—l for the state next year. Our motto must be 'never say die.'" "We must keep this battle up and nominate a true blue anti-monopolist for Governor & we will win," White agreed. "No compromise is my watchword. Field is the damned rascal in the US in my judgment & ought to be impeached. As for the miserable poodles who trot after RR favors I have no use for them.... We must not weaken. The people at large are with us: to yield to a craven fragment of the organization would be suicide." At the August 1885 reception for Congressman Henley, the Stocktonites had publicly endorsed these views, repudiated compromise, and vowed to continue their ideological fight.[1]

Three months later, in November, anti-monopoly Democrats again gathered in San Francisco to honor Henley on the eve of his departure for Washington. This time it appeared, at least on the surface, that some change in sentiment had occurred within the Stockton wing. Henley's farewell speech rehearsed the usual anti-monopoly grievances against the Southern Pacific Railroad, but it concluded

[1] English to White, Oct. 3, 1885, White to G. W. Graves, May 16, 1885, WP. See also White to James Budd, May 17, 1885, White to Henley, Sept. 24, 1885, White to Stoneman, Nov. 28, 1884, WP.

with a muted appeal for Democratic harmony. The congressman urged, in the words of a reporter covering the affair, "that whatever local dissension there might exist in party ranks in this State, and he understood there was some dissension, should be healed, for only in union was there strength." English then addressed the meeting in a similar vein. The change of heart was slight; if the two men praised the benefits of unity, their remarks suggested that they would accept unity only on their own terms. Nonetheless, a conservative Democrat sent newspaper descriptions of the gathering to President Cleveland "to show you the altered tone and better temper manifested by our politicians at this time."[2]

The November meeting signaled the tentative beginning of an important transitional phase in which the California Democratic party departed significantly from the patterns established early in the decade. As Democratic politicians sought to adjust to changed conditions in the party and state, the anti-monopoly coalition began to disintegrate, the Stockton "read-outs" were restored to prominent positions in the party organization, and the party officially adopted a policy of compromise. The major influences that contributed to these developments would have profound and lasting effects on California politics.

II

The most notable and pervasive influences were the fundamental changes taking place in the state's economy and population. During the mid-1880's California's economy finally showed signs of recovery from the severe depression of the previous decade. Improvement was gradual, uneven, and incomplete. With the exception of 1884, when harvests reached record levels, adverse weather conditions damaged agricultural production through 1887.[3] Crop prices remained low, prompting farmers to fill warehouses in anticipation of price

2 SF *Exmr*, Nov. 24, 1885; SF *Chron*, Nov. 24, 1885; J. F. Linthicum to Cleveland, Nov. 25, 1885, CP.
3 "Report of the State Board of Agriculture, February 1, 1884," *J App*, 26 sess. (1885), 2: 12; "Report of the State Board of Agriculture, February 1, 1885," *ibid.*, p. 11; "Report of the State Board of Agriculture, February 1, 1886," *J App*, 27 sess. (1887), 2: 13; "Report of the State Board of Agriculture, February 1, 1887," *ibid.*, p. 14.

increases. Related difficulties beset other industries. Partial crop failures in 1885 cut railroad receipts and forced the Southern Pacific to discharge workers and cancel planned expansion.[4] But indications of returning prosperity overshadowed these troubles. By mid-decade the governor could report a "reasonably prosperous" situation throughout the state; and early in 1886 the San Francisco *Examiner* observed that "the long-existing crisis might be considered as definitely at an end."[5]

To some extent all segments of the economy contributed to the recovery. Although reliable figures are not available for the middle years of the decade, the total value of goods manufactured in California nearly doubled between 1880 and 1890. California's industrial output remained small in comparison to that of New York and Pennsylvania, but it included large quantities of shoes, clothing, lumber, chemicals, flour, and liquor.[6] By 1885 the California Sugar Refining Company's new Potrero Point plant employed hundreds of men and refined some 70,000 tons of sugar annually. Naval contracts awarded by the Cleveland administration to the Union Iron Works of San Francisco stimulated the shipbuilding industry, and iron and steel production more than tripled in value during the 1880's.[7] Although the output of California's mines gained only slightly during the decade, minerals retained a prominent role in the state's economy, with a value in 1889 of nearly $20,000,000. Gold accounted for more than half of this amount, and silver was mined in sizable quantities. At the end of the decade, foreshadowing future development, California registered 89 producing oil wells.[8]

In no sector was the quickened pace of economic growth more

[4] "Sixth Annual Report of the Board of Railroad Commissioners," *J App*, 27 sess., 5: 13–19.

[5] *J App*, 26 sess., 1: 3; SF *Exmr*, Jan. 1, 1886. See also SF *Chron*, Jan. 1, 1885; Ira B. Cross, *A History of the Labor Movement in California*, Univ. of California Publications in Economics, vol. 14 (Berkeley, 1935), p. 151.

[6] *Compendium of the Eleventh Census: 1890*, pt. 2 (Washington, D.C., 1894), pp. 860–61, 982–87; and pt. 3 (Washington, D.C., 1897), pp. 670, 706–11. In 1890 California ranked twenty-second in population but fourth in the number of people employed as saloon-keepers. *Ibid.*, pt. 3, pp. 400–439.

[7] SF *Exmr*, Jan. 1, 1885; SF *Chron*, Dec. 2, 1886; Lothrop L. Bullock to William C. Whitney, Feb. 14, 1887, William Collins Whitney Papers, Manuscript Division, Library of Congress; *Eleventh Census*, pt. 3, pp. 708–11.

[8] *Eleventh Census*, pt. 2, pp. 467–88.

apparent than in agriculture. California farm products increased in value by almost thirty million dollars during the decade, and agriculture continued to dominate economic development in most sections of the state. As in the 1870's, wool and the cereal crops played a major part in agricultural expansion. Newspapers reported the wool clip in the mid-1880's at about fifty million pounds, and though it had declined significantly from that figure by the end of the decade, California still ranked second in the nation in wool production. Farms also produced substantial amounts of barley, oats, and rye, and in wheat output the state moved during the 1880's from seventh to second in the country. In 1885 an estimated 3,750,000 acres had been planted to wheat.[9]

Although wool and wheat remained prominent, the important agricultural developments of the period lay elsewhere. Spurred by continued low prices for staple crops and aided by the spread of irrigation, which opened vast areas of the state to agricultural exploitation, California farmers during the 1880's concentrated on specialized commercial agriculture.[10] Vegetables and nuts became major crops. Viticulturists began to reap profits from the planting boom at the beginning of the decade. Wine production almost doubled between 1880 and 1886, reaching 18,000,000 gallons in the latter year. By 1889 more than 200,000 acres and some 120,000 people were engaged in the wine industry. One Southern California grower, the conservative Democrat J. DeBarth Shorb, annually produced 500,000 gallons as the sweet wines of the region started to penetrate Eastern and European markets.[11]

Orchard and fruit products made similar gains. "In 1875 nothing

[9] Ibid., pt. 3, pp. 618–27, 638–39; SF Chron, April 30, 1886; Alta Cal, Jan. 1, 1886, Jan 1, 1887; "Report of the State Board of Agriculture, February 1, 1888," J App, 28 sess. (1889), 6: 14. An excellent summary of California's agricultural development is provided in Gilbert C. Fite's The Farmers' Frontier: 1865–1900 (New York, 1966), pp. 166–74.

[10] Fite, Farmers' Frontier, pp. 169–71; Gerald D. Nash, State Government and Economic Development: A History of Administrative Policies in California, 1849–1933 (Berkeley, 1964), pp. 139–40; "Report of the State Board of Agriculture, February 1, 1886," J App, 27 sess., 2: 13–15.

[11] "Report of the State Board of Viticultural Commissioners," J App, 28 sess., 6: 18; "Report of the State Board of Viticultural Commissioners," ibid., 30 sess. (1893), 5: 7–8; Alta Cal, July 5, 1888; Eleventh Census, pt. 3, p. 603; Glenn S. Dumke, The Boom of the Eighties in Southern California (San Marino, Cal., 1944), p. 13.

worthy of the name orange could be seen in California," wrote one contemporary, Theodore S. Van Dyke. "Thick-skinned, sour, pithy, and dry, it was an insult to the noblest of fruit to call the California product by that name." The state's raisins, he continued, were "a laughing-stock," and its lemons, "great overgrown things, with skin half an inch thick over a dry and spongy interior, were more worthy of pity than contempt." Change came rapidly, though marketing problems, spoilage, and inadequate inspection procedures continued for years to betray the industry's immaturity. Within a decade the introduction of new varieties and improved transportation facilities had begun the transformation of the fruit industry.[12]

By the close of the 1880's growers had formed organizations, such as the California Fruit Union, to assist the promotion and sale of their crop. They annually dispatched several thousand carloads of oranges and lemons to Eastern outlets. Shipments of apples, apricots, peaches, pears, and canned fruit also expanded considerably. Raisin production leaped from 175,000 boxes in 1884 to 500,000 boxes the next year, and observers were predicting "gigantic dimensions" for the industry. In 1889 output reached 1,372,195 boxes. The Riverside, Orange, and Santa Ana areas became raisin-producing centers, and Fresno County, which dominated the industry, accounted for about one-third of the state's total production.[13]

Emerging from a decade of depressed conditions, Californians took enormous pride in the state's agricultural growth and diversification. Abundant harvests in the late 1880's added to their sense of well-being and fostered "unusual prosperity" among farmers, according to the State Board of Agriculture. "In all occupations contentment reigns supreme." Contentment, for Californians, was never something to be savored in private. In letters, pamphlets, and newspaper articles, they told others of their bounty, employing a mixture of fact and fantasy reflected in the current saying that Coast dwellers "irrigate, cultivate, and exaggerate." Hoping to attract new residents

---

[12] Theodore S. Van Dyke, *Millionaires of a Day: An Inside History of the Great Southern California "Boom"* (New York, 1890), pp. 31–32; Earl Pomeroy, *The Pacific Slope* (New York, 1965), pp. 107–11; Fite, *Farmers' Frontier*, pp. 169–70.

[13] "Report of the State Board of Agriculture, February 1, 1884," *J App*, 26 sess., 2: 12; "Report of the State Board of Agriculture, February 1, 1888," *ibid.*, 28 sess., 6: 17–18; "Annual Report of the State Board of Horticulture for 1889," *J App*, 29 sess. (1891), 4: 430; *Eleventh Census*, pt. 3, pp. 603, 664.

to the state, they represented California as "a modern Canaan, a land flowing with milk and honey, where moderate labor, under smiling skies, yields the husbandman a wonderfully bounteous reward."[14]

They succeeded beyond expectations. A rapid rise in population accompanied the economic revival. Having grown at an average of about 250,000 each decade between 1850 and 1880, the population increased by more than 340,000 during the 1880's. The 1890 census credited California with 1,208,130 inhabitants, and San Francisco, whose population approached 300,000, became the eighth most populous city in the nation. The state's population growth, as the 1890 census noted, was "most marked in its great cities and southern part." The latter development, more than any other in the 1880's, altered the shape of California politics. While prosperity and immigration touched all sections of the state, Southern California experienced a boom that changed the backward "cow counties" into the focus of expansion within the state and a center of attention for much of the nation as well.[15]

The boom had its immediate origins in the entrance into California of the Atchison, Topeka, and Santa Fe Railroad. After overcoming the Southern Pacific's maneuvers to bar it from the state, the Santa Fe reached San Diego in November 1885. Crews then rushed to complete a short line between Barstow and Colton that gave the new railroad its essential link with a leased line into Los Angeles. By early 1886 Santa Fe officials were ready to contest the Southern Pacific's dominance of California transportation. First seeking a pooling agreement, they demanded half the Southern California business and 28 percent of the remaining Pacific Coast traffic. When the Southern Pacific refused, the Santa Fe on February 19, 1886, announced a cut in rates. Its rival followed, passenger and freight charges dropped rapidly, and delighted Californians for the first time experienced a major rate war between domestic railroads.[16]

[14] "Report of the State Board of Agriculture, February 1, 1889," *J App*, 28 sess., 6: 13; Kate Sanborn, *A Truthful Woman in Southern California* (New York, 1893), p. 18; LA *Times*, Feb. 4, 1889.
[15] *Compendium of the Eleventh Census: 1890*, pt. 1 (Washington, D.C., 1892), pp. xliii, 2–4, 438.
[16] Lewis B. Lesley, "The Entrance of the Santa Fe Railroad into California," *PHR*, 8 (1939): 89–96; "Eleventh Annual Report of the Board of Railroad Commissioners," *J App*, 29 sess., 7: 21; LA *Times*, Feb. 20–21, April 3, 1886.

Questioned by reporters in New York City, Collis P. Huntington displayed no concern over the Sante Fe's challenge: "We are and have been all along in favor of low rates," he told one correspondent. Californians were jubilant. Encouraged by a transcontinental rate that sank as low as 25 dollars, Eastern visitors flocked to San Francisco and other communities, where they filled hotels, stimulated the real estate market, and brightened business prospects. "This competition and reduction of rates is a great thing for California," exulted an observer in San Francisco.[17] Southern Californians noticed a changed attitude among local railroad representatives, including new courtesy to passengers and eagerness to expedite freight traffic. "How sharp the contrast between this conciliatory language and the tone of the [magnates] towards the public a few years ago!" the Los Angeles *Times* boasted after a Southern Pacific official promised better service to customers. "Verily, railway competition is a mighty good thing for the people."[18]

The rate war ended a few months after it began, but the pattern was repeated a year later when the Santa Fe acquired its own tracks into Los Angeles. The ensuing drop in freight and passenger rates, combined with the extensive publicity given to Southern California by railroads and newspapers, among others, touched off the great boom of 1887.[19] Rates falling as low as one dollar from Kansas City to Los Angeles and seven dollars from Chicago to Los Angeles drew tourists and home-seekers in record numbers. Travelers returned home with glowing reports of the area's resources, and doctors praised the benefits of its climate for afflictions ranging from hay fever to senility. Sparked by the influx of people, the rising real estate values in Los Angeles and surrounding towns captured nationwide attention. Most satisfying to Southern Californians, the 1887 boom was limited almost exclusively to their region. As one bragged during a

[17] Cornelius Cole to Olive Cole, April 6, 1886, Cole Papers; interview with Huntington in LA *Times*, Feb. 20, 1886. See also Cole to Olive Cole, March 21, 1886, Cole to Olive Cole, March 25, 1886, Cole Papers.

[18] LA *Times*, Feb. 26, 1886.

[19] The best account of the boom is Dumke's *Boom of the Eighties*. Van Dyke's *Millionaires of a Day* offers a contemporary description. For the Santa Fe's entry into Los Angeles, see LA *Times*, May 1, 14–16, 1887; and Franklyn Hoyt, "The Los Angeles and San Gabriel Valley Railroad," *PHR*, 20 (1951): 227–39.

visit to San Francisco: "The travel from the East don't seem to come up this way. It all points towards Southern California, & seems to stick there." "It looks as if the east had just waked up to what Southern California is like," rejoiced another. "People are pouring in here at a great rate."[20]

The Southern Californians' elation reflected their awareness that the boom offered escape from the subordinate position they had long been relegated to in the state's political and economic life. In the course of the 1880's their section experienced the most rapid population increase of any section of California. Los Angeles County jumped from 33,381 inhabitants at the beginning of the period to 101,454 at the end, a figure that did not include the 13,500 people who withdrew in 1889 to form Orange County. The city of Los Angeles, the center and financier of the boom, grew from 11,183 in 1880 to 50,395 in 1890, and unofficial estimates placed it at about 80,000 during the peak of the excitement. While a few residents resented the city's transformation—one called the new metropolis a "hurly-burly of toughs and boors, crowded, sticky, malarial and vehemently Philistine"—most accepted the preconceptions of a growth-minded era. They welcomed swift expansion, boasted of their new status as the second city in the state, and proudly labeled Los Angeles "the Kansas City of the Pacific Coast."[21] Neighboring areas shared their good fortune. During the 1880's Ventura County doubled in population, San Diego quadrupled, and San Bernardino and Fresno counties more than tripled.[22]

The composition of the new population also pleased Southern Californians. Although many immigrants continued to come from New York, Massachusetts, and Pennsylvania, the influx of the 1880's was composed primarily of Midwesterners, particularly from Illinois, Iowa,

[20] Cole to Olive Cole, Dec. 3, 1886, Cole Papers; Charles Dwight Willard to Harriet E. Willard, Nov. 17, 1887, Willard Papers. See also LA *Times*, Jan. 1, 1887; Blanton Duncan to Thomas F. Bayard, Jan. 11, 1888, Bayard Papers.
[21] Willard to Sarah W. Hiestand, April 11, 1888, Willard Papers; LA *Times*, Jan. 1, 1887. Ironically, in view of his early scorn for Los Angeles, Charles Dwight Willard became secretary of the promotion-minded Los Angeles Chamber of Commerce.
[22] *Eleventh Census*, pt. 1, pp. 9, 434; Dumke, *Boom of the Eighties*, pp. 41, 46; Henry Markham Page, *Pasadena: Its Early Years* (Los Angeles, 1964), pp. 69–106; Leo J. Friis, *Orange County Through Four Centuries* (Santa Ana, Cal., 1965), pp. 86–95. The impact of rapid growth on Los Angeles is discussed in Robert M. Fogelson, *The Fragmented Metropolis: Los Angeles, 1850–1930* (Cambridge, Mass., 1967), pp. 63–84.

Ohio, and Indiana.[23] Contemporaries noted that the newcomers were generally more well-to-do than any previous group of immigrants. Attracted by climate and resources, they came in quest of town lots, orchards, or vineyards rather than dirt farms, wheat fields, or cattle ranches. "The ever increasing swarm of immigrants to the State do not come to seek for gold, but for homes—for ten or twenty acres upon which they may raise the vine, the fig, the olive or the orange," remarked the Los Angeles *Times*. Van Dyke observed that the migrants were arriving in "palace-cars instead of 'prairie schooners,' and building fine houses instead of log shanties, and planting flowers and lawn-grass before they planted potatoes or corn."[24]

Inevitably, the immigration of the 1880's had a profound impact on Southern California. It spurred agricultural growth, encouraged the spread of intensive and diversified farming, and gave long-awaited corroboration to the confidence of Southern Californians in the economic potential of their region. Politically, it brought the section much greater leverage: the southern counties sent larger delegations to conventions and the legislature and had a more influential voice in party councils. Recognition of this new status came when the 1886 Republican and 1888 Democratic state conventions were held, for the first time, in Los Angeles. The 1887 boom also sharpened sectional animosities between Northern and Southern California, accentuating the relatively milder tensions of past years. "Was it not plain," asked Van Dyke, "that the once despised 'cow counties' which the northern part of the State had long sneered at were fast becoming the most valuable part of the State for the area?"[25]

Visitors in Northern California found "inordinate jealousy" of Southern California's success, while the Southern California press seized every opportunity to deride the "Northern Citrus Belt."[26] The

[23] *Eleventh Census*, pt. 3, pp. 14–19, 38–41; Morrow Mayo, *Los Angeles* (New York, 1933), pp. 91–103; Charles Dwight Willard, *The Herald's History of Los Angeles City* (Los Angeles, 1901), pp. 317–18.

[24] LA *Times*, Feb. 4, 1889; Van Dyke, *Millionaires of a Day*, p. 45. "It is not so much the fortune-seeker as the health-seeker who is coming to us now," claimed the San Francisco *Examiner* (March 14, 1887). See also E. Pomeroy, *Pacific Slope*, p. 107; John E. Baur, "Los Angeles County in the Health Rush, 1870–1900," *California Historical Society Quarterly*, 31 (1952): 13–31.

[25] Van Dyke, *Millionaires of a Day*, p. 37.

[26] Cole to Olive Cole, Aug. 23, 1890, Cole Papers; LA *Times*, Jan. 17, 1888.

hostility took practical form in renewed agitation for the division of
the state. A mass meeting in Los Angeles in 1888 urged the formation of a separate state, the district's representative introduced a bill
in Congress to that effect, and the issue attracted widespread support. Stephen M. White noted that once reapportionment had registered recent population gains, San Bernardino, Los Angeles, and
San Diego counties together would have more representation than
the entire state north of San Francisco. "If this is the case," he argued,
"it will manifestly be to the interests of our northern brethren to let
us go, because by means of a very slight combination with the Saints
of San Francisco, we could leave the Northern Citrus Belt to freeze
alone." Although interest in dividing the state soon dwindled, a new
sectional dimension had been added to the "country"-"city" divisions
already characteristic of California politics.[27]

Together, these developments—economic recovery, the boom in
Southern California, and immigration—worked in the years after
1885 to alter the fortunes of the California Democratic party. For
one thing, the wave of newcomers introduced an uncertain element
into the state's political life. In the fall of 1886, when the real influx
had only just begun, White estimated that his senatorial district
already contained several thousand new voters; in the presidential
election two years later, more than twice as many votes were cast in
Los Angeles County than ever before. Such increases, which occurred
in all the southern counties and to a smaller degree in the San Francisco Bay Area as well, had an unsettling effect on state politics. Confronted with a rapidly changing electorate, California politicians
found it necessary to reformulate issues and programs to appeal to
the immigrants and to create new bases of political support.[28]

Unfortunately for the Democrats, to the extent that the prior voting habits of the newcomers could be determined, it appeared that

[27] White to W. W. Bowers, June 30, 1887, WP; Willard, *Herald's History of Los Angeles*, pp. 342–43; John Dillingham to William Vandever, Jan. 27, 1889, AP, Cal., Collector of Customs, San Diego, Treasury Dept., RG 56; SF *Chron*, July 18, Aug. 12, Sept. 28, 1887. Sectional tensions, of course, had always been present in state politics, but only after the developments of the 1880's did Southern Californians have the power to act on them.
[28] White to English, Oct. 3, 1886, White to A. W. Potts, Oct. 6, 1886, White to A. F. Jones, Nov. 13, 1888, WP; W. Dean Burnham, *Presidential Ballots, 1836–1892* (Baltimore, 1955), pp. 292–305.

most were Republicans who had come from Republican states in the Midwest. White ruefully observed, "It is supposed that the majority of the new voters are Republicans," and Republican newspapers confidently anticipated that the recent arrivals had strengthened their party. Creed Haymond, the Southern Pacific attorney, voiced the general conviction of political leaders when he predicted that unless the Democratic party could make inroads among the newcomers, the immigration of the 1880's would change the basic complexion of California politics. "I have thought since 1867," Haymond wrote, "that this State, as between the Democrats and Republicans, was very close, chances in favor of the Democrats; but I now incline to the opinion that the immigration will put California in the list of Republican States." To the Democrats' dismay, the coming years would demonstrate the accuracy of Haymond's prediction.[29]

The events of the mid-1880's also had a more immediate impact on the Democratic party: they lessened hostility toward the railroad and undercut the anti-monopoly sentiment that had guided the party since the beginning of the decade. The Southern Pacific and the Santa Fe had played a leading role in the return of prosperity, and among both immigrants and older residents, there was increased appreciation for the railroads' contributions to economic development. Railroad publicity and low railroad rates had helped lure the newcomers into the state, where some of them had settled on company lands. The railroads had speeded freight shipments and provided improved facilities for the movement of fruit and other perishable products to Eastern markets. In 1886, for example, the Southern Pacific inaugurated a system of special trains designed to enable fruit growers to tap new outlets in New York and Boston. None of the experiments proved entirely successful, but they reduced dependence on local markets, offered promise of future benefits, and gratified California shippers. As the railroad commission reported in 1888, "A better understanding and feeling now exists between the railroad companies and their customers than has ever before existed in this State."[30]

---

[29] White to J. M. Miller, Oct. 16, 1886, Haymond to White, Nov. 28, 1884, WP; SF *Chron*, Aug. 17, 1886.

[30] "Ninth Annual Report of the Board of Railroad Commissioners," *J App*, 28 sess., 2: 44; "Report of the State Board of Agriculture, February 1, 1887," *ibid.*, 27 sess.,

Among the causes for the improved situation, the commission added, "The most potent . . . is railroad competition." To Californians,
who had long believed in the blessings of competition, such a conclusion would have come as no surprise. As the Los Angeles *Times*
had earlier declared, "Our one paramount necessity is railroad competition. This will prove more potent in regulating freights and fares
than all the constitutional provisions, all the legislative enactments,
and all the railroad commissions." The Californians' faith appeared
justified by the sharp drop in railroad rates following the arrival of
the Santa Fe in Southern California and its subsequent expansion
up the San Joaquin Valley toward San Francisco. The presence of
two railroads in the state, it seemed, would permanently reduce transportation costs and promote better service. As the editor of a Los
Angeles newspaper recalled, the coming of the Santa Fe "meant
everything to the people of Southern California, and would solve
the distracting question of railroad monopoly which had hung over
the lower part of the State like a dark pall. . . . The spirit of the people
was animated with new hopes."[31]

These new hopes quickly affected the fortunes of the anti-monopoly
Democrats. In the changed conditions after 1885 the anti-monopoly
program no longer seemed quite as relevant to the state's needs, a
feeling that was reinforced early in 1887, when Congress established
a federal agency, the Interstate Commerce Commission, to supervise
railroad affairs. Like most of their contemporaries in the late nineteenth century, Californians blended a basic confidence in the virtues
of expansive capitalism with an underlying distrust of government
activism. They had been willing to demand regulatory legislation
when the need appeared urgent, but they now believed that private
enterprise, through the operation of natural laws of competition, had

2: 15–16; "Report of the State Board of Agriculture, February 1, 1888," *ibid.*, 28 sess.,
6: 16–17; SF *Exmr*, Dec. 29, 1887; Mayo, *Los Angeles*, pp. 91–103; Edna Monch
Parker, "The Southern Pacific Railroad and Settlement in Southern California," *PHR*,
6 (1937): 103–19.
[31] "Ninth Annual Report of the Board of Railroad Commissioners," *J App*, 28 sess.,
2: 44; LA *Times*, May 31, 1885; James J. Ayers, *Gold and Sunshine: Reminiscences
of Early California* (Boston, 1922), pp. 327–28. See also LA *Times*, Jan. 6, 1885, Nov.
19, 1886; Maurice H. Newmark and Marco R. Newmark, eds., *Sixty Years in Southern
California, 1853–1913: Containing the Reminiscences of Harris Newmark* (New York,
1926), pp. 549–83.

solved the problem itself. "The railroad question," one observer noted, "...measurably passed out of existence with the entry of new Transcontinental lines."[32]

Popular support began to slip away from Henley, White, English, and the other anti-monopolists. They would soon regain it. During the following decade, when depression returned to the state and when it became evident that neither competition nor federal regulation had solved the monopoly problem after all, Californians would once again demand vigorous remedial action against the railroads. By then, however, it was too late to salvage the anti-monopoly coalition of the 1880's. The Stockton Democrats in the meantime had been forced to adjust to the altered mood of their state, a mood that, as White lamented, "rendered it out of the question to get an intelligent public opinion upon the railroad issue."[33]

III

Although it was spread over several years, the erosion of anti-railroad sentiment gave immediate encouragement to Democrats who sought an end to dissension within the party. A few party members had refused to take sides in the dispute, regarding it as a wasteful diversion of the party's energies. The party's defeat in the 1884 election had added to their numbers, as had the Democrats' troubles in the 1885 session of the legislature. The storm of public outrage over the stalemate at Sacramento persuaded many Democrats that continued factionalism would discredit the party. "The past," they urged, "should be completely wiped out and a new start made." Through most of 1885 the confident anti-monopolists ignored this advice, for the compromise-minded Democrats still lacked a major leader and had little influence. During the winter of that year, however, they suddenly acquired both. George Hearst decided to desert the anti-monopoly coalition.[34]

Hearst's decision stemmed only in part from the maneuvering of a politician sensitive to shifts in the public temper. It was also the

[32] H. Z. Osborne to E. W. Halford, Nov. 30, 1888, HP.
[33] White to William W. Foote, Nov. 22, 1886, WP.
[34] Richard Bayne to Francis G. Newlands, Sept. 21, 1885, Francis G. Newlands Papers, Yale Univ.

product of long-standing tensions in the anti-monopolist camp. Relations between Hearst and the other anti-monopolists had been strained since the 1882 convention, when he had been denied the gubernatorial nomination. New problems had arisen in the January 1885 senatorial caucus. The powerful Hearst had managed to secure the caucus endorsement, but his victory had been achieved by a narrow margin and only after a protracted struggle with Henley's supporters. Needing Hearst's financial resources, the support of his newspaper, and his influence in San Francisco, the "country" anti-monopolists had hurriedly repaired the coalition, but the experience had convinced Hearst that he could not rely on his allies to fulfill his senatorial ambitions. At the end of 1885, the caucus nomination in his grasp, Hearst apparently concluded that only a reunited party could elect a Democratic legislature that in turn could send him to the Senate.

Significantly, Hearst's movement toward compromise also came shortly after the formation in September 1885 of the Democratic League of California. Organized and largely financed by Francis G. Newlands, who had defended Field at the Stockton convention, the league was an overt attempt to overthrow the anti-monopoly wing of the party. Its membership comprised almost every conservative Democrat of prominence in the state, including Samuel M. Wilson, Jesse D. Carr, John P. Irish, John Daggett, Charles W. Cross, and J. DeBarth Shorb. In an address issued to Democrats, the league claimed to have "no factional affiliation" and called for the immediate restoration of party harmony, but at the same time it criticized the existing "gross mismanagement" of the party, denounced the Stockton platform, and referred to Field's "incalculable service" to the nation. In effect, it was clear that conservative Democrats still intended to end the party's factionalism on their own terms.[35]

The league's sole importance lay in its impact on Hearst and the Democratic organization in San Francisco. Elsewhere it attracted few members not already committed to the conservative cause, and

[35] A list of league members and copies of the address are in the Newlands Papers. Newlands and Carr each contributed $10,000 to the league. In all, members pledged approximately $50,000. Undated financial statement, Democratic League of California, Newlands Papers.

most Democrats recognized that, as one told Newlands, "instead of
tending to promote harmony in the party, it will tend to widen the
existing gap.... It would seem to me like adding fuel to the flame."
To Hearst, however, the abrupt appearance of a well-financed league,
based in San Francisco and composed of a number of leading San
Francisco Democrats, endangered his position in the city party and
perhaps his alliance with the unreliable Buckley. The likelihood that
Newlands had formed the league partly to advance his own aspirations for a Senate seat increased Hearst's apprehension. In sum, the
challenge presented by the league gave Hearst an additional reason
to break away from the anti-monopolists.[36]

On December 18, 1885, Hearst fired Clarence R. Greathouse as
editor of the San Francisco *Examiner*. The railroad and anti-monopoly issues soon disappeared almost completely from its editorial pages.
Instead the newspaper began to call for "harmony and concert of
action" in the California Democratic party. "We have had enough
of dissension and petty strife," the paper declared. "It has resulted in
nothing but harm, and evil is sure to come of it again if not thoroughly and definitely abandoned. We want a united and harmonious
party, relegating personal feuds and bitterness to the individuals who
devised them." Even the Stockton "read-outs," who had previously
been the target of much abuse, found themselves being praised in the
Examiner.[37]

"Alas, how the mighty hath fallen," commented English on
Hearst's new stance. White angrily complained that "the attitude
of the *Examiner* is far from satisfactory," and he concluded that
Hearst, "a natural RR man, a warm friend of Field, only nominally
on our side," could no longer be trusted by the anti-monopolists. Resentful of Hearst's action and concerned for their own position in
the party, the remaining Stocktonites resolved to repudiate the *Examiner*'s compromise pronouncements and undermine Hearst's influence in the Democratic organization. Their opportunity came early
in March 1886, when the death of John F. Miller, a Republican, cre-

---

[36] Richard Bayne to Newlands, Sept. 21, 1885, Newlands Papers; William Lilley III,
"The Early Career of Francis G. Newlands, 1848–1897" (Ph.D. diss., Yale Univ.,
1965), pp. 167–70; SF *Exmr*, Sept. 22, 1885.
[37] SF *Exmr*, June 16, 1886.

ated a vacancy in the Senate and precipitated a serious crisis in the Democratic party.[38]

As soon as news of Miller's illness reached the state, White and English, along with their allies, decided to contest Hearst's bid for the Senate seat and to secure the appointment instead for the loyal anti-monopolist Delphin M. Delmas. Hearst's defeat, they reasoned, would severely damage his prestige and weaken his hold on the San Francisco party. The selection of Delmas, an author of the celebrated Stockton platform and the attorney in charge of the railroad tax cases now before the Supreme Court, would also serve notice to Democrats that the anti-monopoly forces remained firmly in control and that there would be no compromise between the factions. It was a dangerous strategy, as English was aware: "You realize," he wrote to White, "that if our friend is ignored, it will be a slap in the face to all of us." But in light of Hearst's recent apostasy, the anti-monopolists believed their strategy necessary in order to avert the consequences that would follow his victory. "Should anyone not thoroughly identified with the cause get this place it will end us as a party," argued White. "'Compromise' [and] 'harmony' are words of pleasant sound but the ideas conveyed are fatal when applied to political conditions like ours."[39]

Unfortunately for the anti-monopolists, one obstacle doomed their efforts almost from the beginning: the senatorial appointment would be made by Governor Stoneman. In the four years since they had nominated and elected the governor, the anti-monopolists had become totally disillusioned with him. To them he had proved "a well meaning but weak man, wholly unequal to the circumstances in which he was placed." He had, they believed, mismanaged the tax negotiations with the Southern Pacific Railroad. Only under pressure had he agreed to call the 1884 extra session. He had privately criticized the exclusion of the conservatives from the presidential campaign, had wavered in the patronage struggle, and had commented favorably on Leland Stanford's election to the Senate. Months before

[38] English to White, June 24, 1886, White to J. A. Filcher, July 13, 1886, White to English, March 23, 1886, WP.
[39] English to White, Feb. 15, 1886, White to James J. Ayers, March 14, 1886, WP.

the matter of the senatorial seat arose, the Stockton Democrats had resolved to abandon Stoneman in the 1886 campaign.[40]

Stoneman was aware of their intentions. "No man in politics," he had pointedly written to White, "ever can know who his friends are until they have weighed in the balance." Now, by virtue of his appointive power, the governor could determine the fortunes of the anti-monopolists, and despite a frantic effort that lasted throughout March 1886, they found themselves unable to overcome his hostility. Even a pointed hint from White that a wise selection might earn him another term in Sacramento failed to allay Stoneman's suspicions.[41]

Instead the governor chose to bargain with Hearst, who in return for the appointment could offer the convention votes of the large San Francisco delegation. Reports of such an agreement appeared in several newspapers, and after an interview with Stoneman in mid-March, White lamented that the governor "refuses to express an opinion and the bad feature of it is that he talks of the necessity of *harmony*. This of course means defeat.... I fear that there is something behind the curtain; that maybe promises have been made to aid his, S's, gubernatorial aspirations & that he is to reciprocate. He talks too much of 'harmony.' "[42] On March 23, arguing that his choice had been dictated by the earlier caucus nomination, Stoneman appointed Hearst to the vacant Senate seat.[43]

The defeat was a severe blow to the anti-monopolists, and it was followed by another fully as damaging. On May 10, 1886, a few weeks later, the Supreme Court handed down its long-awaited decision in the Santa Clara and other railroad tax cases. In an important step, the Court affirmed at the outset the railroad's contention that the Fourteenth Amendment protected corporations, but it then refused to rule on the constitutionality of the California tax system. Over the

[40] John T. Doyle to Abram S. Hewitt, March 4, 1885, CP; White to Delmas, Nov. 8, 1885, English to White, March 26, 1886, WP; LA *Times*, Jan. 6, 1885.

[41] Stoneman to White, n.d. [June 1884?], White to Stoneman, March 16, 1886, WP. See also John T. Doyle to Stoneman, March 8, 1886, Doyle Papers; English to White, March 9, 1886, White to English, March 14, 1886, James J. Ayers to White, March 17, 1886, White to Ayers, March 19, 1886, WP.

[42] White to English, March 10, 1886, WP. See also SF *Chron*, Feb. 6, 1886; White to Delmas, March 23, 1886, William W. Foote to White, March 24, 1886, WP.

[43] SF *Chron*, March 24, 1886; James J. Ayers to White, March 22, 1886, WP.

objections of Field, who urged a broader ruling, the Court simply voided past assessments on the technical ground that the State Board of Equalization had improperly included the value of the fences along the railway.[44] The decision settled nothing and necessitated another lengthy appeals process involving reassessment on the new basis, contests in lower courts, and final adjudication by the Supreme Court. Jubilant over the outcome, conservatives recognized that the limited ruling represented a serious reversal for the anti-monopolists. "All must now perceive," exulted one journal, "that [the Stocktonites] are demagogic cranks, equally ignorant of law and destitute of common sense, and that the purblind people who accepted the guidance of these blind demagogues have been led into the ditch."[45]

The anti-monopoly Democrats never recovered from the two setbacks. They had promised to compel the railroad to pay taxes, but the Supreme Court's decision left the matter entirely unresolved. It indicated only that a long campaign still lay ahead, and most Californians had grown weary of long campaigns. Thoughtful observers were troubled by the decision, which illustrated a recurrent problem. Cautious, limited rulings may have hoarded the Supreme Court's institutional strength, but they gravely undercut the nation's lawmakers and in a sense damaged rather than advanced the law. They especially hurt elected officials, who faced a public impatient with ambiguity and eager for clear-cut solutions. In California the Stockton Democrats would have preferred a firm decision, even one that overturned the state's tax system, for then they could have proposed immediate measures to satisfy judicial objections. As it was, the Court's 1886 evasion did maximum harm: it unnecessarily kept the issue in the courts instead of the legislature, it precluded an effective response from political leaders, and it in effect postponed needed tax reforms for two decades. Legislative committees studied the issue during the 1890's, and in 1893 an aroused Democratic majority in the legislature managed to push through a Railroad Reassessment Act that

---

[44] *Santa Clara County* v. *Southern Pacific Railroad Company*, 118 U.S. 394 (May 10, 1886). Earlier views of the decision's fundamental constitutional importance are revised in C. Peter Magrath, *Morrison R. White: The Triumph of Character* (New York, 1963), pp. 220–25, and Howard Jay Graham, "The Waite Court and the Fourteenth Amendment," *Vanderbilt Law Review*, 17 (1964): 525–47.

[45] San Francisco *Argonaut*, May 15, 1886. See also SF *Chron*, May 11, 1886; LA *Times*, May 11, 1886; White to George A. Johnson, May 24, 1888, WP.

collected a sizable proportion of the railroad's unpaid taxes. But significant reform, addressed to the kind of fundamental questions raised by the anti-monopolists, would now have to await the 1906 California Tax Commission, a progressive body that would build on the unhappy experience of the earlier period.[46]

If the 1886 tax ruling dampened popular support for the anti-monopolists, Hearst's appointment to the Senate revealed their weakened position within the Democratic party. Gambling on victory, the Stocktonites had attempted, through the senatorial question, to discredit Hearst, repudiate compromise, and demonstrate their continued dominance of the party—and they had been beaten. In the coming months, as White dejectedly acknowledged, the anti-monopoly Democrats would have to confront "some disagreeable facts." Outmaneuvered, their prestige diminished, they had no recourse but to give the new senator their reluctant endorsement and to watch helplessly as their party veered toward compromise. As White ruefully remarked, "The tables are now turned."[47]

The Democratic state convention, which met in San Francisco during the first week of September, confirmed the changed conditions in the party. The San Francisco *Chronicle* provided an accurate appraisal of the party's temper as the convention approached: "The ultra-radicals want to swing the tomahawk again, the ultra-read-outs want to draw the scalping-knife, but a large body of both factions want peace." The new leader of the compromise movement also began to exert his influence. When the delegates arrived they were greeted by an editorial in Hearst's *Examiner* that suggested: "It is the duty of the convention to look forward and fight the enemy, and not look behind for pretexts for factional bickerings. It is the present and future that are to be dealt with, and not the past. It is a time for healing

[46] C. K. Yearley, *The Money Machines: The Breakdown and Reform of Governmental and Party Finance in the North, 1860–1920* (Albany, N.Y., 1970), p. 196; Newton W. Thompson, "Separation of State and Local Revenues," *Proceedings of the National Tax Association* (Ithaca, N.Y., 1915), pp. 42–49; Edwin R. A. Seligman, "Recent Reports on State and Local Taxation," *American Economic Review*, 1 (1911): 284–85; *JS*, 30 sess., p. 461. The California constitution's distinctive mortgage provision remained in effect, but mortgagors (aided by an 1898 decision of the California Supreme Court) managed to pass on their share of the taxes by imposing higher interest rates or by requiring the borrower to pay the full assessment. Carl C. Plehn, "The Taxation of Mortgages in California, 1849 to 1899," *Yale Review*, 8 (1899): 31–67.

[47] White to English, March 23, 1886, WP.

all differences instead of paying off old scores. In one word, harmony is the thing wanted."[48]

Meeting in Odd Fellows' Hall, the convention made it clear from the beginning that the editorial's advice would be followed. "This convention is going to keep in the middle of the road," declared one delegate, "and the first fellow that tries to raise a row will be sat down on hard." In the opening-day contest for the position of temporary chairman, White, who had won easily at Stockton two years before, barely managed to defeat the candidate of the compromise forces, N. Greene Curtis of Sacramento. White's narrow triumph, by a margin of only 36 votes out of 484, revealed the altered situation in the party, for it depended on the delegations from his own Los Angeles County and English's Alameda organization. In a conciliatory gesture Hearst and Buckley gave most of San Francisco's votes to White. But significantly, several areas that had formerly been centers of anti-monopoly strength, including San Joaquin County, Tuolumne County, and numerous interior counties, gave their support to Curtis and compromise.[49]

Unable to contain his anger, Henley "with flushed face and clenched fist" told the delegates that the opposition to White had originated in railroad company headquarters. "Sir," he appealed, "let it not be said, when this convention terminates its labors, that it has bent the knee to railroad influences." The *Examiner* retorted that such "ill-considered and intemperate" accusations "stand in the way of Democratic harmony and Democratic success," while the conservative *Alta California* charged that "Mr. Henley could not permit the party to be peaceable, to be harmonious, to be successful, and so he took the floor to disturb the peace." Even White, alert to the mood of the delegates, sought in his acceptance address to minimize Henley's remarks. Calling the first day's vote "a great change from the old arrogant sway that the radicals held at Stockton," the San Francisco *Chronicle* concluded that during the remainder of the convention the anti-monopolists "must be conservative to a degree, or they will be superseded in power."[50]

---

[48] SF *Chron*, Aug. 22, 1886; SF *Exmr*, Aug. 30, 1886.
[49] SF *Exmr*, Sept. 1, 1886.
[50] *Ibid.*; *Alta Cal*, Sept. 1, 1886; SF *Chron*, Sept. 1, 1886.

The last four days of the gathering continued the pattern established at the opening session. White won election as permanent chairman, but the Stocktonites had to make frequent and extensive compromises with the rest of the party. The delegates rejected an antimonopolist attempt to permit White to select the platform committee, and in the committee itself the anti-monopoly forces failed to secure an endorsement of the Stockton convention. The platform instead stressed the Democratic party's determination to end Chinese immigration, an emphasis that responded to a recent surge of hostility against the Chinese in California and other areas of the West.[51] Besides its appeal to Coast voters, the issue had obvious attractions to a party determined to end factionalism. All Democrats could unite in opposition to the Chinese.

Michael F. Tarpey, an anti-monopolist from Alameda County and a close friend of English, was named the Democratic candidate for lieutenant-governor, but the nomination stemmed more from Tarpey's Irish birth than from his anti-railroad record. With Stoneman having meanwhile removed himself from consideration, the gubernatorial nomination went to Washington Bartlett, the conservative, economy-minded mayor of San Francisco, who owed his political success to the Buckley organization. To ensure that the anti-monopolists recognized the significance of Bartlett's nomination, the *Alta California* hailed it as "an appeal and a concession to the conservative, property-holding, law-abiding elements of the State."[52] In its final

[51] Earlier in the year a convention in Sacramento had organized the California Anti-Chinese Nonpartisan Association and called for a statewide boycott of those employing Chinese or purchasing the products of Chinese labor. Similar meetings occurred in other California communities, and there were anti-Chinese riots in Wyoming and Washington territories. SF *Chron*, March 11–13, 1886; LA *Times*, Feb. 5–7, 28, 1886; Alexander Saxton, *The Indispensable Enemy: Labor and the Anti-Chinese Movement in California* (Berkeley, 1971), pp. 206–13; Lynwood Carranco, "Chinese Expulsion from Humboldt County," *PHR*, 30 (1961): 329–40.

[52] *Alta Cal*, Sept. 4, 1886; Winfield J. Davis, *History of Political Conventions in California, 1849–1892* (Sacramento, 1893), pp. 519–23. In July, at the behest of over two-thirds of the members of the legislature, Governor Stoneman had called an extra session to resolve the problem of water rights and irrigation in the state. The session passed few measures of importance except appropriations for its own expenses; it also promptly deposed George Hearst from the Senate and elected a Republican in his place. Somewhat unfairly, Stoneman received most of the blame for the session's outcome, and in a letter to the Democratic convention he withdrew his name from consideration. Nash, *State Government*, pp. 188–94; James J. Ayers to White, Aug. 4, 1886, White to Ayers, Aug. 6, 1886, White to Henley, Aug. 6, 1886, WP.

act the convention elected a new state central committee that included Jesse D. Carr and other conspicuous opponents of the Stockton platform. Although English was again made committee chairman, John Daggett—the primary target of anti-monopolist bitterness since 1884 —won unanimous election as first vice-president.[53]

IV

Collis P. Huntington was delighted with the new developments. Arriving in San Francisco shortly after the convention adjourned, he told reporters that changed attitudes on the railroad question would spur Southern Pacific expansion across the state. "Now the days of demagoguery have gone beyond recall," he quietly declared.[54] At the same time Huntington also reviewed plans to ensure the elevation of Aaron A. Sargent to the United States Senate. Still resentful of the "somewhat equivocal position" in which he had been placed by Stanford's maneuvers the previous year, he had consulted his associates in May 1886 and reported that "we were all agreed as to the man who ought to be our next Senator." Portions of the Republican legislative ticket were arranged in accordance with this agreement.[55] Writing to a company attorney after the election, Huntington relayed Sargent's acknowledgment that "you and others at the corner of 4th & Townsend streets did all you could for him."[56]

The Democrats ignored the evidence of the railroad's involvement in the election. Illustrating the transformation that had occurred within their party, they gave the railroad question minimal consideration during the 1886 campaign. Democratic newspapers focused

[53] SF *Exmr*, Sept. 4–5, 1886.

[54] LA *Times*, Sept. 19, 1886.

[55] Huntington to Stephen T. Gage, May 8, 1886, Hopkins Collection. On the legislative ticket, see Sargent to Thomas R. Bard, May 12, 1886, Sargent to Bard, May 28, 1886, Bard Papers; SF *Chron*, Sept. 26, Oct. 15–18, 1886.

[56] Fourth and Townsend streets was the location of Southern Pacific headquarters in San Francisco. Huntington made it clear that personally he did not feel his California representatives had worked hard enough for Sargent, "for if you had the results would, in my opinion, have been different. I am quite sure that if you and the others at 4th and Townsend streets had worked earnestly for the Republican ticket from the very commencement of the campaign there would have been very little trouble in securing a handsome majority for the ticket." Huntington to Stephen T. Gage, Nov. 26, 1886, Hopkins Collection. A draft of Gage's reply, denying the charge, is also in the Hopkins Collection.

instead on personal attacks on opposition candidates. They described John F. Swift, the Republican gubernatorial nominee, as "a public pillager" and assailed the "vile hypocrisy and downright dishonesty" of Robert W. Waterman, the candidate for lieutenant-governor. In connection with the Chinese issue, the press charged that Swift employed a Chinese servant, bought vegetables from Chinese peddlers, and patronized a Chinese laundry—conclusive proof, it was said, of Republican duplicity. Party harmony, it appeared, sometimes carried a high price. Since unity could be preserved only by avoiding divisive issues, the Democratic campaign became notable primarily for the absence of any meaningful approach to the problems confronting the state. As one Democrat wrote President Cleveland, "The struggle is confused, bitter, and personal."[57]

The sudden growth of a new organization, the American party, added to the confusion. One of numerous splinter groups that emerged in the political flux of 1886, the American party tapped rising anti-foreign and anti-Catholic sentiment directed particularly against California's sizable Irish population. Guided by the San Francisco *Argonaut*, which inveighed against papal conspiracies and "the vicious foreign element," the party demanded immigration restrictions and other measures to curtail foreign penetration. It offered an outlet for hostility against Buckley and other Irish politicians in San Francisco, and exploited grievances voiced by an earlier observer: "The knowledge that ... Irish, Catholic, corrupt bosses sit in the back room of a grog shop, and arrogate to themselves the power, and actually exercise it too, and dictate to free American-born citizens, whom they shall or shall not vote for, it is more than I can stand."[58] Rather than name its own ticket, the new organization in September 1886 endorsed Swift and Waterman for the state's two highest offices, but the blunt and courageous Swift immediately repudiated the endorsement. The party then selected a separate gubernatorial candidate, further encouraging the Democrats, who had already concluded

[57] SF *Exmr*, Sept. 23, Oct. 11–14, 22–26, 1886; *Alta Cal*, Oct. 12, 1886; Charles D. Cleveland to Cleveland, Oct. 23, 1886, CP.

[58] T. H. Merry to Bard, Oct. 21, 1884, Bard Papers; San Francisco *Argonaut*, April 24, May 1, 1886. The rise of the party is examined in John Higham's "The American Party, 1886–1891," *PHR*, 19 (1950): 37–41.

that Swift "has got his foot in it" no matter what policy he adopted.[59]

The election results bore out the Democrats' expectations. The American party drew fewer than 8,000 votes, most of them in San Francisco and Alameda counties, but it provided the margin of difference in a close election. Aided by defections from Swift, the Democratic candidate, Washington Bartlett, won the governorship by only 654 votes out of more than 195,000 cast. By discreetly remaining silent on the American party issue, Waterman managed to avoid his running mate's problems; he won the race for lieutenant governor by a narrow margin. His triumph would assume greater importance a year later, when Bartlett's death elevated Waterman to the governorship. Quarrels among Republicans over Sargent's senatorial ambitions and a poor turnout in Southern California assisted other Democratic candidates. Although they were held to only two of California's six congressmen, the Democrats elected most state officials, swept the San Francisco municipal contests, and captured a majority in the next legislature. On January 19, 1887, as the final outcome of the election, a joint session of the legislature elected George Hearst to a full term in the Senate.[60]

Hearst's triumph marked the close of an eventful year for the California Democrats. A major shift in the Democrats' outlook, reflecting important developments in both the party and the state, had occurred in the course of 1886. Anti-railroad Democrats had suffered a series of setbacks, party members had chosen to place less emphasis on the railroad and Stockton issues, and a compromise policy had been adopted. The Stockton "read-outs" had been restored to prominent positions in the party, as Democrats sought to end the public display of their personal and ideological dissension. The dissension itself remained, of course, for few Democrats lost the views that had originally caused the split. The familiar struggles between conserva-

[59] English to White, Sept. 20, 1886, WP; LA *Times*, Sept. 19, Oct. 13, 1886; James H. Wilkins, ed., "The Reminiscences of Christopher A. Buckley," SF *Bul*, Jan. 10–11, 1919.
[60] Davis, *Political Conventions*, pp. 532–33; Higham, "American Party," p. 41; Edith Dobie, *The Political Career of Stephen Mallory White: A Study of Party Activities Under the Convention System* (Stanford, Cal., 1927), p. 251; SF *Exmr*, Nov. 24, 1886; W. H. Chickering to Benjamin Harrison, July 6, 1888, HP; LA *Times*, Nov. 10, 1886, Feb. 2, 1888.

tives and anti-monopolists, though under different names, continued to mold Democratic politics in California. Conservatives would still denounce activist Democrats as "frothing demagogues," and in December 1887, more than a year after the party reconciliation, English could predict "another epidemic of the Stockton Convention." "Are you ready," he asked White, "to man the two-hundred-pound gun and fight as in the days of yore?"[61]

But though factionalism would persist, the conservative and anti-monopoly coalitions would never again function quite as they had between 1882 and 1886. Among the conservative Democrats, dispersal came with remarkable rapidity. Few conservatives shared John P. Irish's devotion to the political process and his eagerness to press on with the battle for "decent people" against the "professional and amateur criminals" who controlled the party.[62] Most leaders of the conservative wing felt an intense distaste for politics and its practitioners, and had been lured into a sustained commitment only by their deeper aversion to anti-monopoly doctrines. The emergency ended, conservatives like Samuel M. Wilson hurriedly retreated to private affairs and limited their subsequent public activity to occasional outbursts about the scarcity of able men in politics. Justice Stephen J. Field headed the withdrawal. Disappointed with his past political failures, Field gradually made his peace with former enemies and focused his attention on the Supreme Court. In 1895 he sent a complimentary copy of his printed reminiscences to White, who had presided over his censure at Stockton.[63]

The anti-monopoly coalition underwent change of a different sort. Caught up in a major realignment of political forces within the party, it succumbed to individual ambition, the weakening of anti-railroad sentiment among Californians, and the Democrats' weariness with internal quarrels. Hearst had started its disintegration at the end of 1885 by shifting to a policy of compromise, and his prominent ally,

[61] *Alta Cal*, April 22, 1887; English to White, Dec. 16, 1887, WP.

[62] Irish to Parker, July 26, 1888, "Letters Written by John P. Irish to George F. Parker," *Iowa Journal of History and Politics*, 31 (1933): 427.

[63] White to Field, Nov. 9, 1895, WP. For Field's increasing preoccupation with the Supreme Court, see the illuminating folder of Field letters in the Dickinson Papers; see also Carl A. Pierce, "A Vacancy on the Supreme Court: The Politics of Judicial Appointment, 1893–94," *Tennessee Law Review*, 39 (1972): 558–71.

Buckley, had also lent support to the party's new direction. Both men profited from their defection. Hearst won his coveted Senate seat, and Buckley emerged as the most powerful figure in the Democratic party. The triumph of his municipal ticket in the 1886 campaign consolidated his hold on San Francisco politics, the victories of Hearst and Bartlett gave him close ties to the new senator and governor, and the city's Democratic delegation to the legislature increased his leverage at Sacramento. "I was then in the zenith of my power," Buckley later remarked of the election's aftermath.[64]

English could not resist the blandishments of the influential Hearst and Buckley for long. A tireless politician whose angular features, bright gray eyes, and pointed reddish-brown beard had appeared in the rear rows of anti-monopoly meetings since the early 1880's, English had turned his organizational talents to the cause, becoming an important anti-monopolist leader. His incessant letters and visits to party workers across the state had arranged details and ensured success for gatherings where more skilled orators had received the credit. At first he vigorously opposed the compromise movement led by Hearst, but his opposition soon gave way to his keen instinct for political survival. Promotions, he knew, came rarely to Alameda politicians who ignored the wishes of dominant Democrats in nearby San Francisco. In January 1887, signaling his conversion, English managed Hearst's senatorial campaign and exerted the authority of the state central committee in Hearst's behalf. Thereafter he cooperated closely with the Hearst organization, though with steadily diminishing enthusiasm as the elder Hearst's departure for Washington brought to power the erratic and dictatorial William Randolph Hearst, who against his father's advice assumed responsibility for the San Francisco *Examiner* and for the course of California politics as well.[65]

Less pragmatic than English, Barclay Henley resented the party's comparative neglect of the railroad issue. Through the summer of 1886, rejecting the signs of impending compromise with the conserva-

[64] Wilkins, ed., "Reminiscences of Buckley," SF *Bul*, Jan. 13, 1919.
[65] English to White, Nov. 24, 1886, English to White, Nov. 27, 1886, White to J. D. Lynch, Jan. 14, 1887, WP; SF *Chron*, Jan. 5–8, 1887.

tives, he had predicted that the anti-monopoly Democrats would "make these fellows dance to our music" at the state convention.[66] The ensuing defeat embittered the Sonoma County congressman. Refusing renomination to Congress, he became one of the few anti-monopolists to withdraw from politics. Several years later, after moving to San Francisco, he would take a measure of revenge by joining a successful campaign to overthrow Buckley. But for the present, robbed of influence and unwilling to adjust to the new situation, Henley could only retire with a flourish. "Whenever our party takes the backward track on this monopoly question I am done with it," he declared in August 1886. "Whenever the Democracy bends the knee to corporate influence, and seeks to harmonize into the party a few corrupt scoundrels with the railroad collar around their neck, then they harmonize me out of it, and I don't care a d—n who knows it."[67]

Although he sympathized with Henley's feelings, White never considered retirement. He deeply regretted the virtual disappearance of the railroad issue, but offset regret with continued zest for politics, reluctance to fight battles already lost, and willingness to wait patiently for a change in public opinion. Elected to the state senate in 1886, he carefully constructed new personal alignments to replace the old. His opposition to Hearst's senatorial bid in early 1887 established his independence of the San Francisco organization, yet it was accomplished in a manner that permitted him to stay on friendly terms with English, Buckley, and other allies of Hearst.[68] White then worked to win the leadership of the "country" forces in the party, acquiring the reputation and gathering the support that eventually enabled him to eclipse all Democratic rivals. In the end, despite his momentary dismay, the events of the mid-1880's gave an enormous boost to White's political fortunes. The preeminent figure in Southern California politics, "Our Steve" shared his home region's swift rise to national prominence.

Heedful of the financial needs of a growing family, White also seized the opportunity to expand his Los Angeles law practice. When a particularly lucrative offer arrived in March 1887, he accepted it:

[66] Henley to White, June 5, 1886, WP.
[67] Henley to White, Aug. 13, 1886, WP.
[68] White to J. D. Bicknell, Jan. 1, 1887, White to I. W. Hellman, Jan. 2, 1887, White to D. H. Pinney, Jan. 12, 1887, White to Thomas Raines, Jan. 25, 1887, WP.

White and his law partner became the Southern Pacific's legal representatives in Southern California, thereby displaying the extent of White's own adjustment to the altered conditions in party and state. During his eighteen months in the position, he conscientiously defended the company's legal interests, a course of action that contrasted markedly with his previous attacks on "the miserable poodles who trot after RR favors." Since close scrutiny of his correspondence and career reveals the genuineness of his concern with the railroad problem, White's acceptance of the position likely stemmed from a pragmatic response to the abatement of anti-railroad sentiment. Convinced that politicians must reflect the public will, he did not lose interest in reform but awaited a revival of popular support for regulatory measures. When the revival came in the following decade, White again took the lead in the fight to curtail the Southern Pacific's power in California.[69]

At the close of 1886 White and the other anti-monopolists undoubtedly felt a sharp sense of disappointment as they looked back on the previous half-dozen years. They had promised much and accomplished relatively little. They had pledged to invigorate the railroad commission, solve the railroad tax problem, assert the public's interest in corporate property, and establish the supremacy of the state over the corporation. None of these pledges had been fulfilled. The anti-monopolists could cite small advances, to be sure. They could contend that their intervention had prevented an early, unsatisfactory resolution of the tax dispute. They could argue that their campaigns had educated Californians on the railroad question and that their ouster of recalcitrant Democrats at Stockton had been a novel attempt to tie politicians firmly to their platform. They could claim to have acquired techniques of coercion and persuasion that would prove valuable in later battles with the railroad. Certainly they had learned that in a framework dominated by court, commission, and committee, action was easier to block than to undertake. Many of their proposals had been simplistic, others misdirected. But all had been honest attempts to apply untested remedies to important problems. It was, perhaps, some consolation for years of effort.

[69] White to Creed Haymond, March 18, 1887, White to Haymond, Sept. 27, 1888, WP; Dobie, *White*, p. 101.

CHAPTER FIVE

Cleveland, the Tariff, and the Chinese
1887-1888

GROVER CLEVELAND had profited from the preoccupation with local problems among Californians. As late as 1887, two years after his inauguration, they still had only a vague sense of the president's views, plans, and accomplishments. They were aware that he shared the general Democratic commitment to states' rights, administrative economy, and limited government. They had followed his brief battle with the Republican-dominated Senate over presidential authority to remove unwanted subordinates, had seen evidence on the Coast of his sporadic attempts to enforce civil service reform, and had watched his close supervision over pensions for Civil War veterans. Such limited achievements reflected the president's own modest goals: frugal government, a sound financial system, an "unstrained" interpretation of the Constitution, and appointments based on merit instead of "party subserviency." "The people," Cleveland had declared in his inaugural address, "demand reform in the administration of the Government and the application of business principles to public affairs."[1]

During his first years in office Cleveland's stubborn and courageous pursuit of these aims won widespread public acclaim and earned a new respectability for the Democratic party. No longer would California Democrats have to surmount the fear of "Rebel rule"[2] that had worked to the advantage of their Republican opponents as recently

---

[1] James D. Richardson, ed., *A Compilation of the Messages and Papers of the Presidents, 1789–1897*, 10 vols. (Washington, D.C., 1897), 7: 4884–88. Detailed coverage of Cleveland's first years in the presidency is given in Allan Nevins, *Grover Cleveland: A Study in Courage* (New York, 1932), pp. 212–79, 322–66.

[2] Cornelius Cole to Olive Cole, July 12, 1884, Cole Papers.

as 1884. Though scornful of publicity, Cleveland skillfully used scattered actions to acquire a reputation for political independence and uncompromising honesty. His cautious outlook and conservative approach suited the mood of many Californians in the 1880's. They came to respect his dignified demeanor, to admire his zealous pursuit of administrative efficiency, and to praise his aversion to government interference in private concerns. Some even applauded the president's mediocrity. "This country does not want a brilliant administration," Francis G. Newlands boldly asserted in 1887. "The brilliant events of history have generally been at the expense of the lives, happiness or prosperity of thousands."[3]

But disagreement over specific issues somewhat tempered the general admiration for Cleveland. The president's land reform policies aroused opposition, and his frequent pension vetoes "disgruntled the G.A.R. almost past endurance."[4] Until 1887 contention stemmed primarily from Cleveland's repeated demands for the immediate suspension of silver coinage. Owing to a combination of self-interest and genuine conviction, the great majority of Californians favored the free coinage of silver. An identity of interests with adjacent silver-mining regions, where California merchants conducted a thriving business, contributed to pro-silver sentiment, as did the belief that farmers and other groups would benefit from an expanded currency. California's own mines annually produced over a million dollars' worth of silver in the late 1880's. "*Go for free coinage,*" Robert W. Waterman, owner of the Calico and Barstow mines and later governor of the state, urged a Republican congressman. "Just think how many mines of low-grade ore could be worked at *Calico* with free coinage." Echoing this feeling, both state parties were recorded in favor of silver.[5]

[3] San Francisco *Call*, April 21, 1887, clipping in Newlands Papers.

[4] John R. Kittrell to White, June 28, 1887, WP; SF *Exmr*, March 24, 1887; F. J. Clarke to Cleveland, June 18, 1887, CP. Cleveland's land and pension policies are treated in Nevins, *Cleveland*, pp. 223–28, 322–32.

[5] Waterman to Henry Harrison Markham, Jan. 11, 1886, Markham Papers; *Compendium of the Eleventh Census: 1890*, pt. 2 (Washington, D.C., 1894), p. 474; LA *Times*, June 3, 1888; Charles D. Cleveland to Cleveland, Oct. 16, 1885, William F. White to Cleveland, Feb. 11, 1885, John J. Burke to Cleveland, Nov. 10, 1885, CP. For a rare statement against silver, see John T. Doyle to Abram S. Hewitt, May 25, 1885, Doyle Papers.

Cleveland's anti-silver stand irked California Democrats and to some degree weakened his popular support. At the outset of his presidency all six California congressmen, including Barclay Henley, had joined congressmen from other states in rejecting his financial policy. Republicans had found the contrast between Cleveland's pronouncements and the California Democrats' position an easy target in the 1886 election.[6] In response, the Democrats tried either to ignore or more often to distort the president's views. "I think that Cleveland is with us," George Hearst announced, "but being a New Yorker he dare not say so." In the relatively calm atmosphere of the 1880's the silver dissension was muted, but it embarrassed local Democrats and foreshadowed the animosities of the following decade. "A majority of the Representatives from the West and South are actually mad as wild Texas steers on this silver dollar business," Cleveland's secretary of the treasury commented early in the year 1886. "As we pass each other in the streets they seem to sneer, and hiss through their teeth the words 'gold bug,' and look as if they would like to spit upon one."[7]

Offset by respect for Cleveland's courage and candor, even the silver dispute failed in the end to damage seriously his stature on the Pacific Coast. As public esteem for the president grew, political observers revised their unfavorable assessment of the Democrats' prospects in the approaching presidential election. "California has been opposed to Cleveland on every one of his great proposals (civil service reform, silver question, tariff reform), and yet the Republicans must nominate a very strong man to get this State this year," noted the journalist Franklin K. Lane in February 1888. "The people admire old Grover's strength so much, he is a positive man and an honest man, and when the people see these two exceptional virtues mixed happily in a candidate they grow to love and admire him out of the very idealism of their natures."[8]

[6] A. J. Warner et al. to Cleveland, Feb. 11, 1885, CP; *Congressional Record*, 48th Cong., 2d sess. (Feb. 26, 1885), pp. 2210–11; Winfield J. Davis, *History of Political Conventions in California, 1849–1892* (Sacramento, 1893), pp. 515–19; *Alta Cal*, Oct. 8, 1886.

[7] Hearst interview in *Alta Cal*, May 8, 1887; Daniel Manning to Manton Marble, Feb. 15, 1886, Marble Papers.

[8] Lane to John H. Wigmore, Feb. 27, 1888, in Anne Wintermute Lane and Louise Herrick Wall, eds., *The Letters of Franklin K. Lane: Personal and Political* (Boston,

II

One significant element refused to join in the general praise. In the spring of 1887 William D. English accidentally encountered David R. Risley, a conservative Democrat who had recently been appointed to a federal office in Southern California. Risley informed English that "he was prepared to bury the hatchet and all take common ground for the good of the party in the next campaign. Risley's only reservation was that we should all support Cleveland." English considered this proposal "rather a cheeky one, coming as it did from such a source," and his reply was not cordial: "I told him I was not prepared to make any such arrangement at this time, in fact it was too early to talk of individuals." "Are we Cala. Democrats," asked English, "quietly to throw up our arms & bend the knee to the man that has scourged us? While I believe Cleveland will be nominated I don't feel like supporting him. After his nomination as good party men we will all have to stand in."[9]

By 1887, as English's remarks indicated, Coast Democrats were in open rebellion against the president. His patronage course had early alienated both factions of the party, and subsequent events had done little to recapture their sympathy. A survey in late 1886 showed many influential Democrats, including such diverse figures as English, John Daggett, and Christopher A. Buckley, unwilling to endorse Cleveland for another term.[10] There were reports of a serious break between the president and Senator Hearst when the latter found his recommendations ignored. Stephen M. White believed Cleveland "has antagonized so many people that I think it very improbable that he would receive the popular vote." Assured of a place in the California delegation to the party's national convention, White promised that "if I see a ghost of a show to beat him for the nomination I will do it."[11] On balance, with the exception of the federal office

---

1922), pp. 18–19; James H. Wilkins, ed. "The Reminiscences of Christopher A. Buckley," SF *Bul*, Jan. 18, 1919.

[9] English to White, May 25, 1887, WP.

[10] St. Louis *Globe-Democrat*, Sept. 2, 1886, clipping enclosed in Thomas Beck to Cleveland, Sept. 14, 1886, CP.

[11] White to John McCafferty, Dec. 17, 1886, White to English, May 29, 1887, WP; Hearst to Daniel S. Lamont, Dec. 28, 1886, Jesse D. Carr to Cleveland, April 10, 1887, J. H. Woodard to Cleveland, April 12, 1887, CP; SF *Exmr*, April 8, 1887.

holders and certain conservative Democrats, the party leadership uniformly opposed the Cleveland administration.

Like dissatisfied Democrats in other states, however, the Californians could take no practical action to supplant the president with a candidate more to their liking. To deprive Cleveland of his party's nomination would be to court total defeat in 1888. "He is the first Democratic President in a quarter of a century," the San Francisco *Examiner* candidly noted, "and to set him aside would be to repudiate his policy, which the party cannot afford to do, even if it wished to, which it does not." Should Cleveland desire renomination, agreed Buckley, "nothing can stop him." By the summer of 1887, when it had become clear that the president would not withdraw voluntarily from the race, English and other leaders had concluded that "Cleveland seems to be the dose we have got to swallow. It's bitter, but guess we can take it."[12]

Then, on December 6, 1887, the president took the first decisive step of his administration. Alarmed by the growing surplus in the Treasury and perhaps conscious of the need to rally his party for the approaching election, he devoted his entire annual message to an attack on the present tariff laws, "the vicious, inequitable, and illogical source of unnecessary taxation." In a single move Cleveland committed himself and his party to reform the protective system. Congratulations poured in from many California Democrats. As the *Examiner* recalled some months later: "By one splendid stroke of courage and statesmanship he lifted his party out of its bog of timid irresolution, drove the tariff-fattened monopolies from the insolent aggressive to the alarmed defensive, awakened the people to the infamies they have been patiently enduring for a quarter of a century and marked the lines of the coming campaign beyond the power of shifty politicians to change."[13]

[12] SF *Exmr*, March 18, July 28, 1887; English to White, Aug. 5, 1887, WP.
[13] Richardson, ed., *Messages and Papers of the Presidents*, 7: 5165–76; SF *Exmr*, June 7, 1888. See also SF *Exmr*, Dec. 7, 1887; Ventura *Democrat*, Dec. 8, 15, 1887; *Alta Cal*, Dec. 7, 1887; Thomas Beck to Cleveland, Dec. 11, 1887, Edward Curtis to Cleveland, undated (1887), Max Popper to Cleveland, Jan. 12, 1888, CP. Never considered a brilliant senator, George Hearst reportedly remarked: "Well, I haven't read the message yet, and I did not listen attentively to it; but it seems to be popular with our side, and I guess it will be all right." SF *Chron*, Jan. 11, 1888.

Tariff revision, Democratic leaders knew, had major drawbacks as a political issue. Protectionist sentiment within their own party was strong. Mindful of the tariff's broad appeal, Coast Democrats in the past had often wavered on the question. Their most recent platform, formulated in 1886, had called specifically for higher duties on wool and protective safeguards for the raisin industry. In the same year Congressman Henley, whose district figured prominently in wool production, had voted against the consideration of a tariff reduction.[14] A few party members repudiated Cleveland's reform message. Remarking that "I have always been a high protective tariff man even before I had any property or interests to protect," J. DeBarth Shorb, a winegrower, labeled tariff revision "erroneous in principle and injudicious in a political sense."[15] Others exhibited continued reluctance to embrace reform that touched home industries. When the House reduced the duty on raisins in mid-1888, the *Examiner* complained that "revision should begin at the top, and not at the bottom.... Since the country adheres to the protective system, the raisin industry is entitled to as much protection as any other."[16]

Local Democrats also recognized that their opponents would ignore the president's promise of "safe, careful, and deliberate reform" and his plea against "bandying epithets" like free trade. They would be branded as free traders and accused of unsettling the state's economy, and they could suffer losses among Irish voters, who linked tariff reform with English interests. Above all, they would have to overcome the long-established Republican argument that tied the tariff to prosperity and patriotism in a national framework of protection for manufacturers, farmers, and laborers. In the aftermath of Cleveland's message, Coast Republicans echoed James G. Blaine's clever assault on the Democrats' intentions. The protective system, declared John F. Swift, "is in deadly peril and must fight for its life."[17] Like Blaine, Swift and his allies suggested that the Treasury surplus serve

[14] Davis, *Political Conventions*, pp. 519–20; SF *Exmr*, June 18, 1886.
[15] Shorb to Francis G. Newlands, Nov. 11, 1888, Shorb Papers; LA *Times*, Oct. 25, 1888. See also Shorb to Newlands, Oct. 30, 1888, Shorb Papers; SF *Chron*, Jan. 11, 1888.
[16] SF *Exmr*, July 13, 1888.
[17] LA *Times*, Feb. 2, 1888; H. Wayne Morgan, *From Hayes to McKinley: National Party Politics, 1877–1896* (Syracuse, N.Y., 1969), p. 278.

as a fund for domestic improvements rather than as an excuse to undermine economic development. Most California interests, they contended, qualified as infant industries, especially deserving of protection. Their appeals found a prompt response among wine, wool, and fruit growers that dismayed some Democrats. "I thought we were going to have a walk over," wrote one worried Democrat of the party's prospects in the 1888 election, "but the tariff issue seems to me to leave the outcome rather in the dark."[18]

Shrewder observers, however, realized that Cleveland's message was an astute political move. On the national level a determined campaign to lower the tariff offered the party a much-needed opportunity to expand its electoral base. Adroitly used, the issue could gather new recruits from Eastern importers and merchants, Southern and Western farmers, and New England manufacturers who desired cheaper raw materials. Throughout the country Democrats could argue persuasively that high duties meant high prices for consumers and that the tariff accumulated surplus funds in the Treasury that dampened national economic growth if they remained unspent. Conscious of the narrowness of Cleveland's 1884 victory over Blaine, party strategists saw the issue as a way to penetrate Republican areas of the Midwest and unite New England, New York, and the Democratic South in a powerful and permanent anti-tariff coalition. Exploited with skill and vigor, the tariff reform issue would put the Republicans on the defensive and lay the foundation for Democratic hegemony.[19]

In California the president's message offered additional benefits. For a time at least, it diverted attention from patronage grievances and fostered a spirited sense of commitment and cohesion within the Democratic party. It inspired some party members, rejuvenated others who had despaired of tariff reform, and made available to all Dem-

[18] Charles Dwight Willard to Samuel Willard, Aug. 12, 1888, Willard Papers; SF *Chron*, Nov. 11, Dec. 14, 1887, Jan. 27, 1888; Vincent P. Carosso, *The California Wine Industry: A Study of the Formative Years* (Berkeley, 1951), pp. 108, 147; J. F. Linthicum to Thomas L. Thompson, Dec. 26, 1887, CP.

[19] Festus P. Summers, *William L. Wilson and Tariff Reform* (New Brunswick, N.J., 1953), pp. 49–68; William L. Wilson, *The National Democratic Party: Its History, Principles, Achievements, and Aims* (Baltimore, 1888), pp. 225, 235–36; Geoffrey Blodgett, *The Gentle Reformers: Massachusetts Democrats in the Cleveland Era* (Cambridge, Mass., 1966), pp. 69–80; Joseph Frazier Wall, *Henry Watterson: Reconstructed Rebel* (New York, 1956), p. 198.

ocrats the popular war cry of ending subsidies to special interests. Tariff reform had a positive and constructive sound, though in reality it fit neatly into the traditional Democratic demand for the separation of government and business. It also merged in obvious ways with the general anti-monopoly doctrines so many California Democrats had fought for during the first half of the decade. Politicians noted the issue's strong appeal to young voters and its marked effect on the president's standing in the California party. "The Cleveland boom here is simply colossal," a Democratic editor reported to the administration in the spring of 1888.[20] White and others shifted from enmity to support. They guided through local party conventions resolutions containing fulsome praise for the president and his reform demands. At the Democratic state convention, held in Los Angeles in mid-May, Cleveland was cheered repeatedly. The delegates adopted a platform that lauded the president, "heartily" endorsed his message, and called for "just and comprehensive" tariff reform.[21]

Ironically, however, Cleveland's own reform ardor had meanwhile cooled. Growing fearful of the political hazards of his tariff position, he had decided to press for an evasive plank in the party's 1888 platform. Carried to the national convention at St. Louis by Sen. Arthur Pue Gorman of Maryland, the president's proposed plank ignored his recent message and did not even include the word tariff.[22] But Gorman and his cohorts were unable to stem the new-found enthusiasm of the tariff reformers, led by Henry Watterson of Kentucky. To Cleveland's equivocal draft the convention added a direct commendation of his message and a strong endorsement of tariff reduction. Unaware of the president's desire to retreat on the issue, the San Francisco *Examiner* exulted that the platform "escaped the fatal blunder of timidity." Cleveland and his advisers sulked. "The change in the platform was so great that you could hardly recognize it," Gorman complained after adjournment. "The Convention was com-

[20] Joseph D. Lynch to Daniel S. Lamont, April 17, 1888, CP.

[21] SF *Exmr*, May 18, 1888; LA *Times*, May 6, 1888; A. C. McGlachlan to Lamont, Aug. 27, 1888, CP.

[22] George Tilden McJimsey, "The Life of Manton Marble" (Ph.D. diss., Univ. of Wisconsin, 1968), pp. 417–18. Reminiscing in 1896, Cleveland told a friend that an endorsement in the platform of his earlier tariff message was "a change wh[ich] had occurred to him but which thro' modesty he had not put in." Entry for Dec. 28, 1896, Charles S. Hamlin Diary, Manuscript Division, Library of Congress.

posed of gentlemen who were carried away by sentiment and it is simply wonderful that we were able to prevent more radical measures being adopted."[23]

Other events at St. Louis boosted the spirits of California Democrats. For the first time their delegates played a significant role in a Democratic national convention. The delegation itself, headed by White, English, and Michael F. Tarpey, represented the consummation of a lengthy campaign to defeat the aspirations of the conservatives John P. Irish and Jesse D. Carr to represent California at the convention. As English put it, "The banner of the stalwarts still floats from the masthead."[24] Moreover, the *Examiner* correspondent in St. Louis may not have exaggerated when he reported that the Californians, with their flame-colored clothes, their supply of twenty-dollar gold pieces, and their one hundred cases of wine, "have attracted more attention here than any other set of delegates." They brought in addition three thousand red bandanas, the symbol of Allen G. Thurman of Ohio, and helped lead Thurman's victorious fight for the vice-presidential nomination. The Thurman boom, acknowledged a disgruntled Indiana delegate, "came from the Pacific coast, and I hope they will enjoy it as well after the November elections as they evidently enjoy it today."[25]

Most important, White was named temporary chairman of the convention. His selection, which stemmed in part from the defeat of San Francisco's ambition to become the convention site, owed much to the efforts of Senator Gorman, who had met English during a visit to California in the fall of 1886.[26] After enlisting Gorman in the enterprise, English wrote White: "It would be the crowning act for

23 SF *Exmr*, June 8, 1888; Gorman to Manton Marble, June 12, 1888, Marble Papers; New York *Times*, June 7, 1888; Henry Watterson, *"Marse Henry": An Autobiography*, 2 vols. (New York, 1919), 2: 134; *Official Proceedings of the National Democratic Convention* (St. Louis, 1888), pp. 94–101.
24 English to White, May 4, 1888, WP. The preconvention maneuvers can be followed in English to White, March 14, 1888, White to English, April 22, 1888, English to White, April 24, 1888, White to English, April 26, 1888, English to White, April 28, 1888, White to English, May 1, 1888, WP.
25 SF *Exmr*, June 6, 1888; *Official Proceedings of the National Democratic Convention* (1888), pp. 103–5, 128–30; James A. Barnes, *John G. Carlisle: Financial Statesman* (New York, 1931), p. 140; Thomas Wilkinson to Cleveland, June 11, 1888, CP.
26 SF *Exmr*, Oct. 5–7, 1886; Gorman to Lamont, Dec. 10, 1886, CP; Thomas J. Clunie to White, March 23, 1888, WP.

the Stockton Conventionites to have their chairman honored with this position. Old Field's bowels would drop out."[27] White's performance before the convention was worthy of the honor. A figure of medium height, stoutly built, with a full brown beard and a voice that carried easily throughout the convention hall, he was called "the best presiding officer that has held a gavel in such a gathering within the period of this generation." White's designation as temporary chairman furthered his own career in California and laid the groundwork for his later prominence in the national party. Combined with the subsequent selection of Morris M. Estee to chair the Republican national convention, it also signaled the emergence of California as a growing power in national politics.[28]

III

Grover Cleveland both inspired and bewildered his Democratic followers. To his ardent supporters he was already a symbol, the embodiment of virtue and courage in politics. They drew fresh hope from his example, and agreed with John P. Irish, who told the president, "You have kindled the accumulated political convictions of my whole life with inspiration." Skepticism and a close scrutiny of Cleveland's record alerted other Democrats to the flexible personality that lay behind the facade of fixed beliefs and unswerving rectitude. "You know when I make up my mind I am considered a stayer," the president once boasted to a group of visiting Californians, but they found that in this instance, and many others, he did not prove to be "a stayer" at all.[29] Cleveland's contempt for politics and politicians masked an immense pride in his own political ability and a tendency to indulge privately in the same maneuvers he condemned in public.

[27] English to White, April 24, 1888, WP. Field made no public comment, but John P. Irish protested White's selection: "I deem it my duty to let you know that Mr. White and those who back him here are opponents of Mr. Cleveland." Irish to William L. Scott, May 9, 1888, CP.
[28] Chicago *Globe*, n.d., quoted in Ventura *Democrat*, June 14, 1888. See also New York *Times*, June 6, 1888; White to William Cardwell, June 10, 1888, WP; LA *Times*, June 23, 1888.
[29] Irish to Cleveland, Nov. 18, 1888, CP; Cleveland's remark quoted in White to William W. Foote, Aug. 21, 1886, WP. The boast came in connection with a promised appointment to a judicial office in Southern California, an appointment that Cleveland in the end did not make. Henry Harrison Markham to Cleveland, Dec. 3, 1886, AP, Cal., Judicial File, Justice Dept., RG 60.

His instructions to representatives at St. Louis revealed his eagerness to retreat on the tariff issue; and earlier he had made clear his willingness to exploit foreign policy for domestic political ends.

Pressure on the president for action against the Chinese had mounted steadily since 1886. By then it was evident that past efforts to check Chinese immigration had failed. A futile attempt that year to organize an economic boycott to drive the Chinese from California had once again demonstrated the ineffectiveness of local measures. Federal legislation had also encountered obstacles. Court decisions had hampered the enforcement of the 1882 Chinese Restriction Act, and almost 40,000 Chinese had entered the country in the five years after its passage.[30]

The experience convinced Californians that effective exclusion, removed from judicial purview, depended on negotiating a new treaty with China. Democrats repeatedly informed President Cleveland of this sentiment and warned of dire consequences if nothing were done. "What can we say? What excuse can we offer?" asked a troubled party member. "In a few months the Presidential campaign will be upon us and agitation will be renewed. We shall be violently attacked and be without a weapon to defend ourselves with, and we shall be beaten, for the Chinese question overshadows all others on this Coast and will inevitably determine the result."[31]

There was no cause for alarm. Early in 1887 the administration had begun negotiations with the Chinese government on a treaty to exclude Chinese laborers from the United States. Cleveland outlined his political motivation in confidential communications with the secretary of state, Thomas F. Bayard. "The present condition [regarding Chinese immigration] should be remedied, or an attempt in that direction made at once and by us—that is *our party*," he instructed Bayard on December 18, 1887. "I am fearful almost to conviction that our people in Congress will so botch and blunder upon the tariff question that all benefits of the stand already taken will not be real-

---

[30] W. W. Morrow to Cleveland, March 3, 1888, CP; SF *Chron*, March 11–13, 1886. "It would excite no surprise in this country if at the end of every opinion in the Federal Courts on the Pacific coast, was recited a legend something like the following: 'The Chinese are the lords of the earth, and we kiss their feet.' " SF *Exmr*, April 2, 1886.

[31] J. F. Linthicum to Thomas L. Thompson, Dec. 26, 1887, CP.

ized. If my fears should appear to be well founded, a proper movement upon the Chinese question would furnish a compensation in the way of another string to our bow." Replied Bayard, "It certainly is best to restrict them by treaty, and I will again essay it and at once." Later he added, "As to satisfying the Californians, I fear the effort would be idle—but I am pressing a treaty of exclusion."[32]

By March 1888 the two governments had reached agreement on a pact that prohibited for twenty years the entrance of Chinese laborers into the United States. Californians called it, approvingly, a "radical" treaty. But then unexpected problems arose. The Republican Senate, delaying ratification until May, attached minor amendments that drew ironic charges of political expediency from President Cleveland.[33] Given time to reconsider the treaty, the Chinese government wavered; then it requested a loosening of the treaty's provisions. Secretary of State Bayard understood: "When one reflects upon the attitude among the family of nations that China would occupy by consenting in formal treaty to the exclusion of the great body of her people from equal entry into other lands with the population of other countries—it is scarcely to be wondered that they are inclined to withdraw from such a covenant."[34] Cleveland was frantic. The delay, already extending into September 1888, threatened to nullify the treaty's political effects in the election.

The obvious vulnerability of the Republican presidential candidate, Sen. Benjamin Harrison of Indiana, sharpened Cleveland's disappointment. Cautioning that Harrison's past votes against Chinese exclusion measures meant certain defeat in the fall contest, California Republicans had tried desperately to head off his nomination.[35] On the eve of the party's national convention Michael H. De Young, the

---

[32] Cleveland to Bayard, Dec. 18, 1887, Bayard to Cleveland, Dec. 19, 1887, Bayard Papers; Bayard memo, Jan. 5, 1888, CP.

[33] SF *Exmr*, May 8, 1888; John P. Irish to Bayard, April 25, 1888, Cleveland to Bayard, April 26, 1888, Bayard Papers; Thomas L. Thompson to Lamont, March 25, 1888, CP; Mary Roberts Coolidge, *Chinese Immigration* (New York, 1909), p. 194.

[34] Bayard to Cleveland, Sept. 5, 1888, CP. See also Charles Denby to Bayard, Sept. 6, 1888, Denby to Bayard, Sept. 21, 1888, Bayard Papers.

[35] Stephen B. Elkins to Louis T. Michener, March 3, 1888, John F. Swift to Michener, May 3, 1888, Louis T. Michener Papers, Manuscript Division, Library of Congress; Michael H. De Young to Whitelaw Reid, May 5, 1888, Whitelaw Reid Papers, Manuscript Division, Library of Congress; *Official Proceedings of the Republican National Convention* (Minneapolis, 1903), pp. 153–99.

publisher of the San Francisco *Chronicle* and a member of the Republican national committee, warned a conference of Republican leaders: "It is absurd to talk of agreeing on Harrison; he cannot carry the Pacific Coast, nor can he carry several other States, which would be Republican, on account of his record on the Chinese question." With Harrison as the party's candidate, De Young declared, "we might as well give up the fight in California."[36] Leaked to the press, De Young's remarks found an eager audience among Coast Democrats. "Certainly," exulted White, "Harrison is the weakest man so far as California is concerned who could have been nominated."[37]

From the moment of his nomination Harrison came under heavy attack on the Chinese issue. Letters from alarmed Republicans poured into Indianapolis urging the senator to take a strong position against Chinese immigration. Californians gave the harried candidate a quick education on the evils of the Chinese. "It is difficult," John F. Swift informed Harrison headquarters, "for you who have not lived among the Chinese to realize in your mind the whole extent and force of the degradation and outlandish nastiness that is conveyed to our minds... by the term '*Chinaman*.' On this Coast to compare a man to a Chinaman is more insulting than to compare him to a '*Nigger*' by far."[38] Aware of the consequences of refusal, Harrison responded in July with suitable expressions of hostility toward the Chinese. In his letter of acceptance, issued September 11, he promised to support such legislation "as may be necessary and proper to prevent evasions of the laws and to stop further Chinese immigration."[39]

Signs that Harrison might escape his predicament, combined with continued delay on the part of the Chinese government, persuaded President Cleveland of the need for additional measures. To the em-

[36] SF *Chron*, June 24, 1888; *The Campaign Text Book of the Democratic Party of the United States for the Presidential Election of 1888* (New York, 1888), p. 405.

[37] White to C. S. Bridges, July 19, 1888, WP; W. H. H. Russell to Cleveland, June 26, 1888, J. C. Maynard to Lamont, July 4, 1888, CP; SF *Exmr*, June 26, 1888.

[38] Swift to Michener, July 17, 1888, HP. See also George W. Steele to Harrison, July 5, 1888, W. H. Dimond to Harrison, July 6, 1888, Symmes H. Hunt to Harrison, June 26, 1888, Sen. William M. Stewart to Harrison, June 29, 1888, Sen. Preston B. Plumb to Harrison, July 3, 1888, Michael H. De Young to Harrison, Aug. 24, 1888, HP.

[39] *Official Proceedings of the Republican National Convention* (1888), p. 247; SF *Exmr*, July 14, 1888; Harry J. Sievers, *Benjamin Harrison*, vol. 2: *Hoosier Statesman, 1865–1888* (New York, 1959), pp. 221–24, 409.

barrassment of his secretary of state, who recognized the impropriety of action with the treaty still under consideration, the president resolved to add yet another string to the Democratic bow. William D. English provided the impetus. On September 2 he sent an urgent telegram to the administration, noting rumors that China had rejected the treaty and pleading for the immediate passage of restrictive legislation by Congress. "Our people are at fever heat," English insisted.[40]

The next day, at Cleveland's behest, William L. Scott of Pennsylvania introduced in the House of Representatives a bill to prohibit the return of any Chinese laborers who left the United States. With the presidential election only weeks away, the bill passed the House on the same day and cleared the Senate four days later. "Both Houses," remarked Sen. George F. Edmunds, "appear to have gone crazy on the Chinese question, taking, as the President appears to have done, a false rumor that the Chinese government had refused to ratify the last treaty as a basis for very hasty &, as I think, dishonorable legislation." Dishonorable or not, the measure was triumphantly signed by Cleveland on October 1, 1888. "Hang the banner on the outer wall," English wired White. "President Cleveland has signed the Scott Exclusion bill."[41]

To the elated California Democrats victory in the election now seemed in sight. "You can call of[f] your Orators," one party member told the president, "and use them where they will do the most good; your last Act on the Chinese bill has fixed California." Another reported that "the Republicans are dazed."[42] Denis Kearney, the former sandlot orator, offered Cleveland his services in the battle against the "Yellow Pests." The Democratic state central committee ordered

[40] English to Lamont, Sept. 2, 1888, CP. Lamont replied: "Your telegram received. Bill in accordance introduced by Scott and passed House this morning." Lamont to English, Sept. 3, 1888, Daniel S. Lamont Papers, Manuscript Division, Library of Congress. For Bayard's feelings, see Charles Callan Tansill, *The Foreign Policy of Thomas F. Bayard, 1885–1897* (New York, 1940), pp. 166–76.

[41] Edmunds to Harrison, Sept. 11, 1888, HP; English to White, Oct. 1, 1888, WP. See also John P. Irish to Lamont, Sept. 15, 1888, Marion Biggs to Cleveland, Sept. 30, 1888, CP; White to English, Sept. 18, 1888, WP; John A. S. Grenville and George Berkeley Young, *Politics, Strategy, and American Diplomacy: Studies in Foreign Policy, 1873–1917* (New Haven, Conn., 1966), pp. 59–63.

[42] Thomas Wilkinson to Cleveland, Oct. 1, 1888, CP; Joseph Naphtaly to William C. Whitney, Oct. 2, 1888, Whitney Papers.

a one-hundred-gun salute to the president. Cannons also boomed in Los Angeles, Fresno, and other communities, where thousands of people gathered to hear Democratic speakers compare the Scott law to the Declaration of Independence.[43] San Francisco had the largest celebration. "When I reached the City," recounted Michael F. Tarpey, "I saw people greeting one another with the enthusiasm of school boys, and congratulations alone were in order. This feeling grew hour by hour and by nightfall bonfires were blazing in the Streets and cannon roared out the thanks of the people.... This now places us in a position that we feel justified in saying our electoral vote will be given for the Democracy."[44]

IV

California Republicans kept Harrison informed on the impact of Cleveland's anti-Chinese policy. The passage of the Scott law brought gloomy predictions from some, including Michael H. De Young, who observed its effect on the Democrats' spirits and pessimistically warned that the law would give the party "considerable trouble." But most Republicans remained confident. They acknowledged the Democrats' sizable gains but believed that an aggressive campaign could blunt their opponents' attack. In particular they questioned the influence of the Chinese issue among the thousands of recent immigrants to California. Republican canvassers found new residents less responsive than older residents to anti-Chinese appeals.[45]

Moreover, surveys made of Southern California registration lists in the summer of 1888, showing Republican backgrounds for about 60 percent of the new voters, convinced party leaders that the tariff issue might outweigh the Chinese issue. Congressman Thomas B. Reed of Maine confirmed their assessment. "The signing by the President of the Exclusion Bill is being used for all it is worth and much more," he reported to Harrison in late October, while touring California for the Republican ticket. But the Scott law would not determine the

[43] Kearney to Cleveland, Aug. 27, 1888, Kearney to Cleveland, Oct. 1, 1888, CP; LA *Times*, Oct. 2, 1888; Ventura *Democrat*, Oct. 4, 1888.
[44] Tarpey to Lamont, Oct. 3, 1888, CP; SF *Exmr*, Oct. 2, 1888.
[45] De Young to Harrison, Oct. 2, 1888, Morris M. Estee to Harrison, Sept. 12, 1888, George W. Powell to Harrison, Oct. 4, 1888, HP.

outcome, Reed concluded. "The tariff question ... is taking a strong hold and the immigration into the State has been from the right quarter and these two things will pull us through."[46]

A Democratic tariff bill introduced in Congress in March 1888 gave the Republicans a convenient target. Sponsored by Congressman Roger Q. Mills of Texas, the bill proposed only a moderate reduction in average tariff duties, but it lowered the tariff on raisins and placed on the free list such California products as wool, lumber, salt, nuts, mercury, and various fruits. Still under the spell of Cleveland's tariff message, the *Examiner* labeled the measure "too timid" and urged that coal and iron be added to the free list. Republican newspapers assailed the bill's threat to local interests, complained that it favored the South, and printed interviews with protection-minded Democrats, who called it "a step too far in tariff reform."[47] "California has been selected for special destruction of her home industries," charged the San Francisco *Chronicle*. The Democrats "could not have done much worse for California if they had deliberately attempted to ruin her domestic industries and to turn her orchards and vineyards into pastures for sheep and cattle."[48]

Seizing the moment, Republicans rallied to defend the protective system. "Protection to American Industries & American Labour is the Battle Cry," declared an exuberant party worker. "And that is what will win the Fight." Some businessmen joined the campaign. "If we don't get a change of administration this time," announced an official of the Pioneer Woolen Mills Company, "we will have to close the concern up, and let it rot."[49] Wool growers, horticultural societies, raisin growers, viticulturists, and other groups expressed similar sentiments.[50] Among workingmen the Republicans identified their opponents with free trade, low wages, and the interests of English

[46] Reed to Harrison, Oct. 26, 1888, E. H. Lamme to Harrison, Aug. 16, 1888, HP.

[47] SF *Exmr*, March 5, 1888; LA *Times*, Oct. 25, 1888; Summers, *William L. Wilson and Tariff Reform*, pp. 79–82.

[48] SF *Chron*, March 2, 1888; LA *Times*, March 2–3, 1888.

[49] Paris Kilburn to Henry Z. Osborne, Aug. 18, 1888, Henry Zenas Osborne Papers, Division of Special Collections, Univ. of California, Los Angeles; LA *Times*, July 7, 1888.

[50] Carosso, *California Wine Industry*, pp. 145–48; George W. Powell to Harrison, Oct. 4, 1888, HP; SF *Exmr*, Jan. 12, 1888; SF *Chron*, March 21, May 8, Sept. 7, 1888.

manufacturers. Late in the campaign they pointed to the apparent corroboration of their charges that came when the British minister to the United States, Lord Sackville-West, replying to an inquiry from a California citrus grower, implied his government's approval of the Cleveland administration.[51] The incident had little effect on the election, but it illustrated the skilled efficiency with which Republicans exploited the tariff's economic and emotional appeal.

The Democrats countered with one of the most vigorous campaigns ever undertaken in the state. Their hopes of victory remained high through the summer months, and party leaders recognized that even if defeat should follow, an educational campaign could establish a base for future triumphs. As White observed, "The great proposition is to make the people understand the question." Dispatching campaigners throughout California, the state central committee went deep into debt. Friends alerted Harrison that "the Democracy is flooding this State with speakers; possibly at no time in the history of politics has there been so many Democratic speakers on the stand."[52] Democrats issued broad attacks on tariff-bred monopolies and appealed to specific interests, such as fruit canners and grain farmers, who would profit from the removal of duties on tin and jute, and the influential San Francisco importers, who would benefit from lower tariffs in general. Their efforts impressed the Democratic national headquarters. "We must sustain these people," wrote the head of the executive committee. "They are making a great canvass."[53]

As the campaign drew to a close, however, the Democrats' confidence dwindled. Less than a year had passed since Cleveland's tariff message, too short a period to overturn Republican tariff doctrines. Doubts grew about the party's expectations in Southern California,

[51] LA *Times*, Oct. 21, 24–25, 1888; T. C. Hinckley, "George Osgoodby and the Murchison Letter," *PHR*, 27 (1958): 359–70; "Story of the 'Murchison Letter' as Remembered by George Merritt" (transcript, Bancroft Library, Univ. of California, Berkeley); Harrison Gray Otis to Whitelaw Reid, Oct. 25, 1888, Otis to Reid, Nov. 16, 1888, Reid Papers; Otis to Harrison, Jan. 1, 1889, HP.

[52] White to Marion Biggs, Aug. 6, 1888, WP; Morris M. Estee to Harrison, Sept. 22, 1888, HP. See also English to White, Oct. 31, 1888, WP; Frank Tagliabue to Harrison, July 9, 1888, HP.

[53] Calvin S. Brice to W. W. Ransom, Oct. 10, 1888, CP; White to English, June 19, 1888, White to John H. Wise, July 27, 1888, White to O. K. Gardner, Aug. 11, 1888, WP; SF *Exmr*, June 13, Aug. 13, Oct. 19, 1888; *Alta Cal*, Oct. 24, 1888.

where Democrats had worked to minimize losses. "There is only one thing that can defeat us, and that is the new immigration...," a Democrat lamented to the administration a few days before the election. "No other State has to contend with so large an influx of men, who will vote in California this year for the first time."[54] National party leaders had proved a disappointment, with the president himself unwilling to campaign actively on the tariff issue. Apparently convinced that his educational task had ended in 1887, Cleveland stayed quietly at the White House or his summer home throughout the crucial contest. He also acquiesced in the selection of two known supporters of high tariffs to direct the Democratic campaign.[55]

Grievances mounted in California against Cleveland and "those sleepy congressmen and committee-men." Until as late as September the national committee ignored urgent requests for campaign documents and copies of congressional tariff speeches. The committee's unresponsiveness angered California campaign workers: "Every one is complaining about it," White told English.[56] With no assistance from party headquarters, local Democrats had run out of funds long before election day, forcing many to cancel planned activities. San Francisco party members managed to hold an election-eve parade in which marchers carried signs reminding voters of the president's zeal in promoting anti-Chinese measures:

> Mary had a little lamb,
> Its fleece was white as snow,
> It used to have a Chinese shearer,
> But Cleveland made him go.

Party newspapers printed the usual victory predictions, but in private Democratic leaders foresaw defeat. White closed his final letter be-

[54] Edward Curtis to Cleveland, Oct. 23, 1888, CP; English to White, Oct. 18, 1888, English to White, Oct. 31, 1888, WP.

[55] Horace Samuel Merrill, *Bourbon Leader: Grover Cleveland and the Democratic Party* (Boston, 1957), pp. 127–31; Summers, *William L. Wilson and Tariff Reform*, p. 89; H. C. Kinne to Cleveland, Aug. 11, 1888, CP.

[56] White to English, Aug. 6, 1888, White to English, Aug. 28, 1888, White to John E. Kenna, Aug. 6, 1888, WP. In a period when many voters read campaign literature, the inefficiency of the national committee in this regard was particularly damaging. As White argued, "It often happens that careful reading will convince a man where casual oral statements have no effect." White to Edward E. Biggs, Sept. 3, 1888, WP.

fore the election to English by expressing hopes "that the result may be better than any of us anticipate."[57]

A short time later White was mourning, "How infernally we were whipped.... We are used to being defeated but not so badly." Harrison led Cleveland in California by slightly more than seven thousand votes. Large pluralities in Alameda and Sacramento counties combined with huge margins in Southern California to give Harrison his triumph in the state. The totals bore out the Democrats' apprehension over the "tenderfoot vote" in the South. In Los Angeles County nearly 14,500 more ballots were cast in 1888 than in the presidential election four years before. There Republicans increased their plurality from 912 votes in 1884 to 3,695 in 1888. San Bernardino County registered smaller gains, but in San Diego the Republican plurality leaped from 320 to 1,472. Harrison emerged from the three Southern counties with an edge of almost six thousand votes, a margin that dwarfed Democratic victories elsewhere. As White wryly commented, "I believe we have elected a Constable in a remote, rural precinct which has as yet been undefiled by the tread of the tenderfoot."[58]

Returns from other sections were somewhat more encouraging. Cleveland improved substantially on his 1884 performance, especially in San Francisco, where the Chinese question and the aggressive local campaign turned his earlier defeat by 4,300 votes into a victory by almost 3,000. In California as a whole he carried 23 counties—six more than he had in the previous election—and reduced his margin of defeat by over 6,000 votes from 1884. To a large degree, however, the president's gains only reflected the return to normal patterns after the Blaine landslide. Cleveland's triumphs in tariff-conscious counties like Fresno and Tuolumne offered some encouragement, but failed to offset the numerous Democratic setbacks in which the tariff issue played a significant role. The Democrats lost four congressional seats.

---

[57] *Alta Cal*, Nov. 3, 1888; White to English, Nov. 2, 1888, WP.
[58] White to A. Caminetti, Nov. 16, 1888, White to A. F. Jones, Nov. 13, 1888, WP; W. Dean Burnham, *Presidential Ballots, 1836–1892* (Baltimore, 1955), pp. 292–305. Suggested White: "If you throw out these three lower counties, and had to contend only with the old elements, I mean if you had the same voters to deal with, that we had in the Blaine campaign, there would have been no difficulty in carrying California." White to English, Dec. 8, 1888, WP.

Voters in the first district ousted Congressman Thomas L. Thompson, whose support of the Mills bill had antagonized wool growers there. Another outspoken tariff reformer lost heavily in Southern California's sixth district, where protectionist sentiment swelled Republican majorities. Except for the San Francisco returns, the beaten Democrats found little to comfort them. "I have been sick and demoralized," wrote English, the state party chairman. "California going back on us nearly broke my heart."[59]

English and other Democratic leaders were fully aware of the election's unpleasant implications. In its aftermath they pledged success in 1892, arguing that another campaign could persuade voters of the need for tariff reform, but their assurances concealed a pervasive feeling of despair. Months of hard work had resulted only in failure. They had lost stature among national party figures, who had heeded their advice that the Chinese issue would determine the winner on the Pacific Coast. The defeat would require a reassessment of the issue's importance.[60] Most disheartening of all was the party's rout in Southern California in the first election to register the impact of the recent influx of immigrants. Immigration, and the attendant publicity, had helped thrust California into national prominence, but apparently it had also changed the basic complexion of state politics. Chagrined, White voiced the discouragement among Southern California Democrats: "The only chance that the Democrats of San Francisco and the Northern part of the State have now," he suggested, "is to set us off as an independent commonwealth, and then even if we are lonesome, we will have the consolation of knowing that our section does not interfere with the election of our friends in other localities."[61]

Scrutinizing the returns, other Democrats reached similar conclusions. Like White, they sensed that the 1888 outcome might signal the close of an era in California politics. If not quickly reversed, it

[59] English to White, Nov. 28, 1888, WP. See also SF *Exmr*, May 17, 1888; White to Thomas J. Clunie, Feb. 28, 1888, WP; John F. Ellison to Harrison, Nov. 21, 1888, HP; Davis, *Political Conventions*, pp. 552–53.

[60] SF *Exmr*, Nov. 8–9, 1888; *Alta Cal*, Nov. 9, 1888.

[61] White to J. F. Sullivan, Nov. 8, 1888, WP; Ventura *Democrat*, Dec. 13, 1888; Charles M. Leary to Harrison, Nov. 15, 1888, HP; Wilkins, ed., "Reminiscences of Buckley," SF *Bul*, Jan. 18, 1919.

threatened to end two decades of closely contested politics and mark
the emergence of the Republican party as the dominant party in the
state. It presaged a subordinate position for Democrats, unless they
could consolidate their strength in northern areas, particularly San
Francisco, and penetrate the new Republican bastion in Southern
California. The latter effort would make Democratic strategists especially receptive to the Populist movement of the 1890's, which promised to disrupt the Republican party in its southern stronghold. But
without such improvement, either through outside assistance or
through the direct conversion of Republican voters, the future held
little hope for the Democrats. Temporarily at least, the immigration
of the late 1880's had altered the political balance in the state.

"The truth is," confessed the *Alta California*, "that on the lines that
have divided the parties for the past few years there are several thousand more Republicans in the State than Democrats." Agreeing, the
San Francisco *Examiner* spoke with some exaggeration of "The New
California." Dismayed by the voters' failure to endorse the administration's anti-Chinese policy, the paper ventured a far-reaching explanation: "California has voted for Harrison. The meaning of this
event is that we are living in a new State. The old California has disappeared. The Eastern migration has annexed us to the Atlantic. The
considerations that swayed Californians a few years ago are powerless
now. The Chinese question is dead. The railroad question excites no
interest." "There are new people among us," the paper concluded,
"and instead of our assimilating them they are assimilating us. Very
well."[62]

[62] *Alta Cal*, Nov. 9, 1888; SF *Exmr*, Nov. 9, 1888.

CHAPTER SIX

The Harrison Years
1889-1892

ꝺꙫꙫꝺ

ON MARCH 4, 1889, as a light rain fell in Washington, Benjamin Harrison became the twenty-third president of the United States. In his inaugural address the new president briefly reviewed the nation's progress since 1789, defended Republican tariff doctrines, urged Congress to reduce the Treasury surplus, and promised to enforce civil service reform. The day's ceremonies concluded, Grover Cleveland retired to New York City to practice law. Cleveland had found little time for relaxation during his presidential term, and he wrote friends of his relief at being released from official burdens. His departure disappointed some California Democrats and delighted others. Busy organizing a tariff reform league, Franklin K. Lane thought Cleveland had revolutionized his party. He had created a "new Democracy —a party aggressive, filled with reform spirit, and right in the direction it takes." Democratic professionals like Stephen M. White admired Cleveland's reform principles, but still resented his patronage policy and his refusal to provide leadership in the 1888 campaign. When White's wife gave birth to a son in the fall of 1889, William D. English jokingly suggested that he name the boy Cleveland. "I don't propose to have any such connection with a defeated candidate," White retorted.[1]

Like his predecessor Harrison encountered serious problems in Cal-

[1] Lane to John H. Wigmore, Dec. 2, 1888, in Anne Wintermute Lane and Louise Herrick Wall, eds., *The Letters of Franklin K. Lane: Personal and Political* (Boston, 1922), pp. 20–21; English to White, Sept. 25, 1889, White to English, Sept. 27, 1889, WP; James D. Richardson, ed., *A Compilation of the Messages and Papers of the Presidents, 1789–1897,* 10 vols. (Washington, D.C., 1897), 7: 5440–49; Allan Nevins, *Grover Cleveland: A Study in Courage* (New York, 1932), pp. 448–51.

ifornia from the outset of his presidency. The state's Republicans, conscious of their role in his election, confidently expected him to select a Cabinet member from the Far West. Sen. Leland Stanford joined several Republican congressmen in requesting that someone from the Pacific Coast be named secretary of the interior. Creed Haymond, the Southern Pacific attorney, told the president-elect that such a move would prove politically profitable, and other Californians advanced the familiar argument that the state's distance and different interests from the East entitled it to a voice in the administration. Murat Halstead, the editor of a Cincinnati newspaper and a presidential adviser, urged Harrison to use a Cabinet appointment to encourage the recent trend toward Republicanism on the Coast.[2] Responsive to these suggestions, Harrison clearly intended to name a Californian to his Cabinet, and in the months after his election he employed various intermediaries to discover the best man for the position.[3]

In a development characteristic of politics in California—where, as one party member complained, "Factions are thicker than sage brush" —the Republicans found themselves unable to agree on a candidate. Leland Stanford was recommended by a few, including Halstead, who argued that the senator "is awfully rich, but he is a man of lofty views, and his enormous fortune places him above all temptation." Some requested the selection of John F. Swift, the unsuccessful gubernatorial nominee in 1886, but Stanford quietly undermined Swift's chances.[4] The governor, the Republican members of the legislature, and a large number of the party's county committees supported the aspirations of Morris M. Estee, known as "Much Mentioned" Estee for his repeated failure to obtain political office. Michael H. De Young,

[2] Stanford et al. to Harrison, Feb. 18, 1889, Haymond to Harrison, Nov. 30, 1889, Halstead to Harrison, Dec. 7, 1888, Loring Pickering and George K. Fitch to Harrison, Dec. 5, 1888, HP.
[3] T. W. Palmer to Harrison, Dec. 18, 1888, Palmer to Harrison, Dec. 20, 1888, Palmer to Harrison, Dec. 29, 1888, Matthew S. Quay to Harrison, Dec. 28, 1888, George W. Steele to Harrison, Feb. 14, 1889, HP.
[4] Edwin H. Lamme to W. H. H. Miller, Dec. 12, 1888, Halstead to Harrison, Dec. 7, 1888, T. W. Palmer to Harrison, Dec. 29, 1888, A. K. Hollis to Harrison, Nov. 26, 1888, Louis T. Michener to Harrison, Dec. 26, 1888, Marcus D. Boruck to Harrison, Dec. 8, 1888, Robert W. Waterman to Harrison, Dec. 15, 1888, HP.

who had Cabinet ambitions of his own, made clear his opposition to Estee.[5] Faced with this dissension, Harrison decided to avoid appointing anyone from California at all. As Halstead himself reluctantly concluded, "There are so many jealousies on the coast among the republicans that it would be really the better policy to leave them all out—the secondary chunks of patronage being duly distributed."[6]

Despite their own responsibility for the outcome, many Republicans blamed it on the president. De Young's San Francisco *Chronicle* charged that "President Harrison has committed a serious error, and one which must militate against the success of his Administration."[7] Discontent grew as Harrison dispensed the remainder of the spoils. Unlike his predecessor the new president paid strict attention to the recommendations of the dominant wing within his party's state organization. Between 1889 and 1892, in partial cooperation with the central committee, Senator Stanford and the Republican congressional delegation virtually dictated the allocation of the California offices. Shortly after the inauguration the delegation submitted a list of candidates for most major positions, and without exception Harrison followed its recommendations. In several instances the delegation's solitary endorsement overcame numerous petitions for rival candidates.[8]

While this result pleased the delegation, it aroused resentment among those elements of the party opposed to Stanford. Republicans in Los Angeles and San Diego, proud of their decisive role in Harrison's California victory, were ignored in the appointment process. "I cannot believe that the President understands the situation here,"

[5] Robert W. Waterman et al. to Harrison, Feb. 20, 1889, De Young to Harrison, Feb. 7, 1889, J. N. E. Wilson to Harrison, Jan. 10, 1889, S. A. Scott to Harrison, Dec. 15, 1888, E. Heackock to Harrison, Dec. 24, 1888, HP.

[6] Halstead to Harrison, Jan. 19, 1889, HP.

[7] SF *Chron*, March 6, 1889; SF *Exmr*, March 7, 1889; De Young to Harrison, Feb. 19, 1889, HP.

[8] Stanford to Harrison, March 30, 1889, HP; SF *Exmr*, March 16, 1889. For examples of Harrison's compliance with the delegation's recommendations, see Timothy Guy Phelps File, AP, Cal., Collector of the Port of San Francisco, Treasury Dept., RG 56; and Paris Kilburn File, AP, Cal., Surveyor of the Port of San Francisco, Treasury Dept., RG 56. Harry J. Sievers (*Benjamin Harrison*, vol. 3: *Hoosier President, 1889–1901* [New York, 1968], pp. 41–43, 73–82) and David Saville Muzzey (*James G. Blaine: A Political Idol of Other Days* [New York, 1934], p. 468) contend that Harrison resisted the patronage demands of state organizations.

wrote one angry party member.[9] Harrison Gray Otis, the editor of the influential Los Angeles *Times*, was particularly bitter. The nomination of a Stanford crony as postmaster of Los Angeles damaged his prestige. The selection of Stanford men to head the district's federal land office threatened to cost the *Times* thousands of dollars in annual advertising revenue. Enraged, Otis used his newspaper and political power to avenge "the persistent efforts to fill these offices with personal enemies of mine."[10] By 1892 he had abandoned Harrison. The president, the *Times* asserted, was "a chunky icicle" and "mediocre."[11]

Opposition to Harrison's patronage decisions also came from De Young, who planned to contest Stanford's reelection in 1891 and was stung by the senator's control over federal appointments. From the beginning of the administration Democrats noted encouraging signs in the *Chronicle* that, as one put it, "De Young is becoming a fire brand and is disposed to fight the programme, both Federal and State."[12] In September 1891 James S. Clarkson, an Iowa Republican, encountered De Young in New York in "a state of mind" over the appointments and arranged for the president to talk with him. "His paper is important, & he wields much power on the Coast," Clarkson reminded the administration. It was already too late. Three weeks earlier the *Chronicle* had deserted Harrison and declared in favor of the nomination of James G. Blaine in 1892.[13] Harrison's patronage policy had won him the support of the Stanford wing of the party, but at the cost of alienating powerful factional leaders.

II

The president's patronage troubles only symbolized the larger misfortunes of his administration. Agricultural discontent and a general recession after the summer of 1890 combined to produce, in Harri-

---

[9] Edwin H. Lamme to E. W. Halford, Jan. 8, 1890, HP; W. W. Bowers to Harrison, March 15, 1891, AP, Cal., Collector of Internal Revenue File, Treasury Dept., RG 56.
[10] Otis to Henry Harrison Markham, Jan. 4, 1890, Otis to Harrison, Jan. 7, 1890, Lamme to Halford, Jan. 8, 1890, Lamme to Halford, May 7, 1890, HP; LA *Times*, May 9, 1890.
[11] LA *Times*, April 10, 1892.
[12] English to White, Sept. 13, 1889, White to English, Sept. 15, 1889, White to John F. Swift, Jan. 13, 1890, WP.
[13] Clarkson to Halford, Sept. 17, 1891, HP; SF *Chron*, Aug. 21, 1891.

son's words, "the wild demands and theories that spring from crop failures and business depression." On the Coast economic problems ended the brief business revival of the late 1880's. An especially hard winter in 1889–90 disrupted rail connections with the East, injured San Francisco commercial interests, and damaged farms and vineyards. Heavy rains early in 1890 cut wheat output. Raisin growers, beset by overproduction and low prices, held mass meetings to devise remedies. "Times have been rather dull in California," wrote White in March 1890, "not merely in the Southern part of the State, but particularly in San Francisco, where there are a great many people without employment."[14]

During March the unemployed in San Francisco were estimated to number as many as 25,000. The mayor requested public subscriptions to aid them. One thousand men were given work in Golden Gate Park, and a citizens' group dispatched telegrams to Washington urging that government rations be issued to avert starvation. Gen. Nelson A. Miles, commander of the army's Division of the Pacific, became concerned for the safety of the United States Treasury in San Francisco. There were, he notified his superiors, at least seventy secret organizations in the city, some with "the avowed purpose of taking possession of property which does not belong to them." Miles noted with alarm the prevalence of "disaffection and communistic feeling" in California.[15]

The worried general probably considered among those subject to "communistic feeling" the five Nationalist clubs that had recently been formed in San Francisco. The Nationalist movement had grown rapidly in California after the 1888 publication of Edward Bellamy's utopian novel, *Looking Backward*. Appealing to those unhappy with the nature of American development, the novel advocated a nationalized, cooperative state in which economic equality would be attained by the substitution of public for private control over the econ-

[14] Harrison to Creed Haymond, Sept. 24, 1891, HP; White to John F. Swift, March 24, 1890, WP; Rendigs Fels, *American Business Cycles, 1865–1897* (Chapel Hill, N.C., 1959), pp. 159–76; "Report of the State Board of Agriculture, February 1, 1891," *J App*, 30 sess. (1893), 5: 15–16; "Annual Report of the Board of State Viticultural Commissioners for 1891–92," *ibid.*, p. 8.

[15] Miles to adjutant general, U.S. Army, March 6, 1890, HP; SF *Exmr*, Feb. 16, March 16, 1890; *Alta Cal*, March 7–8, 12, 1890.

omy. The Nationalists' concern with corporate abuses fit easily into California's anti-railroad tradition, and their evolutionary, pragmatic outlook attracted followers who might have been alienated by a more radical program.[16]

Oakland enthusiasts formed a Nationalist club early in 1889, and from there the movement spread swiftly throughout the state. By the next year California had 62 such organizations, more than a third of the national total, with a reported membership of nearly 3,500. As the *Examiner* remarked in April 1890, "Their clubs are springing up everywhere, and California seems to have an especially prolific soil for that sort of product."[17] Nationalist strength centered in Los Angeles and San Francisco, which together had twelve clubs, and in small towns, particularly in Southern California. "In fact," commented the Los Angeles *Times*, "there is probably more Nationalism to the square inch in this county than in all the rest of the State together." The movement found some support among newcomers to the area, perhaps because they were disappointed with their initial experience. It drew a diverse following that included socialists and labor leaders, utopian experimenters, and businessmen.[18]

The movement peaked in the spring of 1890 and then vanished almost as quickly as it had begun. A bitter dispute at the Nationalists' only state convention between those in favor of immediate nationalization and those interested in currency inflation and antitrust legislation split the movement and enfeebled the clubs in San Francisco. Los Angeles Nationalists suffered a severe setback when they ran a socialist for Congress in the 1890 election. Despite endorsements from Bellamy and the local Farmers' Alliance, the candidate received only a thousand votes, and the Los Angeles movement never recovered.[19] Finally, the decline was hastened when many of the disillusioned

---

[16] SF *Chron*, April 6, 1890; SF *Exmr*, April 19, 1890; Arthur E. Morgan, *Edward Bellamy* (New York, 1944), p. 172.

[17] SF *Exmr*, April 19, 1890; F. I. Vassault, "Nationalism in California," *Overland Monthly*, 15 (1890): 659-60; LA *Times*, March 17, 1890.

[18] LA *Times*, Oct. 7, 1890; Vassault, "Nationalism in California," pp. 659-60; A. Morgan, *Bellamy*, pp. 266-69; Robert V. Hine, *California's Utopian Colonies* (New Haven, Conn., 1966), pp. 78-100.

[19] *Alta Cal*, April 10, 1890; Howard H. Quint, "Gaylord Wilshire and Socialism's First Congressional Campaign," *PHR*, 26 (1957): 330-39.

Nationalists "transferred their energies, hopes and plans, with vitality undiminished," to a new movement centering on the Farmers' Alliance and the People's party of California.[20] A. G. Hinckley, a former Nationalist from Los Angeles, soon appeared on the national committee of the People's party. J. W. Hines, a leading Bellamyite, helped organize the Farmers' Alliance in the state, and the Nationalist *Pacific Union*, edited by Hines, became the *Pacific Union Alliance*, an important spokesman for the farm group. In rural sections of Southern California, many Bellamy clubs were turned into local units of the Alliance.[21]

Thomas V. Cator exemplified this smooth transition from Nationalism to Populism. In 1887, at the age of 36, Cator left a New Jersey political career to seek relief in California from a physical ailment. Captivated by the climate, he settled in San Francisco, devoted himself to "the great fight against plutocracy," and passed quickly through the stages of Nationalist, reform Democrat, and Populist. In 1890, in the midst of this transitional period, he accepted a nomination for Congress from the remnants of the nativist, anti-Catholic American party, a move that would hinder later Populist efforts to attract foreign-born and Catholic voters in San Francisco and other California cities. But by that year Cator's personal flair and talent for politics had already won him a leading position among those eager to defy or reform the two major parties. "He combines the erudition of the college professor with the tongue of a Cicero and the dash of a cavalryman with the polish of a courtier," observed the New York *Herald*. Eloquent, ambitious, and opportunistic, Cator would completely dominate the California People's party during the 1890's.[22]

Aided by converts from the Nationalist movement, the Alliance expanded rapidly after its first appearance in Santa Barbara County on April 11, 1890. Like its predecessor, the Alliance was centered in

[20] Donald E. Walters, "The Feud Between California Populist T. V. Cator and Democrats James Maguire and James Barry," *PHR*, 27 (1958): 284.

[21] *Ibid.*; SF *Exmr*, May 21, 1891; Quint, "Wilshire and Socialism's First Congressional Campaign," p. 335.

[22] Cator to Burdette Cornell, Jan. 8, 1895, Thomas Vincent Cator Papers, Stanford Univ.; New York *Herald*, Jan. 15, 1893; Cator to J. R. McPherson, Dec. 9, 1887, CP; Harold F. Taggart, "Thomas Vincent Cator: Populist Leader of California," *California Historical Society Quarterly*, 27 (1948): 311–18, and 28 (1949): 47–55.

Southern California, in economically depressed, native-stock counties, and in areas that had experienced swift population growth during the previous decade. It won some followers in towns as well as in fruit, raisin, and other agricultural districts. A number of Los Angeles residents joined, including the former Republican senator Cornelius Cole. "The alliance will result in great good," Cole contended. "The farmers must protect themselves."[23] Encouraged by the response, representatives from thirteen county Alliance groups met in San Jose at the end of November 1890 to organize a state Farmers' Alliance and Industrial Union. The convention chose Marion Cannon, a 56-year-old Ventura rancher, to head the new body and adopted an aggressive platform that inveighed against Wall Street, "the foreign money power," and the "abject subserviency" of the country's legislators to "the narrow and selfish demands of a purse-proud oligarchy."[24]

For a time Alliance leaders resisted the temptation to involve the organization directly in politics. As late as mid-1891 polls showed that most members favored limited endorsements of Alliance-oriented candidates rather than the formation of a third party. President Cannon agreed. "Our greatest danger," he cautioned, "lies in the possibility of selfish intrigues in politics, in which our lofty principles will be forgotten in a mad struggle for *immediate* power."[25] The California Alliance consequently played little part in the 1890 election, but the political success of the movement in other areas, particularly in several Southern and Plains states, boosted the California Alliance's membership and made it more willing to enter politics.[26] In March 1891 Cannon reported 302 sub-Alliances with 22,000 members; at the close of the year there were some 30,000 members in over 500 sub-Alliances and 34 county Alliances. On October 22, 1891, signaling the group's changed attitude, an Alliance conven-

[23] Cole to Olive Cole, Sept. 7, 1890, Cole Papers; Michael Paul Rogin and John L. Shover, *Political Change in California: Critical Elections and Social Movements, 1890–1966* (Westport, Conn., 1970), pp. 8–16; Tom G. Hall, "California Populism at the Grass-Roots: The Case of Tulare County, 1892," *Southern California Quarterly*, 49 (1967): 194–95.

[24] SF *Exmr*, Nov. 21–23, 1890.

[25] Ventura *Democrat*, Feb. 7, 1891; SF *Exmr*, July 24, 1891.

[26] See statements by the Alliance's state organizer in SF *Exmr*, Nov. 21, 1890; *Alta Cal*, Nov. 12, 1890.

tion in Los Angeles formally created the People's party of California.[27]

This event, together with the rise of Nationalism and the Alliance, worried established politicians, who tended to overlook the fact that Alliance membership in California lagged far behind that in other states. "I don't think in my time I have seen so many evidences of disintegration in politics as now," wrote the Republican John F. Swift in April 1890. Swift feared that "the Bellamyites and the other cranks" would hurt the Republicans' prospects. "Confidentially between friends," he told Stephen M. White, "I am very uneasy. Your party has all the vices of ours except the cranks." White and his Democratic allies shared Swift's uncertainty, but they welcomed the threat to Republican hegemony in Southern California. Predicting that the Populists there might poll as many votes as either of the old parties, they began a campaign to convince the farmers that their interests lay with the Democratic party. Leaders of both parties agreed that the new organization would pose a serious problem in the coming presidential campaign and that in California at least, it promised to draw more strength away from the Republicans than from the Democrats.[28] With a mixture of eagerness and apprehension, they waited to see whether their speculations would be borne out in the 1892 election.

III

Of more immediate concern to political leaders was the marked resurgence of anti-railroad sentiment that accompanied the return of economic hardship and the growth of the Alliance in California. Resentment over railroad rates surfaced again. Following their first frenzied activity, Santa Fe and Southern Pacific officials had shown a greater interest in corporate profits and stability than in rate wars. In part a natural outgrowth of the economics of competition in an

[27] LA *Times*, Oct. 21–23, 1891; Ventura *Democrat*, March 21, July 31, 1891; Walters, "Feud Between California Populist Cator and Democrats Maguire and Barry," p. 287.
[28] Swift to White, April 29, 1890, Swift to White, Dec. 7, 1890, White to Swift, Jan. 24, 1891, White to T. W. H. Shanahan, May 10, 1891, Shanahan to White, May 15, 1891, WP; SF *Exmr*, May 22, 1891; *Alta Cal*, March 20, 1890; Z. Montgomery to Cleveland, Nov. 7, 1890, CP.

industry characterized by high fixed costs, their decision to cooperate rather than compete soon dampened the hopeful mood that had so altered the fortunes of the anti-monopoly Democrats during the late 1880's. As anti-railroad feeling again mounted, many Californians abandoned their earlier faith in the virtues of competitive enterprise and turned instead to a different solution. "After all has been said and done on this subject," concluded the Los Angeles *Times*, formerly a vigorous defender of the benefits of competition, "the fact will probably remain, that no effectual regulation of freights and fares will be possible, until the Government owns the roads."[29]

Nationalists, Populists, and other groups also assailed the efforts of Central Pacific managers to minimize or if possible to avoid paying the company's debt to the federal government for financial aid granted under the legislation of 1862 and 1864. Scheduled to become due in the mid-1890's, this debt amounted to almost $26,000,000. While it worried Central Pacific officials, it intrigued anti-railroad leaders, who sensed an excellent opportunity to harass, punish, or even foreclose the railroad. Citing the debt, the Farmers' Alliance soon after its formation demanded government seizure of the railroad, "a monopoly in this State that charges 'all the traffic will bear.' " Instructing Alliance lecturers to focus on the Central Pacific, President Cannon confidently predicted government ownership by 1894.[30] Meanwhile, revelations that were adverse to the railroad had unexpectedly come from within the company management itself.

The source was Collis P. Huntington, who had decided to use the Southern Pacific's 1890 annual meeting to take public revenge on Leland Stanford. Unwilling to forgive the senator's 1885 treachery to Aaron A. Sargent, Huntington had also been irritated by Stanford's frequent inattention to railroad business and his extravagant personal expenditures at a time when the company sought to demonstrate its inability to pay the government debt. Stanford knew about part of his colleague's plan in advance. In February 1890, at

[29] LA *Times*, May 7, 1889; Hall, "California Populism at the Grass-Roots," pp. 198–99.

[30] Ventura *Democrat*, Dec. 13, 1890, Jan. 24, July 31, 1891; LA *Times*, Oct. 7, 1889; Stuart Daggett, *Chapters on the History of the Southern Pacific* (New York, 1922), pp. 370–403. The railroad debt question is treated in more detail in Chapter Nine below.

a conference of Southern Pacific leaders in New York City, he was forced to sign an agreement providing that Huntington would replace him as president of the railroad. In return Stanford received certain papers "in reference to the Sargent matters" then in Huntington's possession, and all parties promised to "refrain from hostile or injurious expressions concerning each other" and to work "in good faith" for Stanford's reelection to the Senate. Stanford, the agreement made clear, could remain a senator, but only if he relinquished the railroad presidency, which he had held for three decades.[31]

Five weeks later, at the annual meeting in San Francisco, Huntington revealed the full extent of his scheme to embarrass and humiliate his partner. Stanford was unsuspecting. Interviewed en route to the meeting, he told reporters that ill health might necessitate his resignation. "If I have my way," he said, "I'll turn over the presidency to another man at the directors' meeting next week." Already in San Francisco, Huntington continued the charade, expressing surprise and regret over the senator's announcement.[32] But despite the New York agreement, he had no intention of allowing Stanford to retire quietly.

At 10 o'clock Wednesday morning, April 9, the Southern Pacific directors gathered in Stanford's private offices in the company's headquarters at the corner of 4th and Townsend streets. As was now expected, Stanford opened the meeting by announcing his resignation, and the directors turned to routine business until the time came for Huntington to make a few remarks as the newly elected president of the company. Replacing Stanford at the head of the table Huntington thanked his associates and promised to serve the railroad faithfully. But then, continuing to read in the same firm voice from his prepared address, he attacked Stanford and the way in which he had won his Senate seat in 1885. "In no case," Huntington said, "will I use this great corporation to advance my personal ambitions at the expense of its owners, or put my hands into its treasury to defeat

---

[31] A copy of the agreement, dated February 28, 1890, is in the Hopkins Collection; Oscar Lewis, *The Big Four: The Story of Huntington, Stanford, Hopkins, and Crocker, and of the Building of the Central Pacific* (New York, 1938), pp. 188–91. It is likely that Huntington also suspected Stanford of a role in the defeat of the Republican legislative ticket in 1886.

[32] LA *Times*, April 6, 8, 1890; SF *Chron*, April 7, 1890.

the people's choice and thereby put myself in positions that should be filled by others.... Corporations should not be used to advance the interests of this party or that, or to raise up any one man, or to pull down another, and this corporation shall not be so used henceforth for any such purpose if its President can prevent it." As the stunned directors left the meeting early in the afternoon, Huntington's men were already distributing copies of his remarks to waiting newsmen.[33]

The subject of headlines and gossip for weeks afterward, Huntington's address caused consternation in railroad headquarters and fascinated political leaders across the state. For two days Stanford remained in seclusion, but Huntington for once was most accessible to reporters. Interviewed in his office at 4th and Townsend streets, he restated his charge that politics had entered too much into the Southern Pacific's affairs. "This building has been overrun with politics, and it is time to call a halt." Told that the address was creating a sensation, Huntington answered: "I intended to create no sensation. I'm a business man, and want to operate the railroad property as such and to make it a profitable investment." Pausing, he leaned back in his chair. "From this time on," he emphasized, "we are going to follow one business. We are railroad men and intend to conduct a legitimate railroad business.... Politics have worked enough demoralization in our company already, and they have gone out of the door never to return."[34]

Bringing into the open long-standing animosities, the quarrel between the two railroad leaders split the Southern Pacific's ranks. "The various newspapers and other flunkies throughout the State, who have been on the payroll of the railroad, are at a loss to know what to do," Stephen M. White noted with delight. "At present, they seem to be non-plussed." Emerging from seclusion on April 11, Stanford denied Huntington's charges and demanded an investigation. "I never in my life used a penny of the company's money for my individual benefit," he declared. Huntington promptly replied that there had been no mistake. "I, of course, have doubts and hesitancies

[33] *Alta Cal*, April 10, 1890; SF *Exmr*, April 10, 1890.
[34] SF *Exmr*, April 10, 1890; SF *Chron*, April 11, 1890; LA *Times*, April 11–13, 1890.

on many subjects," he remarked to a reporter, "but I hardly make mistakes on so important a matter as my address."[35] Incensed by the whole affair, Stanford's supporters rushed to his defense. The San Francisco *Argonaut* blamed the squabble on jealousy, for Stanford "was beloved and honored" while Huntington "remained a village trader, unknown and unnoticed." In the succeeding weeks Huntington repeated his promise to remove the railroad from politics, though in reality he fired only a few Stanford henchmen and continued to employ experts, as he put it, to "look after the large outside —I might almost say semi-political—interests that the Company has in the State of California."[36] Under pressure from the other Southern Pacific directors, Huntington soon apologized to his colleague, but observers believed he deeply resented the attacks of Stanford sympathizers. As one wrote in late April, "He is now in a worse temper, in my opinion, than he was when the original break was made."[37]

Elated by the unexpected quarrel, the Democrats for a time hoped to use it to thwart Stanford's bid for reelection. "The RR row will help us," White predicted. "Collis P. seems to be dead in earnest in his hostility to Stanford."[38] Rumors spread that the senator, hurt by the publicity and fearful of defeat, would withdraw from the contest. Huntington's charges emboldened anti-Stanford Republicans like De Young, whose paper called the senator "a total failure" and urged his replacement.[39] Encouraged, White decided to run for the seat himself and sought to enlist Huntington's financial support. During August and September he made various appeals to Huntington through Calvin S. Brice, chairman of the Democratic national committee, and Patrick A. Collins, a prominent Boston Democrat. But Huntington, apparently content with verbal assaults, declined

[35] White to English, April 13, 1890, WP; SF *Exmr*, April 12–13, 1890; LA *Times*, April 11, 18, 1890; Stanford to Stephen T. Gage, April 29, 1890, Hopkins Collection; SF *Chron*, April 12, 1890.
[36] San Francisco *Argonaut*, April 21, 1890; Huntington to Henry Harrison Markham, March 24, 1893, copy in WP; Huntington to Benjamin Harrison, Dec. 19, 1892, HP; SF *Exmr*, May 20, 1890; San Francisco *Argonaut*, May 19, June 2, 1890.
[37] J. W. Woodard to E. W. Halford, April 28, 1890, HP; Huntington to Stanford, April 15, 1890, Hopkins Collection.
[38] White to A. F. Jones, April 13, 1890, WP.
[39] SF *Chron*, Sept. 11, 1890; White to G. G. Goucher, May 23, 1890, White to English, May 25, 1890, WP.

to aid the Democratic candidate.[40] Convinced that only a well-financed campaign could oust his old enemy from the Senate, the anti-railroad Republican John F. Swift wondered whether Huntington, accustomed to ready obedience, expected voters simply to heed his April address. "He has been flattered and fawned upon...," Swift suggested, "till he actually believes that if he gives it out that the people must not do a certain thing they will stop and not do it."[41]

Without Huntington's help White's candidacy never had a chance. His entry in the race alarmed Republican leaders, but he could not match Stanford's financial resources. Stanford's money strengthened Republican legislative candidates and ensured the selection of weak Democratic opponents. "All purchasable newspapers, all purchasable politicians are being called into camp," White reported.[42] Their finances inadequate, the Democrats were unable to turn the Huntington-Stanford feud into sufficient political profit. Of the two men Stanford had long been the more popular: he had maintained his residence in the state, had served as governor and senator, and had recently announced plans for the Leland Stanford Junior University. Huntington, by contrast, had moved to the East, had made public statements favorable to Chinese immigration, and had become to Californians the symbol of railroad oppression. Even Democratic newspapers defended the senator against Huntington's attacks. "Mr. Stanford is a Californian, with Californian ideas," explained the San Francisco *Examiner*. "Mr. Huntington has become a New Yorker, and a bitterly anti-Californian, pro-Chinese one at that."[43]

Internal dissension, offsetting the squabbles in the Republican camp, delivered the final blow to the Democrats' prospects. White's

[40] White to Patrick A. Collins, Aug. 4, 1890, Collins to White, Sept. 8, 1890, John P. Irish to White, Aug. 26, 1890, Calvin S. Brice to White, Sept. 12, 1890, White to Brice, Sept. 18, 1890, White to John F. Swift, Sept. 28, 1890, WP.

[41] Swift to White, Aug. 22, 1890, WP.

[42] White to Patrick A. Collins, Aug. 4, 1890, English to White, April 21, 1890, WP. For Republican fear of White, see M. R. Higgins to Henry Harrison Markham, Aug. 28, 1890, Markham Papers. There are no reliable figures for Stanford's expenditures in the 1890 campaign. Estimates ranged as high as one million dollars, a figure suggested by Christopher A. Buckley. While that amount seems unlikely, political leaders agreed that Stanford spent a substantial sum, perhaps more than necessary. James H. Wilkins, ed., "The Reminiscences of Christopher A. Buckley," SF *Bul*, Jan. 22, 1919; Wilkins, ed., "Martin Kelly's Story," *ibid.*, Sept. 12, 1917; SF *Exmr*, Nov. 1, 1890.

[43] SF *Exmr*, April 10, 1890; SF *Chron*, April 12, 1890; *Alta Cal*, April 10, 1890; R. B. Carpenter to Henry Harrison Markham, April 13, 1890, Markham Papers.

drive for the Senate seat revived old animosities within the San Francisco organization. Mindful of White's refusal to back "Uncle George" Hearst in 1887, William Randolph Hearst and the *Examiner* worked to undermine him.[44] White's decision to focus his campaign on the direct election of senators, assailing a Senate in which wealth was a qualification for office, did not improve the situation. "The trouble is," he suggested, "that the Examiner people understand that the principle which will result in the overthrow of Stanford will also bury Uncle George."[45]

Pressure from "country" Democrats on the two Hearsts had no effect. The senator had long since delegated complete authority over the *Examiner* to his son, complaining that "the *damn paper* was giving him a great deal of trouble" and calling it foolish "to pay much attention to what an infernal newspaper said anyhow."[46] William Randolph Hearst, who distrusted White and feared a possible challenge to his father's reelection in 1893, bitterly opposed White's candidacy. The factionalism, coupled with efforts to undermine the ticket in San Francisco and Stanford's ability to overwhelm opponents with a well-financed campaign, destroyed the Democrats' hopes of victory. On November 4, 1890, the Republicans won resoundingly, emerging with 88 legislators to the Democrats' 31. Two months later a joint session of the legislature returned Stanford to the United States Senate.[47]

[44] White planned to ask the Democratic state convention to endorse his candidacy, believing that this would give voters the opportunity in effect to choose between specific senatorial candidates in electing the state legislature. He had the necessary party support but encountered opposition from Hearst and the *Examiner*. Calling for Democratic harmony, White withdrew his request for endorsement, a shrewd move that focused the hostility of "country" delegates on the San Francisco organization and strengthened his position in the party. SF *Exmr*, Aug. 18–21, 1890; Ventura *Democrat*, Sept. 6, 1890; White to Barclay Henley, May 5, 1890, White to Arthur Kearney, June 15, 1890, Frank J. Moffitt to White, July 31, 1890, John T. Gaffey to White, Aug. 5, 1890, WP.

[45] White to Brice Grimes, July 6, 1890, White to F. J. Clark, May 30, 1890, White to A. F. Jones, June 16, 1890, WP.

[46] White's report of a conversation with George Hearst in White to G. G. Goucher, May 2, 1889, WP.

[47] George T. Clark, *Leland Stanford: War Governor of California, Railroad Builder and Founder of Stanford University* (Stanford, Cal., 1931), pp. 446–47; Edith Dobie, *The Political Career of Stephen Mallory White: A Study of Party Activities Under the Convention System* (Stanford, Cal., 1927), p. 251; *Alta Cal*, Jan. 14–15, 1891; Thomas L. Thompson to William C. Whitney, Nov. 23, 1890, Whitney Papers. The legislative totals include fourteen Republican and six Democratic holdover senators, elected in 1888.

IV

Elsewhere in the country the 1890 elections resulted in overwhelming victories for the Democrats. Local conditions in the Midwest, unique to the area, produced major Democratic gains, indicating that the Democrats might at last become the region's dominant political party.[48] The nationwide reaction against the Republican Fifty-first Congress gave the Democrats an even greater boost. Labeled the "Billion Dollar Congress" for its appropriations, subsidies, and pension grants, the session discredited the Republicans and gave Democrats an opportunity to attack the Republicans' expenditures and government activism. The high-tariff McKinley Act, passed in the fall of 1890, raised fears of higher prices and underscored the Democrats' demand for tariff reform. An abortive attempt to enact a Federal Elections bill protecting the rights of Negroes and other voters aroused antagonism in the North as well as the South.[49]

From his New York City law office, Grover Cleveland watched the Republicans "getting deeper and deeper into the mire" and advised Democratic leaders to "let them flounder" rather than propose alternative policies. Cautious in outlook and negative in approach, such advice mirrored major weaknesses that would shortly bring disaster to the party. But for the moment, as the elections displayed the enormous increase in Democratic strength, it seemed sound enough. Republican representation in the House dropped from 166 to 88, while the Democrats won 235 seats. Traditional Republican strongholds like Ohio, Illinois, Michigan, and Kansas witnessed Democratic victories. Nebraska elected its first Democratic governor. Massachusetts also elected a Democratic governor, along with seven Democratic congressmen—a victory that marked the first important penetration of New England by the Democrats in three decades.[50]

[48] Richard J. Jensen, *The Winning of the Midwest: Social and Political Conflict, 1888–1896* (Chicago, 1971), pp. 89–153; Paul John Kleppner, *The Cross of Culture: A Social Analysis of Midwestern Politics, 1850–1900* (New York, 1970), pp. 130–78; Roger E. Wyman, "Wisconsin Ethnic Groups and the Election of 1890," *Wisconsin Magazine of History*, 51 (1968): 269–93.

[49] Sievers, *Harrison*, 3: 144–53, 163–72; H. Wayne Morgan, *From Hayes to McKinley: National Party Politics, 1877–1896* (Syracuse, N.Y., 1969), pp. 332–56.

[50] Cleveland to John G. Carlisle, April 7, 1890, in Allan Nevins, ed., *Letters of*

Unfortunately, California party members could not share in the jubilation. Relieved of the pressures of a national campaign, they had lapsed into their old disunity and indecision on the tariff issue. Instead of mounting an aggressive campaign for lower tariffs, they accepted the McKinley Act's higher duties on wool, oranges, brandy, and raisins, joined Coast Republicans in assailing the removal of duties on sugar, and failed to counter the act's popularity among influential "vine & wine men" and other tariff-affected groups.[51] The California Democrats also found it difficult to accuse the Republicans of excessive government activism. During the 1889 session of the legislature Democratic representatives had sanctioned expenditures that rivaled, on the state level, those of the Billion Dollar Congress. Economy in government became a dominant issue in the local campaign, as it did in much of the nation, but discontent with the Democrats' extravagance at the state level partially offset discontent with the Republicans' extravagance at the national level.[52] The Democrats' gubernatorial candidate—Edward B. Pond, the economy-minded mayor of San Francisco—did not provide the expected assistance on the question, for he proved an ineffective campaigner. Moreover, he owed his nomination to Christopher A. Buckley, and the Republicans were quick to link him to the Buckley regime, "the most corrupt and shameless political organization on the American continent."[53]

In a significant departure from the national pattern, the Democrats' defeat in California could scarcely have been more complete. Besides their large majority in the legislature, the Republicans cap-

Grover Cleveland, 1850–1908 (Boston, 1933), pp. 221–22; Geoffrey Blodgett, *The Gentle Reformers: Massachusetts Democrats in the Cleveland Era* (Cambridge, Mass., 1966), p. 99; Gerald W. McFarland, "The Breakdown of Deadlock: The Cleveland Democracy in Connecticut, 1884–1894," *The Historian*, 31 (1969): 394–95.

[51] Viticultural Protective League of California to Henry Harrison Markham, May 29, 1890, Markham Papers; Vincent P. Carosso, *The California Wine Industry: A Study of the Formative Years* (Berkeley, 1951), p. 148; LA *Times*, Oct. 23, 1890; SF *Exmr*, April 2, 1890; Fred Eaton to John Sherman, July 2, 1890, John Sherman Papers, Manuscript Division, Library of Congress.

[52] Winfield J. Davis, *History of Political Conventions in California, 1849–1892* (Sacramento, 1893), p. 567; SF *Chron*, Aug. 16, 1890; James A. Waymire to Markham, Aug. 30, 1890, Markham Papers.

[53] LA *Times*, Sept. 14, 1890; Paris Kilburn to Markham, Aug. 23, 1890, M. R. Higgins to Markham, Aug. 28, 1890, Markham Papers; D. M. Burns to Henry Zenas Osborne, Aug. 22, 1890, M. R. Higgins to Osborne, Oct. 15, 1890, Osborne Papers.

tured the governorship by a plurality of almost eight thousand votes, won every other state office, and elected four congressmen and all three railroad commissioners. The returns reflected the continuation of the state's recent trend toward Republicanism as well as the influence of more immediate considerations. In some sections, particularly in railroad-oriented counties like Sacramento and Alameda, Stanford's senatorial bid strengthened the entire ticket and helped blunt the effect of a small turnout in Southern California. Alone among the states, California registered Republican gains over the figures for the 1888 presidential election. President Harrison called the result "exceedingly gratifying, and all the more so that it is exceptional." White spoke wryly for the disheartened Democrats: "Our Eastern brethren must have a very exalted opinion of California Democracy. I think we have earned two or three cabinet positions."[54]

Most startling was the outcome of the election in San Francisco. "Country" Democrats were, as one remarked, "perfectly thunderstruck" over the city returns.[55] Only three Democratic candidates for state office took San Francisco, all by narrow margins. Pond carried his home city by barely two hundred votes. Democrats entered the election in control of 23 of the city's 30 seats in the legislature; they emerged with 6. In the mayoralty contest the Democratic candidate ran third behind a Republican and an independent. The party also lost the offices of assessor, sheriff, and auditor, among others the city organization depended on for revenue and patronage. To Democratic leaders, who had hoped to consolidate their 1888 triumph in San Francisco, the rout suggested one conclusion. As Pond himself put it, "Our party was sold out here lock, stock & b[arre]l."[56]

For Pond and others the San Francisco debacle substantiated the persistent rumors during the campaign that George Hearst and Christopher A. Buckley intended to betray the party. Hearst, it was widely reported, had reached an agreement with Stanford whereby

[54] Harrison to Henry Zenas Osborne, Nov. 7, 1890, HP; White to Frank J. Moffitt, Nov. 15, 1890, WP; *California Blue Book, or State Roster, 1893* (Sacramento, 1893), pp. 95–112; Charles Dwight Willard to Mary Francis Willard, Nov. 9, 1890, Willard Papers.

[55] J. DeBarth Shorb to William W. Foote, Nov. 10, 1890, Shorb Papers.

[56] Pond to White, Nov. 17, 1890, WP; *California Blue Book, 1893*, pp. 95–112; SF *Exmr*, Nov. 30, 1890.

the latter would deliver a Democratic legislature in 1893, when Hearst would be up for reelection, in return for a Republican legislature in 1890. Hearst's death in February 1891 precluded certainty about the existence of such an agreement, but enraged Democrats had meanwhile found a more vulnerable target in Blind Boss Buckley. To them the outcome of the city contest supplied convincing proof of allegations that Buckley had received from Stanford large sums, estimated by some observers at eighty thousand dollars, to ensure the election of the Republican legislative ticket.[57]

"The air here is full of reports of the purchase of our leaders and voters by Stanford through his coin," wrote a San Francisco party worker. "I can not figure the result in any other way than that Buckley sold us out for coin." "The fact is," insisted another Democrat, "we have 'wolves' in our own party—*worse than the 'lambs'*—who must be cleaned out before we can hope for success."[58] Even the San Francisco *Examiner*, while denying that its ally had betrayed the party, declared that "Mr. Buckley has proved too heavy a load for the Democracy to carry.... The name of Buckley in the popular mind has become a synonym for political corruption. Before we can have a healthy Democratic revival the boss must retire."[59]

In the end Buckley's retirement from politics was one of the most significant consequences of the 1890 campaign. Even prior to the election many Democrats had come to view Buckley as a liability to the party. In the summer of 1890 a group of dissident city Democrats, led by Stuart M. Taylor, Thomas V. Cator, and the old anti-monopolist Barclay Henley, had formed a rival organization designed to eliminate Buckley from San Francisco politics. The group, called the Regular (or Reform) Democrats, drew noticeably little support in the election, but it focused attention on the Buckley regime.[60] In the course of his career, moreover, Buckley had inevitably alienated

[57] Alexander Callow, Jr., "San Francisco's Blind Boss," *PHR*, 25 (1956): 277; SF *Chron*, Nov. 3, 1890.
[58] Wiley J. Tinnin to White, Nov. 12, 1890, James H. Barry to White, Nov. 14, 1890, WP. Buckley's San Francisco followers were known as his "lambs." See also Thomas V. Cator to White, Jan. 8, 1891, WP; Gavin McNab to Cleveland, Nov. 13, 1890, CP.
[59] SF *Exmr*, Nov. 7, 1890.
[60] SF *Chron*, July 10, Sept. 23–26, 1890.

a number of influential Democrats, including in recent months William D. English, who seized this opportunity to undermine their opponent's position. Finally, Buckley's cause suffered from mounting public disenchantment with his rule, exploited by the Republicans in the 1890 campaign, and from revelations during the campaign that the former Bush Street saloon-keeper could now claim investments and property valued at $900,000. Californians wondered about the source of Buckley's wealth.[61]

Once the erosion of his power had begun, Buckley's downfall was surprisingly swift. The first blow came in the immediate wake of the election, when party leaders throughout the state inaugurated efforts to displace him from city politics. "We can not win again unless we discard Buckley...," argued a Democrat in November. "Buckley has led us to disgrace and defeat—then why not get rid of him?" By the following January, after extensive correspondence and discussion on the matter, White could conclude, "It seems to be pretty thoroughly settled that Buckley is disposed of. Even those who always acted with him in subordinate capacities seem radically denunciatory of his course."[62]

A few months later several hundred San Francisco Democrats formed a reorganization committee to supervise the ouster of Buckley and the elimination of his Democratic club system. A diverse coalition of serious reformers, ambitious politicians, and ward heelers, the committee included Edward B. Pond, the beaten gubernatorial candidate; William T. Coleman, the leader of two historic vigilante groups; Edward McGettigan, the dispenser of Democratic patronage at the Vallejo navy yard; James D. Phelan, a future mayor of San Francisco; and Gavin McNab, Buckley's eventual replacement as boss of the city party. For a time it appeared that Buckley would attempt to defy the committee, but in July 1891, deserted by many of his followers, he announced his withdrawal from politics.[63]

[61] *Ibid.*, Nov. 2, 1890. English blamed Buckley for the failure of his bid for the gubernatorial nomination at the 1890 Democratic state convention. So bitter was the feeling that English's brother tried to assault Buckley as he left the convention hall. SF *Exmr*, Aug. 22, 1890.

[62] Wiley J. Tinnin to White, Nov. 12, 1890, White to Thomas V. Cator, Jan. 10, 1891, White to John P. Irish, Jan. 11, 1891, WP.

[63] SF *Exmr*, June 22–30, July 2, 1891.

If Buckley still hoped for a clandestine return to power, the possibility ended with his indictment by a San Francisco grand jury, on November 10, 1891, on charges of bribing the Board of Supervisors to grant an electric-railroad franchise. The indictment represented the climax of an investigation of political corruption in San Francisco and Sacramento. During its 1891 session the legislature had been accused of so many irregularities that it became known as the "Legislature of a Thousand Scandals." In mid-March, as the legislators were voting for a successor to George Hearst, the "wastebasket scandal" surfaced when one senatorial aspirant discovered, in a wastebasket in the state library, empty currency wrappers and a list of assembly members.[64] The scandals received widespread publicity and obscured the session's real accomplishments, including passage of measures to institute the Australian secret ballot system, improve care for the insane, establish an eight-hour day on public works, and determine popular sentiment on the direct election of senators. Remarked the *Examiner* as the body adjourned, "This Legislature goes home more heavily loaded with public contempt than almost any other we have ever had."[65]

With public opinion aroused, Judge William T. Wallace, sponsor of the 1884 Wallace resolutions, assembled a grand jury in August 1891 to investigate the exposures. To knowledgeable observers the jury's composition suggested that it had another objective besides honesty in government—that of discrediting Buckley and advancing the political fortunes of the anti-Buckley Regular Democrats. Wallace himself had been a candidate for a judicial nomination at the 1890 Democratic convention but had been defeated by the almost solid vote of Buckley's city delegation. Barclay Henley, the jury's foreman, had opposed Buckley since the mid-1880's and had helped lead the 1890 fight against him. One juror was the group's unsuccessful mayoralty nominee, and another had recently written a bitter pamphlet against Buckleyism. In all, at least eight of the jury's mem-

---

[64] SF *Chron*, Nov. 11, 1891; Alexander Callow, Jr., "The Legislature of a Thousand Scandals," *Historical Society of Southern California Quarterly*, 39 (1957): 340–50.
[65] SF *Exmr*, March 26, 1891; *JS*, 29 sess. (1891), pp. 943–90; Erik Falk Petersen, "The Struggle for the Australian Ballot in California," *California Historical Quarterly*, 51 (1972): 227–43.

bers had participated in the anti-Buckley movement of the previous year.[66]

The California Supreme Court soon ruled the Wallace grand jury illegal, but not before indictments had been handed down against Buckley and several others for bribery and corruption.[67] Buckley, meanwhile, had chosen not to await the indictment or to test the jury's legality. In late September 1891 he fled to Montreal and then to London for reasons, he declared, of health. Reporters noted that for some reason Buckley's health necessitated his absence from the United States. In London Buckley called the affair "a little party fight" and derided his former supporters like William Randolph Hearst, "an undeveloped young man who bangs his hair," who had deserted him. The *Examiner*, he charged with some justification, "has always been with me, when it could make anything by it, but now thinks to fool the public by fighting me." Although he returned to San Francisco in 1894, Buckley's career had ended. Faced with insurmountable opposition in his own party and with public criticism of his political methods, the Blind Boss would never again be an important force in California politics.[68]

V

Buckley's downfall and the party's overwhelming defeat in the 1890 election ushered in another period of reorganization, comparable to the events after 1886, as Democrats again moved to adjust to a changed situation. Externally, the growth of the Farmers' Alliance and People's party presented a major challenge, one that politicians believed would alter, if only temporarily, the complexion of state politics. Political leaders noted the attractiveness of the Populist platform, with which many of them substantially agreed, and predicted a large role for the new party in the 1892 presidential contest. "It is a menace to existing political parties," wrote the prominent Republican John F. Swift. "No party that does not embrace all interests

---

[66] SF *Exmr*, Aug. 22, 1890; SF *Chron*, Aug. 23, Oct. 8, 1891; Jeremiah Lynch, *Buckleyism: The Government of a State* (San Francisco, 1889); Wilkins, ed., "Reminiscences of Buckley," SF *Bul*, Feb. 3, 1919.

[67] SF *Chron*, Dec. 13, 1891; SF *Exmr*, Oct. 22, 31, Nov. 7, 11, 1891.

[68] Interview with Buckley in SF *Exmr*, Dec. 27, 1891; SF *Chron*, Sept. 26, 1891; Callow, "Blind Boss," pp. 277–78.

and at least pretend to protect them all can expect more than brief success. But a 'farmers party,' like a 'labor party,' is apt for a certain brief period to attract a vast, uneasy, floating element outside of agricultural interests, and they may act together and make a winning."[69]

Significant changes had also occurred within the Democratic party itself between 1889 and 1891. In San Francisco, where Buckley had ruled for eight years, there began a struggle for control of the party organization that, before it finally ended, would make many city Democrats long for the stability they had known under the Buckley machine. The death of George Hearst early in 1891 removed another familiar and influential figure from California politics. William D. English, rebuffed in a bid to gain the 1890 gubernatorial nomination, had fought with Buckley and had been dropped from the Democratic central committee that he had headed since 1884. English retained an important patronage post as state harbor commissioner, but suffered diminished prestige and authority. As younger San Francisco Democrats like James D. Phelan, Max Popper, and Gavin McNab started to assume positions of power, Stephen M. White became the only Democratic leader to emerge from these years with increased influence. A shrewd and diligent politician, with a reputation as the party's ablest orator, White had skillfully established his mastery of the "country" forces in the party, earned widespread popularity by his actions during the 1890 campaign, and strengthened his prospects for a seat in the United States Senate.

Despite the magnitude of their 1890 setback, Coast Democrats displayed considerable confidence as they awaited the presidential election of 1892. The recent nationwide reaction against the Republican party promised to put a Democrat in the White House. In two years the current political flux could shift California voting patterns in a Democratic direction, the Republican record in the 1891 session of the legislature would come under review, and Democrats could call attention to the ouster of Buckley. The Republican Swift expressed a common conviction when he discounted his party's enormous plurality in the 1890 returns. The plurality "is only important if parties remain exactly as now," he observed. "And I have never seen at any

[69] Swift to White, Dec. 7, 1890, WP.

time stronger premonitions of change and break up than now."
Swift also admitted to White his belief that Grover Cleveland would
be the next president.[70] White no doubt welcomed the prediction of a
Democratic victory and hoped finally to carry California for a Democratic presidential nominee, but he and other party leaders had already
begun making plans to substitute another candidate for Cleveland.

[70] *Ibid.*; White to Swift, Jan. 24, 1891, WP; SF *Exmr*, Nov. 8, 1890.

First row: GROVER CLEVELAND, BENJAMIN HARRISON
Second row: LELAND STANFORD, COLLIS P. HUNTINGTON
Third row: GEORGE HEARST, WILLIAM RANDOLPH HEARST

Governor Stoneman shepherds the Wallace resolutions through the railroad wolves
San Francisco *Wasp*, April 12, 1884

Competition between the Southern Pacific and the Santa Fe lowers
railroad rates while the railroad commission sleeps
San Francisco *Wasp*, March 27, 1886

Plaza of Los Angeles, 1890
Wide World

GEORGE STONEMAN
Men of California

JOHN DAGGETT
Overland Monthly

The Republicans tie
Christopher A. Buckley to
the Democrats' 1890
gubernatorial candidate,
Edward B. Pond. In the
background is Henry
Harrison Markham,
Pond's Republican
opponent

San Francisco *Wasp*,
October 18, 1890

THE LILY IS IN IT.
That Root of All Political Evil—BUCKLEYISM!

The 1892 Cleveland-Harrison campaign in the small California town of San Andreas
United Press International

CALIFORNIA CURIOSITIES.
No. 10.
THE CALIFORNIA DEMOCRACY RATIFIES THE CHICAGO NOMINATION. *(See page 6.)*

William D. English falls
into line behind Grover
Cleveland's nomination
for the presidency
San Francisco *Wasp*,
June 25, 1892

STEPHEN J. FIELD
*History of the Bench and Bar of
California*

SAMUEL M. WILSON
*Contemporary Biography of California's
Representative Men*

San Pedro harbor, about 1895
Land of Sunshine

JOHN P. IRISH
History of Iowa

STEPHEN M. WHITE
La Reina

THOMAS V. CATOR
Courtesy of Harold F. Taggart.

WILLIAM T. WALLACE
*History of the Bench and Bar of
California*

The Free Harbor celebration, San Pedro, April 26–27, 1899
Title Insurance and Trust Company, Los Angeles

Democratic party leaders, including Senator White of California, take aim at President Cleveland

CHAPTER SEVEN

The Democrats in Victory
1892-1893

AS THE 1892 presidential election approached, neither Benjamin Harrison nor Grover Cleveland, the two most likely candidates, aroused much enthusiasm among California politicians. Michael H. De Young, Harrison Gray Otis, and other prominent Republicans continued to denounce Harrison. The San Francisco *Argonaut*, widely considered a spokesman for the Stanford wing of the party, labeled the president "a small accident" and "a monometalist of the yellow stripe." In February 1891 Cleveland revealed the same yellow stripe when he issued a letter condemning free-silver agitation. Hoping to stem the growing silver sentiment in the Democratic party and to counteract rumors that he had become more sympathetic to it, Cleveland predicted "disaster, if in the present situation we enter upon the dangerous and reckless experiment of free, unlimited and independent silver coinage."[1]

Cleveland clearly expected to reap political profit from his letter, which he had deliberately phrased to remain ambiguous on a program of limited silver coinage. "Note carefully the wording of the letter and see how much room after all there is for the action of judgment and conviction below the line of free coinage of the silver of the world," he remarked to William F. Vilas of Wisconsin. A friend who visited the former president in late February recalled that Cleveland, his eyes twinkling, had exclaimed: "You'll find there's some pretty good politics in that letter too!" On the Pacific Coast Cleveland's pronouncement brought the usual praise for his

---

[1] San Francisco *Argonaut*, Feb. 17, May 26, 1890; Cleveland to E. Ellery Anderson, Feb. 10, 1891, in Allan Nevins, ed., *Letters of Grover Cleveland, 1850–1908* (Boston, 1933), pp. 245–46.

courage, along with warnings against his financial views. The former president, charged the San Francisco *Examiner*, had been "enveloped by Eastern influences."[2]

Cleveland's letter on the silver issue, coupled with lingering resentment against his patronage policy, prompted many Democratic leaders to oppose his bid for a second term. "California will never vote for Cleveland," insisted Stephen M. White, who believed that Cleveland's nomination would be "utterly suicidal" in view of party divisions in New York, his home state. William D. English judged that "most of our active workers in California politics are against Cleveland." As for himself, English added, "I am heartily tired of Cleveland and hope he has finally been disposed of. He and his friends act as though the Demo. Party had been created for their sole use and benefit." Party newspapers like the *Examiner*, the Oakland *Times*, and the Los Angeles *Herald*, the three most influential Democratic papers in the state, agreed that a new candidate should be found. As one put it, Cleveland "is no longer indispensable" to the Democratic party.[3]

Most anti-Cleveland Democrats favored the nomination of Sen. David B. Hill of New York. Thought to be more flexible than Cleveland on the silver issue, Hill had also demonstrated his ability to carry New York and his responsiveness to the patronage demands of local party organizations. Newspapers contrasted Hill's open political methods with Cleveland's hidden equivocations and called Hill "refreshingly frank." White observed: "Of course, we want Hill. I am convinced that if he were nominated and elected president, his surroundings are such that we would have no difficulty in getting proper recognition."[4] During the first months of 1892 the New York senator and his advisers, encouraged by reports of widespread anti-Cleveland sentiment in the Coast party, solicited support from Cali-

[2] Cleveland to Vilas, Feb. 18, 1891, in Nevins, ed., *Letters of Cleveland*, p. 246; Joseph Bucklin Bishop, *Notes and Anecdotes of Many Years* (New York, 1925), p. 184; SF *Exmr*, Feb. 13, 1891; Ventura *Democrat*, Feb. 28, 1891; Richard Watson Gilder, *Grover Cleveland: A Record of Friendship* (New York, 1910), pp. 31–33.

[3] White to J. D. Spencer, Feb. 21, 1892, White to David B. Hill, April 1, 1892, English to White, March 6, 1892, WP; SF *Exmr*, Aug. 24, 1891; Ventura *Democrat*, June 17, 1892; I. Allen to William C. Whitney, June 30, 1892, Whitney Papers.

[4] SF *Exmr*, Feb. 5, 1892; White to English, Feb. 29, 1892, WP; LA *Times*, March 5, 1892.

fornia Democratic leaders. They even made a misguided attempt to enlist John P. Irish, a Cleveland loyalist, who retorted in characteristically blunt fashion that Hill's following came from "a herd of swine" and "the sordid elements in the country."[5] White and English, unaware of the kind of company they kept, promised to work for a Hill delegation to the party's national convention. White considered it possible to give Hill "the lion's share of this end" if he could attract significant backing elsewhere.[6]

Peaking early in 1892, Hill's prospects dwindled as party conventions across the country declared for Cleveland. A decision by Coast strategists, later much regretted, to subordinate the silver issue to the tariff issue in the 1892 campaign also gave Cleveland an advantage over Hill. The national party "is united on the tariff," explained the *Examiner*. "Let the issue on which it is divided wait."[7] Most important, a vigorous and genuine Cleveland movement, increasing in intensity as the state convention neared, simply overwhelmed its opponents. Guided by the fervent Irish, the movement drew low-tariff enthusiasts and many pragmatic party members who felt a Cleveland candidacy offered the best chance of victory. The diverse elements that came to Cleveland's aid included Gavin McNab, a tariff reformer; Edward B. Pond, a conservative; and Denis Kearney, the former Workingmen's movement leader.[8] Alert to the party's mood, White and his allies backed a pro-Cleveland resolution at the state Democratic convention, held in Fresno in May. "The feeling in favor of Cleveland turned out to be practically unanimous...," White commented after the convention adjourned. "I have never seen anything like the strength of the sentiment in favor of C."[9]

[5] Irish to Manton Marble, March 1, 1892, Marble to Irish, Jan. 21, 1892, Irish to Marble, Jan. 29, 1892, Marble to Irish, Feb. 22, 1892, Marble Papers.

[6] White to Hill, April 1, 1892, English to White, March 13, 1892, Hill to White, March 24, 1892, W. Bourke Cockran to White, Feb. 15, 1892, WP.

[7] SF *Exmr*, March 18, 1892; Herbert J. Bass, *"I Am a Democrat": The Political Career of David Bennett Hill* (Syracuse, N.Y., 1961), pp. 201–33; George Harmon Knoles, *The Presidential Campaign and Election of 1892* (Stanford, Cal., 1942), pp. 25–29.

[8] Jesse D. Carr to Cleveland, April 8, 1892, McNab to Cleveland, April 14, 1892, Kearney to Cleveland, April 27, 1892, W. S. Leake to Cleveland, April 20, 1892, CP; English to White, March 6, 1892, WP.

[9] White to W. Bourke Cockran, May 20, 1892, WP; SF *Exmr*, May 19, 1892.

The momentum gathered in California and other states carried
Cleveland to an easy first-ballot triumph at the party's national convention, meeting in Chicago during the third week of June. With
delegates in accord on the nominee, the convention's only major
contest involved the tariff plank in the platform. Cleveland had once
again decided that expediency dictated moderation on the issue, and
he instructed his representatives to procure a restatement of the party's equivocal 1884 resolution. But Henry Watterson of Kentucky
and other ardent tariff reformers took the fight to the convention
floor, where they secured a substitute plank that branded the Republicans' protectionism "a fraud, a robbery of the great majority of
the American people for the benefit of the few." "My God," Watterson exclaimed to the delegates, "is it possible that, in 1892, we have
to go back for a tariff plank to the straddle of 1884?" Cleveland was
"very much annoyed and fearful" about the plank. Predicting that it
would "make us more trouble than anything else in the campaign,"
he sought to moderate the party's stand in his letter of acceptance.[10]

II

Despite some misgivings of their own over the Watterson plank—
the California delegation had voted unanimously against it—California Democrats were optimistic at the outset of the 1892 campaign.
Even those opposed to the former president's nomination, noted English, "are all standing in for Cleveland and now declare that he is the
greatest living American." The Democrats' confidence stemmed in
part from the obviously troubled situation in the Republican camp.
Personal animosities, exacerbated by patronage grievances, conflicting ambitions, and Leland Stanford's senatorial victory, had flared
into the open after the 1890 election. A concerned Republican had
earlier summarized party relationships: "Senator Stanford don't like
Swift. No more does ... Estee. And none of these gentlemen lay
awake at night to love each other."[11]

[10] Cleveland to William C. Whitney, July 9, 1892, Whitney Papers; *Official Pro-
ceedings of the National Democratic Convention* (Chicago, 1892), pp. 76–101, 235–37.
The Watterson statement is from *ibid.*, p. 88.
    [11] SF *Exmr*, June 22–24, 1892; English to White, Sept. 7, 1892, WP; Edwin H.
Lamme to W. H. H. Miller, Dec. 12, 1888, HP; Thomas L. Thompson to Whitney,
July 11, 1892, Whitney Papers.

Harrison Gray Otis detested Stanford, the "American Caesar." Michael H. De Young disliked both Stanford and Estee, and Henry Zenas Osborne, the editor of a Los Angeles Republican newspaper, considered De Young "a boor." Nearly everyone thought the strong-willed Otis a "d—n cuss" who "don't seem to feel well unless he is in a row with someone."[12] In San Francisco local supporters of Stanford and Collis P. Huntington were again at war. The renomination of Benjamin Harrison added to the Republicans' discouragement. Most considered it a "disappointment" and would have preferred James G. Blaine as their candidate instead.[13] With defeat in prospect the normal sources of Republican campaign revenue disappeared. By September 1892 the chairman of the party's central committee was privately predicting a Democratic victory.[14]

The presence in the campaign of the California People's party gave the Democrats a second major reason to be optimistic. The Populist national convention at Omaha, attended by Thomas V. Cator and Marion Cannon, had adopted an aggressive platform and nominated James B. Weaver of Iowa for the presidency. Cannon, the head of the Farmers' Alliance in California, had won nationwide attention at the convention when he denounced a proposal to negotiate with railroad companies that had refused to grant fare reductions for the Populist delegates. "I do not want this convention, so far as California is concerned, to go back to that railroad, cap in hand, and ask for any privileges whatever. [Tumultuous cheers.] The Democrats and Republicans secured half fare, but we producers of the earth have been refused equal terms. We can stand the refusal. [Cheers.] We can tell those railway companies that the people will own and operate those roads yet."[15]

A month later, during early August, Weaver and Mary E. Lease of Kansas, a well-known Populist orator, toured California, speaking

[12] LA *Times*, Jan. 17, 1891; Osborne to Nellie Osborne, March 6, 1891, Paris Kilburn to Osborne, Aug. 18, 1888, Osborne Papers.
[13] LA *Times*, June 11, 1892; SF *Chron*, June 5–9, 1892; James A. Waymire to E. W. Halford, Oct. 17, 1892, HP; *Proceedings of the Tenth Republican National Convention* (Minneapolis, 1892), pp. 108–13; Otis to Walter Q. Gresham, July 14, 1893, Walter Quintin Gresham Papers, Manuscript Division, Library of Congress.
[14] Chairman's prediction in Frank J. Moffitt to White, Sept. 29, 1892, WP; Waymire to Halford, Oct. 17, 1892, Marcus D. Boruck to Harrison, Oct. 21, 1892, HP.
[15] SF *Chron*, July 5, 1892.

to large crowds at Los Angeles, Fresno, Oakland, and Sacramento. In San Francisco, at afternoon and evening meetings, thousands gathered to hear Weaver and Mrs. Lease demand free coinage of silver and condemn the "Barons of the Rail."[16] Heartened by the tour, local Populist leaders believed the party would show impressive strength in Ventura, Los Angeles, Santa Cruz, Monterey, San Luis Obispo, Santa Barbara, and Tulare counties. In the months before the election, the Populists held twice-weekly meetings at the Bijou Theater in San Francisco, where they attempted to attract city laborers into the party with campaign songs like "We'll Bid Farewell to the Shylock Crew in 1892."[17]

Rudimentary polls in the summer of 1892 bore out earlier predictions that the People's party, with its following centered in traditionally Republican areas, would draw large numbers of Republican voters. Stephen Bowers, the editor of the Ventura *Observer* and a Republican for 36 years, transferred his allegiance to the Populists. "It is no small task for a man who has been somewhat prominently connected with a political party for almost a life-time to sever his connection with it," Bowers observed. But, he complained, the Republican party was tending "to plutocracy. It now yields a servile obedience to Wall Street." Besides, Bowers added in explanation of his transition to Populism, "I believe God is in the latter movement. I believe He is raising it up to settle the conflict between labor and capital peaceably."[18]

Members of the Democratic executive committee thought the third party would garner 60 percent of its votes from the Republicans. The Populist editor of the San Francisco *People's Press* raised the figure to at least 75 percent. The Los Angeles *Times* repeatedly warned Republican leaders to expect serious losses in Southern California, "honeycombed" as it was with Populism.[19] Democrats estimated that if the new party could poll twenty or thirty thousand of the eighty

16 Fred Emory Haynes, *James Baird Weaver* (Iowa City, Iowa, 1919), pp. 319–22; Ventura *Democrat*, Aug. 12, 1892; SF *Exmr*, Aug. 10, 1892.

17 SF *Exmr*, July 17, Sept. 16, 27, 1892.

18 Bowers to Thomas R. Bard, Sept. 26, 1892, Bard Papers; Bowers to Henry Zenas Osborne, May 25, 1891, Osborne Papers.

19 LA *Times*, July 2, 1892; interview with Populist editor in SF *Exmr*, July 17, 1892; John Markley to White, Aug. 29, 1892, WP.

thousand votes it was predicting, they could carry the presidential contest and possibly the legislative contest as well. Stephen M. White expressed a common opinion among Democrats when he noted that Populism "is decidedly powerful in the rural regions of Los Angeles, but to this we can have no rational objection—this section is so strongly Republican."[20]

Armed with these figures, a number of prominent Democrats sought to unite with the Populists on nominations in Republican districts. With elements of both parties in bitter opposition to the policy, the fusion negotiations were a delicate matter. Bowers, corresponding with White, cautioned him: "Please destroy this letter, as silence is better for us both." Undertaken at various levels throughout the state, including several offices in San Francisco, the fusion effort proved most successful in the southern counties, where White, Jesse D. Carr, and Marion Cannon arranged a series of trades on legislative candidates.[21] White and his allies also persuaded a reluctant Democratic convention in the sixth congressional district to endorse Cannon, the Populist nominee for Congress. Anticipating the election of a dozen or more Populists to the legislature, White had begun to include their votes in his plans to bid for a seat in the United States Senate.[22]

Fusion with the Populists also gave the Democrats a better chance to tap the renewed anti-railroad hostility in California. The Democratic platform adopted at Fresno had dealt harshly with the railroad, leading Huntington to hint that he was prepared to "use the railroad in every way possible to protect its property ... against such agrarian and communistic theories as were enunciated at that convention."[23] Interpreted as a threat of railroad interference in the

[20] White to G. S. Berry, Aug. 21, 1892, English to White, Sept. 7, 1892, White to J. D. Spencer, Aug. 21, 1892, White to Michael F. Tarpey, Sept. 4, 1892, WP.

[21] Bowers to White, Aug. 16, 1892, Carr to White, Aug. 17, 1892, Bowers to White, Sept. 14, 1892, Carr to White, Sept. 18, 1892, C. A. Storke to White, Sept. 24, 1892, Cannon to White, Sept. 29, 1892, WP; SF *Exmr*, Sept. 29, 1892.

[22] White to W. V. Gaffey, Sept. 3, 1892, WP; Ventura *Democrat*, Aug. 26, Sept. 16, 1892.

[23] Huntington interview in SF *Exmr*, Sept. 20, 1892; Winfield J. Davis, *History of Political Conventions in California, 1849–1892* (Sacramento, 1893), pp. 576–81. See also James W. McDill to Harrison, July 29, 1892, James A. Waymire to E. W. Halford, Aug. 29, 1892, HP; LA *Times*, Nov. 14, 1892.

campaign, Huntington's statement added to rising resentment against railroad rates and the inactivity of the state's regulatory commission. Whereas the railroad problem in the 1880's had split the Democrats into anti-monopoly and conservative wings, its resurgence in the early 1890's fostered no immediate divisions in the party. The formerly conservative Democrat Carr, who now urged a vigorous campaign against the railroad, and the Populist-Democrat Cannon, who toured his district "making it red hot for the S.P.R.R.," found themselves united on the issue.[24]

Obvious as the Democrats' gains were, the election returns still came as a severe shock to the Republicans. For the first time in 12 years, and only the second time in 36 years, a Democratic presidential candidate carried California. With a total of 118,174 votes, Cleveland defeated Harrison by 147 votes. Reduced Republican margins in the southern counties and a Democratic plurality in San Francisco of some 6,600 votes were the essential elements in Cleveland's California victory. The Democrats also elected five of seven congressmen, elected 59 legislators to the Republicans' 51, and seemed assured of electing a United States senator. In San Francisco, where an intense struggle for control of the city Democratic organization had been imperfectly resolved only several months before, the Democrats registered a significant recovery from their 1890 disaster. Combined with the party's success in the rest of the nation, the California outcome was, as one Californian remarked, "a glorious victory."[25]

After studying the returns, political leaders acknowledged that much of the credit for Cleveland's having carried California belonged to James B. Weaver and the People's party. Weaver's share of the California vote was only a little more than 9 percent, but it had come in large part from strategic Republican areas. "I vote the People's Party Ticket," read a terse election-day entry in Cornelius

<hr />

[24] Carr to White, Sept. 12, 1892, Cannon to White, Sept. 29, 1892, WP.

[25] Michael F. Tarpey to William C. Whitney, Nov. 9, 1892, Whitney Papers; *California Blue Book, or State Roster, 1893* (Sacramento, 1893), pp. 113–22; Edith Dobie, *The Political Career of Stephen Mallory White: A Study of Party Activities Under the Convention System* (Stanford, Cal., 1927), p. 137. The election figure for congressmen includes the Democrat Warren English, who was not seated until 1894 owing to contested returns. The pre-election struggle in San Francisco can be followed in SF *Exmr*, April 7–20, 1892; White to A. T. Spotts, Sept. 8, 1892, White to J. J. Dwyer, Sept. 9, 1892, WP.

Cole's diary, reflecting the Republicans' losses to the Populists. In Republican counties like Alameda (where Weaver polled 2,118 votes), Los Angeles (3,086), and San Diego (1,519), the Populists had cut into Harrison's pluralities to such an extent that he was unable to overcome the Democrats' wide margin in San Francisco. Weaver had accumulated nearly one-third of his entire vote in the state's seven southernmost counties. The Democrats' estimates of twenty to thirty thousand Populist votes had proved strikingly close to Weaver's final total of 25,311. The Populists had also helped elect Marion Cannon to Congress, and eight Populists had won seats in the legislature. Of these, five had run with Democratic support and two with Republican, while one had campaigned on a straight Populist ticket.[26]

Overall, however, the California People's party had displayed certain weaknesses in the election. A predominantly rural movement, Populism had achieved electoral success only in the state's poorer, native-stock, agricultural sections. Despite the Populists' efforts to appeal to city dwellers, Weaver in the end had garnered only some 2,500 votes in San Francisco, less than 5 percent of the city's total. Similar returns in Sacramento and other urban areas revealed the Populists' failure to attract a significant following in the cities. In Tulare County, for example, the Populist vote ran no higher than 21 percent in any of the towns, whereas it ranged from 38 percent to 75 percent in the rural precincts. The pattern presented party leaders with a gloomy prospect. "Like you," one told the prominent Populist Thomas V. Cator, "I have fears that we have a great task to win a large mass of those city laborers but we must hold out the olive branch and do the best we can for them."[27]

The 1892 campaign, moreover, had exposed internal conflicts in the People's party between those genuinely committed to reform and

[26] Entry for Nov. 8, 1892, Cole Diaries, Cole Papers; *California Blue Book, 1893*, pp. 94, 116; Alexander Saxton, "San Francisco Labor and the Populist and Progressive Insurgencies," *PHR*, 34 (1965): 424; Donald E. Walters, "The Feud Between California Populist T. V. Cator and Democrats James Maguire and James Barry," *PHR*, 27 (1958): 292.
[27] J. L. Gilbert to Cator, Nov. 18, 1893, Cator Papers; Tom G. Hall, "California Populism at the Grass-Roots: The Case of Tulare County, 1892," *Southern California Quarterly*, 49 (1967): 193; Michael Paul Rogin and John L. Shover, *Political Change in California: Critical Elections and Social Movements, 1890–1966* (Westport, Conn., 1970), pp. 10–16.

those who had joined the movement in anticipation of personal gain. These conflicts again surfaced in the period following the election, when a number of prominent Populists opened negotiations with Democrats for federal patronage as the price for past and future assistance. Apparently forgetful of his earlier contention that God had enrolled in the People's party, Stephen Bowers asked Stephen M. White for a consular appointment. "You know," Bowers wrote, "that in my work during the last campaign I indirectly worked for Cleveland, and I rejoiced in his election. I shall never return to the Republicans. . . . So far as the Populists are concerned I think the Democratic party can absorb them."[28]

In January 1893 the internal conflicts erupted in a divisive quarrel that disrupted the People's party momentarily and resulted in the ostracism of one of its founders. Stemming from a disagreement over party policy in the senatorial contest that month, the dispute involved the troublesome question of cooperation with the Democrats, which continually plagued the People's party in California and other states. With 61 votes necessary to elect a senator, the eight Populists and two independents in the legislature held the balance of power between the Republicans and the Democrats. To rally the party and advance his own ambitions, Cator urged the Populist legislators to give him all eight votes until, weary of the stalemate, one of the other parties would elect him. In this strategy he received encouragement from Herman E. Taubeneck, the chairman of the Populist national executive committee; Mrs. Annie L. Digs, a Kansas Populist "deeply anxious" for Cator's election who promised to write the eight legislators on his behalf; and James B. Weaver, who wired the legislators that "millions of true hearts expect the eight to stand by their guns and receive the fire of the plutocrats without a quiver."[29]

Several influential Populists, however, including congressman-elect Marion Cannon, believed their party had incurred an obligation to unite with the Democratic party in electing Stephen M. White sena-

---

[28] Bowers to White, March 17, 1893, E. F. Bernhardt to White, Dec. 22, 1892, WP.
[29] Taubeneck to George D. Gillespie, Dec. 21, 1892, Digs to Cator, Nov. 27, 1892, C. S. Barlow to Cator, Nov. 17, 1892, B. W. Batchelor to Cator, Jan. 3, 1893, Batchelor to Thomas J. Kerns, Jan. 9, 1893, Cator Papers; Weaver telegram quoted in Harold F. Taggart, "The Senatorial Election of 1893 in California," *California Historical Society Quarterly*, 19 (1940): 66.

tor. "But for Mr. White we would probably not have a Congressman from California," Stephen Bowers reminded his fellow Populists. "At least six out of the eight P.P. men in our Legislature were
elected by Dem. votes." White himself could name three Populist
assemblymen who would not have been nominated without his intervention. As it happened, he had already secured enough votes to
win the election without the Populists by persuading one of the independents to vote for him and arranging for a Republican assemblyman to be absent on the day of the balloting. But he needed a show
of Populist support to justify his past action in urging fusion on his
own party. "I have done my part of this work," he angrily told Bowers, "and it remains for the rest to do theirs."[30]

Through December 1892 Cator and his allies labored to brace up
their forces, countering efforts by the Democrats to put pressure on
the eight legislators through the offices of James B. Weaver and William Jennings Bryan of Nebraska.[31] At Cator's request the California Farmers' Alliance lobbied on his behalf. Cator also instructed
John S. Dore, a prominent Populist from Fresno County, to concentrate on keeping the influential Cannon in the fold. At first Dore
reported success. Cannon "will *not* be found working against us, I
am sure," he wrote Cator early in December. But three weeks later
Dore had to confess defeat, reporting that Cannon had changed his
mind and would support White.[32] Worse, he planned to go to Sacramento in January to talk with the Populist legislators. Though
aware that Cannon's defection was a severe blow, the Populists still
hoped for a symbolic victory if their eight men held firm. As Dore
declared, "I want every P.P. man in the legislature to swear by every
drop in his veins to stand by T. V. Cator ... during the *whole length*
of this contest."[33]

[30] Bowers to J. S. Barbee, Dec. 30, 1892, Cator Papers; White to Bowers, Dec. 7,
1892, White to H. C. Dillon, Jan. 9, 1893, WP.
[31] Charles Whitehead to Weaver, Dec. 30, 1892, Weaver to Whitehead, Jan. 11,
1893, Whitehead to White, Jan. 14, 1893, Bryan to White, Jan. 17, 1893, WP; White
to Bryan, Jan. 2, 1893, William Jennings Bryan Papers, Manuscript Division, Library
of Congress.
[32] Dore to Cator, Dec. 3, 1892, Dore to Cator, Dec. 29, 1892, Cator Papers. See also
J. S. Barbee to unnamed correspondent, Jan. 4, 1893, B. W. Batchelor to Cator, Dec. 4,
1892, J. L. Gilbert to Cator, Dec. 27, 1892, Cator Papers.
[33] Dore to Cator, Jan. 3, 1893, Cator Papers.

The strategy failed. During the first ballot on January 18, 1893, Thomas J. Kerns, a Los Angeles Populist who was a close friend of both White and Cannon, voted for the Democratic candidate. Over the shouts of the cheering Democrats, Aaron Bretz, a Populist assemblyman from Alameda County, yelled "Bah! Bah! Bah!," and cries of "Traitor!" and "Scoundrel!" came from other Populists on the floor. Pale and trembling, Bretz leaped to his feet. "I charge that [Kerns] was wrenched from our ranks by the corrupt use of money, and that Marion Cannon was the negotiator." "Liar!" shrieked Cannon from the rear of the chamber. He began to make his way toward Bretz. The sergeant-at-arms meanwhile had moved to protect Kerns, who was the subject of hostile glares from the other Populist legislators. Bretz was not finished. "The Democracy does not grasp the situation here," he shouted. "You are on a slumbering volcano. I—." Interrupted by jeers from the Democrats, Bretz grabbed his hat and stalked out.[34]

The legislature promptly investigated the charges of corruption and, finding no basis for them, censured Bretz and suspended him for one week. Kerns remained under heavy guard, as rumors spread of a possible attempt on his life.[35] But Cator and his supporters had chosen more peaceful means to avenge their defeat. Populist meetings in Sacramento and Los Angeles voted to oust Cannon and Kerns from the California People's party, along with anyone else who shared their desire to cooperate with the Democrats. The Republicans were jubilant. The senatorial quarrel, they believed, had enhanced their prospects for 1894, since the Democrats' only hope "was to keep in with the Populists."[36] For the moment Democratic leaders were too busy celebrating to worry about future contests. John P. Irish expressed a common mood, hailing White's victory as "the beginning of a new era in Democratic politics in this State. Mr. Cleveland will find White a man of brains, not influenced by prejudice and capable of reasoning. He has not made concessions to the political empirics

---

[34] SF *Exmr*, Jan. 19, 1893; SF *Chron*, Jan. 19, 1893; *JS*, 30 sess. (1893), pp. 110–11.

[35] SF *Exmr*, Jan. 21, 31, Feb. 3, 1893.

[36] *Ibid.*, Jan. 19, 26, 31, 1893; Kerns to White, Jan. 28, 1893, Melvin Snow to White, June 1, 1893, WP; J. S. Barbee to Cator, Jan. 26, 1893, Cator Papers.

and will be found in line with the great purposes of the coming Administration."[37]

III

The members of all political parties had reason to be pleased with the legislative session that ran from early January into March, 1893. The struggle between White and Cator, though fraught with a bitterness that would have long-term effects, proved only a momentary distraction to the legislators themselves, as they set about compiling one of the most constructive records in California history. By the time the session had ended, the Republican senate and the Democratic assembly together had passed 301 laws, many of them of major importance. Their work had also attracted nationwide attention, drawing praise from Eastern journals for their "progressive" achievements. At adjournment the San Francisco *Examiner* led California newspapers in calling the session "the most fertile in good measures of any since the passage of the New Constitution." All in all, the 30th session of the California legislature was one of those events that long since should have called into question the stereotyped notions about politics in the Gilded Age.[38]

Though limited in duration to 60 days, a constitutional limitation that measured the period's distrust of its elected officials, the session attacked two broad issues: election reform and the railroad. Building on the advances of two years before, it amended the successful Australian ballot system to make it easier for independent candidates to run for office and to remove all party headings from the ballot, which henceforth would simply list candidates in alphabetical order. A Populist-sponsored bill establishing statewide initiative and referendum succumbed to a dispute over the percentage of voters entitled to initiate legislation, but a similar scheme for the counties, enabling 50 percent of a county's voters to force legislative action, passed without

[37] Irish to Parker[?], Jan. 20, 1893, "Letters Written by John P. Irish to George F. Parker," *Iowa Journal of History and Politics*, 31 (1933): 438; Charles Dwight Willard to Mary F. Willard, Feb. 5, 1893, Willard Papers. Once a bitter enemy, Irish had cooperated closely with White during 1892, motivated in part by recognition of White's growing power and in part by hopes that White would help him win a Senate seat for himself. Irish to White, Nov. 21, 1892, Irish to White, Nov. 26, 1892, WP.

[38] New York *Times*, April 28, 1893; SF *Exmr*, March 16, 1893.

difficulty. Several laws fought corruption in San Francisco. One re-stricted the franchise-granting authority of the Board of Supervisors, long a problem area in the city government, and another set fixed salaries for San Francisco officials to replace the corruption-inducing fee system that had formerly prevailed. The session also established harsher penalties for attempts to bribe or defraud voters, raising the charge for such crimes from a misdemeanor to a felony.[39]

The session's proudest achievement was the Purity of Elections Act. Shepherded through the senate by Guy C. Earl, a young Re-publican attorney from Oakland, and through the assembly by T. W. H. Shanahan, a young Democratic attorney from Shasta County, the act laid down strict rules for the conduct of elections. Its sponsors modeled it on the English Corrupt Practices Act of 1883 and on laws recently adopted in New York and Massachusetts, though they were quick to point out that they had borrowed only the strengths of these laws. In its final form the California act required every candidate for office to choose a five-member committee to oversee his campaign. Within 21 days after the election, this committee had to file as a public document a sworn, itemized statement of all money collected and spent, showing the names of contributors, the amounts contrib-uted, the names of those to whom the committee had paid money, the amount paid to each, and the specific service each had rendered. Such a statement, the act's sponsors predicted, would at one stroke reduce corruption, end the influence of secret campaign contributors over elected officials, and throw the valuable light of publicity over the whole election process.

Unlike its Massachusetts counterpart, the act also set firm limits on campaign expenditures, using a formula based primarily on the term of the office at stake. Under this formula a candidate for a four-year term as governor could spend no more than $1,200, an amount equal to 20 percent of one year's salary. Lower percentages were set for offices with shorter terms. Candidates for the senate and assembly, positions paid on a per diem basis, could spend only $120. Stiff penalties for violations, including fines, imprisonment, and au-

[39] SF *Exmr*, Jan. 14, Feb. 17, 21, 24, March 16, 1893; Erik Falk Petersen, "The Adoption of the Direct Primary in California," *Southern California Quarterly*, 54 (1972): 363–64.

tomatic forfeiture of office, completed the provisions. Signed into law on February 23, 1893, the California Purity of Elections Act sought to curtail the burgeoning power of wealth and to place rich and poor on an equal footing in the race for public office. It also reflected several characteristics that often marked late-nineteenth-century legislation: it was bipartisan in origin and passage; it tried to bring citizens more fully into the political process; it relied on publicity and respect for law to solve the problem; and it attempted to profit from the experience of other states and nations. Though in the end the act failed to accomplish all that its supporters had hoped, it represented a significant stage in the general movement for election reform that extended into the twentieth century. As one newspaper predicted, "It will make the elections of the future much different from those of the past."[40]

The elections act safely through, the legislature turned its full attention to the railroad issue. A large number of railroad-related bills, passed by the Democratic assembly at the beginning of the session, awaited action by the senate. During February and early March the senate debated and then rejected two of these, one removing the present railroad commissioners from office, the other abolishing the commission altogether. The senate also turned down, as too inflexible, an assembly-backed plan to insert a schedule of maximum freights and fares in the state constitution.[41] Angry over the senate's action, the Democrats in the assembly hoped for better results on another bill, which they had passed by a unanimous vote on January 17. Introduced by T. W. H. Shanahan, who divided time between his elections and railroad bills, Assembly Bill No. 10 attacked the familiar problem of railroad taxes, providing for the reassessment and collection of all unpaid taxes for the years 1882 through 1887. As the attorney general noted in a special report shortly after the bill passed the assembly, the Southern Pacific still owed $2,974,-116.23 in back taxes.[42]

[40] SF *Exmr*, Feb. 24, 1893. See also *ibid.*, Jan. 7, 10, 27, Feb. 17–18, 1893; SF *Chron*, Feb. 24, 1893; Geoffrey Blodgett, *The Gentle Reformers: Massachusetts Democrats in the Cleveland Era* (Cambridge, Mass., 1966), pp. 116–17.

[41] *JA*, 30 sess., pp. 202, 871–77; *JS*, 30 sess., pp. 1026–27, 1041; SF *Exmr*, Jan. 27, Feb. 23, 28, March 1, 11, 1893.

[42] SF *Exmr*, Jan. 13–18, 20, 1893; *JS*, 30 sess., pp. 460–64. The railroad tax issue

The Shanahan bill reached the senate on January 19, amid conflicting rumors about the Southern Pacific's position on the tax issue. Some observers believed that the company strongly desired a settlement in order to strengthen its securities, then being pushed in European money markets. Others suggested that since the date was fast approaching for the Central Pacific to pay its huge debt to the federal government, the railroad might want to create a favorable atmosphere in which to negotiate a reduction of the debt. Adding credence to the speculation, the attorney general on January 19 reported an offer by the Southern Pacific to settle the taxes for 1885, 1886, and 1887—amounting according to official figures to more than $2,000,000 —at 60 percent of face value, along with reasonable interest.[43] But then hopes suddenly plunged. On January 24 Charles W. Cross, the former conservative senator and now a railroad attorney, testified before the senate committee on corporations, which was holding public hearings on the Shanahan bill. Reviving old memories of the 1884 extra session, Cross expressed scorn for anti-railroad agitation and bitterly assailed the tax provisions of the 1879 constitution. The Southern Pacific, he told the committee bluntly, "does not owe a single dollar in back taxes."[44]

In the outcry that followed, it quickly became clear that Cross's statement had been designed to test legislative and popular sentiment. Within 24 hours the railroad had retreated to different ground. Southern Pacific attorneys sought out reporters to reaffirm their eagerness to reach a settlement, and the next day Cross himself made a second appearance before the committee to clarify his statement. He had been misunderstood, Cross said. "The railroad wants to be at peace with the people. Three of its projectors and owners have gone from earth, while the two remaining projectors are fast going down the path of life. One of them has no fortune for himself, having given it all to endow a university that is destined to become a great blessing to California. The other of the two living projectors has

---

was divided into three periods: the years 1879–84, when tax officials collected or compromised some taxes and failed to collect most taxes; the years 1885–87, when the railroad paid no taxes at all; and the years after 1887, when the railroad dropped its claim that the federal franchise was included in the assessment and paid all taxes.

[43] SF *Chron*, Jan. 20, March 10, 1893; SF *Exmr*, Jan. 24–26, 31, 1893.

[44] SF *Exmr*, Jan. 25, 1893.

stated publicly that he wants to be let alone to run the railroad as a business proposition." The legislators should seize this opportunity to solve the tax problem, Cross insisted. They should mark paid all taxes before 1885, years when the issue was clouded by the numerous compromises between tax officials and the railroad, and focus instead on settling the taxes for 1885 through 1887. The railroad, for its part, would cooperate with any such settlement. "Now, what more can we do to have you meet us half way and settle this old question? Can any one ask more?"[45]

On January 31 a bill containing Cross's suggestions was introduced in the senate by Russell B. Carpenter of Los Angeles, the respected Republican chairman of the corporations committee and a part-time attorney for the Southern Pacific. It forgave the unpaid taxes before 1885 and ordered that the taxes for 1885–87 be assessed at a new rate, much lower than the one originally in effect. Its opponents promptly countered with a substitute bill, sponsored by J. H. Seawell of Ukiah, that required the reassessment and collection of all taxes since 1879. Arguing that the Seawell bill would only produce further litigation, the senate defeated it by a wide margin but then had somehow to quell the mounting opposition to the Carpenter bill. When 46 Democratic legislators caucused on February 28 and resolved to accept no measure that did not make the railroad pay its taxes to the last dollar, Carpenter saw the need for a conciliatory gesture. On March 3 he amended his bill to include unpaid taxes back to 1882, and in that form it passed easily the next day.[46]

Attention shifted to the assembly, where the Democrats were at work undermining the bill with predictions that it would net the state little more than a million dollars. Cross retorted that the figure would be closer to twice that, "a freight-car load of twenty-dollar pieces," but the assertion changed no minds. Democratic newspapers stepped up their campaign against the bill, and several influential citizens' groups came out against it.[47] The end of the battle near, Max Popper, the chairman of the Democratic state central commit-

[45] *Ibid.*, Jan. 26–27, 31, 1893.
[46] *JS*, 30 sess., pp. 460–64; SF *Chron*, Feb. 1–3, 15–18, 1893; SF *Exmr*, Feb. 25, March 1–5, 1893.
[47] SF *Exmr*, March 7–8, 1893; SF *Chron*, March 8, 1893.

tee, arrived in Sacramento to rally the Democrats. Carpenter's lenient terms "will not do," he announced on arrival. "Why should we accept any compromise? We have the railroad in the door and they know it. They know that sooner or later they must pay all those taxes, and they are anxious to compromise."[48]

Popper, it turned out, was right. Southern Pacific officials were anxious to compromise, though no outsider could be certain of their exact motivation. All resistance crumbled after March 11, when the assembly in a show of strength endorsed the Seawell bill 47 to 21. Carpenter and other senate leaders met to discuss ways to combine the two bills, but the approaching adjournment of the legislature, scheduled for noon on March 14, gave the discussions a frantic air. For once the constitutional limitation on the length of sessions actually worked to the advantage of the anti-railroad forces. On March 13, only hours before adjournment, Carpenter rose in the senate and reported the refusal of the assembly Democrats to make concessions of any kind. Amid hushed silence he moved that the senate accept the entire Seawell bill. Within minutes it was done, and the bill was on its way to the governor.[49]

The Railroad Reassessment Act capped the achievements of the 30th session. Ten months later state officials completed the tax levy called for in the act. Errors in previous assessments still prevented a final settlement for 1886 and 1887, but for the years 1879–85 the railroad owed $2,251,039.78, about three-quarters of which it had paid. In January and April 1894 two further payments, amounting to over $500,000, ended the railroad tax problem as it had been known since the early 1880's.[50] For the Democrats in the legislature, especially those who had participated in the disputes of the anti-monopoly years, the Reassessment Act had special meaning, even though it left unresolved some of the larger questions of state authority that had so preoccupied the anti-monopolists. As the Democratic legislators turned homeward in March 1893, they exchanged satisfied congratulations. Their stands on the elections and railroad issues, among

48 SF *Exmr*, March 9, 1893.
49 *Ibid*., March 10–15, 1893; SF *Chron*, March 14, 1893.
50 SF *Chron*, Jan. 21–24, 1894; SF *Exmr*, Jan. 23, 1894.

others, had kept the party's pledges and had demonstrated its commitment to reform and social responsibility at the state level. The Democrats' work in the legislature had also continued the record of success begun with their victory in California's presidential balloting a few months before. Their spirits soaring, California party leaders noted excitedly that a Democratic administration had taken power in Washington at the same time as the 30th session drew to a triumphant close. Together, the more optimistic among them thought, the two events seemed an auspicious beginning to the era of Democratic hegemony.[51]

IV

As Cleveland assumed office on March 4, 1893, the outlook for Democrats everywhere could scarcely have been brighter. In the 1892 election Cleveland had carried the South, New York, New Jersey, Connecticut, Indiana, and California. He had also become the first Democratic candidate to have carried Wisconsin and Illinois since the 1850's. For the first time since before the Civil War, the Democrats had captured control of the White House and both branches of Congress. It was the most decisive triumph won by either party in twenty years. When Inauguration Day arrived, Democrats across the nation believed they had ended the stalemate that had characterized American politics for two decades. Confident Democratic leaders even predicted that the Republican party would soon disintegrate and disappear. "It is a revolution," said the New York *Times*, "and no Republican can even hope to see his party again in power for a long term of years."[52]

Unfortunately, the Democratic party after 1893 had neither the favorable conditions nor the skillful management necessary to convert its recent gains into permanent sources of support. Within a short time of Cleveland's inauguration, tested by a severe economic depression, the party was thoroughly divided and discredited. Its lead-

[51] SF *Chron*, March 14–15, 1893; SF *Exmr*, March 14–15, 1893; New York *Times*, April 28, 1893; Popper to White, May 9, 1893, Popper to White, May 23, 1893, WP.
[52] New York *Times*, Nov. 10, 1892; SF *Exmr*, March 5, 1893; Woodrow Wilson, "Mr. Cleveland's Cabinet," *Review of Reviews*, 7 (1893): 289; Carl N. Degler, "American Political Parties and the Rise of the City: An Interpretation," *Journal of American History*, 51 (1964): 46–47.

ership, inept and ineffectual when confronted with the problems of
the decade, enfeebled the party organization and alienated the electorate. For these related developments Grover Cleveland bore a large
responsibility. To his party he provided no possibility for compromise
and accommodation; to the nation he offered no hope for escape from
economic hardship. By 1896 Cleveland had become the target of almost unprecedented resentment. Wrote one Californian, who counted
him among the "worse despised" presidents in American history:
"God forgive me for writing the name of cleveland, and I will always
write it hereafter with a little c if I ever write it again."[53]

For California Democrats disillusionment set in almost immediately as a result of the president's patronage policies. Even John P.
Irish, whom Cleveland correctly regarded as his most devoted Coast
follower, found his wishes inexplicably ignored. Flushed with enthusiasm over Cleveland's election victory, Irish had boasted of his friendship with the president-elect and predicted far-reaching influence for
himself. "*I am in a position to deliver,*" he had told patronage-hungry
Democrats. The experience of a few months changed Irish's mind.
Forgetful that the spoils rewarded the faithful and measured an individual's standing in the party organization, Cleveland rejected
Irish's applications for three important offices. "For years I have supported him, propagated his ideas and promoted his leadership...,"
the disconsolate Californian wrote wistfully in March 1893. "I confess
that I would have liked to have been placed in a position of national
prominence by him."[54]

Events also forced White to repudiate his earlier optimism about
the president's policy. "The distribution of patronage in California
will, I fear, come out almost as badly as it did during Mr. Cleveland's
first term," he observed in May. "He seems desirous of settling everything to suit himself, and in this I think he is making a great mistake." Since taking office Cleveland had inadvertently done much to
undermine White's position in the state party. As a San Francisco

---

[53] Unknown correspondent to William Jennings Bryan, Nov. 5, 1896, Bryan Papers.
[54] Irish to White, Nov. 21, 1892, WP; Irish to Parker, March 27, 1893, "Letters
Written by Irish to Parker," pp. 441–42; Jesse D. Carr to Cleveland, Dec. 28, 1892, CP.
Irish was later appointed naval officer of the port of San Francisco, a position with
little prestige or authority.

Democrat informed the new senator, "There is many a sneer here on your lack of influence with the Administration."[55]

The sneers, soon directed at all the members of the Democratic congressional delegation, came in response to Cleveland's action in connection with two of the most significant offices in the state: the collector of the port of San Francisco and the superintendent of the United States Mint. In the former post the president, overlooking impressive recommendations for several other candidates, installed John H. Wise, who as Irish remarked was "an old man, of very infirm habits and in no way a factor in California politics." Though politically impotent himself, Wise had a brother who was a congressman from Virginia. Democrats believed that Cleveland had made the appointment in an effort to please Southern congressmen. But whatever his motive, it offended party leaders and deprived them of a patronage-rich office with which to satisfy the voracious demands of local party members.[56]

More unfortunate from the standpoint of the California party was the president's choice in regard to the second major position, the superintendency of the United States Mint in San Francisco. On May 17, 1893, after personally reviewing the credentials of the various candidates, he named John Daggett to the post. Most California Democrats were aghast, unable for a moment to believe that Cleveland could have made an appointment so completely out of step with the Coast party. Expelled from the party by the anti-monopolists at the 1884 Stockton convention, Daggett was one of the few remaining targets of the intense bitterness felt within the party that year. In late April 1893, when rumors began to circulate that Daggett might be appointed, White and other Democratic leaders sent President Cleveland detailed explanations of the California situation. Daggett's appointment, they pointed out, would gravely undercut the party's record on the railroad question in the 1892 election and during the

[55] White to E. J. Rector, May 24, 1893, J. J. Dwyer to White, May 15, 1893, J. J. Scriver to White, June 22, 1893, WP.
[56] Irish to Parker, March 27, 1893, "Letters Written by Irish to Parker," p. 441; SF *Exmr*, March 19, 1893; Frank McCoppin to Daniel S. Lamont, May 1, 1893, Lamont Papers. For the recommendations given other candidates, see the files for Thomas Beck, William D. English, and Russell Stephens in AP, Cal., Collector of the Port of San Francisco, Treasury Dept., RG 56.

recent session of the state legislature. "While I do not desire to agitate old issues," wrote White, "I feel under these circumstances that it would be highly impolitic to appoint Mr. Daggett." Irish joined the opposition, eager to cooperate with Coast leaders and fearful of the effect of an unpopular choice on his own chances for office. He wired the administration to avoid a "hasty appointment."[57]

But informants in Washington soon reported that Senator Stanford had taken Daggett to the White House for a personal interview with the president. The two men "came away greatly encouraged," it was learned, and a month later Daggett received the appointment.[58] Aware of Stanford's role in the affair, angry Democrats regarded the appointment as "the personal victory of Stanford and the railroad element." Cleveland's action had severely compromised his party in California. White called it "a very serious blunder"; Max Popper was furious. Proud of the party's achievements in the legislature, he resented any action that undermined them. In the period after Daggett's appointment Popper gradually broke off relations with the administration, commenting disgustedly, "If the administration continues to recognize men who have by the past proven their allegiance to the S.P.R.R. in preference to their party, why the future of our party is indeed gloomy."[59]

Barely two months after assuming office, therefore, Cleveland had once again thoroughly frustrated the patronage expectations of the Coast party. To the most important posts he had appointed men whose views were uncongenial to those of the majority of the party and men unconnected with the Democratic leadership on which he would have to rely. His subsequent consent to some of the organization's requests, including a relatively minor position awarded to William D. English, failed to repair the damage. Democrats considered

[57] White to Cleveland, April 21, 1893, CP; Irish to John G. Carlisle, April 6, 1893, AP, Cal., Superintendent of the Mint, Treasury Dept., RG 56. Daggett's file in the Appointment Papers carries Cleveland's handwritten notation "Appoint John Daggett."

[58] Thomas Beck to White, April 15, 1893, WP; SF *Chron*, May 18, 1893. See also Beck to White, May 17, 1893, WP.

[59] White to Barry Baldwin, May 28, 1893, White to T. W. H. Shanahan, May 25, 1893, Popper to White, May 9, 1893, Popper to White, May 23, 1893, White to Hilary A. Herbert, May 18, 1893, James G. Maguire to White, July 7, 1893, WP; SF *Exmr*, May 18, 1893.

English's appointment as surveyor of the port of San Francisco, a post with little prestige and little control of subordinate patronage, only "a bit of balm to the bruised flesh of the California Democracy."[60]

Unhappily for Cleveland, his inept distribution of the spoils proved only the beginning of a severe party crisis that would persist through the remainder of his administration. Under normal conditions Democrats would have quietly nursed their patronage wounds. They had, after all, managed to live with the president's policy during his first term, much as they had grumbled about it. But the troubled 1890's soon gave Democrats a sharper perspective on questions involving party relationships and responsibilities. Time and again in the coming years Cleveland would demand rigid obedience to his wishes without ever understanding that he incurred party obligations in return. Amid difficult problems concerning silver, the tariff, and other issues, Cleveland increasingly lost the sympathy and allegiance of Democrats in California and other states. In the process he shaped American politics for decades to come.

V

For the moment the new president had more immediate worries. On May 3, 1893, in a sudden release of tensions that had accumulated over the previous months, panic struck the stock market, which took its steepest plunge in almost ten years. The following day several businesses closed, and the terrible panic of 1893 had begun. Economic depression, reflected in dwindling sales, slumping business confidence, and rising unemployment, spread swiftly across the country. Precipitated by a sharp drop in investment, particularly in the critical railroad and construction industries, the depression represented a cyclical contraction of unprecedented severity. Depressed agricultural prices, a decline in exports, and a drain on the gold reserve all contributed to the extreme hardship that beset the nation during 1893. In the course of that year one-sixth of the country's railroads went

[60] SF *Exmr*, Nov. 15, 1893; Sidney Lacey to White, April 5, 1893, WP; Michael F. Tarpey to Cleveland, April 17, 1893, James G. Maguire to Cleveland, June 25, 1894, CP. English's appointment brought Stephen J. Field out of political retirement to protest against English as an "offensive, cowardly and base opponent." Field to Don M. Dickinson, Nov. 22, 1893, Dickinson Papers.

into bankruptcy, and some 15,000 business firms and more than 600 banks failed. At the depression's worst point, in mid-1894, the number of unemployed stood at somewhere between two and three million, about 20 percent of the labor force. Continuing through much of the decade, depressed conditions presented a harsh challenge to President Cleveland and the Democratic party. Cleveland himself would later refer to the 1890's as the "luckless years."[61]

Unlike earlier panics, the panic of 1893 reached California within a few months of its beginnings in the East. It struck first among the banks in the southern part of the state, where banking facilities had been overextended during the 1880's. The failure of the Riverside Banking Company on June 14 was followed a week later by the suspension of two banks in San Bernardino, two in San Diego, and one in Anaheim. On June 21 a line of frightened depositors stretched for blocks before the Los Angeles National Bank, which managed to remain open thanks to prompt outside aid. Six other Los Angeles banks, nearly one-third of the city's total, were not so fortunate. In San Francisco, despite the *Examiner*'s proud assertion that "this city remains absolutely unshaken" by the panic, two banks closed in late June and runs began on other financial institutions. During the first eight months of 1893, 21 banks suspended operations in the state. In all, California ranked second to Kansas in the number of commercial and savings bank suspensions.[62]

With the summer banking crisis, depression swept across California. Fearful of further runs, bankers immediately called in available funds and refused requests for new loans. Their action, as the State Board of Agriculture noted, "created havoc throughout the State" and crippled growers of wheat, fruit, and other crops who depended on loans against their harvest. Canneries either closed or slashed orders, adding to the troubles of a fruit industry that already suffered

[61] Grover Cleveland, *Presidential Problems* (New York, 1904), p. 80; Charles Hoffman, *The Depression of the Nineties: An Economic History* (Westport, Conn., 1970), pp. 47–141. See also Rendigs Fels, *American Business Cycles, 1865–1897* (Chapel Hill, N.C., 1959), pp. 184–91; and Charles Hoffman, "The Depression of the Nineties," *Journal of Economic History*, 16 (1956): 137–64.

[62] SF *Exmr*, June 7, 1893; LA *Times*, June 22–26, 1893; Ira B. Cross, *Financing an Empire: History of Banking in California*, 4 vols. (San Francisco, 1927), 2: 571–88, 616–24; Benjamin C. Wright, *Banking in California, 1849–1910* (San Francisco, 1910), pp. 110–11.

from depressed prices and the declining demand in Eastern markets. Prices for wheat and other crops fell to record lows. "This has been an exceedingly unprofitable year for almost every branch of agriculture...," the state board reported. "Never before in the history of agriculture in this State have prices for soil products reached as low figures as during the season just closed."[63]

Conditions worsened during 1894. "Prices of products extremely low," Cornelius Cole wrote in his diary on January 1. "Money very scarce. Hard times." Five days later a severe frost caused extensive damage to the citrus crop. Heavy rains in May and June injured the cherry and peach crops. Winegrowers found that receipts no longer kept pace with expenses. The wine industry, concluded the Board of State Viticultural Commissioners in the fall of 1894, "is probably at the lowest point ever touched since it was first established in this State."[64] Exports from the port of San Francisco dropped far below previous levels; an observer remarked in 1895 that San Francisco harbor was "almost empty of ships."[65] Unemployment mounted as the Southern Pacific Railroad and other companies discharged thousands of workers.[66]

To their dismay, moreover, Californians discovered that their much-publicized climate attracted the nation's unemployed in bad years, just as it drew tourists and health-seekers in good years. The destitute came on foot, in boxcars, and on Southern Pacific freight trains they had commandeered. Newspapers printed worried editorials about California's "tramp problem," while the governor complained of "the rush of unemployed to this State from other localities."[67] Early in 1895 Sacramento residents formed a committee of safety to clear the

[63] "Report of the State Board of Agriculture, February 1, 1894," *J App*, 31 sess. (1894), 2: 11–14; "Horticultural Report," *ibid.* (1895), 5: 23–25; LA *Times*, July 26, 1893.
[64] Entry for Jan. 1, 1894, Cole Diaries, Cole Papers; "Report of the President of the Board of State Viticultural Commissioners," *J App*, 31 sess., 5: 6; "Horticultural Report," *ibid.*, pp. 394–95.
[65] Francis G. Newlands to Henry L. Wright, March 27, 1895, Newlands Papers; Cross, *Financing an Empire*, 2: 618.
[66] LA *Times*, Aug. 6, 1893; SF *Exmr*, Aug. 5, 1893; Ira B. Cross, *A History of the Labor Movement in California*, Univ. of California Publications in Economics, vol. 14 (Berkeley, 1935), p. 217; Gerald T. White, *Formative Years in the Far West: A History of Standard Oil Company of California and Predecessors Through 1919* (New York, 1962), pp. 148–49.
[67] Ventura *Democrat*, Dec. 15, 1893; *JS*, 31 sess., p. 20; SF *Exmr*, Sept. 22, 1893.

city of vagrants. In Los Angeles a local of the Knights of Labor inserted a notice in the union's national publication to discourage the "armies" of unemployed headed for the Southern California area. Officials in Pasadena, whose unemployed population increased suspiciously during the winter months, offered street-repair work in return for meals at a "Cleveland Cafe."[68]

But no city suffered like San Francisco, where the destitute congregated after being forcibly expelled from Sacramento and other communities. Responding to the crisis, San Francisco citizens stretched their local resources to alleviate the hardship. They organized soup kitchens, employment bureaus, and relief committees to aid those without work. By January 1894 some 2,600 men had been given temporary employment in Golden Gate Park, with free box lunches brought from home by the city's elementary schoolchildren, but such emergency measures reached only a small proportion of the estimated 35,000 unemployed in the city. A labor journal asserted that "not for over twenty-five years has San Francisco witnessed such destitution, misery and suffering."[69]

Symptomatic of these conditions was the extent to which California contributed to the armies of unemployed that moved toward the federal capital during the spring and summer of 1894. The state "was perhaps more active in producing these organizations than any other."[70] In April 1894 San Francisco served as the starting point for the largest of all the industrial armies, a 600-man contingent that soon swelled to some 1,500. Gathering recruits as it moved eastward through the heart of the country, the group hoped to persuade Congress to provide government employment on irrigation works in the West.[71] Another large regiment, which its leader called "a living

---

[68] SF *Exmr*, Jan. 6, 1895; Donald L. McMurry, *Coxey's Army: A Study of the Industrial Army Movement of 1894* (Boston, 1929), p. 15, n. 1; Henry Markham Page, *Pasadena: Its Early Years* (Los Angeles, 1964), pp. 182–83.

[69] Cross, *Labor Movement*, p. 217; SF *Exmr*, Jan. 4–9, 1894; SF *Chron*, Jan. 24, 1894.

[70] McMurry, *Coxey's Army*, p. 197; Henry Vincent, *The Story of the Commonweal* (Chicago, 1894), p. 199.

[71] SF *Exmr*, March 28, April 4–7, 1894; John T. Doyle to Abram S. Hewitt, April 19, 1894, Doyle Papers; Donald L. McMurry, "Kelly's Army," *The Palimpsest*, 4 (1923): 325–45; John Ely Briggs, ed., "Tramping with Kelly Through Iowa: A Jack London Diary," *ibid.*, 7 (1926): 129–58.

petition of want and misery, one that cannot be thrown in the waste basket," started from Los Angeles in early March. Several more California armies followed. While none survived the journey intact, they all traveled great distances in their appeal for assistance.[72]

Against this background of unemployment, suffering, and discontent, the Cleveland administration demonstrated the fatal inability of traditional Democratic doctrines to cope with a national crisis. As the dominant party during a depression, faced with unusually complex problems and armed only with rudimentary economic knowledge, the Democrats could hardly have achieved a full measure of success and popularity. But such a conclusion, while central to an understanding of the administration's difficulties, should not obscure the wide field for effective action and spirited leadership that existed in the economic and political conditions of the 1890's. Many Democrats on the state level, where constant contact with the electorate taught the value of flexibility, made the necessary adjustments in party philosophy.

Modifying lifelong commitments to state's rights, administrative economy, and limited government, they advanced remedies that ranged from limited currency expansion and international bimetallism to fundamental revisions in the nation's banking system. In a radical departure from party traditions, some Democrats urged an immediate and massive increase in government expenditures to alleviate want and provide employment for the jobless. "I think a great deal of relief would be occasioned," suggested Senator White of California, "if a number of government buildings which were ordered to be erected quite a while ago were pushed; and then a good deal might be done with reference to harbor improvements and coast defences; even if some of the work turned out to be useless."[73]

But President Cleveland and other national party leaders refused to make similar adjustments. Dogmatic, stubborn, and self-righteous, determined to resist "the unwholesome progeny of paternalism," they

---

[72] SF *Exmr*, March 23, 1894; LA *Times*, March 12–17, 1894; McMurry, *Coxey's Army*, pp. 127–29; Henry Winfred Splitter, "Concerning Vinette's Los Angeles Regiment of Coxey's Army," *PHR*, 17 (1948): 29–36.

[73] White to J. Holloway, April 2, 1894, WP.

clung unwaveringly to the ancient Bourbon faith in "the inexorable laws of finance and trade" that governed human society.[74] "In times like these," explained one Cabinet member, "when every citizen is striving to reduce expenses, the Government, which is merely a collection of citizens, must do the same thing." Another of the president's advisers phrased it more vigorously: the administration's primary task, he declared, was to oppose the unfortunate impulse toward "High Daddy government," to hold fast against " 'reforms' which mean that the Government is to rock the cradle and drive the hearse, weep over the grave and sit up with the widow, and pay every man for cracking his own lice."[75] In keeping with this philosophy—to spur business confidence and reduce outside interference in the natural operation of the economy—Cleveland set to work at the very beginning of his term to end the government purchase of silver.

[74] Cleveland's 1893 inaugural address, in James D. Richardson, ed., *A Compilation of the Messages and Papers of the Presidents, 1789–1897*, 10 vols. (Washington, D.C., 1897), 8: 5822.
[75] J. Sterling Morton to Richard Olney, Aug. 18, 1893, Richard Olney Papers, Manuscript Division, Library of Congress; John P. Irish to Morton, April 27, 1894, CP.

CHAPTER EIGHT

The Democrats in Crisis
1893-1895

JUBILANT DEMOCRATS throughout the country had interpreted their 1892 victory as a mandate for tariff reform. President Cleveland, it appeared, shared their conviction. "The people of the United States," he declared in his inaugural address, "have decreed that on this day the control of their Government in its legislative and executive branches shall be given to a political party pledged in the most positive terms to the accomplishment of tariff reform." In California Senator White, Congressman James G. Maguire, and other Democrats urged an immediate extra session of Congress to respond to the voters' demand. In May 1893, more than two months after the inauguration, they were still pleading with the president to call a special tariff session. "What has become of his boldness since his reelection?" asked the San Francisco *Examiner*. "Who would have believed prior to last November that it would be necessary ... [to] prod Grover Cleveland to activity on the tariff question?"[1]

On June 30, 1893, Cleveland summoned Congress into special session, but not to deal with the tariff. The onset of depression, a rapid decline in the Treasury's gold reserve, and insistent appeals from frightened businessmen had persuaded the president to give precedence to "the silver business." The current economic crisis, he instructed Congress, "is largely the result of a financial policy ... embodied in unwise laws." Its solution was equally simple: the unconditional repeal of the 1890 Sherman Silver Purchase Act, a measure

---

[1] James D. Richardson, ed., *A Compilation of the Messages and Papers of the Presidents, 1789–1897*, 10 vols. (Washington, D.C., 1897), 8: 5824; SF *Exmr*, Nov. 12, 18–19, 1892, May 17, 1893; White to D. A. Ostrom, Nov. 18, 1893, WP.

that required the government to make monthly purchases of silver. Anticipating opposition to repeal from within his own party, Cleveland early advised his subordinates to withhold patronage from "those who bitterly oppose our patriotic attempt to help the country and save our party."[2]

The president quickly encountered stubborn resistance to his policy. To be sure, most proponents of the silver standard disliked the Sherman Act, which they regarded as the product of an unsatisfactory compromise between contending financial views in the Fifty-first Congress. But they would not consent to the act's repeal without the passage of an effective substitute. "I never did think that the Sherman Bill was a wise piece of legislation," wrote Senator White, "but I believe that if it is unconditionally repealed, ... silver will be permanently demonetized."[3] Besides, many silverites argued, the depression stemmed from too little, rather than too much, silver coinage and from the machinations of Eastern and European financiers, who had deliberately precipitated the crisis in order to force repeal. By the time Congress convened in early August, feelings had hardened on both sides of the question. Each side laid sole claim to "sound principles," and respectively blamed the "gold trust" or the "Populist cuckoos" for the nation's economic ills.[4]

In California popular sentiment united behind the pro-silver forces and against Cleveland. A scattering of prominent Democrats and Republicans, as well as some bankers, merchants, and businessmen, spoke in favor of a single gold standard. John P. Irish rushed to

[2] Cleveland to John G. Carlisle, Jan. 22, 1893, in Allan Nevins, ed., *Letters of Grover Cleveland, 1850–1908* (Boston, 1933), pp. 314–15; Richardson, ed., *Messages and Papers of the Presidents*, 8: 5828, 5833–37; Cleveland to Henry T. Thurber, Aug. 20, 1893, CP. The Sherman Act required the Treasury to purchase each month, at the prevailing market price, 4,500,000 ounces of silver. To pay for the silver, the Treasury was instructed to issue legal tender Treasury notes that were redeemable in gold or silver at the Treasury's option.

[3] White to W. M. Eddy, Aug. 22, 1893, WP; LA *Times*, July 2, 1893. Declared Congressman Marion Cannon: "The Sherman act is looked upon rightly as the deadly Enemy of Silver, and we can do nothing for Silver until it is out of the way." Cannon to Cornelius Cole, Sept. 8, 1893, Cole Papers.

[4] White to B. D. Murphy, Aug. 15, 1893, WP; John P. Irish to J. Sterling Morton, undated (probably Sept. 1893, since Morton answered it on Sept. 11, 1893), J. Sterling Morton Papers, Nebraska Historical Society; John R. Berry to Cole, Jan. 29, 1893, Cole Papers.

Washington to asisst the Cleveland lobby in Congress.[5] But in general men of all parties and occupations expressed determined opposition to the unconditional repeal of the Sherman Act. The state's mining traditions and its trade relations with nearby silver-mining regions helped explain this sentiment, as did the spreading conviction, strengthened by the depression, that increased silver coinage would raise wages, boost farm prices, and restore prosperity. By mid-1893 silver had already acquired the special aura that so molded the politics of the decade. As a panacea that promised speedy relief from hardship, it had won a considerable following in urban as well as agricultural areas. In late July a pro-silver mass meeting filled San Francisco's Metropolitan Temple, while a thousand other people, unable to gain admittance, listened to silver speeches in front of the United States Mint. The gathering called on the state's congressional delegation to vote against the repeal measure unless it also provided for "the free and unlimited coinage of silver at the ratio of 16 to 1."[6]

Mass meetings in other communities, from Colusa to Ventura, echoed this demand. Free-coinage petitions deluged California congressmen, including one signed by five thousand residents of San Francisco. The president of the state branch of the American Federation of Labor argued against unconditional repeal, as did the San Francisco Chamber of Commerce.[7] Fusion Congressman Marion Cannon toured Southern California speaking against the extra session, which he labeled Cleveland's Circus. Leading Republican figures like Morris M. Estee and Sen. George C. Perkins worked vigorously for silver.[8] Harrison Gray Otis's *Times* and Michael H. De Young's *Chronicle* joined the Democratic *Examiner* and Los Angeles

[5] Irish to Parker, Aug. 29, 1893, "Letters Written by John P. Irish to George F. Parker," *Iowa Journal of History and Politics*, 31 (1933): 446; Irish to Daniel S. Lamont, July 19, 1893, Lamont Papers; John H. Wise to White, July 23, 1893, White to Collis P. Huntington, Sept. 1, 1893, WP; J. L. Rathbone to Cleveland, Aug. 2, 1893, Frank McCoppin to Cleveland, Sept. 9, 1893, CP; *Congressional Record*, 53d Cong., 1st sess., pp. 284, 1369.

[6] SF *Exmr*, July 23, 1893.

[7] Ventura *Democrat*, July 7, 21, 1893; *Congressional Record*, 53d Cong., 1st sess., pp. 1400–1401, 1670, 1701; White to W. M. Glenn, Aug. 15, 1893, WP; San Francisco Chamber of Commerce to Cleveland, July 18, 1893, CP.

[8] Ventura *Democrat*, July 28, 1893; Harold F. Taggart, "The Party Realignment of 1896 in California," *PHR*, 8 (1939): 436; Perkins to Cole, Sept. 21, 1893, Cole Papers.

Herald to oppose unconditional repeal. Senator White spoke for most Democrats: "The Democratic party has uniformly in California favored silver, and I am not prepared to sacrifice my individual judgment merely because Mr. Cleveland, or somebody else in power, may tell me to do so. Our platforms have never deviated upon this subject; and if we were right upon these numerous occasions, he is wrong now."[9]

The extra session opened in Washington on August 7, 1893, and two weeks later, as anticipated, the repeal bill easily passed the House of Representatives by a vote of 239 to 108. Five of the seven California congressmen (two Democrats and three Republicans) voted against repeal. The other two, Marion Cannon and Thomas J. Geary, a Democrat, addressed public letters to their constituents in which they explained that the repeal of the Sherman Act cleared the way for free silver, but the explanation did not save them from popular indignation. Cannon in particular was denounced as "a pusillanimous, truckling, all-round tool for Grover Cleveland." Of the six pro-silver amendments offered by Richard P. Bland of Missouri, a majority of the California congressmen had favored all except one. For the Democratic party as a whole, the House vote had ominous implications: while most Republicans had supported repeal, the party of Cleveland had divided 138 to 78 on the silver issue.[10]

In the Senate, meanwhile, Arthur Pue Gorman of Maryland led Democrats in an attempt to arrange a compromise that would satisfy both sides and avoid an irrevocable split in their party. In late October, as the final vote neared, 37 of the 44 Democratic senators signed a letter in favor of such a compromise. But the president, determined to secure unconditional repeal, rejected these efforts and used patronage, pressure, and persuasion to force the bill through the Senate.[11]

---

[9] White to D. A. Ostrom, Nov. 18, 1893, WP; LA *Times*, Aug. 9, 1893; SF *Chron*, July 1, 1893; SF *Exmr*, July 23, 1893; Los Angeles *Herald*, Sept. 24, 1893, clipping in WP.

[10] San Diego *Vidette*, n.d., quoted in Ventura *Democrat*, Dec. 1, 1893; *Congressional Record*, 53d Cong., 1st sess. (Aug. 28, 1893), pp. 1004–8; SF *Exmr*, Nov. 5, 1893; White to Irish, Jan. 22, 1894, WP.

[11] Entry for Aug. 18, 1893, Charles S. Hamlin Diary; Irish to Daniel S. Lamont, Sept. 29, 1893, Lamont Papers. California congressmen found a close relationship between their votes on silver and their patronage allotments. See, e.g., White to D. A. Ostrom, Nov. 18, 1893, White to Thomas Beck, July 4, 1893, White to L. L. Boone, Aug. 31, 1893, WP.

"Cleveland is absolutely bull-headed," wrote White, "and is determined to put the country upon a mono-metallic basis and drive silver absolutely out of circulation." As one Cabinet member phrased the administration's attitude, "The President is right," the pro-silver coalition "is wrong, and Right ought to triumph over Wrong, without asking permission from anybody or agreeing to any compromise."[12]

On October 30, with both California senators voting against it, the repeal bill passed the Senate by a margin of 48 to 37. Once again the administration owed its success to Republican support, for the Democrats divided evenly on the question. In the end, too, it had been conscientious silver men like Stephen M. White who had helped make Cleveland's quick victory possible. Joining others to head off a threatened silverite filibuster, White explained: "I do not wish any stones to be placed in the way of speedy action. The country has a right to demand that something be done" to alleviate the depression. Late in the afternoon of November 1, 1893, Cleveland signed the repeal bill into law. He had won a significant victory, but one that would prove very costly for the Democratic party and himself.[18]

II

At first hopefully, then with mounting impatience, Californians awaited the promised economic revival. Impatience changed swiftly to hostility, and in some cases hatred, as it became evident that silver repeal, Cleveland's panacea, had failed to relieve the depression. Fervid silverites depicted Cleveland as the head of a monetary conspiracy committed to gold and the selfish interests of Eastern financiers. Political moderates, Democrats as well as Republicans, resented the president's negative approach to economic hardship. Relying on the repeal of one law, he had offered no constructive program to remedy the economic situation. "The chief criticism against the policy of the administration," noted the Los Angeles *Times*, "has been

[12] White to B. D. Murphy, Aug. 15, 1893, WP; J. Sterling Morton to Richard Olney, Oct. 22, 1893, Olney Papers; J. Rogers Hollingsworth, *The Whirligig of Politics: The Democracy of Cleveland and Bryan* (Chicago, 1963), pp. 16-17.

[18] White to T. V. O'Brian, Aug. 22, 1893, WP; *Congressional Record*, 53d Cong., 1st sess. (Oct. 30, 1893), p. 2958; SF *Exmr*, Nov. 2, 1893; David J. Rothman, *Politics and Power: The United States Senate, 1869-1901* (Cambridge, Mass., 1966), pp. 102-5.

that it has no policy in regard to the financial question, except a negative one. This will not satisfy the people."[14]

Other troubles emerged with time. A tactical error of vast consequence, Cleveland's demand for immediate and unconditional repeal focused national attention on the silver issue, implicitly reinforcing the silverites' belief in the issue's overriding importance. It also ended the Democrats' hopes of submerging their differences on silver in a campaign to reform the tariff. Years later, as the decade drew to a close, Coast Democrats would speculate on what might have happened to the party if Cleveland, like William McKinley in 1897, had sidestepped the volatile silver issue and called a special session devoted to the tariff. For the moment, they watched for signs of economic recovery and angrily recalled their own willingness to subordinate silver to the tariff in the 1892 campaign.

The events of 1893 created a worrisome dilemma for individual Democrats. Their jubilation over the previous year's victory had given way to a growing feeling of discouragement and despair. Under attack from every direction, and identified with the president's unpopular policies, they faced a difficult choice. They could continue to endorse Cleveland's policies, and leave themselves politically vulnerable at home, or they could repudiate the head of their party, and align themselves with the views of their constituents. It was a hard decision to make, involving deep-seated loyalties to the national party, and there were of course those who postponed it or chose to remain silent. But by the end of 1893 every Democrat in the state had been compelled to reexamine his position in relation to the actions of the national administration.

This crucial process was earliest reflected in the columns of the San Francisco *Examiner*, which on September 13, 1893, printed an editorial that marked a major shift in policy. Entitled "The New Cleveland," the editorial charged that the president had "ceased to be a Democrat": "He is no longer the same man who earned the admiration and confidence of the people by the sturdy Democracy of his first term." A review of his actions during 1893, claimed the *Examiner*, revealed that Cleveland had maintained the protective tariff,

[14] LA *Times*, Aug. 29, 1893; SF *Chron*, Oct. 31, 1893.

guarded the gold standard, perpetuated the spoils system through "the use of patronage to bribe or coerce Congressmen into obedience to the Executive," and centralized power in his own hands "to an extent that no other Chief Magistrate has dared to attempt." As a result, "The Democratic party feels that it has been cheated." Concluded the editorial: "The first duty of this Democratic Congress—a duty that it should attend to before it passes a financial, tariff or any other bill—is to bring Grover Cleveland to his senses."[15]

Coming as it did from the most important Democratic spokesman on the Pacific Coast, the editorial crystallized the unspoken opinions of California party members. A few promptly endorsed it; it was read into the *Congressional Record*; and it was echoed by editorials in Democratic papers like the Los Angeles *Herald* and Stockton *Mail*. A larger number of Democrats agreed with the Oakland *Times*, which concurred with the *Examiner*'s criticism but advised that nothing could be gained for the time being from an assault on the president.[16] Finally, the *Examiner*'s editorial spurred many party members to rush to Cleveland's defense.

The editors of the Woodland *Democrat*, Santa Barbara *Independent*, Auburn *Herald*, Fresno *Expositor*, and Antioch *Ledger* assured Cleveland of their continued support. "We still have confidence in your wisdom, integrity and patriotism," one told the president.[17] Other representatives of the Coast press also rallied to Cleveland's side. Several Democratic county committees adopted resolutions endorsing the administration's actions. John P. Irish, who backed everything Cleveland did, advised the president that the *Examiner* editorial meant "the Administration forces within the party must solidly form, be recognized and fight, as under other Administrations that have been attacked by traitors."[18]

The importance of the entire incident lay primarily in what it

---

[15] SF *Exmr*, Sept. 13, 1893. The Republican *Chronicle* promptly retorted: "He is not a 'new Cleveland,' as the *Examiner* calls him, but the same mediocre, slow-witted, obstinate and unschooled Cleveland that he always was" (Sept. 14, 1893).

[16] Excerpts from these papers in SF *Exmr*, Sept. 23, 1893.

[17] Edward E. Leake to Cleveland, Sept. 23, 1893, CP.

[18] Irish to Cleveland, Sept. 12, 1893, Edward E. Leake to Cleveland, Nov. 29, 1893, Thomas Beck to Cleveland, Sept. 25, 1893, S. R. Smith and Oscar Robinson to Cleveland, Sept. 30, 1893, CP; Irish to J. Sterling Morton, Oct. 30, 1893, Morton Papers.

revealed about the dilemma faced by state Democratic parties in the mid-1890's. To most Democrats, however much they disagreed with the administration's policies, a break with the national leadership was a misfortune to be avoided. Partly from traditional fealty, and partly from an awareness of the requirements of practical politics, they were convinced that close relations between national and state organizations must be carefully protected. If Cleveland often overlooked the inseparable connection between principle and party, his followers in California never forgot it. They had learned, many of them during the bitter factionalism of the early 1880's, that the translation of principles into action depended on the smooth and energetic operation of the party.

Knowing this, the vast majority of Democrats strove continuously in the mid-1890's to find common ground with the Cleveland administration. For them, the decision to desert the administration would come neither as early nor as easily as it had for the *Examiner*. As Stephen M. White declared, "We either have a party, or we constitute an affair that cannot be called either an organization or a democratic institution, and if we pretend to be a party we will be forced to stand by our administration." Democrats may criticize their president, White reminded Republicans on another occasion, "but do not flatter yourselves that any process of distintegration is at work here, or that I and my colleagues contemplate suicide.... We are prepared to stand by the Democratic Administration."[19] In California the history of Cleveland's second term was in large part the story of the earnest efforts of individual Democrats to remain loyal to Grover Cleveland and his administration.

III

No single event after 1893 caused the failure of these efforts. A marked economic upturn might have rescued the party, but the depression continued to feed popular discontent and the Cleveland administration became ever more conservative and rigid. Its supporters saw themselves as the last remaining bulwark in defense of the Constitution and sound government. Massed against them, they be-

[19] White to Irish, Aug. 5, 1894, WP; SF *Chron*, Feb. 22, 1894.

lieved, were the forces of radicalism, the "silver bullionaires, industrial tramps and train wreckers, dreamers, dunces, cracked women,
bums, bullies and loafers, who want to repudiate their own debts
and divide the property of the thrifty and well-ordered." If they were
unpopular now, the conservatives constantly reassured each other,
history would vindicate them and their beleaguered president. "That
his integrity of purpose and his wisdom will endure to the end no
one doubts," exulted an ardent Cleveland man, "and his name will
gain in splendor in the high company of the great who have held
fast to the eternal verities in crises when the weak, venal and ignorant have clothed themselves in dreams, or profited by pretenses."
Alone in a hostile world, convinced of their righteousness, the Cleveland Democrats battled in the 1890's for the "eternal verities": property, sound money, limited government, and the Constitution. For
many of them it was an exhilarating experience.[20]

This outlook fostered policies that resulted in a rapid decline in
the California Democrats' fortunes. Evident in the administration's
treatment of the currency, tariff, and labor issues between 1893 and
1895, it early appeared in Cleveland's handling of the Hawaiian
controversy. In the years since the 1875 reciprocity treaty between
Hawaii and the United States, California business interests had established close ties with the islands.[21] When the revolution of January
1893 ousted the Hawaiian queen, most Coast newspapers demanded
prompt annexation. They marshaled commercial and patriotic arguments to overwhelm those who cautioned against assimilating Hawaii's polyglot population.[22] "Hoist the Stars and Stripes," proclaimed
the *Examiner*. "It is a case of manifest destiny."[23] The governor, the

---

[20] Irish to Morton, Aug. 5, 1895, Irish to Morton, Jan. 31, 1895, Morton Papers.
See also Irish to Lamont, Sept. 29, 1893, Lamont Papers.

[21] California's relationship with the islands is examined in Merze Tate, *The United
States and the Hawaiian Kingdom: A Political History* (New Haven, Conn., 1965);
and Jacob Adler, *Claus Spreckels: The Sugar King in Hawaii* (Honolulu, 1966).

[22] For opposition to annexation, see White to J. C. Maccabe, March 2, 1894, WP;
White to Walter Q. Gresham, Dec. 24, 1893, Gresham Papers; Irish to Cleveland,
April 15, 1893, CP; LA *Times*, Jan. 29, Feb. 4, 1893.

[23] SF *Exmr*, Jan. 29, Feb. 2, 1893. Annexation sentiment centered in San Francisco, but it was also significant elsewhere. Of San Francisco's seven newspapers, only
one opposed annexation, and one—the *Chronicle*—wavered on the issue. Tate, *United
States and the Hawaiian Kingdom*, p. 195; SF *Chron*, Feb. 18, April 7, 1893. For
a synopsis of newspaper opinion around the state, see SF *Exmr*, Feb. 4, 1893.

legislature, and the San Francisco Board of Trade voiced similar sentiments. On four different occasions the San Francisco Chamber of Commerce passed resolutions urging "speedy annexation."[24]

In the course of 1893, however, President Cleveland withdrew an annexation treaty from the Senate, appointed a special commissioner to investigate American involvement in the Hawaiian revolution, and ultimately decided that duty required the restoration of the deposed queen. The last stage of this policy failed when the new Hawaiian government politely refused to abdicate in favor of the queen. Prompted by a mixture of admirable principle and blundering naïveté, Cleveland's actions angered and bewildered annexation-minded Californians. The administration, charged the Democratic Congressman Thomas J. Geary, had made "a bad muddle" of the Hawaiian matter. In the next election, Geary complained, it would be difficult "to explain away the stupidity that has characterized the management of this affair. The issue is a pretty big one in my State, and for the life of me I cannot imagine what I am going to say to my people."[25]

Cleveland's policies in connection with the monetary question also met bitter resistance in California. The frequent use of bond sales to buttress the gold standard, including an 1895 issue to a private syndicate headed by J. P. Morgan, aroused widespread discontent and increased suspicions that Cleveland had succumbed to the influence of Eastern financiers.[26] In March 1894, moreover, the president sternly rejected another chance for compromise when he vetoed a bill to authorize the coinage of the silver seigniorage in the Treasury. Ignoring advice that the silver Democrats considered the bill "a great opportunity to unify the party by doing something for their side of the question," Cleveland incensed supporters of the silver standard and once again raised charges that he followed a "purely obstructive"

[24] JS, 30 sess. (1893), p. 268; JA, 30 sess., pp. 256–57, 348; Edward B. Pond to Cleveland, June 1, 1893, Pond to Cleveland, July 18, 1893, W. H. Dimond to Cleveland, Jan. 30, 1894, CP; SF Exmr, Feb. 1–2, 12, 1893.
[25] Geary testimony before House Committee on Foreign Affairs, in SF Exmr, Aug. 5, 1894; Julius W. Pratt, Expansionists of 1898: The Acquisition of Hawaii and the Spanish Islands (Baltimore, 1936), p. 145; Tate, United States and the Hawaiian Kingdom, pp. 228–68.
[26] SF Chron, Feb. 16, 1895; SF Exmr, Feb. 10, 1895.

policy toward the depression.[27] The president's actions throughout had been consistent and courageous, but they had little effect on the economic situation and exacerbated the divisions within the Democratic party. Unhappily for Cleveland, they also intensified the silver sentiment he had intended to dampen.

The seigniorage veto, added to continuing resentment against the repeal of the Sherman Act, crippled the administration's prospects for tariff reform in 1894. The opportunity for genuine reform, seasoned politicians knew, had vanished the previous year with Cleveland's decision to give the monetary question priority over the tariff. A troublesome matter at any time, tariff reform demanded a spirit of unity and enthusiasm that the Democratic party, torn and discouraged by the silver controversy, no longer possessed. Recent events had encouraged a revival of Democratic localism that now found expression in an emasculated tariff bill. "Of course, I am alive to California interests," acknowledged Senator White, voicing the localistic aims of many members of Congress, "and I am seeking to make the reductions there as small as possible."[28]

Under intense pressure from concerned constituents, White and his fellow Coast representatives backed away from extensive reform. Hoping for a few reductions of symbolic importance, they fought to place coal and iron on the free list. That position, involving industries in which Californians had only a small stake, took little courage, but White also worked vigorously for free wool, to the anger and dismay of many Coast sheep ranchers. Beyond that, the delegation's reform ardor did not extend. Duties on raisins, prunes, figs, oranges, lemons, sugar, brandy, wine, and nuts—frequently the products of small farmers as well as large enterprises—all were strenu-

<hr>

[27] George Gray to Cleveland, March 1894, CP; SF *Exmr*, March 30, 1894; Ventura *Democrat*, Feb. 9, 1894; LA *Times*, March 30, 1894; Horace Samuel Merrill, *Bourbon Leader: Grover Cleveland and the Democratic Party* (Boston, 1957), pp. 176–85.
[28] White to Henry C. Gesford, Feb. 22, 1894, White to J. Marion Brooks, July 31, 1894, WP; SF *Exmr*, Jan. 9, 1894. Too often treated as an isolated incident, the tariff debate instead came at the end of a series of events that battered the party and fostered the revival of Democratic localism. Understandably perhaps, as their national prospects deteriorated Democrats became increasingly unwilling to endanger their positions in local districts. This problem was compounded by the extremely narrow Democratic margin in the Senate, which meant that a tariff bill had to satisfy nearly everyone in order to pass.

ously defended.[29] Caught in a difficult situation, the delegation found little guidance or understanding at the White House. Cleveland's one attempt to provide leadership, a public letter that bluntly accused Democratic senators and congressmen of "party perfidy and party dishonor," overlooked his own responsibility for the party's tariff problems and embittered Democrats who pointedly reminded the president of his past evasions on the issue. In mid-August of 1894 the unpopular Wilson-Gorman tariff bill passed Congress, and Cleveland let it become law without his signature. Reflecting divisions within the party, the law supplied a dismal conclusion to the Democrats' tariff reform crusade.[30]

In the meantime, even as Congress and the president struggled over the tariff, the administration had become deeply involved in a major labor dispute that had paralyzed the western half of the nation. On June 26, 1894, Eugene V. Debs's American Railway Union joined the striking employees of the Pullman Palace Car Company, who had walked out in May. With the participation of the ARU, which refused to handle Pullman cars, the strike quickly extended into 27 states and territories, and involved nearly all railroad workers west of Chicago.[31] In California the strike began in Oakland at noon on June 27. By the following day it had completely halted overland traffic on the Santa Fe, Central Pacific, and Southern Pacific systems in the state. "As the matter stands today," noted the San Francisco *Examiner* on June 28, "this State is absolutely isolated from the rest of the world so far as railroad service is concerned."[32]

The strike centered in Sacramento, Oakland, and Los Angeles, where the important terminals and railroad shops were located. Last-

[29] White to Union Iron Works, April 3, 1894, White to J. H. Root, March 29, 1894, White to A. B. Butler, Feb. 2, 1894, White to W. H. Wright, Feb. 6, 1894, White to A. F. Parker, March 1, 1894, White to John T. Doyle, March 5, 1894, White to H. T. Hatch, March 15, 1894, WP.

[30] Cleveland to William L. Wilson, July 2, 1894, in Nevins, ed., *Letters of Cleveland*, pp. 354–57; Festus P. Summers, *William L. Wilson and Tariff Reform* (New Brunswick, N.J., 1953), pp. 174–207; John R. Lambert, *Arthur Pue Gorman* (Baton Rouge, La., 1953), pp. 200–238; White to Edward White, July 25, 1894, White to John T. Gaffey, July 26, 1894, WP; Los Angeles *Herald*, July 25, 1894, quoted in LA *Times*, July 31, 1894.

[31] Almont Lindsey's *The Pullman Strike: The Story of a Unique Experiment and of a Great Labor Upheaval* (Chicago, 1942), offers a detailed account of the strike. See also Stanley Buder, *Pullman: An Experiment in Industrial Order and Community Planning, 1880–1930* (New York, 1967), pp. 147–201.

[32] SF *Exmr*, June 28, 1894.

ing nearly a month, it affected approximately 11,500 railway employees, who lost about one million dollars in wages. Southern Pacific officials estimated the company's losses at $200,000 a day during
the strike.[33] Business and agriculture suffered extensive damage. San
Francisco merchants, cut off from supplies and markets, complained
of "this damnable tie-up." As one lamented, "Everything seems to
conspire to eat into the best interests of our good State this year
(I won't say since your friend Grover took reins)."[34] In Los Angeles
the strike injured commercial interests and threatened to cause a
fuel shortage. "If it continues much longer...," predicted the secretary of the Chamber of Commerce on July 9, "it is going to be ruin-
ous to business of all kinds."[35]

Occurring at the height of the Northern California fruit season,
the stoppage created particular hardship for fruit growers. It stranded
some two hundred cars of fruit on the tracks between Sacramento
and Ogden, Utah, and prevented shipments to Eastern markets.
Sacramento, Placer, San Jose, and Fresno counties reported heavy
damage to the pear, peach, apricot, and plum crops. "In the Valley
of California today there are millions of dollars worth of fruit destined to perish & rot for want of transportation," wrote one Californian.[36] After the strike ended the State Board of Agriculture estimated the loss to fruit growers at more than one million dollars. "The
evil caused by that railroad tie-up will not be eradicated for years to
come," the board asserted.[37]

Yet, in the midst of these dislocations, most Californians lined up
behind the strikers and against the railroad. The virtual unanimity
of the Coast press in this regard led the *Nation* to remark that there
"does not seem to be a voice raised there in favor of law and civil

[33] Ira B. Cross, *A History of the Labor Movement in California*, Univ. of California Publications in Economics, vol. 14 (Berkeley, 1935), pp. 219–20; LA *Times*,
July 4, 1894.
[34] Edward Mills to Jackson A. Graves, July 6, 1894, Jackson A. Graves Papers,
Huntington Library.
[35] Charles Dwight Willard to Samuel Willard, July 9, 1894, Willard Papers; LA
Times, June 30, 1894.
[36] John T. Doyle to Abram S. Hewitt, June 30, 1894, Doyle Papers; SF *Exmr*,
June 30, 1894; SF *Chron*, July 7, 1894; "Horticultural Report," *J. App*, 31 sess.
(1895), 5: 397–99.
[37] "Report of the State Board of Agriculture, February 1, 1895," *J App*, 32 sess.
(1897), 2: 20–21; Porter Brothers Company to Jackson A. Graves, July 18, 1894,
Graves Papers.

government; and the inconvenience and losses to which the public are subjected seem to be accepted willingly, so long as the railroads suffer quite as much or more." The "peculiarity" of the California situation, agreed another observer, was this almost unanimous sympathy with the strikers: "I mean not only the sympathy of what are commonly called the working classes, but that of farmers whose fruit was rotting on the ground, men who were kept from their daily work, business men whose prosperity was imperiled by the strike, professional men who in the ordinary relations of life are counted upright and intelligent, manufacturers who were threatened with ruin, hosts of persons who ordinarily have no direct relations with 'organized labor' or much sympathy with it. Men such as these, with few exceptions, felt a profound sympathy with the strikers, and hoped that they might win."[38]

Although somewhat overdrawn, such observations caught the anti-railroad mood on the Pacific Coast. On July 4, 1894, three regiments of the National Guard, dispatched by the governor, arrived in Sacramento to clear the railroad yards and depot of strikers. "Within two hours," noted a reporter on the scene, "soldiers and strikers were wandering off arm in arm, drinking together, laughing together and having a general good time." As Guard commanders looked on in helpless dismay, the strikers furnished water and lemonade to the exhausted troops. The following day many soldiers sported ARU badges on their uniforms.[39] As one newspaper commented during the strike, "The Southern Pacific was not loved before; it is hated now, and despised, too."[40]

The federal government displayed an entirely different attitude toward the strikers. Under the direction of the attorney general, Richard Olney, a lawyer deeply devoted to the protection of property interests, the Cleveland administration moved swiftly to break the Pullman strike. In California, despite abundant evidence of the strik-

[38] *Nation*, July 12, 1894, quoted in Lindsey, *Pullman Strike*, p. 249; Thomas R. Bacon, "The Railroad Strike in California," *Yale Review*, 3 (1895): 244–45; Cross, *Labor Movement*, p. 220; Ventura *Democrat*, July 6, 1894; SF *Chron*, June 30, 1894.

[39] SF *Exmr*, July 5, 1894; Sacramento *Weekly Union*, July 6, 1894. For the governor's actions during the strike, see the folder of strike-related telegrams in the Markham Papers.

[40] SF *Exmr*, July 12, 1894.

ers' peaceful conduct—"This looks more like a fair than a desperate strike," remarked a United States marshal when he first reached Sacramento[41]—Olney used injunctions and federal troops to ensure the unobstructed passage of the mails and to help the railroads restore overland service. On July 2, a day before soldiers were ordered to Chicago, he sent six companies of troops to Los Angeles. Arriving by special train, the soldiers "gazed with considerable surprise at the peaceful scene before them. There were no derailed trains, or torn up tracks, or demolished depots, or howling mobs of strikers as they had been led to expect."[42]

Eight days later two cavalry companies and four artillery batteries were dispatched to Sacramento, and troops also occupied the railroad yards at Oakland. Trains began to move under guard from Los Angeles on July 6 and from Sacramento on July 14. On July 21, after a stormy meeting, the Sacramento ARU admitted defeat in the state.[43] Some Coast figures welcomed the outcome. Alarmed by labor "radicalism" of any kind, Harrison Gray Otis thought the country had narrowly escaped "national disorder and universal chaos." Stephen J. Field praised Cleveland's bold handling of the "monstrous strikes." Assuring the administration of wide support for its policy, John P. Irish cited a letter he had just received from a California farmer: "I was touched," Irish wrote, "at the simple picture of listening for a train because its roar declared that the law lived. He voices what is in the heart of every patriot here."[44]

---

[41] *Ibid.*, July 2, 1894.

[42] LA *Times*, July 5, 1894. A local paper called the move "entirely farcial and unnecessary" (Ventura *Democrat*, July 6, 1894). Olney did receive inflammatory telegrams from his representatives in Los Angeles, including one stating that "strikers' sympathizers, mostly called People's Party men, have been arriving here for ten days; have from two to three thousand guns and are organizing." But the first of these telegrams arrived two days after the order to send troops to the city. Olney, moreover, had immediately checked the veracity of the dispatch and learned that it was false. Later he reprimanded its author. *Appendix to the Annual Report of the Attorney-General of the United States for the Year 1896* (Washington, D.C., 1896), pp. 22–23; Olney to George J. Denis, Aug. 14, 1894, Olney Papers.

[43] Cross, *Labor Movement*, p. 277; SF *Exmr*, July 11–22, 1894; LA *Times*, July 6–8, 1894. Only after the arrival of the federal soldiers did serious violence occur in the California strike. On July 11 the first overland train to leave Sacramento was derailed, killing the engineer and the five army privates detailed to guard it. SF *Exmr*, July 12, 1894.

[44] Otis to Thomas R. Bard, July 18, 1894, Bard Papers; Field to Don M. Dickinson, Sept. 23, 1894, Irish to Henry T. Thurber, July 17, 1894, David Starr Jordan to

Most Californians, however, resented the administration's interference on behalf of the railroads. Newspapers assailed Cleveland's policy, which they viewed as additional proof of his sordid alliance with Eastern business interests. A federal official alerted Attorney General Olney that there was "an overwhelming sentiment of public feeling, not only against the railroads, but against the Government as well, and we were on the eve of an open rebellion.... This intense feeling against the Government was owing to a conviction among much the larger portion of the people, that the laws of the United States were being enforced with great severity against laboring people and not against the corporations." Discontent grew when subsequent testimony disclosed that many of the deputy marshals sent to Sacramento had been appointed on the recommendation of the Southern Pacific.[45]

To the strikers themselves, and their numerous sympathizers, Cleveland and Olney were to blame for the strike's total failure in the state. Instead of the victory they had expected, the strikers found more than one hundred of their men arrested and all ARU members blacklisted by the Southern Pacific. "We are shadowed every day in our own city to see that employment is not obtained," complained the officers of the ARU local in San Francisco.[46] The labor element, now increasingly hostile to the Democratic party, helped swamp the party's state ticket in the 1894 election and also contributed heavily to the landslide San Francisco triumph of the Populist candidate for mayor, who had befriended the strikers.[47]

Most important, Cleveland's approach to the strike had added to the general belief that the federal government was unresponsive and unsympathetic to the economic plight of the people. This belief,

---

Cleveland, July 18, 1894, CP. See also White to Cleveland, July 8, 1894, White to J. Marion Brooks, July 13, 1894, White to John T. Gaffey, July 17, 1894, WP.

[45] Joseph H. Call to Olney, July 18, 1894, in *Appendix to the Annual Report of the Attorney-General, 1896,* p. 34; SF *Exmr,* July 3, Nov. 16, 1894.

[46] F. S. Oakes and L. E. Stimson to Adolph Sutro, Nov. 20, 1894, Adolph Sutro Papers, Bancroft Library, Univ. of California, Berkeley; Cross, *Labor Movement,* p. 220.

[47] M. McGlynn and James Barry to Sutro, Feb. 6, 1895, American Railway Union, Local 345, to Sutro, Sept. 28, 1895, Sutro Papers; Michael Paul Rogin and John L. Shover, *Political Change in California: Critical Elections and Social Movements, 1890–1966* (Westport, Conn., 1970), pp. 17–18.

which grew steadily during the controversies over currency, labor, and other issues during the mid-1890's, was the largest single influence in the popular repudiation of the president and his party by 1896. While the country demanded positive action, wrote one embittered observer, "this 300 pounds of fat, called Cleveland, sits astride the Nation, pulling and rowelling his steed, and thinking he is a devil of a rider because it kicks so."[48]

IV

The "steed" plainly demonstrated its restiveness in the 1894 state and congressional elections. Recognizing the likelihood of defeat, Coast Democrats attempted to limit the campaign to local issues in order to divert attention from the administration's unpopularity. In line with this strategy the Democratic convention, held in San Francisco during late August, focused on the railroad question. The delegates nominated a prominent anti-railroad figure, James H. Budd, for governor and adopted a platform that urged an average reduction of 25 percent in freight rates in the state. Known as "Buckboard Jim" because he refused to ride the train, preferring a wagon instead, Budd promised an aggressive campaign against the company.[49] His nomination aroused little opposition. As expected, the major struggle of the convention came over the plank that dealt with the Cleveland administration.

In the months before the convention Stephen M. White and likeminded Democrats had lobbied for a general endorsement of the president in the party's platform. "There is nothing else for us to do," White argued. "If we join with the republicans in attacking the administration, we might as well go out of business all together."[50] Opposed to White were those Democrats, led by the San Francisco *Examiner*, who wished to ignore or repudiate the administration. Any endorsement of Cleveland, insisted the *Examiner*, should include several explicit exceptions: the president's failure to call a tariff

---

[48] Francis G. Newlands to Henry L. Wright, Jan. 16, 1895, Newlands Papers.
[49] SF *Exmr*, Aug. 22–24, 1894; LA *Times*, Aug. 21, 1894; Morris M. Estee to James S. Clarkson, Sept. 17, 1894, Clarkson Papers.
[50] White to Frank J. Moffitt, July 23, 1894, White to Henry W. Carter, July 26, 1894, White to Irish, Aug. 5, 1894, White to George S. Patton, Aug. 20, 1894, WP.

session in 1893, his refusal to offer legislation in the interest of silver after the repeal of the Sherman Act, his policy in the Hawaiian matter, and his retention of Richard Olney in the Cabinet.[51]

In the end White and his allies won the debate. The convention jeered a proposal to back Cleveland's Hawaiian policy but then accepted a plank declaring that the party "approves and endorses the Administration of Grover Cleveland, and expresses confidence in his judgment and patriotism, and in his ability to guide the destinies of the republic through the difficulties by which it is beset." Republicans promptly gibed at the "milk-and-water" statement, and the *Examiner* noted with pleasure that it was "not hearty": "Everybody knows perfectly well that there is not in California a corporal's guard of Democrats who really endorse the Cleveland Administration. There is a general willingness to grant that the President is honest and means well, but nobody who is familiar with the history of his second term and possesses common sense is under the impression that he is a great man or a very wise one."[52]

The involvement of the anti-Catholic American Protective Association further complicated the 1894 campaign. First formed in San Francisco in September 1893, the APA movement in California fed on the latent anti-Catholic sentiment that had earlier engendered the unsuccessful American party. Hostility against the Catholic minority mounted during the depression, and by the fall of 1894 the national council of the APA claimed 12,000 members in California. Other estimates ran as high as 17,000 in San Francisco alone.[53] At its peak the movement published at least eleven journals in the state and held weekly "Good Citizenship" meetings where speakers, usually Protestant ministers, declaimed against the Catholic Church. "Romanism," said one, "is the enthronement of folly, the height of absurdity, the climax of foolishness and the apotheosis of the ridiculous."[54]

---

[51] SF *Exmr*, Aug. 9, 1894.

[52] *Ibid.*, Aug. 24, 29, 1894; SF *Chron*, Aug. 24, 1894; LA *Times*, Aug. 24, 1894.

[53] Donald L. Kinzer, *An Episode in Anti-Catholicism: The American Protective Association* (Seattle, Wash., 1964), p. 122; David Joseph Herlihy, "Battle Against Bigotry: Father Peter C. Yorke and the American Protective Association in San Francisco, 1893–1897," *Records of the American Catholic Historical Society of Philadelphia*, 62 (1951): 97; Joseph S. Brusher, "Peter C. Yorke and the A.P.A. in San Francisco," *Catholic Historical Review*, 37 (1951): 129–50.

[54] SF *Exmr*, Dec. 2, 1895; Kinzer, *Episode in Anti-Catholicism*, p. 255; LA *Times*, Jan. 29–31, Feb. 1–3, 1894.

During 1895 APA-endorsed candidates won municipal elections in Stockton and Sacramento, but because of the movement's secrecy, the extent of its influence in 1894 remained unclear. In November a Catholic paper estimated that the movement commanded almost six thousand votes in San Francisco.[55] The APA gained some following among rural Populists, making it difficult for People's party nominees to appeal to urban Catholic laborers.[56] There was also evidence that James H. Budd received a quiet APA endorsement when his Republican opponent, Morris M. Estee, stubbornly refused to discharge a Catholic secretary. But the knowledgeable White, on the other hand, congratulated Budd for having "let the A.P.A. business alone."[57] Post-election Democratic analyses made no mention of the APA, and although no firm conclusion can be reached, it is likely that the movement only added somewhat to the massive 1894 Republican landslide.

Although the Democrats were prepared for a major setback, few of them fully anticipated the magnitude of their defeat. Promising protection and prosperity in contrast to the "utter imbecility" of the Cleveland administration, the Republicans had easily blunted the Democrats' strategy of emphasizing local issues. Budd's anti-railroad campaign, assisted perhaps by the APA, paid off in a narrow victory, and the Democrats elected a majority of the railroad commission. But there the party's success ended. The Republicans swept nearly every other state office, took six of the seven congressional seats, and emerged with 89 legislators to the Democrats' 29.[58] The Populists also made impressive gains in the election, particularly in the state's northern and central counties, where depression brought support from

[55] Herlihy, "Battle Against Bigotry," p. 97; Humphrey J. Desmond, *The A.P.A. Movement* (Washington, D.C., 1912), p. 58; SF *Exmr*, Nov. 5–6, 1895. The APA also had some effect on a local election in Los Angeles in late 1894. LA *Times*, Dec. 4, 1894.

[56] Alexander Saxton, "San Francisco Labor and the Populist and Progressive Insurgencies," *PHR*, 34 (1965): 424–25; Rogin and Shover, *Political Change in California*, pp. 16–17.

[57] White to Budd, Dec. 22, 1894, WP; James H. Wilkins, ed., "Martin Kelly's Story," SF *Bul*, Oct. 5, 1917; Kinzer, *Episode in Anti-Catholicism*, p. 157.

[58] Republican platform quoted in SF *Exmr*, June 21, 1894; SF *Chron*, Aug. 27, 1894; Edith Dobie, *The Political Career of Stephen Mallory White: A Study of Party Activities Under the Convention System* (Stanford, Cal., 1927), pp. 211, 251. Democrats viewed Budd's victory as "close to a miracle." White to Jeremiah Lynch, Jan. 7, 1895, WP.

discontented farmers. In San Francisco the People's party candidate for mayor, Adolph Sutro, garnered over 50 percent of the vote.[59]

Returns across the nation revealed a similar pattern. The Republicans profited from a nationwide reaction that buried the Democratic party in state after state. In one of the largest transfers of congressional strength in American history, the Democrats lost 113 House seats, while the number of Republican seats rose from 127 to 244. Twenty-four states elected no Democrats to national office; six others chose only one Democrat each. A single Democrat represented the party's once-bright hopes in New England. The election virtually destroyed the party in the Midwest. Of the 89 congressmen from that region, only three now bore the Democratic standard. Everywhere the Republicans recouped their 1892 losses and cut deeply into traditional Democratic sources of support.[60] In the aftermath of the election the divisions within the party hardened as administration and anti-administration forces each blamed the other for defeat.[61] On the Pacific Coast, as elsewhere, the Democrats' unity and confidence disappeared. The expectations of political dominance that had accompanied Cleveland's victory in 1892 had not materialized.

V

Defeat reinforced the administration's sense of beleaguered isolation, but it taught no lessons. Some Cleveland supporters found virtue in repudiation. "The extreme result pleases me," insisted John P. Irish, "for reaction is certain, and the work of re-instatement of the party will naturally fall to men of principle, for the expediency mon-

---

[59] Rogin and Shover, *Political Change in California*, pp. 16–18; Saxton, "San Francisco Labor," pp. 424–27; SF *Exmr*, Nov. 9, 1894. Sutro's victory did not provide a measure of Populist strength in San Francisco. Not really a Populist, Sutro had won wide popularity by campaigning against the Southern Pacific Railroad and aiding the strikers in the summer of 1894. See, e.g., Sutro to Hugo Sutro, Aug. 17, 1894, Sutro Papers.

[60] Carl N. Degler, "American Political Parties and the Rise of the City: An Interpretation," *Journal of American History*, 51 (1964): 42; Geoffrey Blodgett, *The Gentle Reformers: Massachusetts Democrats in the Cleveland Era* (Cambridge, Mass., 1966), p. 194; Richard J. Jensen, *The Winning of the Midwest: Social and Political Conflict, 1888–1896* (Chicago, 1971), pp. 209–68; J. Rogers Hollingsworth, "The Historian, Presidential Elections, and 1896," *Mid-America*, 45 (1963): 187–88; Samuel T. McSeveney, *The Politics of Depression: Political Behavior in the Northeast, 1893–1896* (New York, 1972), pp. 108–33.

[61] See, e.g., SF *Exmr*, Nov. 7–10, 1894.

gers are all in the morgue."[62] During 1895 and 1896 Cleveland twice more resorted to bond sales to rescue the Treasury's gold reserve. Deteriorating relations with Congress and the public measured the anti-Cleveland feeling that spread through society and infected the Democratic party. A few of the president's subsequent actions, particularly his blunt opposition to Great Britain in the 1895 Venezuela boundary dispute, brought him praise, but they came too late to stem the party crisis.[63] At first one by one, and then in droves, Democrats deserted the president, leaving him the spokesman for an ever smaller coterie of fervent supporters.

The Democratic party's experience between 1893 and 1896 belies the conclusions of historians who have been "struck by the way in which William Jennings Bryan's campaign for the presidency fractured his own party by forcing Democrats of every persuasion either to commit themselves to his cause or somehow oppose it."[64] The party was deeply fractured at least two years before 1896, and Bryan's candidacy only formalized a process that had begun as early as 1893. It was Grover Cleveland, not Bryan, who compelled Democrats to commit themselves in the 1890's. In the end the 1896 Democratic national convention would reveal, to the president's dismay, the nature of the party's new commitment.

Meanwhile the spreading defections from the administration puzzled the Cleveland Democrats. With unmatched devotion and an unyielding fidelity to party traditions, they had tried, in Irish's words, to keep "the lamps burning in the lighthouse of righteousness." They took pride in their achievements. "The President and his advisers," wrote a member of the Cabinet, "have dared to do that which, in their judgment, is right. They have consulted conscience, rather than convenience. In the Hawaiian matter, in finance,

[62] Irish to J. Sterling Morton, Nov. 8, 1894, Morton Papers; Cleveland to Thomas F. Bayard, Feb. 13, 1895, CP; Shelby M. Cullom, *Fifty Years of Public Service* (Chicago, 1911), p. 269.

[63] White to William Randolph Hearst, April 27, 1895, WP; H. Wayne Morgan, *From Hayes to McKinley: National Party Politics, 1877–1896* (Syracuse, N.Y., 1969), pp. 480–81.

[64] Blodgett, *Gentle Reformers*, p. vii; James C. Olson, *J. Sterling Morton* (Lincoln, Neb., 1942), pp. 383–85; C. Vann Woodward, *Origins of the New South, 1877–1913* (Baton Rouge, La., 1951), pp. 270–84; Paolo E. Coletta, "Bryan, Cleveland, and the Disrupted Democracy, 1890–1896," *Nebraska History*, 41 (1960): 1–27.

and in tariff reform, they have acted together as one man. Their in-spiration has been love of country and a determination to do for the best interests of their countrymen all that their positions and oath of office command and imply that they should do."[65] No one, the Cleveland Democrats thought, could ask for more.

Unhappily, it was not enough. Cleveland's greatest weakness dur-ing his second administration was not his inability to end the depres-sion—no president could have fully accomplished that—or even his stubborn, single-minded pursuit of principles. His greatest weakness was the manner in which he had approached the task, his retreat into unthinking rigidity, his failure to provide positive leadership, and his growing isolation from popular sentiment in the country. Cleveland's inability to accept advice stifled criticism, however con-structive, and produced a small band of loyal adherents who in their enthusiasm constantly misled him about the political and economic situation in their states.

Between 1893 and 1896 Cleveland demanded strict obedience from his Democratic followers, frequently asking them in effect to endan-ger or forfeit their political positions at home, but his own actions plainly displayed an unwillingness to make comparable concessions. Throughout his administration he indulged in a dangerous tendency to classify party members as either statesmen or politicians, assigning to the former category those who unreservedly supported his policies. He never recognized the existence of a middle rank of Democrats who sought to unite principle and party.

It was to this latter group, the large number of party members who conscientiously endeavored after 1893 to maintain the middle ground, that Cleveland had to appeal if he hoped to preserve the party and perpetuate its principles. His failure to make such an appeal, to pro-vide a basis for united action, polarized the Democratic party. It angered and bewildered Democrats who had worked to balance na-tional and local loyalties. As Stephen M. White observed of the Cleveland men in 1895, "I do not know how they expect to keep the party together at all. For my part, it appears clear that some of

---

[65] Irish to Morton, June 23, 1894, Morton to Irish, Jan. 26, 1894, Morton Papers.

our so-called democratic leaders have made up their minds to wreck the entire institution."[66]

No single incident supplied the final cause for Democratic disillusionment with the president. The events of the 1890's each had a different impact on different Democrats. For Max Popper, head of the state central committee, and Michael F. Tarpey, California's representative on the Democratic national committee, disillusionment set in as a response to Cleveland's patronage decisions at the outset of his administration. Their resentment stemmed less from the actual distribution of the offices than from the president's refusal to consult them about the party's desires. William Randolph Hearst's influential San Francisco *Examiner* and a number of other Democratic newspapers deserted Cleveland in the fall of 1893 in indignation at his anti-silver convictions and his decision to postpone tariff reform until the Sherman Act had been repealed.

Cleveland's policies on Hawaii and other issues subsequently antagonized Congressman Thomas J. Geary. Patronage and silver grievances, together with the suppression of the Pullman strike, embittered Congressman James G. Maguire, and continued bond sales finally alienated Thomas J. Clunie, a prominent San Francisco Democrat, who announced his abandonment of the president in August 1895.[67] By that time, too, Sen. Stephen M. White had been brought into open opposition, publicly despairing over the future of the Democratic party under Grover Cleveland. The experience of these California Democrats reflected a nationwide process that shaped party fortunes for years to come. At various points between 1893 and 1896 they and hundreds of other party members had reluctantly reached the same conclusion. They would compromise no longer with an uncompromising administration.

[66] White to Arthur P. Gorman, Sept. 15, 1895, WP.
[67] SF *Chron*, Aug. 22, 1895; Popper to White, May 9, 1893, Popper to White, May 23, 1893, Maguire to White, July 7, 1893, WP; Tarpey to Cleveland, April 17, 1893, Maguire to Cleveland, June 25, 1894, CP.

CHAPTER NINE

The Railroad in California Politics: The 1890's

❧❧❧

IN THE LAST three decades of the nineteenth century one issue over-shadowed all others in California politics: the power of the Southern Pacific Railroad and its affiliated companies, particularly the Central Pacific. Beginning in 1869 every platform of the Democratic party contained at least one plank that dealt in critical fashion with the railroad. Republican pronouncements were only slightly less unanimous, and even the California Prohibition party frequently departed from its temperance admonitions to castigate the Southern Pacific. Preoccupation with the railroad question was almost universal among Californians during these decades. Disturbed by railroad involvement in state politics, unhappy with railroad rates, troubled by the Southern Pacific's control over transportation, Californians early became convinced that the railroad exerted an evil and pervasive influence throughout their state.[1]

There was almost always sufficient evidence of railroad rascality to nurture this conviction. Potential railroad influence ranged from small matters, such as fixing the site of a party convention by manipulating rate discounts, to broad attempts to determine the selection of railroad commissioners or United States senators.[2] Politicians called the Southern Pacific "the great power which rules this land" and feared its wrath. As one Republican told a Midwestern correspondent,[3] "The R.R. powers are everything out here and to openly oppose

---

[1] Winfield J. Davis, *A History of Political Conventions in California, 1849–1892* (Sacramento, 1893), pp. 289–594; SF *Exmr*, June 21, Aug. 24, 1894, May 7, June 18, 1896.
[2] White to William D. English, May 2, 1886, WP; W. W. Stow to Thomas R. Bard, June 8, 1886, Bard to Stow, June 15, 1886, Bard Papers.
[3] Adolph Sutro to Hugo Sutro, Aug. 17, 1894, Sutro Papers; John F. Swift to

them is to be closed out of political life." "According to common report," wrote another observer, "the Southern Pacific runs political conventions, influences elections, controls legislatures, owns railroad commissioners, and frustrates justice. It is the arbiter of trade, fixes the prices of most commodities, determines who (if any) shall prosper and who shall go to the wall, dictates the waxing and waning of prosperity in every community within its grasp." He added, "Some of these charges are proved, more of them are known to be true, all of them are believed."[4]

The common belief in railroad power became the key to Coast politics in the years before 1900. To merchants, farmers, and other groups, it mattered most that Southern Pacific rates were demonstrably higher than railroad rates in the East and that the company's monopoly on transportation enabled it to discriminate among areas and shippers. Californians tended to overlook the fact that aside from the railroad's monopoly position, the topographical difficulties in their state, the relative scarcity of settlement and traffic along many Southern Pacific routes, and the high cost of imported coal also tended to push rates upward.[5] In politics, too, Californians often made of the railroad something it was not: a monolithic tyrant that interfered in elections with uniform regularity and uniform success. Only the virulent divisions in the Southern Pacific management after 1885 and a series of defeats suffered by the railroad during the 1890's began, grudgingly, to convince them otherwise. Except for a few years in the late 1880's, when hostility toward the railroad temporarily subsided, Californians viewed the decades between 1870 and 1900 as a continuous struggle to free their state from railroad thralldom.

Three times in this period anti-railroad sentiment contributed to widespread popular movements that affected the direction of the state's development. The social unrest of the 1870's, reflected in the

Louis T. Michener, May 3, 1888, Michener Papers. Many politicians built their careers on opposition to the railroad, belying the validity of such statements. But in California, as elsewhere, what people believed sometimes counted more than reality.

[4] Thomas R. Bacon, "The Railroad Strike in California," Yale Review, 3 (1895): 248.

[5] "Report of Richard Price Morgan on Existing Rates of Fares and Freights in California," J App, 30 sess. (1893), 2: 339–59; "Thirteenth Annual Report of the Board of Railroad Commissioners," ibid., pp. 50–58, 91–97; Stuart Daggett, Chapters on the History of the Southern Pacific (New York, 1922), pp. 237–92.

Grange and Workingmen's agitation, led to the adoption of a new constitution that established a regulatory commission endowed with unprecedented powers and erected other safeguards against the railroad's influence. In the 1880's both political parties were dominated for a time by an anti-monopoly crusade that attempted to define the railroad's position in California society and to enhance the state's authority over the railroad. Toward the end of the century another reform outburst occurred, more intense than the previous two. Spurred in part by economic discontent, large numbers of Californians decided in the 1890's that the "fight with this Corporation monster is a fight to the death—of the Octopus."[6]

So pervasive was this feeling that it gave a strong anti-railroad cast to Coast politics throughout the 1890's. Republicans as well as Democrats campaigned vociferously against the Southern Pacific, and during these years, unlike the 1880's, there was scarcely a dissenting voice raised in either party. Local Populists feared that their national leaders, unacquainted with California's railroad problem, would mistakenly choose to concentrate on the silver question. "The danger ... is that they will set up the wrong issue for us on this Coast," declared a prominent Populist in 1894. "Admit that the People need more money and its better circulation: we need relief from the burdens of taxation and transportation now put upon us by the S.P. of Ky. For us, the one issue two years hence is and can be none other than 'Down with the Octopus.'" "If the chains of corporate tyranny are not loosed from the chafed limbs of California," cautioned another contemporary, it "may be necessary for the United States to put down an armed rebellion of the people of California.... Desperate men and desperate communities do strange things."[7] Such warnings, common in the 1890's, testified to the depth of resentment against the railroad.

II

To a degree, of course, anti-railroad sentiment in the 1890's came as an outgrowth of the general discontent that accompanied the severe

---

[6] P. O. Chilstrom to Adolph Sutro, May 16, 1894, Sutro Papers; David B. Griffiths, "Anti-Monopoly Movements in California, 1873–1898," *Southern California Quarterly*, 52 (1970): 93–121.

[7] Robert E. Bush to Sutro, Dec. 28, 1894, Sutro Papers; Bacon, "Railroad Strike," p. 250.

depression of that decade. As in the past, the Southern Pacific became a convenient target for popular dissatisfaction with economic conditions on the Coast. More fundamentally, however, the depression served primarily as the catalyst to a deep sense of failure and frustration already felt by most Californians. Beginning in the 1870's they had sought to use the twin instruments of competition and regulation to solve the state's railroad problem. Subsequent experience had convinced them that their efforts had failed, and it was this conviction, exacerbated by economic hardship, that found expression during the 1890's.

Almost from the moment of the Central Pacific's completion in 1869, California citizens had eagerly petitioned for additional transcontinental and internal lines, believing that competition "is our great need; it will prove our salvation; it will strike off the monopoly shackles which must ever bind us in commercial slavery so long as we have but one railroad outlet."[8] The entrance of the Santa Fe into Los Angeles in the mid-1880's aroused momentary hopes that effective competition had at last been achieved, but enthusiasm soon began to wane when rate structures remained basically unchanged. For more than a decade, moreover, the Santa Fe was unable to obtain its own tracks over the Tehachapi range into northern California. There the Huntington-Stanford monopoly continued to rule, and residents pressed for competitive alternatives to the Southern Pacific.

The brief history of the San Francisco and San Joaquin Valley Railway, a 300-mile line projected to run from San Francisco Bay down the Central Valley to Bakersfield, illustrated the continuing demand for competition. Known as the "People's Road" in distinction to its hated predecessor, the line attracted widespread public support. Begun at Stockton in the summer of 1895 amid promises that it would end the Southern Pacific's "reign of terror" in the state, it reached Fresno in October 1896, Visalia in September 1897, and Bakersfield in May 1898.[9] Cheering crowds and flower girls greeted the line's

---

[8] LA *Times*, Jan. 6, 1885; Davis, *Political Conventions*, p. 580; SF *Exmr*, Jan. 1, 1892. Californians also led in the demand for a Nicaraguan Canal to secure water-transport competition to the Southern Pacific. See, e.g., John T. Doyle to White, March 29, 1892, White to Edward Berwick, Dec. 20, 1894, WP; LA *Times*, Feb. 9, 1891; *JS*, 30 sess., p. 16.
[9] SF *Chron*, Feb. 2, 1895.

popular train, the *Emancipator*, as it arrived at each point. The new railroad promptly set rates on grain shipments that ranged from 15 to 40 percent below those on the Southern Pacific, and its admirers estimated that it lured four-fifths of the valley's freight business away from its rival. For two years, until its purchase by the Santa Fe in December 1898, the People's Road supplied on a local level the independent rail competition that Californians had so fervently desired.[10]

Another attempt to provide competition to the Southern Pacific, involving a direct assault on the corporation itself, occurred in the course of the 1894 Pullman strike. Angered by the Southern Pacific's refusal to move trains without Pullman cars, the United States attorney in Los Angeles, George J. Denis, decided to take advantage of the opportunity to divide the entire Southern Pacific system into competitive units. On July 14, 1894, he and his assistant wired Richard Olney, the attorney general, that "the situation, in our opinion, demands enforcement of [the Sherman Antitrust] act of July 2, 1890, against unlawful combines of railroads and transportation companies, and we respectfully suggest bringing suit in name of Government to enforce that law." Olney replied on the same day: "Let act of July 2, 1890, be strictly enforced against all violators, including railroad and transportation companies. You are authorized to bring any appropriate suits under the act named." Accordingly, on July 16 Denis filed suit in the United States circuit court charging the Southern Pacific with combination in restraint of trade and commerce, and requesting that the company and its 34 subsidiaries be required to operate under separate management. Although most Californians enthusiastically welcomed the suit, there was widespread surprise that Richard Olney, well known for his railroad sympathies, had sanctioned it.[11]

No one, however, was more surprised than Olney himself when he learned the nature of the suit. "A most extraordinary bill in equity has recently been filed ... in the Southern District of California," he wrote, "and I am trying to ascertain upon what possible ground they

[10] SF *Exmr*, June 25–28, Dec. 19, 1896; "Fifteenth Annual Report of the Board of Railroad Commissioners," *J App*, 32 sess. (1897), 2: 60–66; James Marshall, *Santa Fe: The Railroad That Built an Empire* (New York, 1945), pp. 255–61.

[11] Denis and Joseph H. Call to Olney, July 14, 1894, Olney to Denis, July 14, 1894, in *Appendix to the Annual Report of the Attorney-General of the United States for the Year 1896* (Washington, D.C., 1896), p. 33; LA *Times*, July 17, 1894.

could suppose they had any authority so to do from this Department."[12] Olney then proceeded to engage in an extensive correspondence with the Southern Pacific, and on August 1, 1894, he instructed Denis to drop the suit.[13] Denis vigorously protested the order: "That Congress did not intend that these various competing lines of railroad, constructed at a cost of hundreds of millions of dollars, as competing lines, should be consolidated and a monopoly created seems self-evident," he told the attorney general. But his efforts were to no avail. Olney reprimanded his overeager subordinates, pointing out that the Sherman Act could not touch prior consolidations and suggesting that the Southern Pacific monopoly facilitated rather than restrained interstate commerce.[14] On August 4, 1894, the angry Denis asked the court to dismiss the suit. The legal challenge to the Southern Pacific had failed.[15]

Along with their attempts to secure competition, Californians had also tried since the 1870's to devise a satisfactory system for supervising and regulating the railroad's affairs. After several initial experiments they had created in 1879 a three-member railroad commission and had given it theoretically broad powers to prohibit unjust discrimination, examine the railroad's accounts, and fix maximum rate schedules. But by the last decade of the century, the vast majority of Californians had reluctantly and bitterly come to believe that their regulatory efforts, too, had met with complete failure.

Troubles beset the commission from the beginning of its existence. Philosophical squabbles impaired the performance of the early commissions, and though these disputes gradually waned, internal debates over the commission's functions continued into the 1890's. Many commissioners took a narrow view of their responsibilities, arguing, as one declared, that it was not their business "to kick up a row in this

[12] Olney to Charles W. Russell, July 20, 1894, Olney Papers; William Letwin, *Law and Economic Policy in America: The Evolution of the Sherman Antitrust Act* (New York, 1965), pp. 128–30.

[13] Olney to Denis, Aug. 1, 1894, in *Appendix to the Annual Report of the Attorney-General, 1896*, pp. 36–37; for Olney's correspondence with the Southern Pacific attorney Charles H. Tweed, see the numerous letters under various dates in July 1894 in the Olney Papers.

[14] Denis to Olney, Aug. 2, 1894, in *Appendix to the Annual Report of the Attorney-General, 1896*, pp. 37–40; Olney's interesting reasoning can be followed in penciled notes he took on the case under the date of July 1894 in the Olney Papers.

[15] SF *Exmr*, Aug. 5, 1894; White to Denis, Aug. 5, 1894, WP.

State."[16] Hasty, sweeping measures, they feared, might damage California's economy as well as the railroad. Despite their relatively high salaries, the commissioners devoted a limited amount of time to their duties, and it was not until 1894 that a political party pledged that its nominees for the commission "shall pursue their official labors unhampered by the demands of any other business or avocation." In 1891, a dozen years after its formation, the commission finally decided to hold weekly instead of monthly meetings.[17]

Although they regarded commission membership as a part-time occupation, the commissioners recognized their potential power over economic development throughout the state. Most assumed office with little knowledge of railroad matters. Some had committed themselves in advance to specific rate reductions, openly violating the commission's quasi-judicial functions.[18] Wary of their power, aware of their ignorance, the commissioners as a rule endeavored to learn the railroad business but found its complexities difficult to master. A few accomplished the task just as their four-year terms expired. Others simply did their best, or gave up in despair. Railroad rate schedules, admitted one commissioner after two years in office, still remained "a great big complex complication to me." Questioned on his limited understanding of railroad affairs, another commissioner replied: "Yes, sir; I see your point, and I ain't dodging it, either, and you need not dodge it."[19]

Commission members complained that railroad accounting procedures, designed more to obscure than to clarify, made it virtually impossible to make accurate rate decisions. Beginning in the early 1880's they repeatedly appealed to the legislature for authority and

---

[16] "Testimony in the Investigation of the Railroad Commissioners," *J App*, 30 sess., 8: 28; "Thirteenth Annual Report of the Board of Railroad Commissioners," *ibid.*, 2: 50–51. Some early influences on regulation are analyzed in Ward M. McAfee, "Local Interests and Railroad Regulation in California During the Granger Decade," *PHR*, 37 (1968): 51–61.

[17] SF *Exmr*, Aug. 24, 1894; "Twelfth Annual Report of the Board of Railroad Commissioners," *J App*, 30 sess., 2: 9; Gerald D. Nash, "The California Railroad Commission, 1876–1911," *Southern California Quarterly*, 44 (1962): 292–93.

[18] [John T. Doyle], "The California Railroad Commission," *American Law Review*, 29 (1895): 896–97; SF *Exmr*, Aug. 24, 1894; "Fourteenth Annual Report of the Board of Railroad Commissioners," *J App*, 31 sess. (1895), 4: 33.

[19] "Testimony in the Investigation of the Railroad Commissioners," *J App*, 30 sess., 8: 6–14, 37–38, 59.

funds to employ expert advisers, but their pleas were ignored.[20] The railroad resisted the commission's own attempts to prescribe a uniform accounting system.[21] Always a major handicap, the commission's inability to decipher railroad ledgers became increasingly injurious in the 1890's, when court decisions dictated that enforced rate reductions could not "unreasonably" deprive the railroad of its property and legitimate profits, a criterion that could be met only through a knowledgeable scrutiny of the railroad's records.[22]

The Southern Pacific's formidable opposition to effective regulation completed the commission's troubles. When the commission proposed lower rates, company officials had a standard and, to some, persuasive response: "Whatever builds up a State builds up the railroad, and whatever helps to build up the railroad helps the State. If you injure the one you injure the other."[23] When commission members persisted, the railroad denied their authority and resorted to delaying tactics. The commission would announce a new rate schedule, the railroad would appeal to the courts, months or even years would pass before a decision was rendered, changed conditions would then necessitate new rates, and the cycle would begin again.[24] In court contests the commissioners encountered jurisdictional difficulties over the Southern Pacific, which could use its status as a Kentucky-based corporation to block state regulation. As a newspaper complained, the railroad "always appeals for local support and sympathy as a California institution and then when an attempt is made to regulate it by State laws it flits into the Federal courts as a sojourner from the blue grass."[25]

"I am glad to notice that you are looking after the Commissioners,"

[20] "Sixth Annual Report of the Board of Railroad Commissioners," *J App*, 27 sess. (1887), 5: 41–42; SF *Exmr*, Jan. 16, 1897.

[21] "Fifteenth Annual Report of the Board of Railroad Commissioners," *J App*, 32 sess., 2: 16, 56–57.

[22] *Southern Pacific Company* v. *The Board of Railroad Commissioners of the State of California*, reprinted in *J App*, 32 sess., 2: 377–415; LA *Times*, Dec. 3, 1896; SF *Exmr*, Jan. 16, 1897.

[23] "Ninth Annual Report of the Board of Railroad Commissioners," *J App*, 28 sess. (1889), 2: 50.

[24] Doyle, "California Railroad Commission," pp. 897–98. For one such cycle in the 1890's see "Fifteenth Annual Report of the Board of Railroad Commissioners," *J App*, 32 sess., 2: 16–56; Nash, "California Railroad Commission," pp. 297–98.

[25] SF *Exmr*, Oct. 15, 1895.

Collis P. Huntington, the most powerful of the Big Four, once wrote to a Coast associate. "I think it very important."[26] Besides court delays and obscure accounting procedures, the railroad had a wide variety of techniques for "looking after" the commissioners. Resistance, persuasion, and in a few cases bribery were used to thwart and discredit attempts at regulation. Huntington made no effort to conceal his hatred of regulatory agencies. "If the State has a right to fix rates," he often declared, "it has a right to confiscate property." He expanded on this theme in an 1891 article in the *North American Review*. Insisting that railroads functioned best under "the fostering care of a paternal government, unrestricted by legislation," Huntington urged that the operation of railroads be left to their owners. "Surely," he said in reference to government regulation, "the time has come to call a halt."[27]

Given the difficult and complex problems it faced, the California railroad commission between 1880 and 1900 performed about as effectively as could have been expected. It reformed a few railroad practices, achieved some rate reductions, and accumulated valuable experience that assisted a subsequent generation of reformers.[28] Impatient contemporaries thought otherwise. They had foreseen large and immediate benefits from the commission system, to which they had turned with increasing frequency in the last quarter of the century. In addition to the railroad commission, California had by the 1890's a state board of health; a commissioner of public works; a Yosemite commission; a debris commissioner; boards of agriculture, viticulture, and forestry; a fish commission; a mining bureau; a bureau of highways; a bank commission; a dairy bureau; a harbor commission; and a host of other supervisory and advisory agencies.[29]

[26] Huntington to David D. Colton, March 31, 1877, in SF *Chron*, Dec. 23, 1883.

[27] LA *Times*, March 23, 1889; Collis P. Huntington, "A Plea for Railway Consolidation," *North American Review*, 153 (1891): 275–82. Neither Huntington's views nor the California experience, therefore, conformed with the conclusions advanced by Gabriel Kolko in *Railroads and Regulation, 1877–1916* (Princeton, N.J., 1965).

[28] Nash, "California Railroad Commission," pp. 287–302; Gerald D. Nash, "Bureaucracy and Economic Reform: The Experience of California, 1899–1911," *Western Political Quarterly*, 13 (1960): 678–91; "Eighth Annual Report of the Board of Railroad Commissioners," *J App*, 28 sess., 2: 7–53; "Fourteenth Annual Report of the Board of Railroad Commissioners," *ibid.*, 31 sess., 4: 22–23.

[29] SF *Chron*, Feb. 3, 1897; Gerald D. Nash, "The California State Board of For-

From few of these bodies did Coast residents receive the technical expertise and the insulation from political influence they had anticipated, and their bitter disappointment was manifested in the widespread outcry in the 1890's against "the extensive and expensive system of commissions in this State." "We are opposed to creating any more public offices or commissions," announced the Republican platform in 1894, "for we believe that there are too many commissions in the State at the present time. We are in favor of ... abolishing and dispensing with all offices and commissions not actually necessary to maintain the State Government."[30]

Most of this disappointment naturally focused on the railroad commission, from which Californians had expected the greatest results. In 1892 the People's party convention labeled the commissioners "traitors and boodlers," and individual Populists resolved, as one wrote, to "knock the office of R.R. commissioner so high it would never light."[31] Many Republican journals favored abolishing the commission, arguing that it "only beguiles the people into fancied security by tempting them to rely upon a reed." The Democrats also denounced the commission's "inaction" and proposed a constitutional amendment to abolish it.[32] Such an amendment passed the assembly during the 1889 and 1893 legislative sessions, but it met defeat in the senate; a similar attempt, again unsuccessful, was made in the 1897 session. In 1894 the commissioners barely escaped impeachment.[33]

In the introspective mood of the 1890's, Californians reviewed two decades of effort and found, they believed, a record of failure and frustration. As the San Francisco *Examiner* recalled, "We have tried to regulate the railroads by Legislatures and Railroad Commissions,

estry, 1883–1960," *Southern California Quarterly*, 47 (1965): 294; Charles P. Korr, "William Hammond Hall: The Failure of Attempts at State Water Planning in California, 1878–1888," *ibid.*, 45 (1963): 307–8.

[30] LA *Times*, Feb. 4, 1893; SF *Exmr*, June 21, 1894; "Report of Committee on Commissions to the Assembly," *J App*, 29 sess. (1891), 7: 3–13; *JA*, 32 sess., p. 4.

[31] SF *Chron*, June 2, 1892; M. Thomas, Jr., to Thomas V. Cator, Nov. 26, 1892, Cator Papers.

[32] LA *Times*, Jan. 23, 1891; Davis, *Political Conventions*, p. 580; White to John T. Doyle, Dec. 30, 1892, WP.

[33] *JA*, 28 sess., pp. 1008–9; *ibid.*, 30 sess., pp. 871–77; *JS*, 30 sess., p. 1041; "Report of the Testimony and Proceedings, Before the Senate Committee on Constitutional Amendments, Relative to Senate Constitutional Amendment No. 8," *J App*, 30 sess., 8: 1–235; *JS*, 32 sess., pp. 283–84.

and the only result has been that legislators and Commissioners have gone on the railroad pay-roll.... Direct regulation by public officials failing, we have tested indirect regulation by competing lines." Neither method had worked, the paper contended: "We have reached the conclusion that when a corporation is greater than the Government the only way to regulate it is to abolish it."[34] Convinced that past campaigns had achieved nothing, and made restive by the state's economic troubles, Californians struggled in the 1890's to rid themselves of the railroad incubus. Their response to two specific issues that arose during the decade involving the funding of a railroad debt and the location for a deep-water harbor in Southern California demonstrated the nature and extent of this struggle.

III

The first of these issues was raised by the debt the Central Pacific owed to the federal government for aid extended under legislation of 1862 and 1864. Amounting without interest to $25,885,120, and secured by a government mortgage on the aided property, this debt was scheduled to become due between January 16, 1895, and January 1, 1899. A series of attempts by Congress to provide an acceptable settlement, including the 1878 Thurman Act, had been unsuccessful. In their annual messages presidents Cleveland and Harrison urged Congress to find a solution before the time came to foreclose the mortgage. "The subject should be treated as a business proposition with a view to a final realization of its indebtedness by the Government," Cleveland asserted in 1888, "rather than as a question to be decided upon prejudice or by way of punishment for previous wrongdoing."[35]

---

[34] SF *Exmr*, July 21, 1894; S. E. Moffett, "The Railroad Commission of California: A Study in Irresponsible Government," *Annals of the American Academy of Political and Social Science*, 6 (1895): 469–77.

[35] James D. Richardson, ed., *A Compilation of the Messages and Papers of the Presidents, 1789–1897*, 10 vols. (Washington, D.C., 1897), 7: 5384; Daggett, *Southern Pacific*, pp. 370–96. Details on the debt can be found in *Senate Report No. 778*, 54th Cong., 1st sess. (Washington, D.C., 1896), pp. 1–10. The Thurman Act required each of the indebted railroads (most notably the Central Pacific and the Union Pacific) to pay annually, according to a prescribed formula, an amount equal to 25 percent of its net earnings. The act proved ineffective, largely because of an unexpected decline in earnings for the railroads over the following two decades.

The Central Pacific managers had plans of their own for a settlement. In private correspondence Leland Stanford proposed that the
entire debt be canceled in view of the incalculable benefits the company had bestowed on the country. "The proof is clear and can not
be contradicted," he told Collis P. Huntington in 1887, "that instead
of the Co. owing the Gov't anything, the Gov't equitably is largely
indebted to the Cos. I think we ought to take that position and decline
to make any offers of future payment." Should this strategy fail, the
railroad leaders hoped to persuade Congress to authorize a substantial
reduction in the amount of the debt or at the very least a lengthy post-
ponement of the date for payment.[36]

Most Californians, for their part, resented the railroad's efforts to
avoid paying the debt. They insisted that the railroad be compelled,
like any other debtor, to redeem its obligations in full. As Stephen
M. White put it, the "people of the State of California are pretty
thoroughly tired of this railroad crowd and would like to see the government claims enforced to the letter." This demand was fed by a desire for revenge and a fear of higher rates, but significantly it also
stemmed from an awareness that the Central Pacific's financial difficulties offered a splendid opportunity to obtain the railroad competition Californians had sought since the 1870's.[37]

Foreclosure of the mortgage, Californians reasoned, would constitute a severe blow to Huntington's rail network. Although it was one
of the less profitable of the Southern Pacific's subsidiaries, the Central
Pacific constituted a vital element in the Southern Pacific's domination of Pacific Coast transportation. "It is the pivot on which Huntington's power turns," commented one observer, "for without control
of the central route the S.P. combination is a failure." In independent
hands it could be used to establish competitive rates, divert traffic
from the southern route, and challenge the Southern Pacific for the
California freight and passenger business. This became the funda-

[36] Stanford to Huntington, Sept. 23, 1887, Hopkins Collection; Huntington to
Benjamin Harrison, July 29, 1892, HP; Huntington to William E. Chandler, April
24, 1896, Chandler Papers; Richard Olney to George F. Hoar, June 8, 1894, Olney
Papers.
[37] White to Thomas H. Bates, June 21, 1894, White to James H. Budd, Jan. 8,
1897, WP; Hugh Craig to Cleveland, Jan. 21, 1896, CP; *JS*, 29 sess., p. 442; *ibid.*,
30 sess., p. 688.

mental objective of the anti-railroad Californians during the 1890's. As one wired John T. Morgan, a senator from Alabama, "Foreclosure Central Pacific R.R. mortgage their only hope for competition."[38]

Californians, moreover, had definite ideas about the proper agency to carry out this task. Few people in the state, at least few of those who made their views public, trusted any longer in private enterprise to provide rail competition, and here lay much of the significance of the railroad debt controversy. It demonstrated the extent to which Coast residents, in their bitter disillusionment with the policies of the Big Four, demanded government ownership and operation of the transcontinental railroads. Thus while some advocated the foreclosure and sale of the railroad to the highest bidder, most believed the Central Pacific's debt should be employed as a device to secure government ownership.[39]

The scheme gathered impressive support. Gov. James H. Budd, Sen. Stephen M. White, Mayor Adolph Sutro of San Francisco, and numerous other public figures gave it their fervent endorsement, as did the state legislature, the San Francisco Chamber of Commerce, the California Farmers' Alliance, and the platforms of nearly every political party. Government ownership, announced Sutro, would "by one great master stroke" provide the Pacific Coast with railroad competition and end "the corruption, the bribery, the enslavement, the evil influences of the Giant corrupt and criminal corporations."[40] Almost all major newspapers agreed, including the San Francisco *Examiner*, the San Francisco *Chronicle*, the San Francisco *Bulletin*, and the Sacramento *Bee*.[41] Even the Los Angeles *Times*, conservative on

---

[38] John T. Doyle to James G. Maguire, April 14, 1898, Doyle Papers; Adolph Sutro to Morgan, Jan. 20, 1890, Sutro Papers.

[39] J. Alfred Kinghorn Jones to Cleveland, Jan. 29, 1895, CP; LA *Times*, May 7, 1889. The owners of the Central Pacific were fairly confident that the government would not resort to foreclosure. Because the mortgage extended only to the aided property, the government could foreclose only on the line from Ogden, Utah, to San Jose, California (by way of Sacramento, Lathrop, and Niles), not including the branch lines and terminal facilities along the route. *Senate Report No. 778*, pp. 5-6; SF *Exmr*, March 15, 1890.

[40] Sutro to Cleveland, June 30, 1894, CP; Budd's views in SF *Exmr*, Jan. 12, 1895; White to W. H. Goucher, June 28, 1894, White to Budd, May 7, 1896, WP; *JA*, 31 sess., pp. 195-96; *JS*, 31 sess., pp. 233-34; Farmers' Alliance petition in *ibid.*, 29 sess., pp. 357-61; Hugh Craig to Cleveland, Jan. 21, 1896, CP; Davis, *Political Conventions*, p. 536.

[41] SF *Exmr*, July 16, 1894; SF *Chron*, Jan. 15, 1891; SF *Bul*, Aug. 28, 1893, San Francisco *Call*, Aug. 27, 1893, Sacramento *Bee*, Feb. 4, 1895, clippings in WP.

most economic matters, declared that with "just one transcontinental line in the possession of the Government, operated in the interests of the public, the rest of the lines would be brought to time very quickly."[42]

Once under government control the Central Pacific could be run either as an independent railroad or as a public track on which everyone had the right to move trains. "Why not make railroads public highways," asked Congressman James G. Maguire, "over which all common carriers may operate their freight and passenger trains upon equal terms, and freely compete with each other for traffic?" White suggested "government proprietorship of the railroad track, giving to transporters the right to use the same upon payment of certain rates or tolls. For instance, the fruit growers of Sacramento Valley might procure two or three locomotives and manufacture cars for a number of trains, and then upon application to the government train dispatcher, procure the right of way for a certain day and send on their product to the Eastern market."[43] Toying with various ideas, the anti-railroad Californians recognized their experimental nature and urged flexibility. They also sensed the potential hostility to such schemes elsewhere in the country and hoped simply to delay action in Congress until the government was forced to foreclose its mortgage.[44]

Watching the situation from his New York headquarters, the wily Huntington noted the nonpartisan basis of the opposition, concluded that Californians "have got a kind of craze on" for government ownership, and decided to abandon plans to ask for a total cancellation of the Central Pacific's debt.[45] Instead, he backed legislation to fund the debt over a long period of time at a low rate of interest. A measure to this effect, extending the debt for 50 years at 3 percent interest, was introduced into the Fifty-third Congress in July 1894. Known as the

[42] LA *Times*, Jan. 24, 1892. In April 1894, students from Stanford University and the University of California held a debate in San Francisco on the question "The National Ownership and Operation of Railroads." Ironically, the Stanford students spoke in the affirmative and won. SF *Exmr*, April 22, 1894.

[43] *Congressional Record*, 53d Cong., 3d sess. (Feb. 2, 1895), p. 215; White to Budd, May 7, 1896, WP; LA *Times*, March 5, 1897.

[44] Sutro to Blanton Duncan, July 18, 1894, Sutro Papers; SF *Exmr*, Nov. 20, 1896.

[45] Huntington to Henry T. Thurber, April 6, 1895, Huntington to Cleveland, April 5, 1895, CP; Huntington to William E. Chandler, Nov. 13, 1894, Chandler Papers.

Reilly bill, it did not entirely satisfy the Southern Pacific management, but a reporter found Huntington confident that Congress would
approve it. Only a few "communistic fellows," he said, desired to foreclose the mortgage.[46]

Although Huntington himself journeyed to Washington to pursue
the quiet lobbying for which he was so well known, the anti-railroad
Californians overwhelmed his forces. Letters, telegrams, and delegations poured into the capital. Mass meetings in San Francisco, Oakland, and other communities denounced the funding proposal. The
virulent Adolph Sutro likened the Reilly bill to an outright sale of
the Pacific states and declared that it would "hand us over to the
mercies of the meanest, most indecent and outrageous despotism that
has ever ruled any country."[47] In late July 1894 the San Francisco
Examiner inaugurated an anti-funding petition in its columns; by
September the petition had nearly 200,000 signatures, and it was presented to Congress in two massive volumes.[48] On February 2, 1895,
responding to the pressure, the House of Representatives voted to
refer the Reilly bill back to committee. In the words of one jubilant
observer, "Californians do not intend quietly to submit to slavery to
the S.P.R.R. any longer and are prepared to fight for their independence."[49]

Heated as this struggle had been, it proved only a preliminary skir-
mish in comparison to the battle that erupted in the course of the
Fifty-fourth Congress. Coast residents held another series of mass
meetings and conventions to condemn funding and demand foreclosure.[50] In an attempt to outflank the Southern Pacific, Sutro appealed to Kentucky officials to repeal the company's charter. "There

---

[46] SF *Exmr*, Feb. 2, 1895; Daggett, *Southern Pacific*, p. 397. According to press
reports, the railroad management desired an extension of 100 years at 2 percent interest. SF *Exmr*, June 8, 1894.

[47] Sutro to Cleveland, undated (1894), Sutro to Cleveland, June 13, 1894, CP; SF
Exmr, June 20–22, 1894. "The Railroad people are becoming very much stirred up,"
Senator White reported from Washington. "Huntington is here a great deal and is
greatly agitated." White to Victor Montgomery, June 21, 1894, WP.

[48] SF *Exmr*, July 21, Nov. 29, 1894; *Congressional Record*, 53d Cong., 3d sess.,
Appendix, pp. 213–14; *JS*, 31 sess., pp. 233–34.

[49] J. Alfred Kinghorn Jones to Cleveland, Jan. 29, 1895, CP; *Congressional Record*,
53d Cong., 3d sess. (Feb. 2, 1895), p. 1711; SF *Chron*, Feb. 3, 1895.

[50] SF *Exmr*, Dec. 8, 18, 1895, Jan. 19, 1896; SF *Chron*, Feb. 1, 1896; James G.
Maguire to Sutro, Dec. 7, 1895, Sutro Papers.

is a cloud on the State of Kentucky which should be cleared off," he informed the governor of Kentucky, J. Proctor Knott. Asked why the Southern Pacific was incorporated there, Huntington retorted: "We wanted to get a charter in some State where the laws were stable and the people were not liable to be changed by the action of such demagogues and charlatans as Adolph Sutro."[51]

A bill to revoke the Southern Pacific charter failed in the Kentucky legislature in early 1896, but this setback did not discourage Sutro, who then began to send letters to congressmen with the words "Huntington wouldn't steal a red-hot stove" stamped prominently on the envelopes. When the postal department impounded these letters as libelous, the mayor's allies urged him to retract by printing on his next envelopes: "The statement that Mr. Huntington wouldn't steal a red-hot stove is false."[52] By the end of the funding fight, Sutro alone had deluged congressmen with so much anti-funding literature that Sen. Benjamin R. Tillman of South Carolina told him: "My mail has been burdened with circular letters from you on the Pacific RR steal & Huntington villainies."[53]

Like the San Francisco mayor, nearly every prominent political figure in California fought against funding. The Populist leader Thomas V. Cator, the Democratic leaders John T. Doyle, Max Popper, and James G. Maguire, and the Republican leaders Morris M. Estee and Michael H. De Young all participated in the diverse anti-funding coalition. Such organizations as the San Francisco Chamber of Commerce and the San Francisco Labor Council found themselves united on the issue.[54] William Randolph Hearst dispatched his well-known

[51] Sutro to Knott, Dec. 31, 1895, Sutro Papers; Huntington interview in SF *Exmr*, Jan. 28, 1896; Huntington to Henry Watterson, Feb. 22, 1896, Henry Watterson Papers, Manuscript Division, Library of Congress; Adolph Sutro, *The People of Kentucky Disgraced*, pamphlet in Yale Univ. Library.

[52] SF *Exmr*, March 5–7, 1896; James G. Maguire to Sutro, Feb. 28, 1896, Sutro Papers; Robert E. Stewart, Jr., and Mary Frances Stewart, *Adolph Sutro: A Biography* (Berkeley, 1962), pp. 200–201.

[53] Tillman to Sutro, Feb. 6, 1896, Sutro Papers. Some Californians thought Sutro's virulence did more harm than good. See, e.g., James McLachlan to Henry Harrison Markham, Feb. 18, 1896, Markham Papers.

[54] SF *Exmr*, Dec. 18, 1895, May 16, 1896; SF *Chron*, Feb. 1, 1896; White to J. P. Fay, Feb. 14, 1896, WP. California Democrats also secured a strong anti-funding plank in the 1896 Democratic national platform. *Official Proceedings of the Democratic National Convention* (Logansport, Ind., 1896), p. 195.

journalist Ambrose Bierce to Washington to lead the newspaper campaign against the railroad. Bierce's commentary, given wide circulation in the Hearst press in New York and San Francisco, castigated the "railrogues" and reported that Huntington, testifying before a Senate committee, "took his hand out of all manner of pockets long enough to hold it up and be sworn."[55]

The turning point came in January 1897. The preceding April, H. Henry Powers of Vermont had submitted, on behalf of the House Committee on Pacific Railroads, a bill designed to settle the debt problem. The Powers bill required the Central Pacific to issue bonds equal to the full amount of the debt, to be redeemed in increasing annual installments over a period of 80 years. It offered several major concessions to the anti-railroad forces, including a provision that the Southern Pacific underwrite the Central Pacific's debt and an extension of the government lien to nonaided properties such as terminals, branch lines, feeders, equipment, and real estate.[56] But the anti-funding Californians regarded the proposal, which set interest at 2 percent, as "distinctly a Huntington bill." To them the Powers bill was even less acceptable than the Reilly bill, which had proposed 3 percent interest and payment over a 50-year period.[57]

Huntington again arrived in Washington, "making every exertion possible" for the bill, but on January 11, 1897, the House defeated it by a vote of 168 to 103. Of the California congressmen only Grove Johnson, the father of the Progressive governor and senator Hiram Johnson, spoke and voted for the bill.[58] In honor of the victory Governor Budd declared the following Saturday a legal holiday, and bands, bonfires, and fireworks marked the day across the state. One celebrant thought the outcome signaled "a new era" for California; others called it "a case of emancipation" and "the most staggering

[55] SF *Exmr*, Feb. 15, March 1, 1896; T. T. Williams to Bierce, March 7, 1896, Williams to Bierce, March 13, 1896, Bierce Papers; Paul Fatout, *Ambrose Bierce: The Devil's Lexicographer* (Norman, Okla., 1951), pp. 214–20.

[56] *House of Representatives Report No. 1497*, 54th Cong., 1st sess. (Washington, D.C., 1896), pp. 1–13; LA *Times*, April 26, 1896.

[57] SF *Exmr*, March 31, April 2, 1896; *Congressional Record*, 54th Cong., 2d sess. (Jan. 9, 1897), pp. 619–20; Sutro to Charles A. Sumner, Jan. 9, 1897, Sutro Papers; *JS*, 32 sess., p. 24.

[58] White to A. M. Stephens, Jan. 5, 1897, WP; Charles A. Sumner to Sutro, Jan. 13, 1897, Sutro Papers; *Congressional Record*, 54th Cong., 2d sess. (Jan. 11, 1897), p. 689.

blow that has ever been dealt to the Huntington monopoly." Sutro compared the bill's defeat to the Boston Tea Party, but then sounded a more cautious note: "The snake is scotched, it is true, but it is not killed."[59]

In a sense the jubilant Californians were right, even though the final debt settlement, a commission plan that slipped through Congress almost unnoticed in the midst of the major battles of the Spanish-American War, did not provide the independent rail competition or the government ownership many had desired. Composed of three Cabinet members, with strict instructions to obtain full payment of the debt within a ten-year period at a minimum interest rate of 3 percent, the commission instituted a repayment program in the form of twenty Central Pacific notes scheduled to mature between August 1, 1899, and February 1, 1909. On the latter date, with the redemption of the last note, the funding problem ended.[60]

Although they would have preferred a different solution, the anti-railroad Californians recognized that they had forced a speedier and more equitable resolution of the debt question. In the process they had gained invaluable confidence, unity, and experience. The funding controversy had sparked a remarkable demonstration of determination and unanimity. Extending over several years, it enlisted diverse forces under a common reform banner and taught techniques of organizing opposition, mobilizing public opinion, and influencing legislative bodies that the participants never forgot. It enabled reform-minded citizens to acquire and test the weapons of coercion and persuasion that their opponents had so often employed to stifle reform in the past. Indeed, even as the battle over funding unfolded, these weapons and techniques proved useful in another fight, one from which the anti-railroad Californians emerged with a complete victory.

IV

The second significant struggle of the 1890's involved the location of a deep-water harbor for the Los Angeles area. Southern California

[59] SF *Exmr*, Jan. 12, 1897; LA *Times*, Jan. 12, 1897; SF *Chron*, Jan. 17, 1897.
[60] LA *Times*, June 30, July 6–7, 1898; Daggett, *Southern Pacific*, pp. 414–24. Had the Powers bill passed, the final payment would not have been made until 1976.

residents had long been convinced that the port of San Pedro, which served Los Angeles, was not commensurate with the economic potential of their region. A submerged sandbar partially blocked the entrance to the inner harbor, compelling ships of any size to anchor outside and transfer their cargoes by lighters. Beginning in 1871 Los Angeles representatives won appropriations from Congress to improve the inner harbor, and by 1893 a fifteen-foot channel had been dug through the sandbar. Meanwhile, stimulated by the Southern California "boom" of the 1880's and the local belief that Los Angeles would become the center of trade with the Orient, agitation had begun to obtain government funds for a deep-water harbor.[61]

The problem arose over the location of the proposed harbor. Until 1892 attention focused on the outer harbor at San Pedro, which seemed the most likely recipient of additional aid because of the extensive work already under way on the inner harbor. San Pedro had further advantages. Two railroads served it, the Southern Pacific and the Los Angeles Terminal Railway, whose tracks ran from the city to wharf facilities on the coast. Moreover, a special commission of army engineers, established by Congress to study the matter, examined the various sites and reported in December 1891 that San Pedro was the best location for a harbor. Encouraged by this report, Southern Californians petitioned Congress for funds to begin the project, but to their dismay they discovered that Collis P. Huntington and the Southern Pacific Railroad had entirely different plans for harbor development in the region.[62]

After wresting the Southern Pacific presidency from Leland Stanford in 1890, Huntington had ended the policy of support for the San Pedro plan that the company had pursued under Stanford. "I

[61] Richard W. Barsness, "Iron Horses and an Inner Harbor at San Pedro Bay, 1867–1890," PHR, 34 (1965): 292–96; Charles Dwight Willard, The Free Harbor Contest at Los Angeles (Los Angeles, 1899), pp. 19–25. An excellent discussion of the harbor question is in Richard W. Barsness, "Railroads and Los Angeles: The Quest for a Deep-Water Port," Southern California Quarterly, 47 (1965): 379–91. Some early observations on San Pedro's inadequacy as a port are contained in Richard Henry Dana, Jr., Two Years Before the Mast: A Personal Narrative of Life at Sea (New York, 1840), pp. 118, 315.

[62] Franklyn Hoyt, "The Los Angeles Terminal Railroad," Historical Society of Southern California Quarterly, 36 (1954): 185–91; LA Times, Jan. 7, 1892; Ella A. Ludwig, History of the Harbor District of Los Angeles (n.p., n.d.), p. 263.

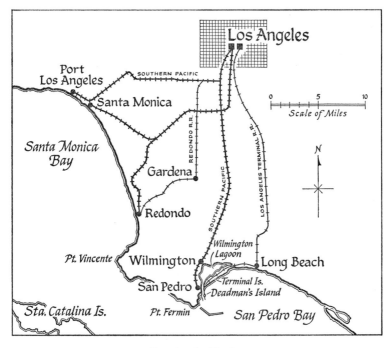

Los Angeles Harbor

became satisfied that San Pedro was not the place for a deep-sea harbor," he later explained, "...as the holding-ground is very bad and it is exposed to the fearful southeast winds that blow up the coast. I carefully inspected the Bay of Santa Monica and, as a result, found that Port Los Angeles (opposite Santa Monica) was decidedly the very best place for a great harbor." Huntington's explanation did not convince Southern Californians, for they knew he had other reasons to oppose San Pedro. At Santa Monica the Southern Pacific would have a virtually unbreakable monopoly on rail transportation to and from the new harbor.[63]

[63] Huntington to Daniel S. Lamont, Jan. 16, 1896, Lamont Papers; Huntington to White, March 29, 1893, Huntington to White, April 4, 1893, WP; Huntington to Cornelius Cole, Oct. 17, 1894, Cole Papers. In the 1870's Huntington had scorned Santa Monica as a harbor site. Huntington to David D. Colton, April 11, 1875, in SF *Chron*, Dec. 23, 1883. For Stanford's support of San Pedro, see LA *Times*, Dec. 7, 1888, Oct. 27, 1889.

Only one railroad reached the ocean at Santa Monica—the Los Angeles and Independence Railroad—and this line had been under the control of the Southern Pacific since the 1870's. In recent years Southern Pacific crews had cut an entrance through the bluffs lining the harbor, laid tracks along the beach, and constructed a large wharf to handle shipping. In the process Huntington and his associates had bought or taken options on much of the property in the vicinity, privately promising in return that the company would use its influence in Congress to locate the proposed port there.[64] More important to the outraged Southern Californians, because of the bluffs and the narrowness of the beach on which tracks had to be laid, other railroads would find it difficult to reach the harbor to compete effectively with the Southern Pacific. Huntington's Santa Monica scheme, charged the Los Angeles *Times*, had been "conceived in sin and brought forth in iniquity."[65]

Led by the *Times*, under the editorship of Harrison Gray Otis, Los Angeles residents launched the free-harbor struggle of the 1890's, which followed almost exactly the pattern of the funding battle that occurred during the same years. They formed a Free Harbor League to lead the anti-railroad forces, won important endorsements from local groups such as the Los Angeles Chamber of Commerce, secured favorable planks in party platforms, held mass meetings, circulated petitions, and recruited support throughout the state. Backed by the weight of public opinion and the report of the government commission, Southern Californians early became confident that San Pedro would be selected as the site for the deep-water harbor.[66]

Huntington, however, had not remained idle while the anti-railroad

[64] Extremely revealing material on Huntington's landholdings and harbor plans can be found in the John P. Jones Papers, Huntington Library, particularly in letters from John P. Jones to Georgina F. Jones, Sept. 24, 1891, Oct. 8, 1891, Feb. 7, 1892. See also LA *Times*, Sept. 6, 1892, July 20, 1894; David Lavender, *The Great Persuader* (New York, 1970), pp. 366–68. It should be noted that land speculation also played a role in the San Pedro side of the battle. See, e.g., the map in the John T. Gaffey Papers, Huntington Library, that shows this San Pedro supporter's holdings of town lots in the vicinity of the proposed harbor.

[65] LA *Times*, May 5, 1896, quoted in Franklyn Hoyt, "Influence of the Railroads in the Development of Los Angeles Harbor," *Historical Society of Southern California Quarterly*, 35 (1953): 205.

[66] Willard, *Free Harbor Contest*, pp. 123–30; LA *Times*, April 7–8, 1894; SF *Exmr*, Aug. 24, 1894; SF *Bul*, Aug. 28, 1893, clipping in WP; *JS*, 31 sess., p. 761.

leaders organized opposition to his Santa Monica project. His first move came early in 1892, as Congress considered a large appropriation for San Pedro. A telegram from the Southern Pacific's chief engineer, questioning the quality of the holding-ground at San Pedro, persuaded Congress to authorize a second special commission of five army engineers to review the matter. The commission held public hearings in Southern California, inspected the two locations, and in October 1892 issued a unanimous report in favor of San Pedro.[67]

Undaunted, and with sympathetic men in charge of the congressional committees that determined harbor appropriations, Huntington managed to delay further action for more than three years. The harbor struggle became a stalemate, as each side maneuvered to gain or preserve control of the crucial committees. To exasperated Californians, impatient with the delay, it appeared that Huntington could overturn the recommendations of two expert commissions and fulfill the angry promise he made in 1894 to the Los Angeles Chamber of Commerce: "Well, I don't know, for sure, that I can get this money for Santa Monica; I think I can. But I know damned well that you shall never get a cent for that other place."[68]

The harbor fight again reached a critical stage during the first months of 1896. As usual Huntington was on the scene in Washington, dividing his time between hearings on the harbor question and on the funding bill. "He is really a remarkable individual," acknowledged his chief opponent, Sen. Stephen M. White. "He has a large number of rooms at his hotel, has an army of lobbyists and attends to more work than any of them himself." San Pedro supporters had also sent a delegation to the capital, with instructions to appeal solely for funds to improve the inner harbor. They had decided on this strategy in the belief that the current depression would preclude appropriations for an expensive deep-water harbor.[69]

[67] LA *Times*, May 29, 1892, Jan. 14, 1893. The commission's report is in *House of Representatives, Executive Document No. 41*, 52d Cong., 2d sess. (Washington, D.C., 1892), pp. 2–26.

[68] Huntington quoted in Willard, *Free Harbor Contest*, p. 107; White to Charles Forman, Jan. 13, 1895, White to John T. Gaffey, Jan. 14, 1895, White to Harrison Gray Otis, Jan. 13, 1895, White to Otis, March 3, 1895, WP.

[69] White to John T. Gaffey, May 4, 1896, WP; James McLachlan to Harrison Gray Otis, Dec. 31, 1895, Markham Papers; LA *Times*, Jan. 21, 1896; SF *Exmr*, Feb. 18, 1896.

The San Pedro forces soon learned, however, that they had under-
estimated the generosity of the House Committee on Rivers and
Harbors. The committee's report, made public in late March 1896,
granted the requested $392,000 inner-harbor appropriation, but it also
allocated $3,098,000 for a deep-water harbor at Santa Monica. South-
ern Californians, recalled a San Pedro leader, were "staggered and
dazed, and at first refused to believe." With a minimum of public
support and against the recommendations of two government commissions, Huntington had been able to obtain congressional backing
for the appropriation he desired.[70]

For a time the so-called double-appropriation scheme threatened to
cause desertions from the free-harbor movement, especially when committee members announced that opposition to the plan would mean
the deletion of both items from the bill. The president of the Free
Harbor League resigned, the Los Angeles City Council resolved in
favor of the two appropriations, and the Los Angeles *Express* joined
the Santa Monica cause.[71] But after hesitating briefly the San Pedro
forces renewed their attack. Early in April 1896 over seven thousand
people attended a mass meeting on the Courthouse steps in Los Angeles. "If you surrender the Southern Pacific octopus will grind you
to death," a speaker told them, and the meeting adopted a resolution
demanding "a free harbor for a free people at San Pedro, or none at
all." Hearst's influential San Francisco *Examiner* again entered the
fray, declaring, "If Mr. Huntington wants a harbor for his wharf at
Santa Monica, let him build it himself with some of the money he has
already stolen from the people." Bolstered by support at home and
from across the state, the Los Angeles Chamber of Commerce, all the
city's labor unions, the Free Harbor League, and other groups reaffirmed their adherence to the San Pedro location.[72]

[70] Willard, *Free Harbor Contest*, p. 141; *Senate Report No. 799*, 54th Cong., 1st
sess. (Washington, D.C., 1896), p. 401; *Report of a Hearing Before the Committee
on Commerce of the Senate of the United States on the Subject of a Deep-Water Harbor in Southern California* (Washington, D.C., 1896), pp. 3–82; White to Charles
Monroe, April 2, 1896, White to T. E. Gibbon, April 7, 1896, WP.

[71] LA *Times*, April 4–8, 1896; Los Angeles *Express*, March 28, 1896, clipping in
WP; Cornelius Cole to Olive Cole, April 22, 1896, Cole Papers; James McLachlan to
Harrison Gray Otis, April 8, 1896, Markham Papers; White to J. A. Hooper, April
16, 1896, White to H. D. Barrows, April 20, 1896, WP.

[72] LA *Times*, April 9, 1896; SF *Exmr*, April 30, 1896; Willard, *Free Harbor Contest*, pp. 145–47; White to W. W. Bowers, March 29, 1896, WP.

Aroused opinion also had its effect in Congress, where Senator White led an assault on the Santa Monica provision. Seeking to divide the Huntington camp, White suggested the creation of a third commission with full authority to settle the question. The Santa Monica forces, headed by Sen. William B. Frye of Maine, fought the proposal vigorously. Attacks on the Southern Pacific, Frye told the Senate, "savor a little bit of the slogan of the sand lots of the Golden Gate, where the name of Huntington is conjured to frighten babies with and used by demagogues to make the knees of weak-kneed politicians tremble." "Oh," Frye exclaimed, "it is too paltry to undertake to stop any legislation with that cheap, demagogical cry that because Huntington has done it no help can be given to Huntington." But the fairness of White's suggestion, coupled with the pressure of public opinion, had already made an impression on many Congressmen. Even those pledged to Santa Monica, noted White, "declared they did not know of any excuse for a refusal to accept my proposition. And so Frye finally accepted and the thing was done." Exulted White: "It is a matter of common talk in the Senate that we got absolutely away with our fight."[73]

In its final form the bill that passed Congress on June 3, 1896, carried a large appropriation for a port in Southern California and established a five-member commission to select its location. In December the new commission began its investigation of the two sites, and on March 2, 1897, it designated San Pedro as the proper location for a deep-water harbor to serve Los Angeles. The reaction in California did justice to a promise Harrison Gray Otis had made to White: "We are waiting for the verdict of the board, and when it is known and found to be right, the eagle on The Times Building will scream a scream which you will hear in your seat in the Senate."[74]

Los Angeles residents held an exuberant celebration. "There was a great deal of cheering and handshaking and drinking of healths," recalled one contemporary. "The fight had been so long, and at times

[73] *Congressional Record*, 54th Cong., 1st sess. (May 11, 1896), pp. 5054–55; White to Charles Monroe, May 15, 1896, White to Harrison Gray Otis, May 15, 1896, WP; LA *Times*, May 13, 1896.
[74] Otis to White, Feb. 7, 1897, T. E. Gibbon to White, March 12, 1897, WP; SF *Exmr*, March 3, 1897. The commission's report is in *Senate Document No. 18*, 55th Cong., 1st sess. (Washington, D.C., 1897), pp. 3–29.

so hopeless, that it seemed quite incredible that it was at last over, and that the invincible railroad had for once gone down in defeat." Work began at San Pedro in April 1899 amid a Free Harbor Jubilee organized to commemorate the event. The harbor contest had ended, and its outcome, an utter defeat for Collis P. Huntington and the Southern Pacific, would shortly assume legendary proportions in Southern California. "The history of the struggle for a free harbor is a rich heritage to the citizens of Los Angeles," Marshall Stimson, a leader of the California Progressive movement, would later write. "Every citizen should know it. It should be taught in all of our public schools."[75]

V

Despite Stimson's plea, the free-harbor struggle, like the anti-funding fight and other anti-railroad efforts in California, has been almost forgotten. Recent scholarship has brought some fresh interpretations, but for the most part the legend of railroad domination has lingered on both in the popular imagination and in histories of the state.[76] From Lord Bryce's early observation that "no State has been so much at the mercy of one powerful corporation" to Sen. Alan Cranston's modern-day description of the railroad's "hammerlock on State and local governments," this legend has remained practically unchanged and unchallenged. "By controlling the governments," Senator Cranston has said of the California railroad lines, "they could fix rates freely, manipulate franchises, smother competition, and commit al-

[75] Willard, *Free Harbor Contest*, p. 179; Marshall Stimson, "A Short History of Los Angeles Harbor," *Historical Society of Southern California Quarterly*, 27 (1945): 7; LA *Times*, March 3, 1897. As late as December 1898 Huntington still refused to admit defeat in the harbor matter. "We are not bothering our heads about San Pedro or what is going to be done there," he told one correspondent, "because the great business of your part of the country is going to be done over the Port Los Angeles pier." Huntington to Cornelius Cole, Dec. 9, 1898, Cole Papers. See also Huntington to Rudolf Axman, June 10, 1898, Gaffey Papers.

[76] Fresh and valuable interpretations, for example, can be found in two articles by Gerald D. Nash: "The California Railroad Commission," pp. 287–305; and "Bureaucracy and Economic Reform: The Experience of California, 1899–1911," *Western Political Quarterly*, 13 (1960): 678–91. See also McAfee, "Local Interests and Railroad Regulation," pp. 51–61. W. H. Hutchinson's "Southern Pacific: Myth and Reality" (*California Historical Society Quarterly*, 48 [1969]: 325–34) reassesses some past views, including the interpretation of railroad power contained in his own "Prologue to Reform: The California Anti-Railroad Republicans, 1899–1905" (*Southern California Quarterly*, 44 [1962]: 175–218).

most any other outrageous abuse to protect or expand their own interests. For four incredible decades, the Southern Pacific ... ran the State and largely controlled both political parties."[77]

This view needs serious reappraisal. Such a reappraisal, if based on the abundant evidence in Pacific Coast archives, would not attempt to minimize the Southern Pacific's considerable impact on California affairs; nor would it praise Huntington and his associates for circumspect behavior in the political arena. But it would recognize that the legend of railroad domination in late-nineteenth-century California obscures the complex relationship between politics and the railroad, assesses the railroad's strength without regard for its divisions and defeats, and perpetuates a myth of passive acquiescence in the railroad's demands that is clearly belied by the activities of railroad opponents in the 1890's and earlier. Worse, the legend of railroad domination misjudges the independence and honesty of a generation of Californians and completely ignores the significant accomplishments of these decades. On the Pacific Coast men acted far more often in opposition to or in disregard of the railroad than in compliance with it, and their actions, not the dictates of the Southern Pacific Railroad, determined the direction of state politics. California politics in the late nineteenth century was not a simple adjunct of railroad enterprise.

If a few Progressives like Marshall Stimson were willing to acknowledge the debt they owed their predecessors, however, historians of the Gilded Age and the Progressive Era have almost totally neglected these early attempts to regulate and restrain the railroad. While this neglect has made their story a compelling one in which a new generation of reformers emerges after decades of corruption to release a state from bondage to the railroad, it has slighted the important contributions made in the years before 1900 and has served to conceal the continuities between the nineteenth and twentieth centuries. The

[77] James Bryce, *The American Commonwealth*, 2 vols. (New York, 1908), 2: 441; Alan Cranston, "Democratic Politics," in Eugene P. Dvorin and Arthur J. Misner, eds., *California Politics and Policies: Original Essays* (Reading, Mass., 1966), p. 30. Probably the most influential exposition of this theme is George E. Mowry's *The California Progressives* (Berkeley, 1951), pp. 1–22. Virtually all histories of the state reflect it. The harbor and funding issues are briefly discussed, though still in the context of railroad domination, in Walton Bean, *California: An Interpretive History* (New York, 1968), pp. 298–310; and Andrew F. Rolle, *California: A History* (New York, 1963), pp. 445–47.

1880's and 1890's were a period rich in significance, marked by meaningful efforts to deal with complex questions of economic instability, corporate power, political change, and urban-industrial growth.[78] On the Coast these questions dominated political discussion and brought concerned citizens together in statewide movements that merged diverse forces and often transcended party lines. In this way late-nineteenth-century Californians achieved substantial reforms of their own and helped lay the groundwork for the achievements of another generation. On the failures and triumphs of these years the Progressives would later build.

[78] See, e.g., H. Wayne Morgan, *From Hayes to McKinley: National Party Politics, 1877–1896* (Syracuse, N.Y., 1969); Geoffrey Blodgett, *The Gentle Reformers: Massachusetts Democrats in the Cleveland Era* (Cambridge, Mass., 1966); Lewis L. Gould, *Wyoming: A Political History, 1868–1896* (New Haven, Conn., 1968); David P. Thelen, *The New Citizenship: Origins of Progressivism in Wisconsin, 1885–1900* (Columbia, Mo., 1972).

CHAPTER TEN

Bryan, McKinley, and 1896

~~~~

IN 1896 THE DEMOCRATIC party faced its gravest internal crisis since the Civil War. The events of the preceding three years had eroded public confidence in the Cleveland administration and divided the party into irreconcilable factions, each convinced that it alone represented Democratic principles. Anti-administration sentiment spread through large areas of the country, particularly in the South and West, angering Cleveland Democrats, who rallied to their leader. Some administration opponents simply sought a scapegoat; others more justly resented the president's failures of philosophy and temperament. His inflexibility and tenacity, qualities that had won praise during the more placid years of his first administration, had become serious liabilities under conditions that demanded experimentation, innovation, and bold leadership.

In a time of national emergency Cleveland had demonstrated the sterility of the Democratic ideal of negative government. As bond issue followed bond issue in the mid-1890's, unaccompanied by spirited leadership, the people lost faith in an administration that appeared irrelevant to their needs and callous to their plight. In growing numbers they turned against the president and resorted, like Cleveland before them, to a panacea that promised to alleviate their condition. By 1896 the twin manifestations of discontent, pro-silver and anti-Cleveland sentiment, pervaded even the ranks of the president's own party. Democrats who had rejoiced at Cleveland's victory in 1892 now eagerly awaited the end of "the reign of Grover the Great."[1]

[1] White to Russell B. Carpenter, May 8, 1896, WP; Stanley L. Jones, *The Presidential Election of 1896* (Madison, Wis., 1964), pp. 36–73.

Blind to the causes of this discontent, Cleveland and his close advisers responded with increasing alarm. As William L. Wilson, the postmaster general, noted in his diary, the silverites "are socialists, anarchists and demagogues of a dangerous type, and a supreme test of our institutions seems ahead of us." Dismayed and discouraged, the secretary of agriculture, J. Sterling Morton, considered the formation of a new political party that would exclude all dissidents. "Is it not possible," he wondered, "for the proprietors of this country—by this I mean the men who own their homes and places of business—to get together and organize a businessmen's sound-money party or a conservative party? Conservatives are those who have something to conserve in the way of homes, good names, and personal property, and generally in all. The radicals are those who have everything to gain and nothing to lose by a currency of violently fluctuating purchasing power."[2]

For the moment Cleveland rejected such suggestions. Unwilling to concede the control of the Democratic party to the silverites, he redoubled his efforts to prevent the inclusion of a silver plank in the party's 1896 platform. Wilson outlined the president's strategy: "If we can keep the platform right, and the National party sound, the future need not greatly worry us. For while defeat seems inevitable this year, and a sound money platform may lead to a bolt from the Convention, or at any rate to a great falling off in the South and West of free silver Democrats to the Populist party, they will eventually come back and the integrity of the organization will be preserved." Accordingly, Cleveland wrote several public letters in which he derided silver and, ironically, urged "a consultation and comparison of views" within the Democratic party. "I refuse to believe," the president said in June 1896, "that when the time arrives for deliberate action there will be engrafted upon our Democratic creed a demand for the free, unlimited, and independent coinage of silver."[3]

[2] Entry for June 26, 1896, in Festus P. Summers, ed., *The Cabinet Diary of William L. Wilson, 1896–1897* (Chapel Hill, N.C., 1957), p. 109; Morton to John P. Irish, March 14, 1896, Morton Papers.
[3] Entry for Feb. 16, 1896, in Summers, ed., *Cabinet Diary of Wilson*, pp. 27–28; Cleveland to the Democratic Voters, June 16, 1896, in Allan Nevins, ed., *Letters of Grover Cleveland, 1850–1908* (Boston, 1933), pp. 440–41; SF *Exmr*, June 17, 1896; Irish to Morton, March 5, 1896, Morton Papers.

To their dismay, however, Cleveland and his supporters made little headway in their anti-silver campaign. Mistakenly convinced that only socialists, anarchists, and demagogues would favor silver, they failed to recognize that the events of the 1890's, including the depression and the administration's own dogmatic approach to the money question, had transformed silver from simply an inflationary instrument into the symbol for a wide range of popular grievances. In 1896, as the Cleveland Democrats soon learned, it was too late to dampen the silver movement in the country. It was also too late for appeals to the Democratic party to remain loyal to the principles and policies of Grover Cleveland. Between April and June, despite the president's last-minute efforts, Democratic conventions in state after state broke with the administration and declared in favor of silver. "Now," lamented Postmaster General Wilson in May, "we find perverts where we least expected them, and a madness that cannot be dealt with or, indeed, scarcely approached."[4]

As Wilson had feared, when the Democratic national convention opened in Chicago on July 7, 1896, the dissidents were firmly in control. By a vote of 564 to 357 the delegates defeated a resolution to commend "the honesty, economy, courage and fidelity of the present Democratic National Administration." They adopted instead a platform that denounced nearly every policy Cleveland had pursued since 1893. The platform demanded the free and unlimited coinage of silver, called the currency question "paramount to all others at this time," and labeled gold monometallism a British policy, "not only un-American, but anti-American." Other planks assailed the president's bond issues, censured his "trafficking with banking syndicates," and condemned his actions in the 1894 Pullman strike.[5]

On July 10 the convention completed its repudiation of the administration by nominating for president William Jennings Bryan of Nebraska, a young silverite whose famous speech during the platform debate had captivated the delegates. Some Cleveland supporters had

---

[4] Entry for May 26, 1896, in Summers, ed., *Cabinet Diary of Wilson*, p. 90; Paolo E. Coletta, *William Jennings Bryan*, vol. 1: *Political Evangelist, 1860–1908* (Lincoln, Neb., 1964), pp. 112–18; Paul W. Glad, *The Trumpet Soundeth: William Jennings Bryan and His Democracy, 1896–1912* (Lincoln, Neb., 1960), p. 54.

[5] *Official Proceedings of the Democratic National Convention* (Logansport, Ind., 1896), pp. 250–56.

already departed, refusing to countenance the party's new direction. "Left Chicago," one administration official wrote in his diary the day before Bryan's nomination. "The platform had been announced and there was nothing more to be done. No respectable man could afford to remain." Vacationing in Massachusetts, Cleveland was "dazed" by the proceedings at Chicago. "I am in no condition for speech or thought on the subject," he told Richard Olney, the attorney general. To another friend the president exclaimed: "If ever there was a penitentiary devoted to the incarceration of those who commit crimes against the Democratic party, how easily it could be filled just at this time!"[6]

II

Cleveland's small band of California followers was aghast at the Chicago outcome. Attending the convention as a spectator, John P. Irish immediately huddled with William C. Whitney and other administration supporters to discuss the creation of a third party. Such a party, they reasoned, would provide a Democratic alternative to the Chicago nominees and establish a base from which control of the main organization could later be recaptured. In California other Cleveland Democrats moved swiftly to "spit out Bryan and populism."[7] They assured the president of their continued loyalty, denouncing "the brutal and entirely indefensible treatment you have received," and gave encouragement to the third-party strategy. As one put it, "I hope Whitney ... and the rest will nominate some good gold Democrat so I can cast a vote for principle if not for success."[8]

Success seemed unlikely indeed. Instead of displaying disgust with the convention's action, most California Democrats were openly jubilant over it. "The gathering at Chicago was certainly a great affair,

[6] Entry for July 9, 1896, Charles S. Hamlin Diary; Cleveland to Olney, July 13, 1896, Olney Papers; Allan Nevins, *Grover Cleveland: A Study in Courage* (New York, 1932), p. 704.

[7] John T. Doyle to Abram S. Hewitt, Nov. 10, 1896, Doyle Papers; "Memorandum of a Meeting of Sound Money Men," July 7, 1896, Whitney Papers; William D. Bynum to Cleveland, July 25, 1896, CP.

[8] Marcus Rosenthal to Cleveland, July 14, 1896, CP; Charles Dwight Willard to Samuel Willard, July 13, 1896, Willard Papers. See also Joseph Allen to William C. Whitney, July 11, 1896, E. W. Britt to Whitney, June 29, 1896, Whitney Papers; Jonathan J. Valentine to Cleveland, July 23, 1896, CP.

and it was not run by any clique or faction," exulted Stephen M. White, who had been honored with the chairmanship of the convention. "It hit straight from the shoulder without any reference to crowned heads or presidents, senators or other office-holders. I think we are going to win. Don't believe the money bags can control us."[9] For three years Coast Democrats had tried to avoid a split with the Cleveland administration. When the final break came in 1896, their reaction was one of mild regret mixed with a sense of relieved exhilaration.

Besides, the convention's outcome offered pragmatic advantages too attractive to ignore. Ending earlier fears of a sound-money platform, it brought new hope and confidence to a party that had anticipated a severe drubbing in the November election. Both candidate and platform would enable the Democrats to exploit silver sentiment, encourage defections from the Republican camp, and perhaps tap the strength of the California People's party. Capitalizing on Bryan's nomination, Democratic strategists quickly planned an aggressive reform campaign, divorced as much as possible from the party's record of the past several years. Senator White sounded the campaign's central theme: "The present conditions are admittedly deplorable. Those who support Mr. Bryan offer relief. Those who oppose him insist upon a continuance of a policy which has been proven to be detrimental to all of our producers, and beneficial only to the limited wealthy class who profit from the trials of their fellow citizens."[10]

In William Jennings Bryan, moreover, the Democrats had a candidate who was already popular on the Pacific Coast. While in Congress Bryan had won Californians' approval by his opposition to railroad-funding legislation; he had maintained close relations with California silver leaders; and in September 1895 he had visited California to speak on behalf of the silver standard. "You have a great

[9] White to G. G. Goucher, Aug. 6, 1896, WP; SF *Exmr*, July 11–12, 1896. Although he had been a United States senator for only three years, White received several honors at the convention. He was first chosen chairman of the platform committee, but he declined this position when he was tendered the permanent chairmanship of the convention. Jones, *Presidential Election of 1896*, p. 222.

[10] White to E. T. Greyson, Sept. 21, 1896, WP. For the Democrats' preconvention fears of a sound-money platform, see White to J. P. Haynes, April 30, 1896, White to A. Kinkead, May 2, 1896, White to J. E. Baker, May 7, 1896, White to J. W. Purdy, June 5, 1896, WP.

many friends in this and adjoining States," a prominent California silverite told him.[11] Bryan's address to the Chicago convention enhanced his appeal, as did his prompt promise to wage a vigorous cross-country campaign. On the night after his nomination thousands celebrated the event in San Francisco. "The enthusiasm here Saturday night was bordering on hysteria," remarked one observer.[12]

The Bryan demonstrations, spreading through Los Angeles and other communities, depressed the Cleveland Democrats. When John P. Irish returned from Chicago in late July, he heard discouraging reports of the emotional fervor that had greeted the news of Bryan's nomination. Combining with Edward B. Pond to form a San Francisco Sound Money Club, Irish could initially persuade only 32 Democrats to join. Most party members, even men such as John Daggett and Gavin McNab who were sympathetic to gold, had chosen to follow Bryan and silver.[13] The Cleveland Democrats fought on but became gloomy and pessimistic. "Unless something is done in this State," one warned the president, "by those who believe in the integrity of the government, as affecting its financial and judicial policy, by those who believe with you, this State in my judgment is irretrievably lost."[14]

With few exceptions Coast Republicans shared this pessimism. During 1895 and early 1896 they had decided to gamble on the nomination of William McKinley, the popular former congressman and governor of Ohio, on a platform advocating free silver or bimetallism. Lending support to the McKinley movement, they had directed their efforts "towards opening the eyes of the leaders of the Republican party throughout this country, to the fact that that party must sooner or

[11] Alva Udell to Bryan, May 28, 1895, George P. Keeney to Bryan, Oct. 22, 1895, Adolph Sutro to Bryan, Sept. 19, 1895, Bryan Papers; Harold F. Taggart, "California and the Silver Question in 1895," *PHR*, 6 (1937): 259.

[12] G. M. Collier to Thomas V. Cator, July 13, 1896, Cator Papers. In California, it might be noted, there was no serious mention of Bryan as a possible candidate, either in the Democratic press or within the delegation, until his address to the convention. The Nebraskan's speech enthralled the Coast delegates, and for them at least, the *Examiner* was substantially correct in asserting that "a speech has made a candidate" (July 11, 1896). For a different, nationwide view, see James A. Barnes, "Myths of the Bryan Campaign," *Mississippi Valley Historical Review*, 34 (1947): 376–82.

[13] SF *Exmr*, July 11, Aug. 19, 1896; SF *Chron*, July 11, 1896; Samuel Braunhart to White, Aug. 4, 1897, WP.

[14] Henry S. Foote to Cleveland, Sept. 18, 1896, AP, Cal., U.S. Attorney File, Northern District, Justice Dept., RG 60.

later come to the side of silver or ... it will be in danger of repudiation by the people."[15] As the first step toward carrying out this policy, the Republican state convention in May 1896 endorsed McKinley, unanimously approved a resolution in favor of the free coinage of silver, and selected a delegation dominated by silverites to attend the party's national convention. In a hopeful mood the delegates journeyed to St. Louis, the convention site, in a special train that bore a giant banner: "California is for the free and unlimited coinage of silver at the ratio of sixteen to one, and no compromise."[16]

To the Democrats' delight, the delegation hastily furled its banner for the return trip. Although the convention nominated McKinley for president, it also declared "unreservedly" for "the existing gold standard." The St. Louis proceedings had abruptly put California Republicans in an awkward position and dampened their expectations of victory in the fall contest. Most refused to bolt the party and, loyal to the national organization, made the transition from silver to sound money with relative ease. But the St. Louis platform, as one contemporary later recalled, "left the Republican rank and file in a state of utter confusion. Probably 80 to 90 per cent of them had for years accepted free-silver leadership."[17] The Sacramento *Bee*, the Santa Rosa *Press*, and a few other party journals came out for Bryan and silver, and some prominent Republicans transferred their allegiance to the Democratic ticket. "Leading republicans here are distributing silver documents and Bryan speeches," noted an observer in Fresno County. "I was astonished."[18]

Continuing into September, defections from the McKinley ticket

---

[15] Charles K. McClatchy to Thomas R. Bard, March 19, 1896, Bard Papers; McClatchy to Henry Harrison Markham, March 13, 1896, Paris Kilburn to Markham, April 3, 1896, John F. Davis to Marcus A. Hanna, April 2, 1896, Markham Papers; James A. Waymire to McKinley, April 13, 1896, William McKinley Papers, Manuscript Division, Library of Congress; Morris M. Estee to James S. Clarkson, Jan. 11, 1896, Clarkson Papers.

[16] Franklin Hichborn, "California in the 1896 National Campaign" (typescript dated 1943, Franklin Hichborn Papers, Public Affairs Service Department, Univ. of California, Los Angeles), pp. 2–12; SF *Chron*, May 7, 1896.

[17] Hichborn, "California in the 1896 National Campaign," p. 4; *Official Proceedings of the Eleventh Republican National Convention* (St. Louis, 1896), pp. 83, 91–96; SF *Exmr*, June 18, 1896; H. Wayne Morgan, *From Hayes to McKinley: National Party Politics, 1877–1896* (Syracuse, N.Y., 1969), pp. 498–500.

[18] O. L. Abbott to Cator, Sept. 7, 1896, Cator Papers; Harold F. Taggart, "The Party Realignment of 1896 in California," *PHR*, 8 (1939): 439–42; SF *Exmr*, July 22, Oct. 6, 1896.

alarmed Republican campaign managers. Worry centered on the party stronghold in Southern California, where silver Republicans busily organized clubs to marshal the Bryan forces in the party. "What does this mean?" a McKinley manager asked after hearing about a Los Angeles club with several thousand members. "Are the Republicans deserting us in a body, or is this Club a sham?"[19] By election eve the Los Angeles group, claiming a membership of five thousand, threatened to throw the region into the Bryan column. The Republican central committee bombarded Southern California leaders with frantic appeals to stem the desertions: "Of course," wrote the committee's secretary, "we cannot get out of our minds the old-time majority of about 10,000 that came up to us from the south of Tehachapi, and it takes our breath away some times to think that we may not come north with any majority at all and we wonder where it is to come from."[20]

Boosted by these developments, the Democrats' spirits soared through the summer of 1896. The Republicans' mounting troubles, silver's obvious allure, and the ardent response to Bryan's candidacy promised victory in November. Republicans grew despondent. "I am satisfied," one admitted toward the end of August, "that if the election were to take place tomorrow it would go strongly Democratic. The business men here appear to be acting sensibly and are very much in earnest in this matter, but where the great mass of laboring men will go is pretty hard to tell. Certain it is that the Bryan fad is having its influence over them." Dispatching favorable reports to national headquarters, Stephen M. White and other Democrats predicted a large Bryan majority in the state. All that remained to clinch the almost certain triumph, White and his allies thought, was fusion with the California People's party.[21]

19 James A. Waymire to Henry Zenas Osborne, Oct. 5, 1896, Irving B. Dudley to Osborne, Sept. 28, 1896, F. H. Heald to Osborne, Sept. 24, 1896, Osborne Papers; G. E. Specht to Bryan, Oct. 31, 1896, Bryan Papers; Harold F. Taggart, "The Silver Republican Club of Los Angeles," *Historical Society of Southern California Quarterly*, 25 (1943): 105–6.

20 M. R. Higgins to Osborne, Sept. 25, 1896, Osborne Papers; SF *Exmr*, Oct. 17, 1896; White to James K. Jones, Sept. 2, 1896, White to John M. McClure, Oct. 9, 1896, WP.

21 Henry Harrison Markham to Irving C. Stump, Aug. 24, 1896, Markham Papers; White to Arthur Sewall, Sept. 2, 1896, White to James K. Jones, Oct. 7, 1896, WP; SF *Exmr*, Sept. 18, Oct. 28, 31, 1896.

To achieve this aim, however, the Democrats first had to overcome stubborn hostility to fusion among the Populists. In recent years the California Populists had been engaged in a divisive dispute over the place of silver in the party's reform program. On one side were those who, impressed with the growth of silver sentiment in the South and West, had become convinced that a free-coinage stance offered the best chance of success in 1896. The leader of this faction, E. M. Wardell, chairman of the Populist central committee, argued "that the Silver issue is the *one* issue we can win on, and that it is the *only one* on which we can win."[22] Opposition to Wardell's strategy came from a powerful "middle-of-the-road" element in the California party. While agreeing that the Populists, as one put it, "must avail ourselves of this Silver racket & get all [the] strength we can out of it," this element demanded that the party continue to campaign on the broad reform platform outlined at Omaha in 1892.[23] The People's party, warned John S. Dore in September 1895, should not become "so blinded by any silver agitation as to think for an instant [that] that question settled is all we need to be a happy & prosperous people." "Can any man of fair intelligence," asked Dore, "for one moment believe our party can be carried bodily away from [the] Omaha platform to a single issue Silver party? I say no! & I can't make myself believe otherwise."[24]

By early 1896 the "middle-of-the-road" Populists had prevailed over the silverite faction, and they moved quickly to kill, in Dore's words, "the snake that was getting into our political garden." The party's state convention in May approved a free-coinage plank, but it also reaffirmed the Omaha platform and adopted a resolution opposing fusion with other parties. Convinced either by the arguments or by the superior number of his opponents, Wardell endorsed the convention's action and agreed with Thomas V. Cator, who insisted that "no leader of the Populist party would think of going into a campaign

[22] Wardell's position reported in John S. Dore to Cator, May 6, 1895, Cator Papers.
[23] Dore to Cator, Sept. 22, 1895, Cator Papers. Populists who opposed the narrowing of the party's platform to one issue, particularly silver, called themselves "middle-of-the-road" Populists. They urged the party to stay "in the middle of the road" and fight for the entire Omaha platform, which called for new national policies toward money, credit, transportation, and land.
[24] Dore to Cator, Sept. 22, 1895, Dore to Cator, Oct. 28, 1895, W. H. Gilstrap to Cator, June 24, 1896, Cator Papers.

on a free silver plank, to the exclusion of the other principles our party holds dear."[25] Cator would soon lead the California Populists in the direction he now scorned, but for the moment the "middle-of-the-roaders" had won. "Isn't it astounding the way our reform ideas are growing ...," wrote one a week after the convention adjourned. "We cannot now drop a single issue or trim a single plank.... Back of us & with us are the millions, the toilers sinking into moral and physical decay. Our party is their last hope. In front of us and around us [are] the old party manipulators actuated by the hell-born power of greed."[26]

July and the Democratic national convention brought a sudden change in the Populists' outlook. Destroying the assumptions on which their plans had been based, the events at Chicago presented the California Populists with an unpleasant dilemma. Some still held out for an independent campaign and urged party leaders to "look rather to the future effect, than to present success. A victory without practical reform following it will be, like the victories of Pyrrhus, barren of results."[27] But Bryan's nomination gave new force to the contentions of the silverites, who could now predict defeat and disgrace if the People's party failed to endorse him. The Bryan candidacy, a San Francisco Populist told Cator, "has struck a responsive chord in the hearts" of the people. "I have talked with hundreds and 9 out of 10 on an average are going to support Bryan.... In him, I think we will have a President that will be a match for the money power of this Country."[28]

Under great pressure from party followers and insistent Democrats who extended fusion overtures, Cator himself began to slip toward Bryan and silver. En route to the Populist national convention at St. Louis, he found "a kind of popular whirlwind for silver, all the way across the continent as I came, meeting many populists of the rank

[25] Dore to Cator, Dec. 1, 1895, Cator Papers; Cator quoted in SF *Exmr*, May 24, 1896; SF *Chron*, May 12–14, 1896.

[26] D. W. Huffman to Cator, May 24, 1896, Dore to Cator, April 12, 1896, Cator Papers. "Let the fundamentals be preserved intact," declared another Populist. "Let the tripod stand: 'Land, Transportation & Finance.'... Fusion with Democracy means speedy dissolution of our party." C. H. Castle to Cator, June 27, 1896, Cator Papers.

[27] C. H. Castle to Cator, July 18, 1896, Cator Papers; SF *Chron*, July 12, 1896.

[28] G. M. Collier to Cator, July 13, 1896, Eureka County Committee to Cator, July 15, 1896, E. J. Richards to Cator, July 16, 1896, Cator Papers; SF *Exmr*, July 16, 1896; Olive Cole to George R. Cole, undated (1896), Cole Papers.

and file, who declared we must not divide the silver vote." On July 21, the day before the convention opened, the pragmatic Cator came out in favor of a union of all forces against gold, and once the convention had nominated Bryan, he used his considerable influence to persuade fellow California Populists to join the Democrats in the campaign.[29] By mid-September 1896, despite the earlier opposition within the People's party to such a policy, the Populists and the Democrats had reached a fusion agreement that covered most of the offices at stake in the election.

The first formal step toward fusion came in late August with the creation of a Democratic-Populist-Silver party conference committee authorized to work out a joint campaign for the three parties. Although neither the Populists nor the Democrats would consent to the withdrawal of their vice-presidential candidate, the committee decided to combine presidential electors, allotting the Democrats five electors and the People's party four.[30] The Silver party—a small party established earlier in 1896 by some of those who believed, mistakenly, that neither major party would endorse free silver—and the Democratic central committee promptly ratified the arrangement, and on August 22 four Democratic electors submitted their resignations. Two days later, over the protests of Dore, who continued to fight for an independent campaign, the Populist executive committee accepted the plan. The conference committee then proceeded to name fusion candidates in the state's seven congressional districts. Meeting during the first week of September, it chose four Democratic and three Populist candidates, the latter concentrated in the normally Republican areas of Southern California.[31] These two agreements made the fusion arrangements for the national campaign virtually complete.

[29] Cator to E. M. Wardell, July 9, 1896, Cator Papers; SF *Exmr*, July 22, 1896. For a detailed treatment of the Populists' problems on the national level, see Robert F. Durden, *The Climax of Populism: The Election of 1896* (Lexington, Ky., 1965).

[30] For vice-president the Democrats had nominated Arthur Sewall of Maine, and the Populists, partly to maintain a semblance of independence, had named Thomas E. Watson of Georgia. Jones, *Presidential Election of 1896*, pp. 244–63.

[31] SF *Exmr*, Aug. 23–25, Sept. 6–9, 1896; Taggart, "Party Realignment of 1896," pp. 443–44. However, two previously nominated congressional candidates, a Populist in the first district and a Democrat in the fifth, refused to withdraw in favor of the fusion candidates. Aided by the failure of the fusion effort, Republican candidates carried both districts in November. SF *Chron*, Dec. 14, 1896.

This success was repeated on the state and local level in California, and as in 1892, it owed much to the combined efforts of Cator and Stephen M. White, who both strove for fusion in every section of the state.[32] With his eye on a Senate seat in 1897, Cator endeavored to trade local offices for Populist nominations to the legislature. His accomplishments in this regard evoked complaints from members of the Democratic central committee: "Some of these interior Democrats would swap an Assemblyman for a ham sandwich in case the man with the sandwich happened along. Cator has been that man. He is getting Assemblymen for Constables, Justices of the Peace and such small deer."[33] Democrats like White, on the other hand, recognized that the lingering disappointment over Bryan's nomination, and the need to placate the influential "middle-of-the-road" elements in the Populist party, had heightened the Populists' demands. They pointed to the 1892 example and argued that fusion alone could produce victory. "It is clear," White remarked, "that we must make some concessions to the populists or we cannot succeed in getting anything." In the end, with the exception of San Francisco, where Democratic factionalism made such agreements difficult, the two parties agreed on fusion candidates for the legislature in all but five assembly districts and one senatorial district.[34]

Rounding out the Democratic strategy, the fusion arrangements made party leaders confident of success in November. Through the campaign's remaining weeks the Democrats focused almost exclusively on the silver issue, assuring voters that free coinage would raise wages, increase farm income, and cure the depression.[35] On October 30 they held their final northern rally in the Mechanics' Pavilion in San Francisco. Some 15,000 people listened to silver speeches and

[32] Henry C. Dillon to Cator, Aug. 11, 1896, Cator Papers; White to Cator, Aug. 17, 1896, White to W. H. Alford, Sept. 2, 1896, White to Cator, Sept. 14, 1896, White to Cator, Sept. 17, 1896, White to Cator, Sept. 25, 1896, White to Cator, Sept. 28, 1896, WP.

[33] SF *Exmr*, Sept. 14, 1896.

[34] White to John C. Fisher, Aug. 28, 1896, WP; SF *Exmr*, Sept. 8, 1896; LA *Times*, Sept. 13–15, 1896; Harold F. Taggart, "Thomas Vincent Cator: Populist Leader of California," *California Historical Society Quarterly*, 28 (1949): 51.

[35] SF *Exmr*, Aug. 21, 30–31, 1896; White to unknown correspondent, Sept. 1896, White to T. T. Williams, Sept. 24, 1896, WP. During the campaign the *Examiner* published a special silver edition claiming with remarkable precision that the demonetization of silver had cost California farmers $381,730,317.40 since 1873 (Sept. 27, 1896).

upon a signal from the stage waved tiny American flags to refute a Republican charge that the party's platform was unpatriotic. Los Angeles Democrats attended a similar meeting. "It seemed as if the whole city was out," wrote one elated participant. "We have strong hopes now of the election of Bryan."[36] On the night before the election, the chairman of the Democratic central committee forecast a 25,000-vote majority for Bryan in the state. Congressman James G. Maguire was even more optimistic. "You have made the grandest campaign in the world's history," he wired Bryan. "California will give you forty thousand majority."[37]

III

Beginning some two months before, however, there had been a perceptible shift in the momentum of the California campaign. Momentarily stunned by the outcome of the summer conventions, the Republicans had spent July and August in quiet reflection, fearful of defeat and uncertain of the best strategy. The Democrats had taken advantage of this lassitude to establish an early lead, but the arrival of fall brought a resurgence of Republican energy. In September a new note of eager confidence appeared in the correspondence of Republican leaders. Reports reached party headquarters that the Bryan fervor, peaking during the summer months, had started to wane. Encouraging signs in San Francisco and other northern areas, coupled with the continuing loyalty of most Republicans to the McKinley ticket, helped offset the discouraging trend in Southern California.[38]

"The prospects for our success are improving daily," the chairman of the Republican central committee wrote in mid-September, "and were the South in as good shape as the Northern section of the State I would be prepared to offer big odds that the electoral vote of California would be delivered beyond all question of doubt to Major Mc-

[36] Olive Cole to George R. Cole, Nov. 2, 1896, Cole Papers; SF *Exmr*, Oct. 31, 1896; LA *Times*, Nov. 3, 1896.

[37] Maguire to Bryan, Nov. 3, 1896, N. J. Manson to Bryan, Oct. 30, 1896, G. E. Specht to Bryan, Oct. 31, 1896, Bryan Papers; SF *Chron*, Nov. 3, 1896.

[38] Harrison Gray Otis to Thomas R. Bard, Oct. 8, 1896, Bard Papers; H. A. Averill to Osborne, June 26, 1896, C. D. Bonestel to Osborne, Sept. 24, 1896, Irving B. Dudley to Osborne, Sept. 28, 1896, Osborne Papers; William M. Osborne to McKinley, Aug. 11, 1896, McKinley Papers.

Kinley." The Republicans worked through September to consolidate their gains in the North, and then turned their attention to conditions south of the Tehachapi.[39] They hoped to exploit the weaknesses of their opponents' one-issue campaign, attract voters who were put off by Bryan's moralistic crusade, and convince moderate silver men to support the McKinley ticket. To accomplish these aims the Republican strategists planned a three-pronged attack designed to undermine the Democratic candidate and platform, defuse the silver issue, and advance the presidential stature of William McKinley.

With a savagery unmatched in previous campaigns, Republican speakers and newspapers assailed Bryan, deftly managing to link him to both the discredited past of the Cleveland administration and the untested future of social upheaval. Identifying him with anarchists, cranks, and misguided fanatics, they depicted Bryan as a radical whose candidacy, backed by "maddened demagogues" and "social revolutionists," threatened the continuation of the republic.[40] "The soldier-haters, the sectionalists, the class-against-mass incendiaries, the socialists, are in the Bryan following, one and all," proclaimed the San Francisco *Chronicle*. The theme was constantly repeated as the campaign progressed. "There has been a new birth of sectionalism and class hatred which revives the memory and arouses the spirit of the war days. With it comes the threat of anarchy. Behind it is the menace of revolution."[41]

William McKinley, the Republicans suggested, embodied an entirely different outlook. Instead of occupational, ethnic, and sectional divisiveness, McKinley stood for a pluralistic approach to American society and offered a benevolent framework in which all sections, religions, and classes would find protection. Rather than social revolution McKinley promised social progress, constructive reform, prosperity, and the fulfillment of time-honored objectives. In place of a single-minded silver crusade, tainted by self-righteousness and irrational prejudice, McKinley spoke for a broad, positive program, highlighted by a protective tariff to guard the interests of farmers, laborers,

[39] Frank McLaughlin to Osborne, Sept. 15, 1896, M. R. Higgins to Osborne, Sept. 25, 1896, Osborne Papers.
[40] SF *Chron*, July 14, 16, 1896; LA *Times*, July 9, 1896.
[41] SF *Chron*, Oct. 9, Nov. 3, 1896.

and manufacturers. McKinley, Coast Republicans repeated again and again, represented national unity and responsibility, progress with stability, and a prosperous departure from the depression-ridden policies of the Democratic party.

With consummate skill Republican campaigners stressed some themes throughout the state and varied others to suit the tastes of particular regions. Everywhere they emphasized the tariff and prosperity. Tariff literature, dispatched in huge quantities by Republican national headquarters and the American Protective Tariff League, flooded the state.[42] Local party workers tapped long-standing loyalties to the protective system and adroitly used the issue in silver Republican districts where fear of a Democratic low-tariff administration often outweighed distaste for the Republican sound-money platform. Those who voted for Bryan, the Republicans suggested, voted against "the advance agent of prosperity" and risked destroying the wine, wool, fruit, lumber, and other important California industries. "The issue," as the Riverside *Press* put it, "is simply McKinley and plenty vs. Bryan and destitution."[43]

The silver question required more careful handling. In agricultural areas, particularly in Southern California, many Republican candidates adopted a simple expedient: they ignored the St. Louis platform and campaigned for silver. To counter doubts about the national party's intentions, they quoted McKinley's promise to seek an international agreement to establish bimetallism and assured voters that "the white metal will be kindly treated by him. He has always been friendly to silver."[44] They reminded people of the Democratic alternative. "Those who feel sore over the defeat of silver [at the St. Louis convention]," remarked one Republican journal, "should remember that all the silver in the world could not compensate this country for another four years of Clevelandism."[45] In this way Coast Republicans avoided an embarrassing break with past positions, kept

[42] Wilbur F. Wakeman to Osborne, Oct. 23, 1896, Osborne Papers; Bard to Otis, Oct. 5, 1896, Bard Papers; SF *Chron*, July 11, 1896.
[43] Riverside *Press*, n.d., quoted in LA *Times*, July 27, 1896; SF *Chron*, July 3, Sept. 1, Nov. 1, 1896.
[44] SF *Chron*, June 19, 1896; LA *Times*, Sept. 16, 1896; SF *Exmr*, Nov. 4, 1896; Durden, *Climax of Populism*, p. 146.
[45] San Pedro *American*, n.d., quoted in LA *Times*, June 21, 1896.

some silverites in the McKinley camp, and ensured that the California campaign would not become a clear-cut contest between silver and gold.

By default as well as by design, they also managed to profit from sound-money sentiment. While Republican speakers canvassed silver districts in behalf of the white metal, party leaders in San Francisco and other centers of gold strength courted groups hostile to the Democratic free silver platform. They devoted particular attention to the gold Democrats who in early September had helped form a new organization, the National Democratic party, and had nominated John M. Palmer of Illinois to oppose Bryan's candidacy. Determined to uphold the Cleveland administration, John P. Irish organized a California branch of the new party and then departed for the Midwest for a series of debates with Bryan.[46] His allies, including John T. Doyle, Edward B. Pond, and William D. English, remained behind to fight the "silver lunatics" and "the great impending peril of national dishonor and socialistic domination."[47] The Republicans carefully followed their activities, fearful that a sizable National Democratic vote might give Bryan the state in a close election. By pointing out this danger they managed to persuade a considerable proportion of the gold Democrats to back the McKinley ticket.[48]

Like the gold Democrats many businessmen felt they had no reasonable alternative to the Republican ticket. If they sometimes rebelled against the silver emphasis in the Republican campaign, they were far more bitterly opposed to the Democratic candidate and platform. Most of them accordingly joined the McKinley fold. Irving M.

[46] *Proceedings of the Convention of the National Democratic Party* (Indianapolis, Ind., 1896), pp. 34–39; William Jennings Bryan, *The First Battle: A Story of the Campaign of 1896* (Chicago, 1896), pp. 602–3; Irish to Parker, Feb. 1, 1897, "Letters Written by John P. Irish to George F. Parker," *Iowa Journal of History and Politics*, 31 (1933): 450. J. Rogers Hollingsworth, *The Whirligig of Politics: The Democracy of Cleveland and Bryan* (Chicago, 1963), pp. 69–83, examines the new party.

[47] Marcus Rosenthal to Cleveland, July 14, 1896, CP; Doyle to Abram S. Hewitt, Nov. 10, 1896, Doyle to Hewitt, Nov. 12, 1896, Doyle Papers; A. B. Butler to William C. Whitney, June 23, 1896, Joseph Allen to Whitney, July 11, 1896, Whitney Papers; SF *Exmr*, Oct. 5, 1896. Once one of the most influential politicians in the state, English had lost power during the 1890's; his brief and ineffective appearance as a Cleveland Democrat in 1896 was ironic in view of his earlier hatred of the president.

[48] Irving B. Dudley to Osborne, Sept. 28, 1896, C. D. Bonestel to Osborne, Sept. 24, 1896, Osborne Papers.

Scott, president of San Francisco's Union Iron Works, urged his employees to vote for McKinley, and the sugar magnate Claus Spreckels, in New York for the Democratic national convention, hurried home to California to work against the Democratic nominees. "The people need not feel the slightest alarm," announced Spreckels. "Insanity is not going to rule this country, and gold for a long time to come will remain the standard coin of the United States."[49] To rally the McKinley forces, a group of San Francisco merchants, bankers, and lawyers formed the California Sound Money League, with branches in the principal towns across the state. The Southern Pacific Railroad reportedly circulated among its workers a pamphlet entitled *Every Man for Himself*, which forecast a general reduction of wages should Bryan win.[50]

This activity prompted the Democrats to complain frequently of improper conduct by businessmen during the campaign. "Monetary disbursements and coercion freely utilized by opposition," Senator White wired the party's national committee.[51] It also left the Democrats impoverished. "It is exceedingly hard to raise money, as banks and large monied interests are all on the other side of the fence," noted White, who lamented that "this is a poor man's campaign, if there ever was one." While silver-mine owners and a few Southern California businessmen helped out, the Democrats were forced to economize on speakers, literature, and campaign rallies. In the midst of the campaign the Democratic central committee had to issue "an appeal to the people" for small contributions. The San Francisco *Examiner* called the state committee "ludicrously poor" and estimated that the Democratic campaign had less money to operate on than any campaign that the state had witnessed since its admission to the union.[52]

[49] SF *Exmr*, July 12, Sept. 20, 1896.

[50] *Ibid.*, Aug. 19, Sept. 15, 1896; Charles Dwight Willard to Samuel Willard, Sept. 12, 1896, Willard Papers; Frank McLaughlin to Osborne, Sept. 15, 1896, Osborne Papers.

[51] White to James K. Jones, Oct. 7, 1896, White to A. N. Soliss, Sept. 4, 1896, WP; SF *Exmr*, Oct. 28, 31, 1896.

[52] White to J. F. Kinney, Sept. 21, 1896, White to Mark R. Plaisted, Sept. 14, 1896, WP; SF *Exmr*, Sept. 20, Oct. 5, 1896; Taggart, "Party Realignment of 1896," p. 444; William Hayward to Bryan, Nov. 6, 1896, Bryan Papers.

For a time the Republicans experienced similar difficulties. Through mid-September the prevailing certainty that Bryan would carry the state held down business contributions, and members of the Republican national committee informed dismayed Coast leaders that the committee planned to focus its efforts on carrying the electoral votes of the Northeast and Midwest. California must "practically take care of herself in this campaign," wrote one committee member.[53] Recognizing the need for a vigorous campaign to reverse the Democrats' early gains, Republican managers were in a quandary: "The fact is," one complained, "that we are already talking through our nose to save the wear and tear on our back teeth, economy being the order of the day."[54] To their relief, rising hopes of victory soon changed the outlook of businessmen and the national committee. In October the committee's treasurer arrived with $35,000 to add to the California campaign chest, an amount that was matched by local sources. The new funds enabled the party to dispatch speakers and literature across the state.[55]

Heartened, the Republicans displayed their strength in a massive parade in San Francisco during the final days of the campaign. To swell the ranks of the marchers, most employers gave their laborers a paid holiday, and the Southern Pacific brought additional contingents into the city from surrounding areas. For four hours army veterans, fruit growers, railroad employees, ironworkers, and other groups marched down Market Street in a parade that even the Democrats, unable to afford a parade of their own, viewed as "an undoubted success." The San Francisco demonstration encouraged Republican leaders who only weeks before had been prepared to concede the state to Bryan. "San Francisco was ablaze with enthusiasm which has not yet abated," exulted the secretary of the party's central committee, "nor do we think it will subside until the desired result is effected. I firmly believe that yesterday's proceedings, coupled with

[53] Charles Dick to Osborne, Sept. 24, 1896, Osborne Papers.
[54] Frank McLaughlin to Osborne, Oct. 6, 1896, C. D. Bonestel to Osborne, Sept. 24, 1896, M. R. Higgins to Osborne, Sept. 25, 1896, James A. Waymire to Osborne, Oct. 5, 1896, Osborne Papers.
[55] SF *Exmr*, Oct. 20, 24, 1896; Taggart, "Party Realignment of 1896," p. 446; LA *Times*, Oct. 28, 1896; Hichborn, "California in the 1896 National Campaign," pp. 17–18; William A. Robinson, *Thomas B. Reed, Parliamentarian* (New York, 1930), p. 349.

the prevailing sentiment in Southern California, assures the vote of California to Major McKinley."[56]

IV

Election day, November 3, 1896, bore out the prediction. The swing in momentum late in the campaign, brought about by the Republicans' adroit use of the silver, tariff, and prosperity issues, carried McKinley to a narrow victory in California. McKinley received 146,688 votes to Bryan's 144,766, a difference of only 1,922 out of the several hundred thousand votes cast. A trailing Republican elector gave Bryan one of the state's nine electoral votes. Bryan would later muse over the returns: "A change of 962 votes from Mr. McKinley's column to mine in California would have given me the entire electoral vote of that State."[57] Republicans were jubilant; Bryan Democrats and Populists disconsolate. "Well,'" remarked one unhappy Populist, "McKinley is to be our next Pres. and trusts, monopolies, bond-holders & bilks generally our rulers for the next four years. The clap-trap cry of 'Sound-money,' 'repudiation' & 'anarchy,' had its effects." Speaking for most Democrats, Senator White charged that business coercion had cost Bryan the state. "To tell the truth," he wrote Bryan, "I felt rather sick at the outcome in California."[58]

White's statement in part reflected his disgust with the important role the gold Democrats had played in the California outcome. The National Democratic party garnered only 2,006 votes, less than 1 percent of the total, but its leaders estimated that an additional 13,000 Cleveland Democrats had voted directly for McKinley. While this exact claim was impossible to corroborate, the returns did indicate that in some areas, particularly in San Francisco, a significant num-

[56] SF *Exmr*, Nov. 1, 1896; M. R. Higgins to Henry Harrison Markham, Nov. 1, 1896, Markham Papers; SF *Chron*, Nov. 1, 1896.

[57] Bryan, *First Battle*, p. 609; *California Blue Book, or State Roster, 1911* (Sacramento, 1913), pp. 201, 304, 428. The *Chronicle* (Nov. 7, 1900) shows the official 1896 returns by counties, in a more useful form than does Edgar Eugene Robinson's *The Presidential Vote, 1896–1932* (Stanford, Cal., 1934), pp. 72–73, 145–50. Perceptive observations on the long-term significance of the election are offered in Michael Paul Rogin and John L. Shover, *Political Change in California: Critical Elections and Social Movements, 1890–1966* (Westport, Conn., 1970), pp. 19–29.

[58] Olive Cole to George R. Cole, Nov. 6, 1896, Cole Papers; White to Bryan, Jan. 6, 1897, White to Cator, Nov. 12, 1896, WP; E. M. Gibson to Bryan, Nov. 4, 1896, Charles Sumner to Bryan, Nov. 6, 1896, Bryan Papers; Paul W. Glad, *McKinley, Bryan, and the People* (New York, 1964), pp. 195–96.

ber of Democrats had cast their ballots for the Republican candidate.[59] Armed with these figures, the Cleveland Democrats were quick to assume complete credit for Bryan's defeat. "The emergency presented by Bryan's nomination was great," the elated John P. Irish declared. "It combined all the vagrant policies and people, put them in one pot and under one lid, where we succeeded in doing them to a turn. Had it not been for the patriotic action of the real Democracy, he would have been elected."[60]

To the further dismay of the Bryan forces, the returns also revealed that the state had essentially been lost in one city, San Francisco. Conditions there had worried Democratic managers throughout the campaign. Factional struggles hindered an effective presidential campaign and defied the efforts of White and others to "smooth things over" in the San Francisco party.[61] The tendency of pietistic elements within Bryan's rural following to assail the evils of the "City of Sin and Syringes" did not aid his cause in San Francisco, nor did the small but noticeable strain of anti-Catholicism and antisemitism that surfaced in Populist ranks during the campaign.[62] As the location of most businesses and government offices, San Francisco also became the focus of business and gold Democratic activity against the Bryan ticket. "Nearly every solitary influential person in San Francisco is fighting against you either openly or secretly ... ," Bryan was told shortly before the election. "Outside of San Francisco you will have a majority, but in San Francisco it is a hard fight on account of the Factories, Whole-sale houses, and the Rail Roads; they are pouring out money like water, to defeat you."[63]

Although they were aware of these complications, the Democrats were still unprepared for the magnitude of their setback in the Bay

[59] *California Blue Book, 1911*, p. 428; Henry S. Foote to Cleveland, Nov. 19, 1896, CP; SF *Exmr*, Nov. 8, 1896; Charles Dwight Willard to Samuel Willard, Nov. 13, 1896, Willard Papers.
[60] Irish to George F. Parker, Feb. 1, 1897, "Letters Written by Irish to Parker," p. 450; John T. Doyle to Abram S. Hewitt, Nov. 10, 1896, Doyle Papers; Foote to Cleveland, Nov. 19, 1896, CP.
[61] White to P. F. Dundon, Sept. 15, 1896, White to R. P. Troy, Sept. 30, 1896, White to Samuel Braunhart, Jan. 20, 1896, WP.
[62] Olive Cole to George R. Cole, undated (1896), Olive Cole to George R. Cole, Oct. 18, 1896, Cole Papers; Rogin and Shover, *Political Change in California*, pp. 16–24.
[63] William H. Emmons to Bryan, Oct. 31, 1896, Samuel Braunhart to Bryan, June 2, 1896, Bryan Papers.

Area. San Francisco, which had given Cleveland a plurality of some 6,600 votes in 1892, went for McKinley in 1896 by 392 votes. That McKinley's victory in San Francisco was at least partly due to an anti-Bryan vote was evident in the pattern of the city returns. While the Bryan electors trailed their Republican opponents, the San Francisco Democratic party elected its mayoralty candidate, James D. Phelan, increased the size of its delegation in the legislature, and returned James G. Maguire to Congress. Both Phelan and Maguire, running on platforms that endorsed Bryan and silver, triumphed by over 8,000 votes, even though Bryan at the head of their ticket failed to carry the city. The anti-Bryan outcome in San Francisco, combined with a Republican margin of more than 5,000 votes in adjacent Alameda County, where many of the same influences operated, practically doomed Bryan's chances in the state. As White lamented after the election, "The vote around San Francisco Bay was severe in the extreme."[64]

The results elsewhere were more comforting to the Bryan Democrats. A comparison of Bryan's totals in 1896 with Cleveland's in 1892 showed that Bryan had run quite well in most of the state. While Cleveland had won in 22 counties, Bryan won in 31 (including two counties that had been created in the intervening years). He bettered Cleveland's 1892 totals in 36 counties and failed to match them in only 18. As expected, Bryan ran particularly well in agricultural and mining districts and in Southern California, where he cut deeply into the Republican vote. Los Angeles became one of the few cities in the nation to support him. The farming population in the Sacramento and San Joaquin valleys generally went for Bryan and silver, as did such mining counties as El Dorado and Nevada. For the first time since before the Civil War, Sacramento County voted for a Democratic presidential candidate, a record almost matched by San Diego County, which until 1896 had not voted for a Democratic candidate in 24 years. In the state as a whole Bryan carried twelve counties that had eluded Cleveland in 1892, and of the counties Cleveland

[64] White to Charles Aull, Nov. 7, 1896, WP; SF *Exmr*, Sept. 19, Nov. 6, 1896; SF *Chron*, Nov. 20, 1896; Taggart, "Party Realignment of 1896," p. 449. For an analysis of the city returns from the Populist viewpoint, see Alexander Saxton, "San Francisco Labor and the Populist and Progressive Insurgencies," *PHR*, 34 (1965): 421–38.

had carried that year, Bryan lost in only four. Of course, owing largely to the returns in one of these counties—San Francisco—Bryan lost the state in 1896, whereas Cleveland had won it in 1892. But in most of California Bryan made a stronger showing than had Cleveland four years before.[65]

In both state and nation Bryan brought the Democrats closer to victory than any other candidate probably could have done. Although he was the nominee of a divided and discredited party, Bryan with the aid of the Populists still drew almost 48 percent of the popular vote in the country. His emotional crusade for silver capitalized on agrarian discontent and attracted voters who otherwise would not have supported the Democratic ticket. Bryan's terse explanation for his defeat—"I have borne the sins of Grover Cleveland"—ignored the basic weaknesses of his own one-issue campaign and the deftness of the campaign waged by his Republican opponents. But to many in the 1890's, conscious of the conditions under which Bryan had labored, the explanation seemed accurate. To them the election's significance lay in how close Bryan came to winning despite grave handicaps. In a fundamental sense the Democratic candidate was "beaten in advance," as the San Francisco *Examiner* noted. "Three years of Clevelandism had reduced the Democracy to a hopeless wreck."[66]

Such reflections consoled Bryan's Coast followers. During the weeks after the election, in letters, speeches, and newspaper editorials, they reaffirmed their commitment and vowed to continue the struggle. "We all feel dreadful over Bryan's defeat, & must work harder than ever," wrote one. "We are going to organize and consolidate our silver

<hr/>

[65] All county comparisons, except where otherwise noted, do not include the new counties. There were 54 counties in 1892, and 57 in 1896. SF *Chron*, Nov. 7, 1900; SF *Exmr*, Nov. 5, 1896; LA *Times*, Nov. 13, 1896; Taggart, "Party Realignment of 1896," pp. 449–50; White to P. A. Byrne, Nov. 17, 1896, WP; D. O. McCarthy to Cator, Nov. 12, 1896, Cator Papers; William Hayward to Bryan, Nov. 6, 1896, Bryan Papers.

[66] Coletta, *Bryan*, I: 197; SF *Exmr*, Nov. 11, 1896; Jones, *Presidential Election of 1896*, pp. 340–50; William Dimond, "Urban and Rural Voting in 1896," *American Historical Review*, 46 (1941): 286–93; Gilbert C. Fite, "William Jennings Bryan and the Campaign of 1896: Some Views and Problems," *Nebraska History*, 47 (1966): 247–64; Lee Benson, "Research Problems in American Political Historiography," in Mirra Komarovsky, ed., *Common Frontiers of the Social Sciences* (Glencoe, Ill., 1957), pp. 155–71; Richard J. Jensen, *The Winning of the Midwest: Social and Political Conflict, 1888–1896* (Chicago, 1971), pp. 269–308.

forces here, and renew the fight for free coinage of silver at once,"
declared another.[67] The closeness of the presidential contest, the numerous victories of silverites in local and state races, and the election of four fusion candidates to Congress encouraged Bryan's supporters. Their continuing determination disheartened the Cleveland
Democrats, who had believed for a moment that defeat had crushed
the silver movement. "I am sorry to say," remarked a dismayed gold
Democrat, "that I am afraid we will all be in the same fix in 1900
because these silver men are in dead earnest and ready for a long
hard fight."[68]

For most California Democrats the major battle was already over.
There would be no more "Clevelandism," at least. After years of
worry and hesitation, when they were beset by the dilemma of conflicting loyalties, they had repudiated the president and sought new
ground. There were few regrets. Following the election they made
no effort to restore their former ties with Eastern Democrats or to
propitiate the Cleveland men in the state. "You say that you are a
democrat of the Cleveland type," Stephen M. White wrote bluntly
to one correspondent. "In my view this means that you are not a
democrat at all." In a similar vein the 1897 convention of the Iro-
quois League, an influential statewide organization of Democratic
clubs, restated the party's support for free silver and resolved: "We
believe William J. Bryan to be the best living incarnation and the
most eloquent exponent of Democratic principles, and we cannot but
feel that Providence has reserved him as the deliverer of this country
four years hence from the evils and dangers in which the vicious
financial policy of the Republican party has involved it." Since 1884
a picture of Grover Cleveland, the head of the party, had hung in
the league's chamber. During the convention league members turned
the picture symbolically to face the wall.[69]

The passing of the Cleveland administration on March 4, 1897, was

[67] Olive Cole to George R. Cole, Nov. 6, 1896, Cole Papers; D. O. McCarthy to
Cator, Nov. 12, 1896, Cator Papers.
[68] Charles Dwight Willard to Samuel Willard, Nov. 13, 1896, Willard Papers; SF
Chron, Dec. 14, 1896.
[69] White to Cassius Carter, Feb. 26, 1897, White to Alexander Montgomery, Dec.
22, 1896, White to William Jennings Bryan, Dec. 22, 1896, WP; SF *Exmr*, Feb. 23,
1897; SF *Chron*, Feb. 23, 1897.

a time for much rejoicing in California. "Today we have a new President, and we hope a good one," wrote a delighted onlooker. "He could hardly be worse than the old one, so far as the interests of the people are concerned."[70] In a perceptive though oversimplified editorial that expressed the bitter feelings of most Coast Democrats, the San Francisco *Examiner* used the occasion to review the party's fortunes during the 1890's. "There never has been an instance in which a President has begun a term so entrenched in power and popularity as Grover Cleveland was four years ago, and ended it in such abject, humiliating failure." In 1892, the paper recalled, the Democrats had campaigned and won on the tariff issue. "Had the President called an extra session in March [1893] to deal with the tariff question he would have been the leader of a strong, united and victorious party. The tariff would have been promptly revised in accordance with the Democratic pledges, and then Mr. Cleveland, with his great popularity enhanced by the triumph of the principles on which he had been elected, would have been in a position to exert a decisive influence in the settlement of the currency question."

Instead, the president gave precedence to currency, and "the issue on which the Democracy was united was postponed to one on which it was divided." When the Democrats finally reached the tariff issue in 1894, they came "not with the impetus of victory and enthusiasm ... but timidly, with doubt and discouragement, in the midst of public distress and party disaster." To a large degree these early events had dictated the party's later course. "The President's challenge was accepted. The currency question replaced the tariff as the paramount issue, the old Democracy was dead, and the new Democracy was born." And now, concluded the *Examiner*, as a Republican, William McKinley, assumed the presidency, "The times are still hard, the warcloud hangs black over Europe, anarchy reigns in Cuba and momentous political and social problems confront this republic. But nevertheless, on this auspicious day the sky is blue, the birds sing and joy is unconfined. It is the last day of the Cleveland Administration."[71]

[70] Olive Cole to George R. Cole, March 4, 1897, Cole Papers; Los Angeles *Express*, March 2, 1897, quoted in James High, "Some Southern California Opinion Concerning Conservation of Forests, 1890–1905," *Historical Society of Southern California Quarterly*, 33 (1951): 303.
[71] SF *Exmr*, March 4, 1897.

CHAPTER ELEVEN

Aftermath

HEARTENED by the close race Bryan had run in the state, and unaware of the changes that would shortly occur in their political fortunes, the California Democrats in the aftermath of 1896 quickly
forgot their initial discouragement and began to look forward with
confidence to the campaigns of 1898 and 1900. By then, they believed,
McKinley would have demonstrated his inability to fulfill the extravagant promises made during the recent campaign. Signs of mounting public impatience in the early months of 1897 reinforced this
belief and alarmed Coast Republicans, who warned national party
leaders that because "hard times continue," popular sentiment had
already turned "overwhelmingly" against the Republican party. Encouraged, Sen. Stephen M. White forecast a swift victory for the
silver forces. "The 'advance agent of prosperity' has done nothing,"
he wrote to Bryan. "Banks are failing, and there seems to be not a ray
ahead.... I honestly think that if there were an election today and
with all of the same influences against us, the judgment would be
reversed."[1]

The Democrats' confidence increased in the summer of 1897, when
Bryan toured California in almost a triumphal procession. In six days
he made fifteen speeches, addressing large and enthusiastic audiences
throughout the state. Welcomed by Gov. James H. Budd and Congressman James G. Maguire, Bryan opened his tour in Sacramento,
and then moved south through the farming communities of the San
Joaquin Valley. An estimated 10,000 people in Stockton, 15,000 in

[1] Morris M. Estee to James S. Clarkson, May 8, 1897, Estee to Clarkson, May 20,
1897, Clarkson Papers; White to Bryan, Jan. 6, 1897, White to John B. Campbell,
Nov. 4, 1896, White to William Randolph Hearst, Nov. 4, 1896, WP.

Fresno, and 12,000 in Los Angeles heartily applauded as Bryan continued to dwell on the currency issue. "Mr. Bryan will receive a great reception in this State," a San Francisco Democrat exulted while noting the preparations for Bryan's visit. "The alacrity with which the endorsers of the Cleveland administration (of unlamented memory) and the advocates of the gold standard vie with each other in rendering homage to the apostle of silver seems quite refreshing. It augurs well for Democratic ascendency."[2]

Unbeknownst to the Democrats, however, the elections of 1894 and 1896 had together closed a distinct era in both state and national politics. In gathering a 600,000-vote plurality in the nation, the largest for either party since 1872, McKinley and the Republicans had consolidated a massive electoral coalition that left only the South and scattered sections of the West to the Democrats. McKinley's victories in Maryland, Delaware, West Virginia, and Kentucky were clear indications that the Democrats were losing their hold in areas of former strength. The urban centers of the Northeast and Midwest, which generally had gone Democratic in 1892, now furnished part of the base on which the Republican coalition rested. Extending the pattern that emerged two years before, the Democrats in 1896 carried only one Midwestern city with more than 45,000 residents, lost in the normally Democratic cities of New York and San Francisco, and won in only seven of Boston's 25 wards; they carried a single county in New York State, and none in all of New England. Bryan's devastating losses in the cities, and among labor, immigrant, and some farm voters, reflected the continuation of the 1894 anti-Democratic trend, as well as his lack of appeal to these elements. More than ever dependent on the South, the Democrats were again the familiar party of opposition. Their search for a permanent national majority, seemingly so close to realization in 1892, had ended in total failure.[3]

[2] Samuel Braunhart to White, July 1, 1897, WP; LA *Times*, July 4–6, 1897; Harold F. Taggart, "The Silver Republican Club of Los Angeles," *Historical Society of Southern California Quarterly*, 25 (1943): 107–8.

[3] Paolo E. Coletta, *William Jennings Bryan*, vol. 1: *Political Evangelist, 1860–1908* (Lincoln, Neb., 1964), pp. 191–92; Richard J. Jensen, *The Winning of the Midwest: Social and Political Conflict, 1888–1896* (Chicago, 1971), pp. 269–308; Geoffrey Blodgett, *The Gentle Reformers: Massachusetts Democrats in the Cleveland Era* (Cambridge, Mass., 1966), p. 238; Stanley L. Jones, *The Presidential Election of 1896* (Madison, Wis., 1964), pp. 332–50; Samuel T. McSeveney, *The Politics of Depression: Political Behavior in the Northeast, 1893–1896* (New York, 1972), pp. 188–221.

The mid-1890's brought a similar realignment of party forces on the state level. Beginning roughly in the 1870's California politics had been characterized by a series of closely contested battles between political parties of relatively even strength. In the seven elections from 1880 through 1892, three Democrats and one Republican had been elected governor, and control over the two houses of the legislature had alternated between the parties. During the same years 22 Republicans and 19 Democrats had been elected to the House of Representatives, and two Democrats and two Republicans had been elected to full terms in the United States Senate. Only twice during the period, in 1880 and again in 1892, had the Democratic presidential nominee carried California, but these contests had generally been decided by fairly narrow margins. In two of the four presidential elections, a difference of less than 1 percent of the popular vote had determined the winner.[4]

After 1896 this political balance came rapidly to an end as California became a solidly Republican state. In 1898 the Republican gubernatorial candidate soundly defeated the popular silver Democrat James G. Maguire, and the Republicans captured six of the state's seven congressional seats. Two years later the Republicans swept all seven congressional districts, and McKinley routed Bryan in California by almost 40,000 votes. In 1904 Theodore Roosevelt increased the Republican plurality to nearly 116,000 votes. In the seven elections from 1898 through 1910, 52 Republicans and five Democrats won seats in the House of Representatives. With rare exceptions California's one-party status continued until 1932 as the Republicans almost completely monopolized the governorship, the legislature, and the congressional delegation. Between 1920 and 1932, the nadir of the California Democrats' fortunes, no Democratic gubernatorial candidate drew even as much as 36 percent of the vote.[5]

[4] The figures include only regularly elected officials and not those who succeeded to office through the death or resignation of a previous official. *California Blue Book, or State Roster, 1893* (Sacramento, 1893), pp. 252–66; Michael Paul Rogin and John L. Shover, *Political Change in California: Critical Elections and Social Movements, 1890–1966* (Westport, Conn., 1970), p. 24.

[5] Robert E. Hennings, "California Democratic Politics in the Period of Republican Ascendancy," *PHR*, 31 (1962): 267–68; *California Blue Book, or State Roster, 1911* (Sacramento, 1913), pp. 304–5; Harold F. Taggart, "The Party Realignment of 1896 in California," *PHR*, 8 (1939): 450–51. After their 1894 gubernatorial victory the Democrats did not elect another governor until 1938.

A number of factors contributed to this transformation. The massive influx of Midwesterners during the late 1880's provided an initial impetus, but it did not automatically determine subsequent political developments in the state. The depression of the 1890's, coupled with the distinctive appeals of the 1896 McKinley and Bryan campaigns, altered party prospects and shifted voter alignments in both transitory and long-lasting ways. After 1897, the immediate enactment of Republican proposals on the tariff and other issues, the return of prosperity to the Pacific Coast, and the advent of the Spanish-American War presented a marked contrast to the lethargy of the Cleveland administration and appeared to corroborate the Republicans' visions of an era of prosperity, progress, and patriotism. Changing recent Republican converts into permanent supporters and luring additional voters into the party fold, the events of the late 1890's and after solidified new patterns of party loyalty, ensured decades of Republican rule, and blunted the occasional promise of a Democratic resurgence.[6]

Finally, Grover Cleveland and the Democrats had managed to preside over their own political demise. After years of stalemate the 1890's had opened with bright prospects for the national Democratic party. The results of two successive elections had overwhelmingly repudiated the Republican party, rejected the Republican concept of the active state, and seemingly presaged the establishment of permanent Democratic hegemony. Yet within a short time, beset by depression, torn by internal division, and glaringly unable to govern, the party had completely squandered its hard-won gains. For this development Cleveland and his Democratic followers had only themselves to blame. Awarded national power in 1892, they failed to meet the challenge in a way that would satisfy the voters, strengthen the party organization, and bring them further electoral victories. In a fundamental sense the actions of Cleveland and the national Democratic party had thrust the Republican party into power.

Cleveland himself attempted to divert the blame elsewhere. "Has it occurred to you," he asked an adviser after the 1896 Democratic national convention, "that in view of the outcome at Chicago no one

6 Rogin and Shover's *Political Change in California* (pp. 35–152) provides the best interpretive analysis of party developments after 1900. For the business revival on the Coast, see Ira B. Cross, *A History of the Labor Movement in California*, Univ. of California Publications in Economics, vol. 14 (Berkeley, 1935), pp. 217–18, 228.

can be fool enough to charge against this administration the disasters that await the Democratic party?" Leaving office in March 1897 as the most unpopular president since Andrew Johnson, Cleveland retired to Princeton, New Jersey, where he found welcome relief from "these last stormy and trying years of official life, when friends fell away and foes were insolent and villainous." Still bewildered by his repudiation, he spoke wistfully of "the rectitude of my intentions and the honesty of my efforts to serve my Country and my fellow citizens."[7] Emerging occasionally from retirement, he continued to fight against Bryanism and the party's new direction. "My feeling," he wrote in 1900, "is that the safety of the country is in the rehabilitation of the old Democratic party." It was a sentiment that would never be realized, though the selection of a Cleveland Democrat to head the party's 1904 ticket provided momentary comfort. Grover Cleveland died in Princeton on June 24, 1908, eighteen days before his party gave William Jennings Bryan a third nomination for the presidency.[8]

During the mid-1890's, discouraged by the mounting opposition to administration policies, Cleveland and his allies had often found solace in the thought that a later generation would praise their course. In large measure they were right. As memories dimmed and participants passed from the scene, generous recollection outgrew reality. The frustrations and hostilities of the 1890's gave way to increasing respect for Cleveland's courage, candor, and unyielding devotion to principle. Some of this admiration was merited; some was not. It justly recognized Cleveland's undoubted rectitude and genuine concern for his nation's ills; it neglected his numerous errors, evasions, and failures of outlook and temperament. But Grover Cleveland bequeathed more than a legend to American politics. Between 1884 and 1897 his comfortable figure had served as the focus for the Democratic party's bid for power. Through him the Democrats hoped to establish political hegemony and realize the party's time-honored objectives of states' rights, decentralization, and limited government.

Spurred by wide public support, the Democrats' hopes rose through

[7] Cleveland to Richard Olney, July 13, 1896, Olney Papers; Cleveland to Jonathan J. Valentine, March 21, 1897, CP.

[8] Cleveland to Judson B. Harmon, July 17, 1900, in Allan Nevins, ed., *Letters of Grover Cleveland, 1850–1908* (Boston, 1933), pp. 532–33; Nevins, *Grover Cleveland: A Study in Courage* (New York, 1932), pp. 729–64.

the 1880's and early 1890's, only to end abruptly in the midst of a nationwide depression. Events then revealed that Democratic leadership and doctrines could neither solve nor survive a national crisis. Rooted firmly in the past, Cleveland and his party had failed to keep pace with the needs of a changing country. By the mid-1890's the Democrats' traditional localism and negativism were no longer satisfying answers in a depression-ridden, increasingly industrialized, interdependent society. As voters moved toward outright acceptance of the Republican tenets of economic nationalism and government activism that they had repudiated a few years before, it became clear that Cleveland and the depression had combined to emasculate a party, discredit a philosophy, and change the course of American politics for decades to come. If the people turned after 1894 to "the party of progress, prosperity, and national authority," they also turned against the party and principles of Grover Cleveland.[9] This was Cleveland's main legacy to his party and the nation.

While the California Democrats suffered through the long period of Republican hegemony, the California People's party failed to survive it. By the close of 1898 Populism as a political force was practically defunct in the state, having declined almost as rapidly as it had appeared at the beginning of the decade. Once a breeding ground of the People's party, the California Farmers' Alliance could muster only 25 delegates to its annual convention in the fall of 1896, and the convention adopted a resolution declaring that political involvement had proved detrimental to the organization.[10] Within the People's party itself the struggle between "middle-of-the-road" elements and those favoring fusion with the Democrats continued with renewed bitterness. When the latter faction gained control of the party's 1898 state convention, Thomas V. Cator, who had become an opponent of fusion, led his followers to another hall, where they nominated a straight Populist ticket. After the Republicans' landslide victory in

9 Carl N. Degler, "American Political Parties and the Rise of the City: An Interpretation," *Journal of American History*, 51 (1964): 49; Lewis L. Gould, "The Republican Search for a National Majority," in H. Wayne Morgan, ed., *The Gilded Age*, rev. ed. (Syracuse, N.Y., 1970), pp. 171–87. For concise statements of the contrasting philosophies of the two parties, see William L. Wilson, *The National Democratic Party: Its History, Principles, Achievements, and Aims* (Baltimore, 1888); and Thomas B. Reed, "Rules of the House of Representatives," *Century Magazine*, 15 (1889): 795.
10 SF *Exmr*, Nov. 18–19, 1896.

California that year, many Populists deserted to the Republican ranks. Others, especially in San Francisco, joined the socialist movement. In late 1898 Cator himself announced his return to the Republican party and issued a statement endorsing the tariff and the gold standard. The dissolution of Coast Populism was hastened by the loss of the man who had dominated the party since its inception, but it would soon have occurred in any event.[11]

For John P. Irish and the loyal remnant of Cleveland Democrats in the state, the years after 1896 were filled with disillusionment and despair. In the mid-1890's, when serious opposition to Cleveland had first arisen, Irish had begun to experience "that torment with which one looks directly upon weakness, selfishness and treachery in places where noble sacrifice, manliness and fidelity should lift a heroic front." His correspondence with national party leaders offered an eloquent glimpse into a dying philosophy, reflecting the blend of bewilderment, outrage, and elation common to the Cleveland Democrats in the 1890's. Though disheartened, Irish relished the struggle and could still believe in the future of the Democratic party. He had, he thought, been given an opportunity few men have in their lifetimes. "I bugle the forces...," he wrote a friend in 1894, "and above the mists and clouds can see and above the clamor can hear the clearer welkin and the shouts of victory. As we pass on in present humiliation the enemy can *vae victis* but I can hear the rumble of our conquering chariots."[12]

The events of 1896 tested Irish's faith. Bryan's nomination angered him, but it also supplied the occasion for a final battle to vindicate "that magnificent personality, that incarnation of Democratic principle, that everlasting moral principle which must pervade all government made incarnate in the flesh—Grover Cleveland."[13] In November Irish rejoiced over Bryan's defeat. "It will not be said," he assured other Cleveland Democrats, "that we constructed a bridge over which

[11] Harold F. Taggart, "Thomas Vincent Cator: Populist Leader of California," *California Historical Society Quarterly*, 28 (1949): 53; Donald E. Walters, "The Feud Between California Populist T. V. Cator and Democrats James Maguire and James Barry," *PHR*, 27 (1958): 295–98; John W. Mitchell to White, June 28, 1898, WP.
[12] Irish to Parker, Jan. 18, 1894, "Letters Written by John P. Irish to George F. Parker," *Iowa Journal of History and Politics*, 31 (1933): 447–49. *Vae victis*—"Woe to the vanquished!"—is Livy's famous phrase.
[13] Quotation from Irish's speech to the gold Democratic convention, in *Proceedings of the Convention of the National Democratic Party* (Indianapolis, Ind., 1896), pp. 34–39; Irish to Mrs. John P. Irish, Feb. 2, 1896, John P. Irish Papers, Stanford Univ.

our party marched to victory, but over which a nation passed to safety." Once his jubilation had worn off, however, Irish recognized that neither the state nor the national party intended to repent its apostasy. He became embittered. In 1900, when the Democrats again nominated Bryan for president, Irish hinted that he would cast his vote for William McKinley.[14]

The passing years brought little modification in his views. He later opposed the direction in which Woodrow Wilson led the Democratic party. Determined to resist the encroachments of "socialism," he fought against labor unions and such political reforms as recall and the direct election of United States senators. In the end, unable to reconcile his principles with the changes that had occurred in his party and country, Irish began to lose confidence in representative government and the democratic process. "We will not live to see the party regenerated or winning a victory that will do any good," he declared in 1903. "I look back, as do thousands of others, upon a life time spent in accumulating a heritage of principles for the party, at last to see it traded for Populist pottage by Bryan and his gang. The only pleasure left me in politics is in fighting them." John P. Irish died on October 6, 1923, at the age of 80, still vibrant, continuing to the end to defend his beliefs, an unabashed relic of another era.[15]

The 1898 election, which gave the Republicans an overwhelming majority in the legislature, retired Irish's former enemy, Stephen M. White, from the United States Senate. Three years later White, the dominant figure in the California Democratic party for more than a decade, was dead at the age of 48. Newspapers printed effusive editorials reviewing White's achievements. Los Angeles residents grieved for "Our Steve" and erected a statue to commemorate his role in the free-harbor struggle of the 1890's.[16] They could as well have commemorated a dozen other events in a career that in many ways symbolized the course of California history between 1880 and 1900. White's career mirrored the concerns of late-nineteenth-century Californians,

14 SF *Exmr*, Jan. 9, 1897; Irish to Parker, Feb. 14, 1900, "Letters Written by Irish to Parker," p. 454; Irish to J. Sterling Morton, Dec. 17, 1900, Morton Papers.
15 Irish to Parker, Jan. 30, 1903, "Letters Written by Irish to Parker," p. 455; SF *Chron*, Oct. 7, 1923.
16 LA *Times*, Feb. 22, 1901; SF *Exmr*, Feb. 22, 1901; Edith Dobie, *The Political Career of Stephen Mallory White: A Study of Party Activities Under the Convention System* (Stanford, Cal., 1927), p. 25.

spanned the era in California politics that witnessed the transition to one-party domination, represented the advent of a new generation of California-born political leaders, and reflected the swift rise of Southern California to a position of power in the state. White's selection as chairman of the 1888 and 1896 Democratic conventions was an early recognition of California's growing influence in national politics.

A knowledgeable contemporary once called White "the best all-around politician that I ever met in my life."[17] White would have savored the compliment, and the description. He was a politician, unashamedly so, and he practiced the art with enormous zest and exceptional skill. He had an unshakable faith in the political process, enjoyed its victories, accepted its defeats, understood its strengths and limitations, recognized it as a path of personal advancement as well as a means to guide and protect the interests of constituents. Like political figures in other periods, he found it difficult to reconcile the popular demand for effective public service with the popular tendency to scorn those who served. But he served nonetheless. For White politics provided an outlet for diverse energies, a chance to test men and issues, and an opportunity to advance certain deeply held principles.

White brought intelligence, dedication, and diligence to the political arena. An able and persuasive orator, he relished public debate, jesting on one occasion that "there is considerable pleasure to be derived from speaking to a crowd in sympathy with you. When you find that you can govern them you develop an opinion of their intellectuality and integrity which you would not have if they howled for the other fellow."[18] It was some measure of White's career that people seldom howled for the other fellow. Although he was a Democrat living in an increasingly Republican district, he moved steadily from local to national prominence. In common with others of his generation, he was a devoted party member who sincerely felt that his party's ideals represented the hope of the country. But he maintained close relations with his Republican opponents and strove to avoid a partisanship that would preclude joint campaigns in pursuit of desirable objectives. Few legislative enactments bore his name—and none of

[17] Frank J. Moffitt to David B. Hill, July 31, 1893, David B. Hill Papers, New York State Library, Albany, provided through the courtesy of Prof. Carl A. Pierce, Univ. of Tennessee College of Law.
[18] White to John F. Swift, Sept. 28, 1890, WP.

these had any major importance—but he nonetheless received continuing recognition for substantial contributions to his people and
his state.

Most important, perhaps, Stephen M. White may have been unusual, but he was not entirely unique. With varying degrees of ability
and commitment, White, Irish, and other California Democrats had
tried to solve the problems and advance the interests of their state and
nation. They had fought a losing battle, however, and like most of
the vanquished, they disappeared from history. As politicians they
lost the contest for party supremacy. As Democrats they unwittingly
helped to undermine their party's doctrines. Fearful of centralized
power, they drew a careful line between state and national action,
and consented to federal intervention only when the need for it
seemed extreme. They relied instead on local measures and worked
on the state level to accomplish their aims. If they demonstrated the
potential fruitfulness of this approach, they also demonstrated its
unfortunate limitations. In the end, during the troubles of the 1890's,
a few of them came to understand that their achievements, though
significant, could only be limited and temporary, that a nation's complex problems demanded complex national solutions.

Later generations would apply glib and unmerited generalizations
to their era. For all their mistakes, the California Democrats of the
1880's and 1890's deserved better than this. Admittedly, they had experienced failure as often as success. They had frequently been short-
sighted. As a group they had suffered from the occasional corruption
and cynicism characteristic of politics in all periods. They had not
conceived grand dreams or pursued radical visions of a remade America. Their proposals had been cautious, ameliorative, on occasion innovative, to some extent experimental, based always on a faith in the
fundamental benefits of an expansive, urban-industrial society. They
had dealt with important issues, confronted difficult problems, and
sought productive solutions. On the whole their record was worthy
of attention and a measure of respect. Certainly Stephen M. White
and John P. Irish, along with numerous others, believed in their goals
and took pride in their accomplishments. Like most men they did not
suspect that they would be so soon forgotten.

Bibliographical Note

Bibliographical Note

꙳

Since most California historians have focused on such periods as the Gold Rush years, the discontented 1870's, and the Progressive era, the historian interested in the 1880's and 1890's has few valuable secondary sources to turn to and must rely almost entirely on manuscript collections, newspapers, printed contemporary documents, reminiscences, and other primary sources. The following note makes no attempt to list all the sources from which the text is documented. Instead, it points out and comments briefly on the materials of major significance to this study.

MANUSCRIPTS

Californians wrote and saved letters in profusion. Pacific Coast archives, particularly those at Stanford University, the Bancroft Library, the Henry E. Huntington Library, and the University of California at Los Angeles, contain a wealth of manuscript collections that, taken together, enrich our understanding of late-nineteenth-century California history. Moreover, whether because of some natural verbosity, or more likely because of a feeling of distance from Eastern centers of power and culture, Californians frequently wrote to national leaders. Letters from Californians—often filled with advice, appeals, and detailed explanations of California affairs —constitute a major element in many late-nineteenth-century manuscript collections.

The Stephen Mallory White Papers, in the Borel Collection, Manuscripts Division, Department of Special Collections, Stanford University Libraries, were the most important source of evidence for this study. White was a diligent politician who maintained an extensive correspondence with Democrats throughout the state and nation. The White Papers offer intelligent, candid insights into the internal deliberations of the Democratic party, the questions of policy and personality that shaped California politics, the workings of the state legislature, the relations of California Democrats with their Eastern leaders, and a host of other matters. White's efforts to cooperate with the People's party and his ability to remain on cordial terms with Republican opponents make his papers valuable for an understanding of Populist and Republican politics as well. The collection's only important weakness, the absence of much of the incoming correspondence, is offset somewhat by White's custom of summarizing a correspondent's letter in his reply. Consisting of more than one hundred boxes of letters, letter books, and newspaper scrapbooks, the White Papers are indispensable for any study of California politics in this period.

Other collections in the Stanford University Libraries were also of great value. The Thomas Vincent Cator Papers are the most useful single source for the problems and policies of the California People's party. The Ambrose Gwinett Bierce Papers contain correspondence relating to the railroad issue and the policies of the San Francisco *Examiner*, the most influential Democratic journal in California. Concerned in the main with family affairs, the John Powell Irish Papers were disappointing, but when used in conjunction with the published Irish correspondence and the Irish letters in other manuscript collections, they help illuminate the personality of this intriguing political figure. According to Irish's granddaughter, none of Irish's political correspondence remains in the possession of the family. Although relatively few in number, the letters in the Timothy Hopkins Transportation Collection provide significant information on railroad affairs, particularly the strained relations between Leland Stanford and Collis P. Huntington after 1885. The David Starr Jordan Papers contain items of interest on politics in the 1890's. Of less use were the John T. Doyle Papers, the Charles N. Felton Papers, the James Carson Needham Collection, and the Joseph J. Evans Papers. Minor material on the 1894 Pullman strike can be found in the Stanford Family Papers, in the University Archives.

The Henry E. Huntington Library, San Marino, has a number of outstanding collections. The scarcity of manuscript materials relating to Republican party leaders makes the Henry Harrison Markham Papers a major source of information on Republican politics. Although incomplete, the Markham Papers include helpful correspondence with other California Republicans, letters concerning Markham's policies while governor of the state from 1891 to 1895, and telegrams in connection with the Pullman strike. The James DeBarth Shorb Papers, also at the Huntington Library, record the convictions of Shorb, who was a conservative high-tariff Democrat, a leading viticulturist, and a bitter enemy of Stephen M. White in Southern California.

Although confined mostly to the twentieth century, the large collection of Thomas R. Bard Papers at the Huntington Library sheds some light on the views of a young anti-Stanford Republican. A few pertinent letters by Bard can also be found in the Charles Fernald Papers. While still subject to restrictions on their use, the John Percival Jones Papers are of vital importance to an understanding of the harbor fight of the 1890's. The papers of Charles Dwight Willard, John T. Gaffey, and Jackson A. Graves also contain important material on the railroad and other Coast issues. Of less value were the papers of Adolph Sutro, Ambrose Bierce, Theodore P. Lukens, James F. Crank, George A. Gillespie, H. H. Haight, Marshall Stimson, Benjamin D. Wilson, William Andrew Spalding, David Jacks, and S. L. M. Barlow.

Among the many manuscripts in the Division of Special Collections, University of California at Los Angeles, two are particularly important. The Cornelius Cole Papers, a large and diverse collection, were an unexpectedly rich source for the entire period. Blending political and family correspondence, the Cole Papers offer a detailed record of life in Southern California as well as helpful information on Republican politics, the harbor controversy, and the growth of Populist and pro-silver sentiment in the southern part of the state. Although the Henry Zenas Osborne Papers are a much smaller collection, they are essential for their coverage of the internal deliberations of the Republican party, particularly between 1890 and 1896. The loss or destruction of most post-1881 political correspondence lessens the value of the William Starke Rosecrans Papers, also at the University of California at Los Angeles. Only scattered items of interest were to be found in the Jones Family Papers and the papers of Edward A. Dickson, Theodore P. Gerson, Charles F. Stern, Hugo Fisher, and C. C. Teague.

The H. H. Bancroft Library, University of California at Berkeley, has several informative collections, including the Adolph Heinrich Joseph Sutro Papers. The builder of the famous Sutro Tunnel on the Comstock Lode, Sutro also achieved prominence as an anti-railroad figure and the Populist mayor of San Francisco. The Sutro Papers offer insights into one aspect of the anti-railroad campaign of the 1890's. Reflecting the outlook of an anti-monopoly Democrat, the John T. Doyle Papers trace the aims of a Californian who was deeply concerned about the power of the Southern Pacific Railroad. The Bancroft Library's holdings of Ambrose Bierce Papers relate more to Bierce's literary career than to his journalistic or political activities. The objectives of a San Francisco socialist and labor leader are revealed by the International Workmen's Association Records in the Burnette G. Haskell Papers. Students of conservation and the controversy over the Yosemite Valley can find useful information in the Robert Underwood Johnson Papers. The Stephen Johnson Field Papers, at the University of California General Library, Berkeley, consist entirely of autograph letters.

The Manuscript Division, Library of Congress, has a large number of relevant collections, nearly all of which proved extremely valuable for this study. The most useful, of course, were the Grover Cleveland Papers, an informative collection that illuminates Cleveland's personality, details his actions in connection with patronage, and records the public's response to his policies on the tariff, silver, and other issues. Other presidential manuscripts examined were the Benjamin Harrison Papers, which provide an unusually full account of Republican policies between 1888 and 1893, and the William McKinley Papers. The correspondence of Cleveland's advisers and Cabinet members supplements the record contained in the Cleveland Papers. The papers of Daniel S. Lamont, Walter Quintin Gresham, Daniel Manning, William C. Whitney, and Charles S. Hamlin all included significant materials. The administration's foreign policy, particularly in connection with the Chinese question, may be followed in the Thomas F. Bayard Papers, and the administration's actions during the Pullman strike are traced in the Richard Olney Papers. Letters from Stephen J. Field, outlining Field's views on a variety of issues, were found in the Don M. Dickinson Papers. The papers of William E. Chandler, James S. Clarkson, Whitelaw Reid, and Louis T. Michener contain important letters from California Republicans. Other manuscripts consulted at the Library of Congress include the papers of Manton Marble, William Jennings Bryan, Henry Watterson, and John Sherman.

The J. Sterling Morton Papers, at the Nebraska Historical Society in Lincoln, include so much correspondence with John P. Irish that they compensate somewhat for the relative scarcity of Irish letters elsewhere. Close friends and allies, Irish and Morton discussed in detail the problems of the Democratic party, and their letters reflect the disgust and despair of two conservative Democrats over the party's abandonment of the principles of Grover Cleveland. The Francis G. Newlands Papers, in the Yale University Library, were a valuable source for Democratic policies in the mid-1880's.

The Appointment Papers collected at the National Archives in Washington are a rich and virtually untapped source of information on California politics. These papers record the struggles over the distribution of patronage in the state's land offices, ports, internal revenue districts, and customs offices. Correspondence on land offices and the selection of surveyors general is filed under the Department of the Interior, Record Group 48. Letters concerning marshals, judges, and United States attorneys are under the Department of Justice, Record Group 60, and recommendations for customs and internal revenue offices are under the Treasury Department, Record Group 56. Broad in scope and value, these Appointment Papers constitute a storehouse of evidence on late-nineteenth-century politics.

NEWSPAPERS

Of the newspapers consulted, the three most important were the San Francisco *Examiner* (1880–97), the San Francisco *Chronicle* (1880–97), and the Los Angeles *Times* (1881–97). Under its two owners, George Hearst and William Randolph Hearst, the *Examiner* became the most influential Democratic journal on the Pacific Coast. Like other newspapers of the time, it mirrors the partisan and personal leanings of its proprietors, though William Randolph Hearst did make some improvements in this regard. But the paper is of great value as a source of political information and as a reflection of the views of the two powerful Hearsts. Similarly, when used with care the *Chronicle*, owned by Michael H. De Young, and the *Times*, owned by Harrison Gray Otis, are essential for an understanding of Republican politics and for coverage of important events and trends in their respective regions.

The *Alta California* (1885–91), edited for a time by John P. Irish, expressed the opinions of conservative Democrats, particularly in opposition to the objectives of the anti-monopolists. The Ventura *Democrat* (1884–94), a Democratic newspaper, and the available issues of the San Francisco *Argonaut* (1886, 1890–91), a periodical with nativist leanings, were also helpful sources.

PUBLIC DOCUMENTS

John G. Ames, *Comprehensive Index to the Publications of the United States Government, 1881–1893* (Washington, D.C., 1905) is a helpful guide to federal documents relating to California. Among other public documents, the *Compendium of the Tenth Census* (Washington, D.C., 1888) and the *Compendium of the Eleventh Census: 1890* (Washington, D.C., 1892) contributed much useful information. The *Congressional Record* (Washington, D.C., 1884–97) records the California delegation's response to the issues of the period, such as the silver question, railroad funding, the location for a deep-water harbor in Southern California, and the tariff. Important telegrams concerning the Cleveland administration's reaction to the Pullman strike appear in the *Appendix to the Annual Report of the Attorney-General of the United States for the Year 1896* (Washington, D.C., 1896). Evidence on the deep-water harbor question appears in *House of Representatives, Executive Document No. 41*, 52d Congress, 2d sess. (Washington, D.C., 1892); *Senate Report No. 799*, 54th Congress, 1st sess. (Washington, D.C., 1896); *Senate Document No. 18*, 55th Congress, 1st sess. (Washington, D.C., 1897); and *Report of a Hearing Before the Committee on Commerce of the Senate of the United States on the Subject of a Deep-Water Harbor in Southern California* (Washington, D.C., 1896).

Among documents printed by the state of California, the *Appendix to the Journals of the Senate and Assembly ... of the Legislature of the State of California* (Sacramento, 1883–97) is a vast cache of information on all aspects of California life. Still waiting to be fully exploited by historians, these volumes contain the official reports of the various state commissions, statistical material on the development of California's economy, and information on a host of other subjects. *The Journal of the Senate and Assembly . . . of the Legislature of the State of California* (Sacramento, 1881–97) is confined largely to motions, bills, memorials, and votes; the legislative debates must be followed in newspapers, nearly all of which printed a Sacramento column when the legislature was in session. The *California Blue Book, or State Roster* (Sacramento, 1893–1913, title and imprint vary) is a mine of factual material concerning elections, laws, politicians, and elected officials.

COLLECTED LETTERS, MEMOIRS, AND CONTEMPORARY ACCOUNTS

A useful collation of the platforms of all political parties appears in Winfield J. Davis, *History of Political Conventions in California, 1849–1892* (Sacramento, 1893). The important Cleveland correspondence is given convenient form in Allan Nevins, ed., *Letters of Grover Cleveland, 1850–1908* (Boston, 1933), and several letters by Stephen J. Field are printed in Howard Jay Graham, ed., "Four Letters of Mr. Justice Field," *Yale Law Journal*, 47 (1937–38): 1100–1108. The valuable correspondence in "Letters Written by John P. Irish to George F. Parker," *Iowa Journal of History and Politics*, 31 (1933): 421–512, reflects Irish's views over four decades. Also of use were Anne Wintermute Lane and Louise Herrick Wall, eds., *The Letters of Franklin K. Lane: Personal and Political* (Boston, 1922), and Festus P. Summers, ed., *The Cabinet Diary of William L. Wilson, 1896–1897* (Chapel Hill, N.C., 1957).

Contemporary indictments of California politics, based in most cases on inadequate evidence, can be found in James Bryce, *The American Commonwealth*, 2 vols. (New York, 1908); Rudyard Kipling, *American Notes* (New York, 1930); and Jeremiah Lynch, *Buckleyism: The Government of a State* (San Francisco, 1889). Two articles by Henry George, "What the Railroad Will Bring Us," *Overland Monthly*, 1 (1868): 297–306, and "The Kearney Agitation in California," *Popular Science Monthly*, 17 (1880): 433–53, offer informative opinions on early events.

Of the vast literature on the blessings and benefits of Southern California, the interested student might examine Charles Dudley Warner, *Our Italy* (New York, 1891); Theodore S. Van Dyke, *Southern California* (New York, 1886); Kate Sanborn, *A Truthful Woman in Southern California* (New York, 1893); Southern California Bureau of Information, *Southern California: An Authentic Description of Its Natural Features, Resources, and Prospects* (Los Angeles, 1892); and Ludwig Louis Salvator, *Los Angeles in the Sunny Seventies: A Flower from the Golden Land* (Los Angeles, 1929). Theodore S. Van Dyke, *Millionaires of a Day:*

An Inside History of the Great Southern California "Boom" (New York, 1890) takes a humorous look at its subject. S. E. Moffett, "The Railroad Commission of California: A Study in Irresponsible Government," *Annals of the American Academy of Political and Social Science*, 6 (1895): 469–77, voices contemporary disillusionment with the railroad commission. A more sympathetic treatment, including a brief analysis of some of the commission's problems, appears in [John T. Doyle], "The California Railroad Commission," *American Law Review*, 29 (1895): 896–98. Collis P. Huntington, "A Plea for Railway Consolidation," *North American Review*, 153 (1891): 272–82, shows Huntington's hostility to government regulation. The Pullman strike is covered in Thomas R. Bacon, "The Railroad Strike in California," *Yale Review*, 3 (1895): 241–50. Although it is a contemporary account, Charles Dwight Willard, *The Free Harbor Contest at Los Angeles* (Los Angeles, 1899), is still among the best treatments of the harbor struggle.

Sentiment on the Chinese question in California is expressed most revealingly in contemporary letters and newspapers, but a number of printed sources provide a sampling of it. Among them are California State Senate, Special Committee on Chinese Immigration, *Chinese Immigration: Its Social, Moral, and Political Effect* (Sacramento, 1878); G. B. Densmore, *The Chinese in California* (San Francisco, 1880); and Willard B. Farwell, *The Chinese at Home and Abroad* (San Francisco, 1885). Benjamin S. Brooks, *The Chinese in California* (San Francisco, 1876), defends the Chinese immigrants.

Several books and articles by Grover Cleveland, notably *The Self-Made Man in American Life* (New York, 1897), *Presidential Problems* (New York, 1904), and *Good Citizenship* (Philadelphia, 1908), suggest Cleveland's views on government and society. Cleveland's distaste for the spoils system may be seen in his article "The President and His Patronage," *Saturday Evening Post*, 174 (May 24, 1902): 1–2. William L. Wilson, *The National Democratic Party: Its History, Principles, Achievements, and Aims* (Baltimore, 1888), is an excellent summation of the Democrats' philosophy. Henry Vincent, *The Story of the Commonweal* (Chicago, 1894), reports on discontent during the second Cleveland administration, while William Jennings Bryan, *The First Battle: A Story of the Campaign of 1896* (Chicago, 1896), gives Bryan's analysis of the considerations that led to Cleveland's repudiation in 1896. Also of value is F. I. Vassault, "Nationalism in California," *Overland Monthly*, 15 (1890): 659–61.

California is rich in memoirs. Valuable for its relatively intimate look at "Blind Boss" Buckley is James H. Wilkins, ed., "The Reminiscences of Christopher A. Buckley," *SF Bul*, Dec. 23, 1918, to Feb. 5, 1919. In the same vein, but less successful, are James H. Wilkins, ed., "Martin

Kelly's Story," SF *Bul*, Sept. 1 to Nov. 26, 1917; and W. S. Leake, "When King Mazuma Ruled," SF *Bul*, March 16 to April 2, 1917. Although it does not extend into the period under review, Stephen J. Field, *Personal Reminiscences of Early Days in California* (New York, 1968), sheds light on Field's background and personality.

Other useful memoirs include David Starr Jordan, *The Days of a Man: Being Memories of a Naturalist, Teacher and Minor Prophet of Democracy*, 2 vols. (New York, 1922); James J. Ayers, *Gold and Sunshine: Reminiscences of Early California* (Boston, 1922); John L. Davie, *My Own Story* (Oakland, Cal., 1931); Maurice H. Newmark and Marco R. Newmark, eds., *Sixty Years in Southern California, 1853–1913: Containing the Reminiscences of Harris Newmark* (New York, 1926); Frank A. Leach, *Recollections of a Newspaperman: A Record of Life and Events in California* (San Francisco, 1917); and Jackson A. Graves, *My Seventy Years in California, 1857–1927* (Los Angeles, 1927).

Although disappointing overall, Henry Watterson, *"Marse Henry": An Autobiography*, 2 vols. (New York, 1919), recalls the Democrats' wavering on the tariff issue. George F. Parker, *Recollections of Grover Cleveland* (New York, 1909), and Richard Watson Gilder, *Grover Cleveland: A Record of Friendship* (New York, 1910), give Cleveland very sympathetic treatment.

SELECTED SECONDARY SOURCES

The standard histories of California devote relatively little attention to the 1880's and 1890's. Of the one-volume histories, John W. Caughey, *California* (New York, 1940), is still one of the best and most thoughtful. Walton Bean, *California: An Interpretive History* (New York, 1968), adds the insights of recent scholarship. Andrew F. Rolle, *California: A History* (New York, 1963), has useful material on developments during the period, as do such older works as Hubert Howe Bancroft, *History of California*, 7 vols. (San Francisco, 1884–90); Theodore H. Hittell, *History of California*, 4 vols. (San Francisco, 1885–97); and John S. Hittell, *A History of the City of San Francisco* (San Francisco, 1878). Two books by Robert Glass Cleland, *A History of California: The American Period* (New York, 1922), and *From Wilderness to Empire: A History of California, 1542–1900* (New York, 1944), cover economic and social developments. John S. Hittell, *The Resources of California* (San Francisco, 1863), is a useful early account of its subject.

California has fortunately attracted the attention of several outstanding scholars. Earl Pomeroy, *The Pacific Slope* (New York, 1965), persuasively places California in a regional and interpretive framework. Gerald D. Nash, *State Government and Economic Development: A History of Ad-*

ministrative Policies in California, 1849–1933 (Berkeley, 1964), is an excellent analysis of the relationship between the government and economy. Nash's article "Bureaucracy and Economic Reform: The Experience of California, 1899–1911," *Western Political Quarterly*, 13 (1960): 678–91, makes some perceptive general comments on the late nineteenth century. Michael Paul Rogin and John L. Shover, *Political Change in California: Critical Elections and Social Movements, 1890–1966* (Westport, Conn., 1970), uses quantitative techniques to shed light on the movements and elections of the 1890's and after. For economic trends and developments, Ira B. Cross, *A History of the Labor Movement in California*, Univ. of California Publications in Economics, vol. 14 (Berkeley, 1935), is indispensable, though dated. Vincent P. Carosso, *The California Wine Industry: A Study of the Formative Years* (Berkeley, 1951), examines a major California industry and includes commentary on the tariff issue and other political matters. Two volumes by Carey McWilliams, *Southern California Country: An Island on the Land* (New York, 1946), and *California: The Great Exception* (New York, 1949), attempt general interpretations of the California character.

A study focusing on one state must profit from comparisons with national patterns and the experiences of other states and regions. H. Wayne Morgan, *From Hayes to McKinley: National Party Politics, 1877–1896* (Syracuse, N.Y., 1969), is essential for the national framework and should replace Matthew Josephson, *The Politicos, 1865–1896* (New York, 1938). Other recent volumes advancing broad interpretations of the period include Robert H. Wiebe, *The Search for Order, 1877–1920* (New York, 1967); Samuel P. Hays, *The Response to Industrialism, 1885–1914* (Chicago, 1957); Robert D. Marcus, *Grand Old Party: Political Structure in the Gilded Age, 1880–1896* (New York, 1971); and John A. Garraty, *The New Commonwealth, 1877–1890* (New York, 1968). C. K. Yearley, *The Money Machines: The Breakdown and Reform of Governmental and Party Finance in the North, 1860–1920* (Albany, N.Y., 1970), is a pathbreaking study of finance and taxation. Fresh interpretations of the era's political history are in Lee Benson, "Research Problems in American Political Historiography," in Mirra Komarovsky, ed., *Common Frontiers of the Social Sciences* (Glencoe, Ill., 1957), pp. 113–83; Carl N. Degler, "American Political Parties and the Rise of the City: An Interpretation," *Journal of American History*, 51 (1964): 41–59; and Samuel P. Hays, "The Social Analysis of American Political History, 1880–1920," *Political Science Quarterly*, 80 (1965): 373–94.

On the state and regional level, Geoffrey Blodgett, *The Gentle Reformers: Massachusetts Democrats in the Cleveland Era* (Cambridge, Mass., 1966), and Lewis L. Gould, *Wyoming: A Political History, 1868–*

1896 (New Haven, Conn., 1968), are models of graceful prose and excellent analysis. Another superb study, Richard J. Jensen, *The Winning of the Midwest: Social and Political Conflict, 1888–1896* (Chicago, 1971), can be supplemented with Paul John Kleppner, *The Cross of Culture: A Social Analysis of Midwestern Politics, 1850–1900* (New York, 1970). Samuel T. McSeveney, *The Politics of Depression: Political Behavior in the Northeast, 1893–1896* (New York, 1972), investigates party trends in three Northern states, and David P. Thelen, *The New Citizenship: Origins of Progressivism in Wisconsin, 1885–1900* (Columbia, Mo., 1972), is a perceptive study of developments in that state.

Historians of California between 1870 and 1900 must deal with the role of the Central Pacific and Southern Pacific railroads. Insight into railroad affairs can be gained from Stuart Daggett, *Chapters in the History of the Southern Pacific* (New York, 1922), still one of the most comprehensive treatments of the California railroad network. George E. Mowry, *The California Progressives* (Berkeley, 1951), is an influential analysis of the twentieth-century response to railroad power, but Mowry slights the contributions made before 1900 and overestimates the extent of the Southern Pacific's influence in the late nineteenth century. W. H. Hutchinson, "Southern Pacific: Myth and Reality," *California Historical Society Quarterly*, 48 (1969): 325–34, advances some fresh observations about railroad influence. The problems and accomplishments of the railroad commission are given excellent treatment in Gerald D. Nash, "The California Railroad Commission, 1876–1911," *Southern California Quarterly*, 44 (1962): 287–305. Richard W. Barsness, "Railroads and Los Angeles: The Quest for a Deep-Water Port," *Southern California Quarterly*, 47 (1965): 379–91, is a good study of one anti-railroad campaign. The subject of railroad power is touched on in Ward M. McAfee, "Local Interests and Railroad Regulation in California During the Granger Decade," *PHR*, 37 (1968): 51–61; David B. Griffiths, "Anti-Monopoly Movements in California, 1873–1898," *Southern California Quarterly*, 52 (1970): 93–121; and Walton Bean, "Ideas of Reform in California," *California Historical Quarterly*, 51 (1972): 213–26.

The men who owned and managed the Central Pacific and Southern Pacific railroads are treated in Oscar Lewis's lively study *The Big Four: The Story of Huntington, Stanford, Hopkins, and Crocker, and of the Building of the Central Pacific* (New York, 1938). David Lavender, *The Great Persuader* (New York, 1970), answers the long-standing need for a good biography of Collis P. Huntington, though it is stronger for the early years of the railroad than it is for the 1880's and 1890's. Cerinda W. Evans, *Collis Potter Huntington*, 2 vols. (Newport News, Va., 1954), is of less value. George T. Clark, *Leland Stanford: War Governor of California, Railroad Builder and Founder of Stanford University* (Stanford,

Cal., 1931), and Norman E. Tutorow, *Leland Stanford: Man of Many Careers* (Menlo Park, Cal., 1971), examine the career of California's most prominent Republican leader.

A major figure who deserves a good biography is George Hearst. At present, Mr. and Mrs. Fremont Older, *George Hearst: California Pioneer* (Los Angeles, 1966), is the only full-length treatment of the mining magnate. W. A. Swanberg, *Citizen Hearst* (New York, 1961), examines the careers of both Hearsts. Other helpful biographies of California figures are Edith Dobie, *The Political Career of Stephen Mallory White: A Study of Party Activities Under the Convention System* (Stanford, Cal., 1927); Carl Brent Swisher, *Stephen J. Field: Craftsman of the Law* (Hamden, Conn., 1963); W. H. Hutchinson, *Oil, Land and Politics: The California Career of Thomas Robert Bard*, 2 vols. (Norman, Okla., 1965); Alexander Callow, Jr., "San Francisco's Blind Boss," *PHR*, 25 (1956): 261–79; and Harold F. Taggart, "Thomas Vincent Cator: Populist Leader of California," *California Historical Society Quarterly*, 27 (1948): 311–18, and 28 (1949): 47–55. Oscar T. Shuck, *History of the Bench and Bar of California* (Los Angeles, 1901), is filled with biographical information.

Among biographies of national political figures, the most important for my purposes was Allan Nevins, *Grover Cleveland: A Study in Courage* (New York, 1932), which presents a thorough and sympathetic portrait of the president. Horace Samuel Merrill, *Bourbon Leader: Grover Cleveland and the Democratic Party* (Boston, 1957), is much more critical. Robert McElroy, *Grover Cleveland: The Man and the Statesman*, 2 vols. (New York, 1923), has useful information. Paolo E. Coletta, *William Jennings Bryan*, vol. 1: *Political Evangelist, 1860–1908* (Lincoln, Neb., 1964), is the best study of Bryan's early years. James C. Olson, *J. Sterling Morton* (Lincoln, Neb., 1942), Horace Samuel Merrill, *William Freeman Vilas: Doctrinaire Democrat* (Madison, Wis., 1954), and Mark D. Hirsch, *William C. Whitney: Modern Warwick* (New York, 1948), are excellent biographies that provide insights into more than just their respective subjects. Other major biographies include James A. Barnes, *John G. Carlisle: Financial Statesman* (New York, 1931); John R. Lambert, *Arthur Pue Gorman* (Baton Rouge, La., 1953); Herbert J. Bass, "*I Am a Democrat*": *The Political Career of David Bennett Hill* (Syracuse, N.Y., 1961); Harry J. Sievers, *Benjamin Harrison*, 3 vols. (New York, 1952–68); and H. Wayne Morgan, *William McKinley and His America* (Syracuse, N.Y., 1963).

Despite its importance, the city of San Francisco still awaits a historian. Walton Bean, *Boss Ruef's San Francisco: The Story of the Union Labor Party, Big Business, and the Graft Prosecution* (Berkeley, 1952), has perceptive observations on the pre-1900 period. But at present there is no study of San Francisco to match the analytical treatment given Los Angeles in Robert M. Fogelson, *The Fragmented Metropolis: Los Angeles, 1850–1930* (Cambridge, Mass., 1967). The plight of the Chinese who lived in San Francisco and other California cities has received considerable attention. Alexander Saxton, *The Indispensable Enemy: Labor and the Anti-Chinese Movement in California* (Berkeley, 1971), is an important investigation of the uses made of the Chinese by labor and political leaders. Other elements of the Chinese issue can be followed in Gunther Barth, *Bitter Strength: A History of the Chinese in the United States, 1850–1870* (Cambridge, Mass., 1964); Mary Roberts Coolidge, *Chinese Immigration* (New York, 1909); and Elmer Clarence Sandmeyer, *The Anti-Chinese Movement in California*, Illinois Studies in the Social Sciences, vol. 24 (Urbana, Ill., 1939). Sandmeyer's "California Anti-Chinese Legislation and the Federal Courts: A Study in Federal Relations," *PHR*, 5 (1936): 189–211, examines the problems that state legislation encountered in the federal courts.

Only recently has the California People's party begun to receive sustained study. Michael Paul Rogin and John L. Shover, *Political Change in California*, already cited, identifies the geographical, economic, and other bases of Populist support. Tom G. Hall, "California Populism at the Grass-Roots: The Case of Tulare County, 1892," *Southern California Quarterly*, 49 (1967): 193–204, treats Populism in one county. More valuable is Alexander Saxton, "San Francisco Labor and the Populist and Progressive Insurgencies," *PHR*, 34 (1965): 421–38. The Populist dilemma concerning cooperation with the Democrats is examined in Harold F. Taggart, "The Senatorial Election of 1893 in California," *California Historical Society Quarterly*, 19 (1940): 59–73; and Donald E. Walters, "The Feud Between California Populist T. V. Cator and Democrats James Maguire and James Barry," *PHR*, 27 (1958): 281–98. Sheldon Hackney, ed., *Populism: The Critical Issues* (Boston, 1971), has a very good bibliographical essay for those interested in the considerable literature on Populism.

The background and nature of the 1896 election in California can be followed in three articles by Harold F. Taggart: "California and the Silver Question in 1895," *PHR*, 6 (1937): 249–69; "The Silver Republican Club of Los Angeles," *Historical Society of Southern California Quarterly*, 25 (1943): 102–16; and "The Party Realignment of 1896 in California," *PHR*, 8 (1939): 435–52. The national campaign is given detailed coverage in Stanley L. Jones, *The Presidential Election of 1896* (Madison, Wis., 1964); Paul W. Glad, *McKinley, Bryan, and the People* (New York, 1964); Robert F. Durden, *The Climax of Populism: The Election of 1896* (Lexington, Ky., 1965); and J. Rogers Hollingsworth, *The Whirligig of Politics: The Democracy of Cleveland and Bryan* (Chicago, 1963). Other interpretations are in two articles by Gilbert C. Fite: "Republican Strategy and the Farm Vote in the Presidential Campaign of 1896," *American Historical Review*, 65 (1960): 787–806, and "William Jennings Bryan and the Campaign of 1896: Some Views and Problems," *Nebraska History*, 47 (1966): 247–64. Paolo E. Coletta, "Bryan, Cleveland, and the Disrupted Democracy, 1890–1896," *Nebraska History*, 41 (1960): 1–27, looks at the Democrats' troubles through the decade. Robert E. Hennings, "California Democratic Politics in the Period of Republican Ascendancy," *PHR*, 31 (1962): 267–80, traces the decline of the California Democratic party during the early twentieth century.

Index

Ohio, 48, 90, 118, 146, 238
Olney, Richard, 196–200 *passim*, 210f,
  236
Omaha platform, 159, 241
Orange County, 86, 89
Osborne, Henry Zenas, 159
Otis, Harrison Gray: opposes Stanford, 68–
  69, 134; attacks Harrison, 134, 155;
  position of, in party, 159; opposes silver
  repeal, 185; and Pullman strike, 197;
  and the harbor issue, 226, 229

Pacific Mail Steamship Company, 10
Pacific Union Alliance, 137
Palace Hotel, 4
Palmer, John M., 248
Pasadena, 180
patronage: Democratic struggle over, 27,
  62–65 *passim*, 70–82 *passim*, 97; importance of, 56–58; Cleveland's problems
  with, 113, 116, 131, 156; and Harrison,
  133–34, 158; Populist desire for, 164;
  in Cleveland's 2d term, 174–77, 205;
  use of, in repeal battle, 184–89 *passim*
Pennsylvania: and California, 33, 84; as
  source of population, 89; mentioned,
  81, 123
People's party: birth of, 137, 139; and railroad issue, 140, 215; challenges old
  parties, 152; in 1892 election, 159–64;
  in 1896 election, 236–44 *passim*; state
  central committee of, 241; decline of,
  262–63. *See also* Populists
—national conventions: of 1892, 159; of
  1896, 242–43
—state conventions: of 1896, 241–42; of
  1898, 262
Perkins, George C., 185
Phelan, James D., 150, 153, 253
Placer County, 195
Pond, Edward B.: gubernatorial race of,
  147–50 *passim*; supports Cleveland, 157;
  and 1896 campaign, 238, 248
Popper, Max: rise of, 153; and railroad issue,
  171–72, 221; attacks Cleveland, 176, 205
population: movements of, 1, 6; in 1880,
  2; trends within California, 3–4, 87–90
  passim; and the railroad, 8f, 92; and the
  boom, 87–92 *passim*; political effects of,
  91–92, 124–30 *passim*, 260
Populists: and old parties, 130; appeal to
  laborers, 137, 160, 201, 252; and Catho-
  lics, 137, 201, 252; in 1892 election, 159–
  64 *passim*; and fusion with Democrats,
  161, 241–45; in 1893 senatorial election,
  164–66; and blame for ills, 184; votes
  in 1894, 198–202 *passim*; and railroad
  issue, 208, 215; in 1896 election, 241–45,

251–54 *passim*; mentioned, 31, 234, 264.
  See also People's party
Port Los Angeles, 225
Powers, H. Henry, 222
progressives: policies of, antedated, 1, 230–
  32; and tax issue, 17f, 100
Prohibition party, 206
Pullman strike, 194–99, 205, 210–11, 235
Purity of Elections Act, 168–69

railroad commission: creation of, 13–17
  passim, 21, 207–8; as 1882 issue, 25f;
  early policies of, 28–31, 51; reform of,
  recommended, 40, 42, 46, 109, 169;
  praises railroad competition, 92f; grievances against, 162; proposed abolition of,
  169; alleged railroad influence over,
  206f; characteristics of, analyzed, 211–
  16; mentioned, 32, 148, 201
Railroad Reassessment Act, 99–100, 169–72
railroads: effects of competition between,
  3–4, 87–94 *passim*, 130; power of, 5, 9–
  10, 206–8; grievances against, 7–14, 136–
  40 *passim*, 159, 207–8; rates of, 10, 15,
  26–31 *passim*, 40, 42, 87f, 92f, 139, 162,
  169, 199, 206f, 212; and Workingmen's
  party, 15–16; and the constitution, 17;
  taxation of, 17, 26f, 31–40, 46, 48, 64–65,
  97–100 *passim*, 109, 167, 169–73; issue
  of, divides Democrats, 18–27 *passim*, 62,
  96, 105; in extra session, 40–46; assailed
  at Stockton, 48; and Stanford's election,
  66–70; depressed conditions on, 84, 179;
  in 1886 election, 103; and funding, 140,
  216–26 *passim*, 230, 237; as issue in 1892,
  161–62; in 1894 election, 199, 201;
  problem of, analyzed, 206–9; and railroad
  commission, 212ff; and harbor issue, 224–
  30 *passim*; reappraisal of, 230–32; alleged 1896 activity of, 252. *See also*
  specific railroads by name
raisin industry: growth of, 86; and the
  tariff, 115, 125, 147, 193; depression in,
  135, 138
Randall, Samuel J., 81
Reconstruction, 1
Reed, Thomas B., 124
Regular Democrats (Reform), 149–52
  passim
Reilly bill, 220, 222
Republican party: characteristics of, 1–2,
  60n, 146, 260; in 1882 election, 26; and
  railroad issue, 26, 28, 41–44 *passim*; 206,
  215; in 1884 election, 51–53, 110–11; and
  the tariff, 53, 115f, 124–26, 147, 246f,
  260; and Stanford's senatorial election,
  64–70 *passim*; profits from immigration,
  92; in 1886 election, 104–5; and silver,

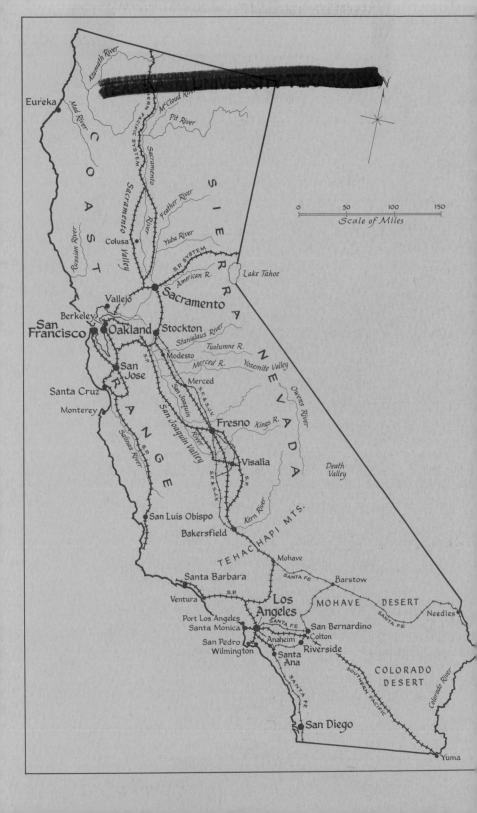